A New English Grammar, Logical and Historical

By

Henry Sweet

Published by Forgotten Books 2012

Originally Published 1892

PIBN 1000035789

A NEW

ENGLISH GRAMMAR

LOGICAL AND HISTORICAL

BY

HENRY SWEET, M.A., Ph.D., LL.D.

Formerly President of the Philological Society
Editor of 'The Oldest English Texts,' Alfred's 'Cura Pastoralis' and 'Orosius'
Author of 'An Anglo-Saxon Reader'
'A First' and 'A Second Middle-English Primer'
'A Primer of Spoken English' 'A History of English Sounds'
'A Primer of Phonetics,' 'Shelley's Nature-Poetry,' etc.

PART I

INTRODUCTION, PHONOLOGY, AND ACCIDENCE

Oxford

AT THE CLARENDON PRESS

1892

Oxford

PRINTED AT THE CLARENDON PRESS

BY HORACE HART, PRINTER TO THE UNIVERSITY

PREFACE

———◆———

THIS work is intended to supply the want of a scientific English grammar, founded on an independent critical survey of the latest results of linguistic investigation as far as they bear, directly or indirectly, on the English language.

Although historical, this grammar is not one-sidedly historical: it is at the same time a logical grammar. It will be seen that I have taken considerable trouble to define accurately not only the parts of speech. but also the primary grammatical categories 'word,' 'inflection,' 'sentence,' etc.. which have hitherto been often neglected, and sometimes ignored, by grammarians. Even in the more beaten tracks I have found many obstacles and difficulties which it has cost me years of hard thought to conquer—often only partially. Practical teachers, who generally confine themselves to one book and one method, are often hardly able to realize how unsettled grammar still is. I remember once reading a paper on grammar before the Philological Society, in which I modestly advanced the view that *cannon* in *cannon-ball* was not an adjective. When I had finished my paper, an English philologist, who was also a teacher, got up, and told me that my criticisms were superfluous, as no practical teacher possessed of common sense would think of calling *cannon* in *cannon-ball* an adjective. Thereupon another eminent philologist, who was not only a schoolmaster, but had written an English grammar, got up, and, to the intense amusement of the meeting, maintained that *cannon* in *cannon-ball* was an adjective and nothing else; and although he refused to commit himself to a comparison *cannoner, cannonest,* he found another speaker to support him. Again, one would imagine that if anything in grammar is perfectly clear, it is the function of prepositions; and yet when I refer to five different grammars, I find the following five definitions, some of which directly contradict the others:—-

1. Prepositions are so named, because they were originally prefixed to the verb to modify its meaning (Morris: Elementary Lessons in Historical English Grammar).

2. A preposition is a word which when placed before a noun or a pronoun denotes some relation in which a thing, or some action or attribute of a thing, stands to something else (Mason: English Grammar).

3. A preposition is a word which shows the relation of one word to another (Smith and Hall: School Manual of English Grammar).

4. A preposition is a word that can be placed before a noun or pronoun, so that the preposition and noun or pronoun together can make up an adjective-phrase or an adverb-phrase (Abbott: How to Tell the Parts of Speech).

5. A preposition is a word prefixed to a noun or its

equivalent to make up a qualifying or adverb-phrase (Bain : A Higher English Grammar).

It is also worthy of note that, with one exception, all the above definitions insist on the prefixing of the preposition, although a preposition that follows its noun-word (such as the Latin *tenus*) is as much a preposition as one that precedes it.

This is evidently the result of an attempt to make the definition harmonize with the etymology of the name. In some grammars the definitions of the parts of speech are literally nothing more than quibbling etymologies. It is a singular fact that some of those who protest most loudly against the servile imitation of Latin grammar are the greatest sinners in this respect.

This is one of the reasons why I have abstained from explaining the etymology of grammatical terms, which is really no more a part of grammar than the etymology of such a word as *oxygen* is a part of chemistry. Although the existing grammatical terminology is objectionable enough in many respects, it has at least the practical merit of affording a certain number of technical terms of definite and generally accepted application, and I see no advantage in substituting a misleading term such as *possessive case* for the traditional *genitive.* Of course, whenever the existing terminology is confusing, ambiguous, or defective, it is our duty to try to improve it. I have myself been as conservative as possible. Where the usage varies, I adopt what seems the best nomenclature, and use it consistently. Thus, in common with the majority of English grammarians, I prefer *noun* to *substantive*—not however for the sake of the quibbling etymological definition of a noun as 'the name of anything,' but simply because it is shorter. Where the

†

existing nomenclature is defective, I have, of course, been obliged to coin new expressions. The multiplication of grammatical terms is certainly an evil, but it is an un-avoidable one: it is only by repeated experiment and by a slow process of elimination and of survival of the fittest that we shall ever attain a uniform terminology. Some of my new names are mere shortenings of familiar expressions, as when I shorten 'verbal nouns and adjectives' into *verbal* as a convenient name to include the 'un-finite' forms of the verb. I have always tried to make the new names suggest associations with the existing terminology. I have also tried to avoid arbitrary restrictions in the application of terms already in familiar use. Thus I prefer to use *sentence* as a general term to include 'clause,' rather than to attempt enforcing a distinction which is not warranted by popular language. On the same principle I reject *phrase* altogether as a grammatical term, because of the endless confusions that arise between the various arbitrary meanings given to it by different grammarians and its popular meaning. I also avoid the arbitrary distinction between 'complex' and 'compound' sentence by using the former only, and short-ening *complex sentence* into *complex*. I have lastly avoided the common English fault of parading German terms when there are good English ones to hand; thus I prefer *mutation* to *umlaut*, *blending* to *contamination*.

As I have already said, this grammar is not one-sidedly or fanatically historical. The old belief in the value of historical and comparative philology as an aid to the practical study of languages has been rudely shaken of late years; but the practice of interlarding even the most elementary English grammars with scraps of historical and comparative philology is still almost universal. In the good old days of Schleicher and Brachet, when the main principles of Arian and Romance etymology could be tabulated in a brief space, and with a delusive simplicity and symmetry, this practice was plausible enough; but nowadays, when even the phonetic changes from Latin to French can hardly be mastered by specialists themselves, and Grimm's Law has to be supplemented by Verner's Law and a host of other Laws, all of them liable to endless complications by analogical influences (which we are no longer allowed to dismiss as irregularities), common sense and honesty command us to give up the attempt to make comparative philology and etymology a part of ordinary education. And now that it is generally admitted that the principles of language and its development can be better explained by English itself than by any dead language, it seems most rational to proceed from the known to the unknown—to learn as much as we can from the history of English itself before attempting a wider survey, for which the student will then be thoroughly prepared. Thus, what better preparation can there be for the study of Verner's Law than an acquaintance with the precisely analogous Modern English change (§ 863)? Again, the results of Comparative Philology are so meagre and so problematical in many cases, that it is more profitable to treat of the origin of inflections, parts of speech, etc. from the point of view of general grammar, as I have done in this book.

A less ambitious program would further allow of greater thoroughness within its narrower limits. If historical English grammar were bounded definitely by Old English (Anglo-Saxon) at one end, an elementary knowledge of Old English might reasonably be made the indispensable prelude to the historical study of English. It

seems strange that at this time of day it should be necessary
to insist that this is the indispensable foundation: that
cramming up a Middle English text is no more a preparation for the study of the English language than it is for
the study of English literature ; that until our whole system
of teaching these subjects and examining in them has
been radically reformed, the Extension movement cannot be
put on that definite footing which every true friend of education wishes it to assume.

In this grammar I have taken pains to make the Old
English foundation as sound as possible, especially by
eliminating the numerous errors that have been handed
down from grammar to grammar, or have resulted from
taking words from the dictionaries without verification. I
have spent many weary hours in hunting up words and
forms given in Matzner's grammar, merely to find that they
have no existence.

I have also paid great attention to the distinctions of
dialect, and the chronology of the language. Dr. Morris
has already made the discrimination of the Middle English
dialects a part of historical grammar teaching. This
grammar is the first to do the same for the Old English
period. It is well known that the German grammars make
a complete confusion between the different periods of
Modern English, all grammars—English as well as German—
ignoring the distinction between the literary and spoken
language. This again has been completely reformed in
the present grammar, in which the spoken language has
had its proper importance assigned to it.

As regards its scope, this grammar is strictly elementary,
as far, at least, as a grammar which is scientific and historical and not purely descriptive can be said to answer

to this description. It confines itself therefore as much as possible to the main grammatical phenomena and main lines of development; and being based on the language of the present time, it ignores historical details which do not bear on Present English.

As one of the most direct practical uses of English grammar is that it serves as a preparation for the study of foreign languages, I have throughout endeavoured to bring out clearly the relation of English grammar to general grammar, with especial reference to the languages that are most studied in England, and to Old English, as may be seen in my treatment of the cases (§ 128) and of the subjunctive mood (§ 294).

As my exposition claims to be scientific, I confine myself to the statement and explanation of facts, without attempting to settle the relative correctness of divergent usages. If an ‘ungrammatical’ expression such as *it is me* is in general use among educated people, I accept it as such, simply adding that it is avoided in the literary language. So also in dealing with such spellings as *honor* (§ 1710), I make no comments, leaving the reader to draw the natural inference from the facts stated, namely that the English retention of the older spelling *honour* is a piece of conservatism which is inconsistent with our abandonment of *emperour*, etc.

I have made my exposition as concrete as possible by embodying every rule or principle in an example. That there are not enough examples I am fully aware ; but this is a defect which could not be avoided in a first edition of limited space.

I am at variance with most German philologists in completely separating the descriptive and logical part of grammar

XII PREFACE.

from the historical: it will be seen that in my introduction I explain fully the grammatical categories, and even treat of the parts of speech in detail before entering on a single historical question, on the principle that it is no use explaining the origin of a phenomenon till the learner has some practical acquaintance with that phenomenon.

In this introduction I may seem to have gone too much into generalities, as, for instance, in the section on the history of language. 'Why not,' the reader may say, 'have simply referred us to Professor Max Müller's *Lectures on the Science of Language*, and Professor Earle's *Philology of the English Tongue?*' But these works, admirable as they are in some respects, are not suited to serve as introductions to my grammar. I have therefore been obliged to introduce my readers to the fundamental principles of linguistic science in my own way.

Like Professor Bain, I treat of the parts of speech in detail apart from their inflections and the details of their formal characteristics.

In my treatment of sentences I may call attention to the new method of organic analysis, which instead of mechanically cutting up a complex sentence into single sentences or clauses, tries to analyse it into lesser groups, each with a definite structure of its own.

An essential feature of this grammar is that it is on a phonetic basis. It is now generally recognized, except in hopelessly obscurantist circles, that phonology is the indispensable foundation of all linguistic study, whether practical or scientific— above all, of historical grammar. I have made my exposition as brief and simple as possible, in consideration of the difficulty of getting instruction in the subject, and the lamentable want of teachers.

The ground having thus been fully prepared, I have been able in the accidence to follow a purely historical exposition.

In the section on Derivation I have been careful to exclude all details that do not belong to grammar, but to the etymological dictionary: from an English point of view *bishop* has nothing whatever to do with the prefix *epi-*.

In preparing this grammar, I have been influenced from so many quarters, that it would not be possible to acknowledge my obligations fully. The grammars I have made most use of are those of Mätzner, Abbott, Bain, Hall, Mason, and Morris. I have also to acknowledge my obligations to the Parallel Grammar Series, especially to Professor Sonnenschein's Latin Grammar, from which nearly all my Latin quotations are taken. My treatment of the suffix *-ate* (§ 1751) will nelp to show what a debt English grammar will some day owe to *The New English Dictionary*. In the Introduction I owe more to H. Paul's *Prinzipien der Sprachgeschichte* than to any one book — at least in the historical sections. I must also specially mention Jespersen's *Studier over engelske Kasus*, which is the most original and stimulating investigation in English grammar that has appeared for a long time. I need not here repeat the acknowledgments that I have made in the prefaces to my History of English Sounds, etc.

There is, on the other hand, much in this grammar that is original. Many of my grammatical investigations have, of course, been already published elsewhere, such as the weakening of Old English *eo* into *ea, a* (§ 1068) in the Philological Society's Proceedings, 1880-1, p. 75. I may call special attention to my paper on *Words, Logic and Grammar* (Phil. Soc. Transs. 1875-6), in which will be

ound the germs of many of the 'new views' which have
)een re-imported into this country from Germany.

In conclusion, I need hardly say that I shall be grateful
or any criticisms and suggestions.

HENRY SWEET.

South Park, Reigate,
15 *Dec.* 1891.

CONTENTS

———◆———

INTRODUCTION.

PHONOLOGY.

PHONETICS.

LAWS OF SOUND-CHANGE 238

OLD ENGLISH SOUNDS.

ACCIDENCE.

INTRODUCTION.

GRAMMAR AND LANGUAGE.

DEFINITION OF GRAMMAR.

1. Grammar may be regarded either from a theoretical or a practical point of view. From the theoretical point of view grammar is the science of language.

By 'language' we understand languages in general, as opposed to one or more special languages.

2. The first business of grammar, as of every other science, is to observe the facts and phenomena with which it has to deal, and to classify and state them methodically. A grammar which confines itself to this is called a **descriptive grammar**. Thus a descriptive grammar dealing with Modern English would state such facts as that *I call* is made into *I called* to show that the action of calling took place in the past instead of in the present; and would go on to state that *I go* is made into *I went*, *I hold* into *I held*, to express the same change of meaning—or, in the technical terminology of grammar, that most Modern English 'verbs' form their 'preterite' by adding *-ed*, the verbs *go* and *hold* having the exceptional or 'irregular' preterites *went* and *held* respectively.

3. When we have a clear statement of such grammatical phenomena, we naturally wish to know the reason of them.

and how they arose.   In this way descriptive grammar lays the foundations of **explanatory grammar.**   There are three chief methods of explaining the phenomena of language, by the help, namely, of (*a*) historical grammar, (*b*) comparative grammar, and (*c*) general grammar.

4. (*a*) **Historical grammar** tries to explain the phenomena of a language by tracing them back to their earlier stages in that language.   Thus, if we go back a few centuries in the history of the English language, we shall find that *went* was originally the preterite of a verb *to wend*, meaning 'to turn'—a meaning still partially preserved in such literary phrases as *to wend one's way, to wend homewards.*   The historical explanation of the preterite of *go* is therefore that it was originally the preterite of another verb of similar meaning.   But if we take the preterite *held*, and trace it back even to the oldest English of the eighth century, we cannot explain its origin.   To do this, we require the help of

5. (*b*) **Comparative grammar,** which compares the grammatical phenomena of a language with those of the cognate languages, that is, languages which are related to it through having arisen from a common parent language.   Just as the Romance languages – Italian, Spanish, French, etc.—are cognate to one another through being independent developments of their parent language Latin, so also English is cognate with Dutch, German, Danish, Swedish, and the other Germanic languages. Now in the oldest Germanic languages the preterite of *hold* appears in some such form as *hehald*, being formed, like many other Germanic preterites, by reduplication, that is, repetition of the beginning of the word.   The Germanic languages themselves are cognate with Greek, Latin, Sanskrit, and the other members of the Arian family of languages ; and as comparative grammar finds reduplicated preterites in these languages also—thus Latin *mordeo*, 'I bite,' has preterite *momordī*, 'I bit'—it infers that such preterites formed part of the Parent Arian language—the hypothetical ancestor of all the

languages mentioned in this paragraph.　We see then that comparative grammar is really a branch of historical grammar, only it takes us a long way further back than we could go by confining ourselves to one language.　The historical explanation of *held* afforded by comparative grammar is, — therefore, that it is a contraction of an originally reduplicated form.　Historical and comparative grammar content themselves with tracing the phenomena of a language—or of a group or family of cognate languages—as far back as possible, without attempting to explain the origin of the oldest forms thus arrived at.　To do this is the task of

6. (*c*) **General grammar** (philosophical grammar), which is not concerned with the details of one special language or family of languages, but with the general principles which underlie the grammatical phenomena of all languages.　In dealing with such a phenomenon as reduplication, general grammar asks (*a*) what are the facts about reduplication in those languages in which we can observe it clearly? and (*b*) what is the explanation of those facts—what are the general principles on which they depend?　Thus general grammar first of all tells us that reduplication is widely used in primitive languages all over the world to strengthen the meaning of words in various ways, as when *man-man* is used to express 'more than one man' or 'many men,' *big-big* is used to express 'very big,' and so on.　Hence it infers that in Parent Arian past time in verbs was regarded as more emphatic—because more definite—than present time, and so was expressed by reduplication.

7. The explanation of grammatical phenomena often seems self-evident—a matter of 'common sense.'　Thus the origin of the preterite of *went* hardly requires to be explained to any one who is acquainted with literary English. But even in such cases as this we can never dispense with historical and comparative grammar, for experience has shown that an examination of the older forms of a language

may at any time prove that what appears at first sight to be a self-evident explanation is untenable. Thus it would seem natural to suppose that the familiar phrase *I'll tell you what* is a shortening of the longer phrase *I will tell you what it is*; but historical and comparative investigation shows that *what* is here used in the sense of 'something,' which was one of its regular meanings in Old English—a meaning which the cognate German word *was* still has, so that the longer phrase is really an expansion of the original shorter one, the result of the meaning of *what* contained in it having become obsolete.

8. Considered from a practical point of view, grammar is the **art of language**.

OBJECTS OF GRAMMAR.

9. The main object of practical grammar is to give—or rather, help to give—a mastery of foreign languages either living or dead, including earlier stages of the native language, as when a modern Englishman sets to work to learn the Old English of King Alfred's time with the help of a grammar and dictionary. This mastery may amount only to understanding the language in its written or spoken form, or may include the power of expression both in speaking and writing.

10. Grammar in the widest sense of the word is therefore both the science and the art of language. But as the scientific study of language is more definitely expressed by 'philology,' the term grammar is generally used to imply a mainly practical analysis of one special language, in which study general principles and theoretical explanations are subordinated to concise statements of facts, and definite rules.

11. We study the grammar of our own language for other objects than those for which we study the grammar of foreign languages. We do not study grammar in order to get a practical mastery of our own language, because in the

nature of things we must have that mastery before we begin
to study grammar at all.　　Nor is grammar of much use
in correcting vulgarisms, provincialisms, and other linguistic
defects, for these are more dependent on social influence at
home and at school than on grammatical training.

12. In considering the use of grammar as a corrective of
what are called 'ungrammatical' expressions, it must be
borne in mind that the rules of grammar have no value
except as statements of facts : whatever is in general use
in a language is for that very reason grammatically correct.
A vulgarism and the corresponding standard or polite expression are equally grammatical—each in its own sphere—
if only they are in general use.　But whenever usage is
not fixed—whenever we hesitate between different ways of
expression, or have to find a new way of expression—then
grammar comes in, and helps us to decide which expression
is most in accordance with the genius of the language, least
ambiguous, most concise, or in any other way better fitted to
express what is required.

13. The native language should be studied from the point
of view of general grammar.　We thus learn to compare the
grammatical phenomena of our own language with those of
other languages, and to criticize impartially its defects, so
that we are better prepared for the divergent grammatical
structure of other languages.　In this way the study of
English grammar is the best possible preparation for the
study of foreign languages.

14. The study of grammar has also a variety of less direct
uses.　　Grammar being itself a science, affords a training
in scientific methods generally.　　It also helps us to get
a clearer knowledge of the things and ideas expressed by
language ; as the poet says of Prometheus : —

　　　　　　He gave Man speech,
and speech created thought, which is the measure of the
　　Universe.　　　　　　　　(SHELLEY, Prometheus.)

15. Lastly, grammar satisfies a rational curiosity about the structure and origin of our own and other languages, and teaches us to take an interest in what we hear and utter every day of our lives.

DEFINITION OF LANGUAGE.

16. Language is the expression of ideas by means of **speech-sounds** combined into **words**. Words are combined into **sentences,** this combination answering to that of ideas into thoughts. Thus in Latin the word *terra* expresses the idea 'the earth,' and *rotunda* expresses the idea 'round,' and these two words are combined together to form the sentence *terra rotunda,* which expresses the thought 'the earth is round.' Different languages have different sounds (sound-systems), and attach different meanings to the combinations of sounds into words, and of words into sentences.

FORM AND MEANING.

17. There are, then, two sides to language—two ways of looking at it: there is the **formal** side, which is concerned with the outer form of words and sentences, and the **logical** side, which is concerned with their inner meaning. Thus the formal side of such a word as *man* is that it is made up of certain sounds standing in a certain relation to one another—following one another in a certain order, etc. So also the form of such a sentence as *the man helped the boy* consists in its being composed of certain words following one another in a certain order, and standing in other relations to one another; and we can alter the form of a sentence by merely changing the order of the words of which it is made up, as in *the boy helped the man.* The study of the formal side of language is based on **phonetics**—the science of speech-sounds ; the study of the logical side of language is based on **psychology**—the science of mind. But phonetics and psychology do not constitute the science of language, being only preparations for it : language and grammar are concerned not with form and meaning separately, but with the connections between them, these being the real phenomena of language.

PROVINCE OF GRAMMAR.

18. But it is only a part of these linguistic phenomena that fall under the province of grammar. Grammar—like other sciences—deals only with what can be brought under **general laws** and stated in the form of general rules, and ignores **isolated** phenomena. Thus grammar is not concerned with the meanings of such primary words as *man*, *tree*, *good*, *grow*, and relegates them to the collection of isolated facts called the **dictionary** or **lexicon**, where they constitute what we may call the **lexical side** of language. But the processes by which words are joined together to form sentences, the changes they undergo in these processes, and the formation of new words by composition and derivation,—all this is the province of grammar as opposed to the dictionary. Thus the fact that *tree* becomes *trees* when we speak of more than one tree is a general one, for in English the plural of nearly all names of things is formed in this way— by the addition of *s* : the formation of the plural of nouns is therefore a part of English grammar. So also if we have once learnt to join the words *tree* and *grow* in such sentences as *the tree grows*, *trees grow*, *the trees are growing*, we are able to construct as many more sentences as we like on the pattern of these, if we only know the words required to make them up : the formation of sentences is therefore an essential part of the grammar of all languages. The business of the grammarian is to find out the general principles on which such processes depend, and to frame a grammatical terminology for stating these general principles in the form of definite grammatical rules, such as 'the regular plural of English nouns is formed by adding *s*.'

Connection between Form and Meaning in Grammar.

19. We have now to consider more closely the connection between form and meaning in grammar. This connection is often imperfect. Different grammatical functions are often marked by the same form, as in *tree-s* and *grow-s*; for the *s* in *trees* has a totally different meaning from what it has in *grows*. On the other hand we often find the same meaning expressed by a variety of forms, as in the plurals *trees, children, men*, the 'singulars' of which are *tree, child, man* respectively. Although there is no formal likeness whatever in these plurals, yet they all not only mean exactly the same, but are used to build up sentences in exactly the same way: wherever in a sentence we put *trees* instead of *tree*, there also we must put *children* instead of *child*, and *men* instead of *man*—in other words, all these forms have exactly the same grammatical function. So also the addition of -*ed* in *I called* as distinguished from *I call*, the change of *I hold* into *I held*, and the substitution of *I went* for *I go*, all mean exactly the same thing—namely the change from present to past time.

Isolation; Irregularity.

20. We have seen that the phenomena of language are of two kinds: those that can be brought under general rules, and those that cannot (**18**). The only phenomena that can be brought under general rules are those that have something in common by which they are associated together in the mind by the psychological process of **group-association**, by which **association-groups** are formed. There are in every language an endless number of these groups, and one and the same word may belong to several such groups at once. Thus the words *trees, towns, boys* form an association-group through having the same 'inflection' -*s*, and having the meaning 'more-than-oneness' in common ; this group is therefore both a formal and a logical one. The plurals *trees*, *children*, *men*, on the other hand, constitute a logical, but not a formal, group—as far, at least, as their inflection is concerned—for they are associated together only by the meaning of their endings. *Tree*, *wood*, *forest*, *park*, etc. are also associated by their meaning only, but in a different way. We see then that the single word *tree* can enter into at least three different association-groups.

21. When a word stands outside an association-group, it is said to be **isolated**. Thus, if we take away *tree* from the group *tree*, *wood*, *forest*, etc., and put it with *town* and *boy*, it is, as far as its meaning is concerned, no longer a member of a group, but is isolated. But although the three words *tree*, *town*, *boy* are isolated from one another in meaning, yet the fact of their all being able to form plurals in -*s*—together with other grammatical characteristics that they have in common—makes them members of another group, which we express grammatically by calling them all 'nouns,' or, more generally, by saying that they all belong to the same 'part of speech.' It is easy to see from this last example that there is no such thing as absolute isolation : every word has something in common with some other word in the language.

22. Hence when we speak of isolation, we generally mean **partial isolation**. Thus the plural *men* forms part of the group *trees*, *towns*, *boys*, etc. by virtue of its meaning, but stands outside this group as far as its form is concerned.

23. When one and the same grammatical function is performed by a variety of grammatical forms, that form which is used in the greatest number of words is called the **regular** form. Thus, as the majority of names of things in English form their plurals by adding *s*, this is called the regular plural ending. Those forms which are in the minority—such as the plural *children*—are called **irregular** forms or **irregu-**

larities. But although such an irregular inflection as the
-*ren* in *children* is so isolated in form that there is no other
word in which it occurs, it still forms part of the group con-
stituted by the whole body of English noun-plurals, both
regular and irregular, by virtue of its grammatical function.
But if every noun in English formed its plural in a different
way, so that we could not tell beforehand what its plural
would be, then such plurals as *men* and *children* could hardly
be called irregular, because there would be no general rule
to which they would be exceptions: they would, from a
grammatical point of view, be as completely isolated grammatically as the primary words *tree, man,* etc., are in meaning;
and the formation of the plural of nouns would belong rather
to the dictionary than to the grammar.

We see from such considerations that it is not always easy to
draw the line between what belongs to the grammar and what
belongs to the dictionary.

Grammatical and Logical Categories.

24. A group of grammatical forms expressing the same
meaning—having the same functions—constitutes a **grammatical category.** Thus the addition of -*s* in *trees,* of -*ren*
in *children,* and the change of *a* into *e* in *men* together
constitute—or help to constitute—the grammatical category
'plural of nouns,' which, again, falls under wider grammatical
categories, such as 'number' (singular and plural number),
'inflection.' So also the inflections in *I called, I held,* etc.
constitute the grammatical category 'preterite tense of verbs.'

25. Every grammatical category is the expression of some
general idea—some **logical category.** Thus the grammatical category 'plural' expresses 'more-than-oneness,' and
therefore falls under the wider logical categories of 'number'
and 'quantity'; and the grammatical category 'tense' corresponds to the logical category 'time.'

Divergence between Grammatical and Logical Categories.

26. But in actual language—which is always an imperfect instrument of thought—the grammatical and logical categories do not always exactly correspond to one another. Thus in the word-group *a ten pound note* compared with *ten pounds*, plurality is not expressed grammatically by any inflection of *pound*, but is left to be inferred from the meaning of *ten*. In such a word-group as *many a man*, the divergence between the grammatical and the corresponding logical category is still stronger; for the word *many* shows that 'more than one' is meant, and yet the combination *a man* is the regular grammatical expression of 'oneness' or the singular number.

27. For this reason it will be advisable to get clear notions of the logical categories commonly expressed in language before dealing with the corresponding grammatical categories—that is, to learn to distinguish between **what** we say and **how** we say it.   Under the head of logical categories we will learn to regard words solely from the logical point of view—to classify them entirely by the ideas they express, making, for instance, no distinction between *a man* in *many a man* and *men* in *many men*, but regarding them both as expressions of the idea of more-than-oneness. Under the head of grammatical categories, on the other hand, we will regard *man*, not only in *one man* but also in *many a man*, as belonging to one and the same category of 'singular number,' although, of course, we shall point out such divergences between form and meaning, and try to explain the origin of them.

LOGICAL CATEGORIES.

Ideas Expressed by Words.

SUBSTANCES AND THEIR ATTRIBUTES.

28. The ideas of which thoughts are made up are concerned mainly with **substances** (material things) and their **attributes**. Substances are known to us solely by their attributes, that is, the impressions these substances make on our senses. Thus the substance 'gold' is known to us by its attributes of 'hardness,' 'heaviness,' 'yellow colour,' etc., which together make up our idea of the substance 'gold.' Such words as *gold, man, house* are, therefore, substance-words; such words as *hard, hardness, heavy, heavily, weight, yellow* are attribute-words.

29. These last all express **permanent attributes**. There are also changing attributes or **phenomena**. Thus 'man' is known to us not only by a number of permanent attributes —'shape,' 'size,' etc.,—but also by the phenomena 'movement,' 'speech,' 'thought,' etc. Hence we call *move, movement, motion, speak, speaking, speech, think, thought, thoughtful, thoughtfully*, etc., phenomenon-words.

30. For convenience, words denoting permanent attributes and those denoting changing attributes or phenomena, are included under the common name **abstract**. Every word which is not a substance-word must therefore be an abstract word. In grammar substance-words are generally called **concrete**. Thus *gold* is a concrete word.

'Concrete' and 'abstract' also have a totally different logical meaning (39). In this—which is the original—sense of the word, substance-words can be abstract as well as concrete.

RELATIONS BETWEEN SUBSTANCES AND THEIR ATTRIBUTES.

31. It is evidently impossible to think of a substance without thinking of its attributes. But it is equally impossible to think of all these attributes at once. When we think of a substance, we are reminded only of some—perhaps only one— of its attributes; and under different circumstances different attributes become prominent in our minds. Thus in comparing 'hair' to 'gold,' we think only of the colour of gold. not of its hardness or weight.

32. It is equally evident that the only way in which we can form an idea of any attribute, such as 'yellow,' is by thinking of a number of yellow substances, such as 'gold.' 'buttercups,' etc.

33. But it is easier to think of an attribute apart from substances than it is to think of a substance apart from its attributes. Phenomena are still more independent than permanent attributes. Thus, although we know that without something to burn—wood, coals, etc.—there can be no fire, and that what we call electricity can only show itself in connection with matter (substances), yet when we see a fire in the distance, a moving light, or a flash of lightning. we are inclined to consider these phenomena as independent objects. Among uncivilised races, indeed, such phenomena as fire and electricity are regarded as living beings, and are even worshipped as gods.

QUALIFIERS.

34. When we distinguish between *a tall man* and *a short man, tall* and *short* are evidently attribute-words. But when we distinguish between *many men, all men*, and *some men* or *few men*, we cannot say that *many, all, some, few* are attribute-words; they are only qualifiers. When we say *some Englishmen are tall*, or *many Englishmen are tall, the majority of Englishmen are tall, Englishmen are mostly tall.* the words *some, many, majority, mostly* do not give us any information about Englishmen : they merely qualify, or limit, or define the idea expressed by *Englishmen*. *Englishmen are tall* by itself might mean 'all Englishmen,' 'many Englishmen,' 'some

Englishmen,' or 'only a few Englishmen'; so we add the words *all, many, some, few,* etc., to qualify the idea expressed by *Englishmen.* Attribute-words may be qualified as well as substance-words. Thus *very* in *a very strong man* qualifies the attribute-word *strong.* Qualifiers themselves may be qualified, as in *very many Englishmen.*

It is easy to distinguish between an attribute-word and a qualifier by asking ourselves, Does this word, which at first sight looks like an attribute-word, give us any direct information about the word it is connected with? Thus it is easy to see that even in such a statement as *we are seven,* the word *seven* does not really tell us anything about the persons designated by *we,* at least not in the same way as *we are young, we are English,* etc. would. In many cases, indeed, a qualifier cannot be used to make a statement with at all. Thus from *these tall men* we can infer *these men are tall,* but we cannot make *some Englishmen* into * *Englishmen are some,* or *half the island* into * *the island was half.*

35. The qualifiers we have hitherto been considering are all **quantitative** words. There is another important class of qualifiers called **mark-words**, which, as it were, put a mark on the word they are associated with, singling it out or pointing to it in various ways. Thus *this* and *that, here* and *there,* as in *this house, the man there,* are mark-words of place ; *now, then* are mark-words of time ; while such mark-words as *the* point out an object in thought, as in *give me the book,* meaning 'the book you know of,' 'the book we were speaking about.' Some mark-words, instead of merely qualifying a word, act as substitutes for it. Thus the mark-word *he* may be used as a substitute for the words *John, the man,* etc., and the mark-word *it* may be used as a substitute for *the book.*

36. Attribute-words may be used as qualifiers. Thus when we say *give me that red book, not the blue one,* although *red* and *blue* give information about the two books, they are not used for that purpose, but simply to distinguish between the two books : *red* and *blue* are in fact here used as mark-words, though they still preserve their full attributive meanings. When attribute-words are used in this way, we call them **qualifying attribute-words.**

General and Special Words.

37. Some attributes are of more general application than others. Thus there are more things that we can call *red* than there are that we can call *dark red* or *yellowish red*, and *red* itself falls under the still more general attribute *colour*. So also the qualifiers *many*, *few*, *some* fall under the more general category of *quantity*. The same gradations are seen also in substance-words. Thus *cast iron* and *wrought iron* go under *iron* ; *iron*, together with *gold*, *silver*, *lead*, etc. goes under *metal*; and *metal* itself goes under *mineral*, and so on.

38. The more special a word is, the more meaning it has. Thus *iron* implies all the attributes implied by the more general word *metal*, and, in addition, all the attributes that distinguish iron from gold and the other metals.

39. Even if we confine ourselves to a single word, we can make the same distinction. Thus the word *man* may suggest the idea either of ' man in general,' as in *man is mortal*, or of one particular man, as when we talk of *this man* or *the man*. We call the former the **generalizing** (abstract), the latter the **specializing** (concrete) use of the word *man*. The specializing use evidently puts more meaning into the word : *the man* not only implies all the attributes that men have in common, but also implies further attributes by which we distinguish ' the man ' from other men.

It must be observed that the logical and the grammatical meanings of the terms **abstract** and **concrete** are distinct and even contradictory. When we talk of ' man in the abstract ' we are using *abstract* in its logical sense, while in grammar *abstract* is a convenient means of including attributes and phenomena under a common name (30). Hence in grammar it is best to restrict these words to their grammatical meaning, using *generalizing* and *specializing* to express their logical meaning.

Combination of Words to express Thoughts.

ADJUNCT-WORDS AND HEAD-WORDS.

40. The most general relation between words in sentences from a logical point of view is that of **adjunct-word** and **head-word**, or, as we may also express it, of **modifier** and **modified**. Thus in the sentences *tall men are not always strong, all men are not strong, tall, strong,* and *all* are adjunct-words modifying the meaning of the head-word *men.* So also *dark, quick, quickly* are adjunct-words in *dark red, he has a quick step, he walks quickly. Stone* is an adjunct-word in *stone wall, wall of stone,* because it modifies (defines) the meaning of *wall.* So also *book (books)* is an adjunct-word in *book-seller, bookselling, sale of books, he sells books, he sold his books,* the corresponding head-words being *seller, selling, sale, sells, sold.*

41. The distinction between adjunct-word and head-word is only a relative one : the same word may be a head-word in one sentence or context, and an adjunct-word in another, and the same word may even be a head-word and an adjunct-word at the same time. Thus in *he is very strong, strong* is an adjunct-word to *he,* and at the same time head-word to the adjunct-word *very,* which, again, may itself be a head-word, as in *he is not very strong.*

SUBJECT AND PREDICATE.

42. As we have seen (**16**), such a thought as 'the earth is round' is made up of the two ideas 'the earth' and 'round' or 'roundness.' All thoughts require at least two ideas : (*a*) what we think of, called the **subject**—in this case 'the earth,' and (*b*) what we think concerning it, called the **predicate**,

namely that it is ' round,' or has the attribute of ' roundness.'
Hence in such a sentence as *the earth is round*, we call *earth*
a subject-word, *round* a predicate-word.   In this example
the predicate-word—or predicate, as we may call it for the
sake of shortness—is an attribute-word ; but the predicate
may be also a qualifier, as in *he is here, we are seven.*

43. Subject and predicate may be joined together in
various ways.   In the above example the connection between
them is affirmed (stated as a fact)—such a sentence as *the
earth is round* being therefore called an ' affirmative ' sentence ;
but it may also be stated doubtfully, as in *perhaps the earth is
round*, or denied, as in *the earth is not flat*, and the relation
between subject and predicate may be modified in various
other ways.

ASSUMPTION.

44. If instead of stating some attribute or qualification
about the subject, we take it for granted, as in—

> *For so the whole round earth is every way*
> *bound by gold chains about the feet of God,*
> (TENNYSON)

the predicate becomes an **assumptive** (commonly called
' attributive '), and the word *round*—as also *whole*—is said to
be used assumptively (attributively).   From such a collocation
as *the round earth* we can infer the statement *the earth is
round*.   Thus assumption may be regarded as implied or
latent predication, and predication itself may be regarded as
strengthened or developed assumption.

Assumption is generally called ' attribution ' in grammars ;
but this term is objectionable because it is liable to cause confusion with the logical term ' attribute.'

It is easy to see that every assumptive word must be an
adjunct-word as well as every predicate, just as every subject-
word must be a head-word.   But every adjunct-word is not
necessarily an assumptive, for in grammar we use this term in
contrast with ' predicative,' so that when we call a word

'assumptive,' we generally imply that it can be used also as a predicate. Thus *the* and *very* in *the earth, very good* are adjunct-words, but there would be no object in calling them assumptives. But in grammar such qualifying words as *whole, all, seven* are said to be used attributively in such word-groups as *the whole earth, all men, seven men* ; for although we cannot make *all men* into the statement **men are all*, we can make the statement *we are seven, there are seven of us*, and, besides, we feel that *all men* is analogous to *good men*, etc.

Subordination and Coordination.

45. The relation of adjunct-word to head-word is one of **subordination**. But ideas can also be connected together with little or no subordination of one to the other—they can stand in a **coordinate** relation to one another. Thus in *you and I will be there before the others*, we cannot say that either of the two words connected by *and* is subordinated to the other : we do not necessarily think of 'you' first and then join 'I' on to it, but we think of the two simultaneously, just as we should do if we expressed the idea of 'you and I' by the single word *we*. *You* and *I* in the above sentence are also coordinate through having the same predicate in common.

46. Even in predication the subordination to the subject-word is often very slight, for although the subject is generally more prominent in our minds than the predicate, the union of subject and predicate in thought is instantaneous, and if the two are of nearly equal importance, it may sometimes be almost a matter of indifference which idea is regarded as subject, and which as predicate. Thus it does not matter much whether we say *the first day of the week is Sunday*, or *Sunday is the first day of the week*, just as in numbering the days of the week we might write either 1 *Sunday*, 2 *Monday*, etc., or *Sunday* 1, *Monday* 2, etc.

47. So also there are degrees of subordination of assumptives to their head-words.

When an assumptive is, as it were, detached from its head-word—as in *Alfred, king of England*, compared with *king Alfred*, where *king* is entirely subordinate—it is said to be in **apposition** to it. (90.)

GRAMMATICAL CATEGORIES.

48. The most general classification according to grammatical categories is into **words, word-groups,** and **sentences.**

49. Sentences are made up of words, but we speak in sentences, not words. although it may happen that a sentence is made up of a single word. A sentence is a word or combination of words capable of expressing a thought, that is, a combination of a logical predicate with a logical subject (**42**). Thus *come !, he went away* are both sentences. When a sentence is expressed by a single word, as in the case of *come !*, the word is called a **sentence-word.**   When two or more sentences are joined together to express a single complete thought, they constitute a **complex sentence**, the simple sentences of which the complex sentence is made up being called **clauses.**   Thus the complex sentence *if you are right, I am wrong* is made up of the two clauses *if you are right* and *I am wrong*.

50. When words are joined together grammatically and logically without forming a full sentence, we call the combination a **word-group.**   Thus *man of honour, the roundness of the earth, the round earth, going away, his going away* are word-groups.

When words come together without there being any special connection between them, they may be said to constitute a **word-collocation.**

Words.

51. In a continuous discourse there is no separation between the words, except where we pause to take breath, or for emphasis : the words of a sentence are run together exactly in the same way as the syllables of a word are.   Thus in ordinary pronunciation the two words of the sentence *tell her* ! are run together exactly in the same way as the two syllables of the word *teller*, the two groups being identical in sound—(telə).   Until we know the meaning of (telə)—which we cannot do without a sufficient context—we not only cannot divide it into words, but we cannot even tell whether it is one word or two words.

52. A word may be denned as an **ultimate independent sense-unit.**   A sentence such as *cats catch mice* is an independent sense-unit, but it is not an ultimate one, for it can be subdivided into the smaller independent sense-units *cats* (or *cat*), *catch*, *mice*.   We call such a sound-group as *cat* an ultimate sense-unit because it cannot be divided into lesser sense-units.   We call *arbitrary* an ultimate sense-unit for the same reason ; for *arbi* and *trary* by themselves make nonsense.   Such a sound-group as *tripod* is also an ultimate sense-unit, because, although its two syllables *tri* (trai) and *pod* are by themselves real sense-units, yet their meaning has no connection with that of *tripod* itself.   *Cat, arbitrary, tripod* are further independent sense-units : they can stand anywhere in a sentence, and enter into any combinations with other words that are not contrary to their meaning and the principles of English grammar.

The inflected word *cats* can be divided into *cat-s*, but the second element, though it has the definite meaning of plurality, is not an independent sense-unit, and the connection between *cats* and the uninflected *cat* is so intimate that we cannot regard the two as distinct words.   Besides, such a plural as *mice* cannot possibly be divided into two sense-units.

53. By **form** words are distinguished by the different sounds of which they are made up, by the different order of these sounds (*tip, pit*), by their length—especially as measured by the number of syllables, and by stress (·*abstract*, *to ab·stract*), and intonation.

Although, as we have seen (**51**), there is no necessary separation of words in sentences, yet in all languages words are to some extent marked off by their form. Thus in some languages the stress is always on the first syllable of a polysyllabic word, so that a strong stress always shows the beginning of a new word, just as a louder note in music shows the beginning of a bar. And in all languages certain sounds and certain sound-groups occur only in certain positions. Thus in English, whenever we hear the sound (n)—as in *king* (kin), we know that it cannot form the beginning of a word.

54. A word may occur in more than one form. Thus in English we have the distinction between emphatic (hiz), as in *it is his, not her s*, and unemphatic (iz), as in *it is his own*. In such cases we do not regard the two forms as different words, being, indeed, generally insensible of the difference between them. Such pairs are called **doublets**.

If a pair of doublets diverge in meaning as well as form, so that the gap between them cannot be bridged over without the help of historical grammar, then we feel them to be distinct words, as in the case of *of* and *off*, which were originally both modifications of Old English *of*.

55. It sometimes happens that a word has a different form when it is absolute—that is, stands alone—from what it has when it is conjoint—that is, grammatically associated with another word. Thus we have the absolute form *mine*, as in *it is mine*, corresponding to the conjoint form *my*, as in *it is my book*.

56. If, on the other hand, the same combination of sounds expresses several distinct meanings which cannot be associated together, as in *bear* (the animal) and *to bear*, then we feel the two sound-combinations to be distinct words, for in language we cannot go by form alone, apart from meaning. Such pairs are called **homonyms**.

57. When we call words ultimate sense-units, we do not

ımply that they represent ultimate ideas. On the contrary, many words—indeed most words—express a good many ideas at once. Such a word as *rain*, for instance, contains in itself the elements of a sentence, though of course not put in the form of a statement: *rain* means roughly speaking 'drops of water falling from the sky.' Such a word as *baker* is still more complex : it implies selling as well as making bread, biscuits, buns, and other food of the same kind. In fact, we put ideas into words not because of their simplicity or primitiveness, but because of their importance to us; and whenever it is convenient to express a group of ideas by a single word, language generally finds the means to do so.

FORM WORDS.

58. In such a sentence as *the earth is round*, we have no difficulty in recognising *earth* and *round* as ultimate independent sense-units expressing the two essential elements of every thought—subject and predicate. Such words as *the* and *is*, on the other hand, though independent in form, are not independent in meaning: *the* and *is* by themselves do not convey any ideas, as *earth* and *round* do. We call such words as *the* and *is* **form-words**, because they are words in form only. When a form-word is entirely devoid of meaning, we may call it an **empty word**, as opposed to **full words** such as *earth* and *round*. It is easy to see that *the* and *is* in *the earth is round* belong to this class of form-words. Although *is* sometimes has the independent meaning 'existence,' as in *Troy is no more*, it is easy to see that in *the earth is round* it has no meaning of its own, and serves only to show that the word which follows it—namely *round* —is a predicate, or, in other words, it serves to connect subject and predicate. We see then that *is*, though it has no independent meaning, has a definite grammatical function —it is a grammatical form-word. *The* in *the earth*, on the other hand, has not even a grammatical function, and serves only to show that *earth* is to be taken in the sense of 'terrestrial globe,' and not in that of 'mould,' which it might otherwise have; so that although formally independent of *earth*—for we can put another word between them, as in *the whole earth*—it is, logically speaking, almost a part of it, as if it were a derivative prefix, like the *un-* in *unknown* (69).

59. It often happens that a word combines the function of a form-word with something of the independent meaning of a full word. *Become*, as in *he became prime minister*, is an example of such a 'full form-word,' for it combines the full meaning 'change' with the grammatical function of the form-word *is*: *he became* means 'he changed his condition,' and the full sentence implies 'he is (was) prime minister.'

60. In most languages there is a natural tendency to subordinate form-words to full words in stress. This is especially the case in English. Thus in *the earth is round* (-ȯi ·əəþ -iz ·raund) we have two full words with strong stress, and two form-words with weak stress; and, as we see in such a sentence as *Troy ·is no more* (58), *is* itself has a strong stress when it has a full meaning.

61. Another practical test of form-words is that they may often be omitted with a slight change in the form of the sentence—sometimes without any change at all—or in translating into some other language. Thus the form-word *of* in *man of honour* is omitted in the synonymous expression *honourable man*, and *the earth is round* may be expressed in Latin by *terra rotunda*, literally 'earth round,' where both form-words are omitted. So also *some* in *·some people think differently*, being a full word has strong stress and cannot be omitted; while in *give me some more bread* it has weak stress, and might be omitted without loss of clearness, being here used as a form-word like the French *du*, literally 'of the,' in *du pain* 'some bread,' 'bread.'

Even such words as *piece* and *lump* are used nearly as form-words in such groups as *a piece of ·bread, a lump of ·lead,* as is shown by their diminished stress, and by their having practically almost the same meaning as the weak *some* in *some ·bread.*

It will, of course, be understood that it is not always easy—or even possible—to draw a definite line between full words and form-words.

Word-formation.

62. We have hitherto confined our attention to **simple** words, that is, words which in their uninflected form cannot be divided into lesser sense-units. But there are also **complex** words, which can be divided in this way. Complex words are of two kinds, (*a*) **compound** words or compounds, such as *blackbird,* formed by composition, and (*b*) **derived** words or derivatives, such as *unknown, keeper,* formed by derivation, that is, by adding derivative elements, such as *un-, -er.* Composition and derivation are included under the common designation of **word-formation** or word-forming processes.

COMPOSITION.

63. A compound is a combination of two words equivalent formally and logically to a simple word. Thus in the compound word *blackbird* the elements of the compound—the words of which it is made up—are as distinct as in the word-group *black bird*; but apart from this, *blackbird* is as much a single, indivisible word as the monosyllabic word *swan* compared with such a word-group as *white·bird.*

64. The formal distinction between a compound and a word-group evidently is that in a compound the elements are associated more closely together. Just as in the simple word *tripod* the two syllables *tri* and *pod* are inseparable from one another, and follow one another in a fixed order, so also the elements of *blackbird* are inseparable from one another and follow one another in an absolutely fixed order. Just as *tripod* forms its plural *tripods,* so also such compounds as *blackbird, hatbox*, form their plurals *blackbirds, hatboxes*, the first elements of these compounds being as incapable of change of form as the first syllable of *tripod* itself.   But such a word-group as *a box for a hat* can be freely altered not only into *a box for hats*, but also into *boxes for hats*; and the elements of the word-group *a black bird* may be modified and separated in various ways, as in *so black a bird, the black-est bird, birds black and white*.

65. The formal unity of a compound is often further strengthened by its having only one strong stress.   Thus, just as the single strong stress in the simple word ·*tripod* makes us feel that it is a single, indivisible word, so also the single stress in ·*blackbird* makes us feel that it is a single, indivisible word as opposed to the group ·*black* ·*bird*, in which both syllables have the same strong stress.

But unity of stress by itself is not enough to constitute a compound ; thus in the group *the man* there is only one strong stress, and yet we cannot call this group a compound, because of its separability and want of isolation.

66. We may sum up the formal characteristics of compounds by saying that they imply formal isolation : the elements of a compound are brought into such close connection with one another that they are isolated from the other words of the sentence in which they occur.

67. Hence a compound word is not only inflected like a simple word, but is capable of entering into fresh compounds, and of taking derivative elements.   Thus the compound *midship* and the simple word *man* are combined together in the compound *midship-man*.   We call such compounds **secondary** compounds, as opposed to **primary** compounds, such as *blackbird.*   From the compound *moonlight* the derivative *moonlight er* is formed.

In such compounds as *firelighter* the *-er* is not a derivative ending added to the whole compound, but the compound is made up of *fire* and the already derived word *lighter.*

68. It is evident that compounds must have special meanings of their own, for otherwise there would be no object in distinguishing them from word-groups—in distinguishing, for instance, between ·*blackbird* and ·*black* ·*bird.* Hence we find that while the meaning of such a word-group as *black bird* is inferred as a matter of course from the meanings of the separate words of which it is made up, this is not the case with a compound such as *blackbird*: there is, for instance, nothing in the meaning of the words *black* and *bird* to tell us that a blackbird is a bird with a yellow beak. *Blackbird* is, therefore, to some extent, an ultimate sense-unit ; and yet it consists of two words, each having an independent meaning of its own, the meaning of both words entering into that of the compound formed by them. We may express this in other words by saying that the meaning of a compound is isolated from the meanings of its elements.

Logical, without formal, isolation is not enough to constitute a compound. The meaning of such a sentence as *how do you do ?* cannot be fully inferred from the meanings of the words of which it is made up; and yet we do not call this group a compound, because it does not differ formally from any other sentence made up of independent words and capable of various modifications of form. Again, although *The Red Sea* means one particular sea—the meaning of the combination being therefore strongly isolated yet as the group does not differ grammatically in any way from *the black bird* and other groups in which there is no logical isolation, we cannot call it a compound.

But there is a class of combinations called **group-compounds** (**440**), which are really intermediate between true compounds and word-groups.

DERIVATION.

69. Such a derivative element as *un-* in *un-known* is an ultimate sense unit with a very definite meaning, being so far on a level with the word *not.* But it is not independent : for

while *not* can stand alone, and can be put before any word
with which the general rules of English grammar allow it to
be associated. *un-* cannot stand alone, and can be used only
with certain words; thus we cannot form such derivatives as
*unwhite, **unreligious*, answering to the word-groups *not white*,
not religious, although there is nothing in the rules of English
grammar to forbid such combinations.

70. When a derivative element comes before the body of
the word, it is called a **prefix** ; when it comes after it, it is
called a **suffix** or **ending.** Thus *un-* and *be-* in *unknown*
and *become* are prefixes, *-er* and *-ness* in *keeper* and *goodness*
are suffixes.

71. Derivation is sometimes accompanied by sound-
change, as in *national* (næʃənəl) from *nation* (neiʃən), *breadth*
from *broad* compared with *truth* from *true.* Sometimes
a process analogous to derivation is carried on by sound-
change alone, without the addition of any derivative element,
as in *to fill* from *full,* compared with *to gladden* from *glad.*

Derivation by sound-change alone can generally be traced
back to an earlier stage of derivation by sound-change and
addition together, which, again, is a later stage of derivation
by addition alone. Thus the difference between *national* and
nation in Present English is the result of the earlier English
tendency to shorten the vowels in the first syllables of longer
words.

72. Derivation, being a process for forming new words,
necessarily alters the meaning of the derived word. The
meanings of derivative elements are often vague and irregular. Thus it is not easy to see much community of meaning
in the prefix *be-* in such words as *become, befall, beset,* nor
between the complex *become* and the simple *come.* The suffix
-ness in *goodness, badness, redness,* etc. is an example of a
derivative which is much more regular in its meaning, but
even here we should not be able to infer the meaning of
business from that of *busy.*

Inflections.

73. By inflection we understand an addition to a whole
class of words expressing some grammatical function, or a
meaning so general as not to constitute a new word. Thus
the inflection *-s* is added to *tree*, etc. to express the meaning
of plurality, this meaning being so general a one that we
feel *trees* to be essentially the same word as the uninflected
singular *tree*. So also the preterite inflection *-ed* is added to
call, *live*, *stop*, etc. to express past time; and the genitive
inflection *-s*—which is distinct in meaning and origin from
the plural inflection—has the grammatical function of making
such words as *tree*, *day*, etc. into a particular class of adjunct-
words, and thus of connecting words together in sentences,
as in *a day s journey*, where *day's* defines *journey* in the same
way as *long* in *a long journey*.

As words are always liable to develop a variety of meanings,
it sometimes happens that the plural of a word has a different
meaning from the singular, as in *sands* = 'sandy shore of the
sea' compared with *sand*. But such changes of meaning are
secondary ones, which took place after the formation of the
plural, and with which the inflection had originally nothing
to do.

74. Inflection by addition is, like derivation, sometimes
initial—at the beginning of the uninflected word, or **base**—
but generally **final**—at the end of the base. We have an
example of initial inflection in the augment of the Greek
verb, which expresses past time, as in *é-tupton* 'I was striking'
compared with the present *tupto* 'I strike,' and the German
and Old English *ge-* by which these languages mark the
preterite participles of verbs, as in German *gemacht*, Old
English *gemacod* 'made,' from German *machen*, Old English
macian 'to make.' As inflection is mainly final in English
and the other languages cognate with it, initial inflection in

these languages is generally accompanied by final inflection —
é-tupt-on, ge-mac-od.   Hence there is a tendency to restrict
the term 'inflection' to final additions to a word, and to
regard *ge-* etc. as derivative prefixes.

75. Inflection is often accompanied by sound-change, as
in the plural *leaves* from *leaf,* preterite *though-t* from *think.*
Sometimes inflection is effected entirely by sound-change,
as in *men* from *man, saw* from *see.*

As in derivation, the forms with sound-change are generally
of later origin.

76. Sometimes an inflectional function is performed by a
variety of distinct forms, as in the plurals *trees, children, men,*
and the preterites *called, thought, saw, held.* As the change of
child into *children* and of *man* into *men* has exactly the same
meaning as that of *tree* into *trees,* we do not hesitate to
regard all these changes as constituting one and the same
inflection, however distinct they may be in origin, and so
also with the preterites *called, thought,* etc.   It sometimes
even happens that different words stand in an inflectional
relation to one another, with or without the help of inflection.
Thus *went, was* stand in the same relation to *goes, is* as
called. saw to *calls, sees* ; and the uninflected *me* stands in the
same relation to *I* as the inflected *hi-m* does to *he.*   Here,
again, we do not hesitate to call *went* the preterite of *go,* and
me the objective case of *I.*

77. The absence of inflection —**negative inflection**—
often has the same function as positive inflection.   Thus
the absence of the plural inflection *-s* in *tree* expresses the
singular number.

78. Inflections have the same grammatical functions as
form-words.   Thus the genitive inflection *-s* in *a day s work*
has exactly the same function as the form-word *of* in *the
work of a lifetime.*

When a form-word is much shortened, it may become pho-netically indistinguishable from an inflection, as in *John is here* (dӡonz hiə), where the (z) is, phonetically speaking, as much a part of the preceding word as the genitive -*s* in *John's book* (dӡonz buk). But we can easily see that in *John is here* the (z) is an independent word in spite of its shortness, by trans-posing it in such a sentence as *here is John* (hiəz dӡon), the in-flectional -*s* in *John's book* being, on the other hand, absolutely inseparable from its base.

79. Inflection is very similar to derivation, not only in form, but also, in some cases, in meaning. Thus although the plural inflection in such a word as *trees* only adds to the meaning of *tree* without otherwise altering it, yet *trees* may to some extent be regarded as a new word—as approximating in meaning to such words as *forest* and *park*. In fact modern English does treat plurals of nouns to some extent as if they were new words; for just as *man* has a genitive *man's*, so also the plural *men* has a genitive *men's*, as if it were an independent word.

80. Conversely, there are some derivative elements which are very similar to inflections. Thus the change of *white* into *whiteness, good* into *goodness*, etc., can hardly be said to form a new word, for it comes to the same thing whether we say *snow is white* or *snow has the attribute of whiteness*. In fact, the only use of the change of *white* into *whiteness* is to give greater freedom in the use of the word in sentences. But, on the other hand, in such derivatives as *business, his Highness*, there is a considerable change of meaning, really amounting to the formation of a new word.

Relations between Words.

81. There are five ways of indicating the relations between words in word-groups and sentences : (*a*) word-order, or posi-tion, (*b*) stress, (*c*) intonation, (*d*) the use of form-words, and (*e*) inflection.

82. The simplest and most abstract way of showing the relations between words is by their **order**. We see how the meaning of a sentence may depend on the order of its words by comparing *the man helped the boy* with *the boy helped the man*, where the distinction between subject and adjunct to the predicate depends entirely on the word-order.

83. We can see how **stress** alters the meaning of a sentence by comparing *that is ˌmy book* with *that is ˈmy book*; the latter really means 'it is my book and not some one else's.'

84. We can see how **intonation** shows the relation between words by comparing a sentence such as *you are ready ?'*, uttered with a rising tone, with the same sentence uttered with the falling tone of such a sentence as *I am ready`*. While the falling tone expresses statement, the rising tone expresses question, so that the rising tone in *you are ready'* has the same meaning as the change of word-order in *are you ready ?*

The above are examples of **sentence-stress** and **sentence-intonation** as distinguished from **word-stress** and **word-intonation**. English uses both sentence-stress and word-stress to express differences of meaning (the latter in such pairs as *ˈabstract* and *to abˈstract*), while intonation is used in English only to modify the meaning of sentences. Word-intonation occurs in many foreign languages, such as Old Greek and Chinese (the 'Chinese tones'), where it is used to distinguish the meanings of separate words. Thus in Old Greek *oíkoi* 'at home' and *oíkoi* 'houses' were distinguished solely by their intonation, both words having the same sounds and the same strong stress on the first syllable.

85. Stress and intonation, however, have not much influence on the grammatical structure of sentences, sentence-stress being used mostly for emphasis, and intonation to express shades of feeling, such as curiosity, dogmatism, contempt, though, as we have seen, it is also used to express purely logical meanings such as question. Variations of stress and intonation are also limited in number. The distinctions that can be made by word-order are still more limited, so that if a language depended entirely on word-order to show grammatical relations, it would have to use the same word-order to express a great variety of different meanings. Hence no language can rely exclusively on these three, but requires the help either of form-words or inflections, which afford as many grammatical distinctions as are necessary.

86. The nature of **form-words** and **inflections** has been already explained. Some languages, such as Chinese, show grammatical relations entirely by means of word-order and form-words. Others, such as Latin, rely mainly on inflections, though they use many form-words as well, with which, indeed. no language can dispense. We call such a language as Chinese an **isolating** language as distinguished from an **inflectional** language such as Latin. English is mainly an isolating language which has preserved a few inflections.

The classification of languages according to their structure, without regard to their relationship, is called the **morphological**, as opposed to the **genealogical** classification. English and Latin are genealogically related by being both members of the Arian family of languages, but they differ widely morphologically. English and Chinese, on the other hand, show great morphological resemblance without being in any way genealogically related.

87. We have now to consider how these means of grammatical expression, especially word-order, form-words, and inflections, are used in language to express logical relations.

88. The first main division is that of **modifying** and **connective**. *The* in *the earth* is a modifying form-word ; *is, and* in *the earth is round, you and I*, are connective form-words. So also the plural inflection in *trees* is modifying, while the genitive inflection in *a day's work* is connective. A modifying form requires only one word to make sense (*the earth, tree-s*), while a connective form requires two words to

make sense (*you and I, a day-s work*). The relations between words in sentences are therefore shown mainly by connectives, while modifiers have almost the function of word-formers (**58**).

89. When two words are associated together grammatically, their relation may be one either of **coordination** or of **subordination** (**45**). Coordination is shown either by word-order only, or by the use of form-words, as in *men, women, and children*, where the first two full-words are connected only by their position, while the last two are connected by the form-word *and*.

90. Subordination implies the relation of **head-word** and **adjunct-word** (**40**). But there are degrees of subordination. When the subordination of an assumptive (attributive) word to its head-word is so slight that the two are almost coordinate, the adjunct-word is said to be in **apposition** to its head-word. Thus in *king Alfred* the adjunct-word is a pure assumptive—as much so as *good* in *the good king*—and has the usual position of an assumptive word in English, that is, before its head-word, while in *Alfred the king* or *Alfred, king of England*, it stands in apposition to its head-word in a different position and in a more independent relation.

91. In the above examples the relation between head-word and adjunct-word is only vaguely indicated by position, being mainly inferred from the meaning of the words. But in such a sentence as *I bought these books at Mr. Smith's the bookseller's*, the connection between the adjunct-words *these* and *bookseller s* and their head-words is shown by each adjunct-word taking the inflection of its head-word. This repetition of the inflection of a head-word in its adjunct-word is called **concord**, and the two words are said to **agree** in whatever grammatical form they have in common: the concord between *these* and *books* consists in their agreeing in number— that is, in both having plural inflection ; and the concord between *bookseller s* and *Smith's* consists in their both having the same genitive inflection. In such groups as *green trees*, *the trees became green*, there is no concord, as if we were to say **this books* instead of *these books*. In a highly inflected concord-language such as Latin, *green* in the above examples would take the plural inflection of *trees* just as much as *this* would.

92. The concord-inflection of an adjunct-word is not only logically superfluous, but often unmeaning. Thus it is evident that the idea expressed by *this* and *green* does not admit of plurality—for we cannot form an idea of 'more than one this' or of 'more than one greenness'—and consequently that the plural inflection of *this* in *these trees* is in itself devoid of meaning. Such concord-inflections have indeed only an indirect grammatical function, namely that of indicating the connection between head-word and adjunct-word : the plural inflection of *this* in *these trees* does not modify its meaning in the slightest degree, but only serves to connect it with another word having the same inflection, namely *trees*.

93. When the relations between words are shown by word-order, concord is not of much use, and consequently is reduced to very narrow limits in such a language as English. Conversely, in a highly inflectional language with a highly developed system of concord, such as Latin, fixed word-order is not required to show the grammatical relations between words. Even in English we might put *these* and *trees* far apart in a sentence and yet easily join them together in thought by their having the same inflection. Hence in such a language as Latin the word-order is much freer than in English, the position of words being determined mainly by considerations of emphasis and euphony.

94. When a word assumes a certain grammatical form through being associated with another word, the modified word is said to be **governed** by the other one, and the governing word is said to govern the grammatical form in question. Thus in *a day's work*, *day's* is governed by *work*, and *work* itself is said to govern the genitive case. So also in *I see him*, *him* is governed by *see*, and *see* is said to govern the objective case *him*. In *I thought of him*, the form-word *of* also governs the objective case.

Parts of Speech.

95. As regards their function in the sentence, words fall under certain classes called **parts of speech**, all the members of each of these classes having certain formal characteristics in common which distinguish them from the members of the other classes. Each of these classes has a name of its own —noun, adjective, verb, etc.

96. Thus, if we compare nouns, such as *snow, tree, man*, with adjectives, such as *big, white, green*, and verbs, such as *melt, grow, speak*, we shall find that all nouns whose meaning admits of it agree in having plural inflections—generally formed by adding *s* (*trees*); that adjectives have no plural inflections, but have degrees of comparison (*big, bigger, biggest*)—which nouns and verbs have not; that verbs have inflections of their own distinct from those of the other parts of speech (*I grow, he grows, grown*); that each part of speech has special form-words associated with it (*a tree, the tree; to grow, is growing, has grown*); and that each part of speech has a more or less definite position in the sentence with regard to other parts of speech (*white snow, the snow melts, the green tree, the tree is green*).

97. If we examine the **functions** of these three classes, we see at once that all verbs are predicative words—that they state something about a subject-word, which is generally a noun (*the snow melts*); that adjectives are often used as assumptive words (*white snow*), and so on.

98. If we examine the **meanings** of the words belonging to the different parts of speech, we shall find that such nouns

as *tree, snow, man,* are all substance-words, while the adjectives and nouns given above are all attribute-words, the adjectives expressing permanent attributes, the verbs changing attributes or phenomena. We can easily see that there is a natural connection between the functions and meanings of these parts of speech. We see that the most natural way of speaking of a substance is to imply or state some attribute about it (*white snow, the snow melts*); and that permanent attributes, such as 'whiteness,' can often be taken for granted, while phenomena, such as 'melting,' being often sudden and unexpected, require to be stated explicitly.

99. But this connection, though natural, is not necessary. In language it is often necessary to state, as well as imply, permanent attributes (*the tree is green*), and it is sometimes convenient to make statements about attributes as well as substances. Thus, instead of using the word *white* as a means of implying something about *snow* or any other substance, we may wish to state or imply something about the attribute itself, as when we say *whiteness is an attribute of snow,* or talk of *the dazzling whiteness of the snow.* It is easy to see that there is no difference of meaning between *whiteness is an attribute of snow* and *snow is white* : the difference between *white* and the noun *whiteness* is purely formal and functional—grammatical, not logical.

Classification of the Parts of Speech.

100. The parts of speech in inflectional languages are divided into two main groups, **declinable**, that is, capable of inflection, and **indeclinable**, that is, incapable of inflection.

101. The declinable parts of speech fall under the three main divisions, **nouns, adjectives,** and **verbs,** which have been already described.　　**Pronouns** are a special class of nouns and adjectives, and are accordingly distinguished as **noun-pronouns,** such as *I, they,* and **adjective-pronouns,** such as *my* and *that* in *my book, that man.* **Numerals** are another special class of nouns and adjectives : *three* in *three of us* is a noun-numeral, in *three men* an adjective-numeral.   Verbals are a class of words intermediate between verbs on the one hand and nouns and adjectives on the other : they do not express predication, but keep all the other meanings and grammatical functions of the verbs from which they are formed. Noun-verbals comprise infinitives, such as *go* in *I will go, I wish to go*, and gerunds, such as *going* in *I think of going.* Adjective-verbals comprise various participles, such as *melting* and *melted* in *melting snow, the snow is melted.*

102. Indeclinable words or particles comprise adverbs, prepositions, conjunctions, and interjections.   The main function of adverbs, such as *quickly* and *very*, is to serve as adjunct-words to verbs and to other particles, as in *the snow melted quickly, very quickly.*   Prepositions, such as *of*, are joined to nouns to make them into adjunct-words, as in *man of honour*, where *of honour* is equivalent to the adjective *honourable.*   Conjunctions. such as *if*, are used mainly to show the connection between sentences, as in *if you do so, you will repent it.*   Interjections, such as *ah ! alas !*, are sentence-words (49) expressing various emotions.

103. For convenience we include nouns in the limited sense of the word, noun-pronouns, noun-numerals and gerunds under the common designation noun-word. So also we include adjectives, adjective-pronouns, adjective-numerals and participles under the common designation adjective-word.

The term ' verb ' is sometimes used to include the verbals, sometimes to exclude them.   When necessary, the predicative forms of the verb as opposed to the verbals are included under the term finite verb : thus in *I think of going, think* is a finite verb as opposed to the verbal (gerund) *going,* although both are included under the term ' verb ' in its wider sense.

104. The following is, then, our classification of the parts of speech in English:

declinable
- { **noun-words**: noun, noun-pronoun, noun-numeral, infinitive, gerund.
- **adjective-words**: adjective, adjective-pronoun, adjective-numeral, participles.
- **verb**: finite verb, verbals (infinitive, gerund, participles).

indeclinable (particles): adverb, preposition, conjunction, interjection.

The distinction between the two classes which for convenience we distinguish as declinable and indeclinable parts of speech is not entirely dependent on the presence or absence of inflection, but really goes deeper, corresponding, to some extent, to the distinction between head-word and adjunct-word. The great majority of the particles are used only as adjunct-words, many of them being only form-words, while the noun-words, adjective-words and verbs generally stand to the particles in the relation of head-words.

Conversion of the Parts of Speech.

105. When we talk of _the whiteness of the snow_ instead of saying _the snow is white_, we make the adjective _white_ into the noun _whiteness_ by adding the derivative ending _-ness_. But in English, as in many other languages, we can often **convert** a word, that is, make it into another part of speech without any modification or addition, except, of course, the necessary change of inflection, etc. Thus we can make the verb _walk_ in _he walks_ into a noun by simply giving it the same formal characteristics as other nouns, as in _he took a walk, three different walks of life._ We call _walk_ in these two collocations a converted noun, meaning a word which has been made into a noun by conversion.

Conversion bears some resemblance to derivation, although the mere change of a verb into a noun can hardly be said to make a new word of it.

But although conversion does not involve any alteration in the meaning of a word, yet the use of a word as a different part of speech naturally leads to divergence of meaning. There is, for instance, in nouns a natural tendency to develop a concrete meaning (98). Thus, while the noun *walk* in the examples given above keeps the abstract meaning of the verb from which it is formed—although there is a slight change of meaning in the second example—it has assumed a concrete meaning in *gravel walk*—a meaning which cuts it off both from the verb *to walk* and the abstract noun *walk*.

106. The test of conversion is that the converted word adopts all the formal characteristics (inflection, etc.) of the part of speech it has been made into. Thus *walk* in *he took a walk* is a noun because it takes the form-word *the* before it, because it can take a plural ending -*s*, and so on. The question, which part of speech a word belongs to is thus one of form, not of meaning. The nouns in *silk thread*, *gold watch* are used as attribute-words very much as the adjective *silken*, but nevertheless they are not adjectives in the above collocations: we could not say *very silk, *more silk, as we could say *very silken*, *more silken* ; in fact *more silk* by itself would suggest a totally different idea, namely that of 'a larger quantity of silk.'

107. But there are cases of **partial conversion**, in which a word really partakes of the formal peculiarities of two different parts of speech. Thus in *the good are happy*, *good* takes the form-word *the* before it like a noun, and stands as the subject of a sentence like a noun, and yet in its want of plural inflection it is an adjective, not a noun. *Goods* in *goods and chattels*, on the other hand, shows complete conversion of an adjective into a noun.

It is sometimes doubtful what part of speech a word belongs to. The less marked the formal characteristics of a word, the more difficult it is to settle what part of speech it belongs to. Hence particles offer more difficulty than declinable words, as we see in the difficulty of distinguishing between adverbs and conjunctions. Hence also the more inflectional a language is, the easier the discrimination of the parts of speech is. Thus in English, where the adjective is nearly indeclinable, it is more difficult to distinguish it from other parts of speech than in Latin.

Relations between Logical and Grammatical Categories.

108. We have already seen that the correspondence between words and the ideas they express is often imperfect (**26**). Even when the grammatical and logical categories do not directly contradict one another, the expression of ideas in language may still be imperfect in various ways. Sometimes we express the same idea twice over, as in concord (**91**), while sometimes we do not express it at all, but leave it to be inferred from the context ; sometimes we have more than one way of expressing the same idea ; and sometimes we can express an idea only imperfectly, or not at all.

It must not be assumed that defective correspondence between logical and grammatical categories is necessarily injurious to language considered as a means of expression. On the contrary, illogical and ungrammatical constructions often add greatly to ease, and even to accuracy, of expression (**528**).

Fullness of Expression ; Ellipse.

109. The two extremes as regards fullness of expression are **redundance** on the one side, and **ellipse** on the other.

110. Redundance is easy to recognise, as in the phrase *I will know the reason why* = *I will know the reason of it* ; here the idea of 'reason' is expressed twice over—by *reason* itself and by *why*. The best example of grammatical redundance is afforded by concord (**91**). From a logical point of view there is redundance not only in such constructions as *these trees* but also in *two trees, ten trees*, etc., where the numeral by itself is enough to show plurality without the noun-inflection.

111. The opposite phenomenon of **ellipse** offers more difficulties. When there are two forms of expressing the same idea, one shorter than the other, it is not always safe to assume that the shorter form is an elliptical variation of the longer one. Thus we cannot say that *come !* is an elliptical form of *come thou !*: *come thou !* is rather an extended or redundant form of *come !*; for, as the pronoun is really super-fluous—commands being generally addressed to some one person—*come !* is the normal form of expression. Such an expression as the colloquial *glad to hear it* = *I am glad to hear it*, is, on the other hand, really elliptical, partly because the meaning is not clear without the pronoun *I*, but still more because the fuller expression is more in harmony with the principles of English grammar, and is in more frequent use than the shorter one. The most unmistakeable ellipses are those which give rise to grammatically impossible constructions. Thus *he is stopping at his uncle's* is elliptical not so much because the missing word *house* after *uncle's* suggests itself without an effort, but because without it the preposition *at* seems to govern the genitive case, which is im-possible in English. In ellipse the addition of the missing word must not involve any change of construction. Thus *this is mine* cannot be expanded into **this is mine hat*, etc., which shows that *this is mine* is not an elliptical form of *this is my hat*, any more than *the trees are green* is an elliptical form of *the trees are green trees*. Hence we cannot assume an ellipse in the parallel construction *this is his*, although it can be expanded without change into *this is his hat*, etc. From this we can see that the practical rule is, never to assume an ellipse unless it seems grammatically necessary.

112. What might at first sight seem to be ellipse is often a different phenomenon, namely what we may call **condensa-tion**. We have seen that in sentence-words subject and predicate are expressed by one word (49). Now as such a sentence-word as *come !* is not either logically or historically a shortened form of *come thou !*, it cannot be regarded as an elliptical, but only as a condensed expression. We have another

kind of condensation in such a construction as *what you say is true*, which is nearly equivalent to *you say something which is true*. Here the word *what* does duty for two words at once: it stands in one grammatical relation to *say*, and in another to *is*. But it would not be good English to expand *what you say is true* into **what you say, that is true*. So there is no ellipse in this case. All we can do is to acknowledge the fact that in such sentences *what* unites the grammatical functions of the two words *something* and *which*; and we do this by calling it a 'condensed relative pronoun' as opposed to the ordinary relative pronoun *which* in *something which is true*.

UNIFORMITY OF EXPRESSION.

113. In a perfect language there would be one distinct form, and only one, to express each separate grammatical meaning. But this uniformity and simplicity of expression is never carried out fully in any actual language. We have already seen that in inflection the same grammatical function is often discharged by a variety of distinct forms, and the same form used to express a variety of distinct grammatical functions (**76**). In languages of mixed morphological structure, such as English, we find the same grammatical relation expressed by different categories of grammatical forms—sometimes by inflection, sometimes by form-words, sometimes by word-order, as in *a day's work, the work of a life, night work*—and the same grammatical relation is often shown by several grammatical forms at once. Thus, while in *the boy helped the man* the different relations in which the two nouns stand to the verb are shown by the word-order only, the same relations between noun-pronouns, as in *he helped him*, are shown by inflection as well as word-order.

ADEQUACY OF EXPRESSION.

114. As regards adequacy, the expression of grammatical categories may be imperfect, or wholly wanting. The grammatical relations between words can be shown only imperfectly by word-order; for as the number of different positions a word can take in a sentence is necessarily limited, the same position must be used to express a variety of grammatical relations, that is, if any great use is made of word-order.   Thus the nouns and pronouns coming after the verbs in the following English sentences stand in various different relations to those verbs: *I saw a man; he became a lawyer; they gave him a house; they made him a bishop.*   In such a language as Latin the different relations in which these words stand would be clearly shown by their inflection.   In Latin, *him* in *they gave him a house* would be put in the dative or 'indirect object' case, *house* in the accusative or 'direct object' case. In English the distinction between direct and indirect object is expressed, not by inflection, but imperfectly by word-order, the indirect coming before the direct object in such sentences as that given above, although in some constructions the order is reversed, as in *give it me !* We can distinguish between the direct and the indirect object by the latter being able to take the preposition *to* before it : *they gave the house to him ; give it to me !* Hence, although it would be quite incorrect to say that *me* in *give it me !* is in the dative case, it is correct to say that it stands in the dative or indirect object relation, for in English we really have a feeling of this grammatical relation, although we cannot express it very clearly.

115. So also, when we say that prepositions govern the objective case in English, we mean that a pronoun such as *I* or *he*, when connected with a preposition, must be put in the objective case *me, him* instead of the nominative *I, he*, as in *with me, to him.*   But as there is no distinction between nominative and objective in nouns, we cannot say that the nouns in *with pleasure, to sea*, are in the objective case, and consequently it is hardly correct to say that they are governed grammatically by these prepositions, although *with me*, etc., would justify us in saying that these nouns stand in the objective relation, and we are tolerably certain that if English nouns had distinct nominative and objective inflections they would assume the latter inflection after prepositions. But the logical connection between preposition and noun-word is just as strong in *with pleasure* as in *with me*: *with* governs *pleasure* logically just as much as it governs *me*. In *you and I*, which means practically the same as *you with me*, there is no grammatical government, and yet *and* may be said to govern *I* logically almost as much as *with* governs *me*. But it will be most convenient to use ' government ' strictly in the sense of grammatical government, and to express logical government by the term **modification**. Thus we can say that *and* in *you and I* modifies *I*, while *with* in *with me* both modifies and governs *me*, government always implying modification as well.

DIVERGENCE BETWEEN LOGIC AND GRAMMAR ; ANTIGRAMMATICAL CONSTRUCTIONS.

116. If, in the divergence between logic and grammar, logic triumphs over grammar, we have an **antigrammatical** construction, as in *the party were assembled,* where a verb in the plural (*were*) is associated with a noun in the singular (*party*) against the grammatical principles of concord. From a logical point of view there is no inconsistency in this, for *party* combines the idea of a single body of people with that of the separate individuals of which it is composed.

117. Antigrammatical constructions are sometimes the result of **attraction**, which is generally a purely mechanical process, being the result of simple contiguity, by which a word is made to agree with another word with which it would otherwise not be connected grammatically, as in *the opinion of several eminent lawyers were in his favour*, where *were*, although grammatically connected with the singular noun *opinion*, is put in the plural as if it were governed by *lawyers*.

118. Antigrammaticalness may lie not in any one con-

struction, but in the relation between two or more constructions. Thus in such a colloquial sentence as *my friend,
when he heard it, he laughed*, the beginning of the sentence
makes us expect *laughed* instead of *he laughed*, which again
makes us expect a different beginning : *my friend heard it ;
when he heard it, he laughed.* This want of grammatical
sequence we call **anacoluthia,** the construction itself being
called an **anacoluthon** or 'grammatical break.' Anacoluthia, then, consists in beginning with one grammatical construction, and then changing to a different one, so that the
first half of the statement remains unfinished, the last half
being connected with it not grammatically but only logically.
Anacoluthia is the result either of forgetting the beginning of
the statement—that is, forgetting its grammatical form—or
of confusion of thought caused by a complex arrangement of
clauses. Thus the anacoluthia in the example given is the
result of *my friend* being separated from *laughed* by the
clause *when he heard it* ; and if this clause is got out of the
way, there is no longer any inducement to make the construction anacoluthic : *my friend laughed when he heard it.*
We have a more marked anacoluthon in the colloquial sentence *he is always polite to people he thinks he can get anything
out of them* = the grammatical sentence *he is always polite to
people out of whom he thinks he can get anything*, or *he is
always polite to people when he thinks he can get anything
out of them.*

119. When a grammatical construction misrepresents the
logical relations of the ideas expressed by it, it is said to be
antilogical.

120. The most frequent cause of antilogical constructions
is **shifting.** In such a sentence as *the majority of Englishmen are tall* (or *the majority of Englishmen are short*) compared with *most Englishmen are tall, Englishmen are mostly
tall*, we have shifting in its most rudimentary form, namely

shifting of prominence. It is evident that in the thought expressed in different forms by these three sentences, the prominent and logically important ideas are those of 'Englishmen' and 'tall,' and that *majority, most, mostly*, all express a mere qualification of the ideas expressed by the other two words. In the last two sentences the logically prominent words are made grammatically prominent as well—as far, at least, as the rules of English grammar will allow—especially in the last sentence, where the subject is put first in the sentence. But in the first sentence not only are the logical relations of head-word and adjunct-word reversed—the word expressing the idea of 'most' being made a grammatical head-word, to which the logical head-word is subordinated— but the word which is the least important logically of all three is put first and made the subject of the sentence. Again, in these sentences the logical predicate is *tall*, for 'tallness' is what we state about Englishmen. But from a purely grammatical point of view *tall* cannot be a predicate-word, for it is not a finite verb. If the term 'grammatical predicate' is to be restricted to a single word, the only word in these sentences that can be called predicate is *are*, and *tall* must be regarded as an adjunct to it, just as it is an adjunct to *grew* in *the boy grew tall*. But as the verb *to be* is entirely destitute of meaning in ordinary English (**58**), it is impossible to regard *are tall*, even grammatically, as equivalent to 'exist in a state of tallness' or anything of the kind, so that the only way of getting out of the difficulty is by regarding *are tall* as a group-predicate, in which *are* is a kind of prefix to make *tall* into a predicate. *Are* in *are tall* has, indeed, much the same function as the *-s* in *the boy grows tall*, and just as we regard the combination *grow-s*—and not the *-s* by itself —as constituting the predicate, so also we are justified in regarding the group *are tall* as the grammatical predicate. So also in the 'group-verbs' *I am seeing, I have seen, I shall have seen*, compared with the simple verbs *I see, I saw*, what we may regard as the logical centre of gravity is shifted from the verbs *see, saw,* to the verbals *seeing, seen,* and yet these groups could not be used as predicates without the logically insignificant form-words *am, have, shall.* We call the logically prominent element of a group the **nucleus.** Thus the nuclei of the groups *the majority of Englishmen, I shall have seen* are *Englishmen* and *seen.* So also the nucleus of the group *a piece of bread* is *bread, piece,* although grammatically the head-word of the group, being really little more than a form-word not only logically, but also to some extent formally—through its weak stress (**61. 1**). In this case, then, the formal criteria may be said to contradict one another.

121. It will be seen that we use the terms head-word, subject, etc., both in a logical and a grammatical sense, distinguishing when necessary between logical and grammatical head-word, etc. We are able to do this because most of the distinctions expressed by these terms have no definite grammatical expression, a grammatical adjunct-word, for instance, being represented by a variety of parts of speech, while different parts of speech share even in predication. Hence we cannot recognise grammatical head-words, adjunct-words, etc., mechanically by their form as we can recognise an inflection or any other definite grammatical form. Such inflections as the genitive case have grammatical functions and often more or less definite meanings of their own, but when we say that such a word as *John s* is in the genitive case, we think more of the fact that it ends in *s* than of anything else. This definiteness would be lost if we were to set up a 'logical genitive' as opposed to a grammatical genitive, calling for instance the group *of John* a logical genitive. The utmost we should allow ourselves would be to call *of John* a ' genitive-equivalent.'

122. We can observe a more marked kind of shifting in the Latin *laudatum īrī* 'to be about to be praised,' which

means, literally, ' to-be-gone to-praise ' instead of ' to-go to-be-praised.'

123. In language the logical connections between words extend over a wider area than the purely grammatical ones. Thus in such a sentence as *I came home yesterday morning*, the grammatical predicate to *I* is *came*, *home* and *yesterday* being grammatically connected with the predicate only, while *morning* is an adjunct to *yesterday* only. But in thought *yesterday* is as much part of the predicate as *came* itself, *came-home-yesterday-morning* being the logical predicate, which, from a grammatical point of view may be regarded either as an extended predicate or a group-predicate.

124. Hence such a sentence as *I like boys when they are quiet* or *I like quiet boys* practically means ' I like quietness ' as much as ' I like boys.' Such a sentence, indeed, as *I like boys to be quiet* does not imply even the slightest liking for boys, as the other sentences do. And yet in this last sentence the only word that *I like* governs grammatically is *boys*, *to be quiet* being only a grammatical adjunct to *boys* ; while from a logical point of view *I like* is connected directly with *to be quiet*, to which *boys* is a logical adjunct, the sentence being logically equivalent to ' I like quietness of boys.' We may call this phenomenon **indirect government**.

125. Grammatical and logical anomalies often arise through the **blending** of two different constructions. Thus in colloquial English the two constructions *these things* and *this kind of things* have resulted in the blending *these kind of things*. So also the plural *themselves* may be regarded as a blending of *himself* and *ourselves*.

PARTS OF SPEECH IN DETAIL.

Nouns.

FORM.

Inflections.

126. The inflections of nouns in English are those of **number** and **case**.

127. As regards number, most languages distinguish between **singular** and **plural,** some having a third number, the **dual.** English has only singular (*tree*), and plural (*trees*). The singular expresses ' oneness,' or else leaves the number indefinite, as in *man is mortal, the lion is the king of beasts.* The dual expresses ' twoness'; thus in such phrases as *to use one's eyes and ears* those languages which have this number would put *eyes* and *ears* in the dual. The plural expresses ' more-than-oneness'; in those languages which have a dual it expresses ' more-than-twoness.' Thus in Old English the plural *we* 'we' implies at least three persons, ' we two' being expressed by the dual *wit.*

We have a trace of the distinction between dual and plural in the reciprocal noun-pronouns *each other* (dual) and *one another* (plural).

128. The most important cases in language generally are the nominative, vocative, accusative, dative, genitive, instrumental, locative.

129. The **nominative** is the 'subject-case,' its main function being to mark the subject of a sentence. Thus in *the earth is round, the earth is a round ball, earth* would be expressed by a noun in the nominative by all languages which have the nominative inflection, such as Latin; and if *ball* were inflected in such a language, it also would be put in the nominative to show that it is an adjunct to the other nominative *earth*; and in a concord-language *round* in both sentences would also be put in the nominative. In English there is no special nominative inflection of nouns, so that all we can say is that in the English sentence *the earth is round*, *earth* stands in the nominative relation, or is nominatival.

130. The **vocative** is the 'exclamation-case,' or, in other words, it is a noun used as a sentence-word; we might therefore call it the 'sentence-case.' *Sir !* is an example of a noun in the vocative relation.

131. The **accusative** or 'direct object case' serves to complete the meaning of a transitive verb (**248**). Thus in *the man beat the boy, the man saw the boy, boy* is in the accusative relation, being regarded as the direct object of the actions expressed by *beat* and *saw*. Every noun which follows a verb in English is not necessarily in the object relation to the verb, but may stand in the subject (nominative) relation. Thus in such sentences as *John became a lawyer, he turned Methodist*, although the nouns *lawyer* and *Methodist* may be said to modify the meanings of the verbs *became* and *turned*, they are much more intimately connected with the subject-words *John, he*, the verb being little more than a link between the two pairs of noun-words *John … lawyer, he … Methodist*; whereas in *he beat the boy, boy* is not connected—except very indirectly—with *he*, and modifies *beat* only, just as in the compounds *boy-beater, boy-beating*. In such a sentence as *he is a lawyer*, where *is* has no meaning of its own, *lawyer* cannot, of course, be said to modify that meaning in any way.

132. If another noun-word is required to complete the meaning of a transitive verb, it is generally in the **dative** or 'indirect object' relation, as in *that man gave my brother an orange*, where *brother* would be put in the dative case in such a language as Latin or German. As we see from this example, the dative generally denotes the person affected by or interested in the action expressed by the verb; the dative is therefore the 'interest-case.' Hence in such sentences as *he helped the man, he injured the man*, the noun would be put in the dative in many languages. In English we should call *the man* in such constructions simply the object of the verb, for in English we recognise an indirect object only by its standing alongside of a noun in the direct object relation (**114**).

133. The **genitive** case, as in *John's book, a day's work*, shows that the noun in the genitive case (*John's*) is an adjunct to another word—generally a noun; it may therefore be regarded as the 'adjective case,' *a day's* being equivalent to *of a day* (**78**), and *of honour* being equivalent to the adjective *honourable* (**102**).

134. The **instrumental** case expresses the instrument or manner of an action. Thus in *struck by lightning, by degrees*, the nouns *lightning, degrees* are in the instrumental relation.

135. The **locative** case expresses place. Thus in *to stop at home, to live in the country*, the two nouns are in the locative relation.

136. The instrumental and locative—especially the former—may be regarded as 'adverb cases,' for, like adverbs, nouns in these cases are used chiefly to modify verbs, and *by degrees* is exactly equivalent to the adverb *gradually*.

137. There are many other meanings which are expressed by case-inflections in different languages. Thus some languages have a 'comitative case' to express 'accompanied by,' and many primitive languages have a variety of cases to express minute distinctions of position, on, in, or near an object, etc.

138. The meanings of cases are often very varied, and when we give a case a certain name we do not imply that it is confined to the functions expressed by that name. Thus in Greek the dative case not only denotes an interest or indirect object relation, but also has the functions of the instrumental and locative cases of more highly inflected languages.

139. All cases except the nominative and vocative are included under the common term **oblique** cases.

140. English has only one inflected case, the **genitive**, (*man's, men s*), the uninflected base constituting the **common case** (*man, men*), which is equivalent to the nominative, vocative, accusative, and dative of such a language as Latin.

141. But in that special class of nouns called personal pronouns we find a totally different system of case-inflection, namely, a **nominative** (*he*), and an **objective** case (*him*), which latter corresponds to the accusative (*I saw him*) and the dative (*give it him!*) of more highly inflected languages. But the nominative case of the pronouns in English, though originally a strict nominative, has lost many of its grammatical functions. In spoken English, such a nominative as *he* or *I* is hardly used except as a conjoint form,—as a kind of prefix to the finite verb (*he sees, he saw, I have seen*), the objective case being always substituted for the nominative when used absolutely in vulgar speech, as in *it is me*, and often also in educated speech.

Gender.

142. Gender is the expression of sex-distinctions by means of grammatical forms.

143. In nature things are distinguished by sex as **male**, such as 'man,' 'son,' 'cock'; **female**, such as 'woman,' 'daughter,' 'hen'; and **neuter**, that is, neither male nor female, such as 'stone,' 'tree,' 'hand.'

144. All languages have separate words for 'man,' 'woman,' 'son,' 'daughter,' etc., with which they can form gender-denoting groups or compounds, such as *man-servant, woman-servant, cock-sparrow, hen-sparrow*, etc. Some languages also mark the distinctions of sex in pronouns, as in the

English *he, she, it.* With the help of these pronouns we are able to mark sex in such compounds as '*he-goat, she-goat.*

145. If we did not know the meanings of such words as *woman* and *daughter*, we should not be able to tell whether they denoted male, or female, or lifeless things. But in many languages there are words which show sex by their **form** : thus in English we know that such words as *authoress, baroness, lioness* denote female beings by the ending *-ess* ; even if we did not know the meanings of these words, we should still be able to guess that they denoted female beings. This denoting of sex by means of grammatical form is called **gender.** The only certain test of gender in all languages is the use of the pronouns *he, she, it,* by which we can distinguish nouns as he-nouns, she-nouns, and it-nouns, according as they are spoken of or referred to as *he, she,* or *it.* Thus *baroness* is a she-word, but *burgess* is a he-word, although it has the same ending, and *business* is an it-noun. In grammar, he-words are called **masculine,** she-words **feminine,** it-words **neuter.**

146. In English the grammatical category gender generally agrees with the logical category sex ; that is, feminine nouns are names of female beings, and so on. When gender agrees with sex in this way, it is called **natural gender.** But gender and sex do not always agree. Thus, even in English we call a ship *she,* and in books the sun is called *he* instead of *it.* In such languages as Latin, German, and Old English this is carried much farther ; thus in Old English, *foot* is a he-noun or masculine, and *hand* is feminine. In such languages not only are names of things made masculine and feminine, but even names of male and female beings have genders which contradict the natural sex. Thus in Old English *wif* 'woman,' 'wife' is neuter, and *wif-mann* 'woman,' literally 'wife-man,' is masculine. When gender diverges from sex in this way, it is called **grammatical gender** ; thus the Old English *wifmann* is a grammatical masculine, while Old English *mann* 'man' is a natural masculine.

Form-words.

147. The most important form-words associated with nouns are the indefinite article *a* (*a man*), the definite article *the* (*the man*), and the prepositions, such as *of, to, with*.

148. The meaning of nouns is often modified by the presence or absence of the articles, as in *where does Baker live?* compared with *where does the baker live?, iron is a metal,* compared with *an iron to iron with.* The presence or absence of an article often goes hand in hand with inflection; thus the plural of *a man* is *men*, and the absence of the articles *a* or *the* in the singular *man* generally shows that it stands in the vocative relation.

149. Putting a preposition before a noun is grammatically equivalent to adding an inflection. Thus *of a man* means exactly the same as *a man's*, and *to him* means the same as *him* in *give it him!* So also *with difficulty* corresponds to the instrumental case in such a language as Sanskrit.

Meaning.

Concrete Nouns.

150. The primary and most characteristic use of nouns as regards their meaning is to express substances. Substance-nouns, or **concrete** nouns, as they are generally called, are divided into the two main classes of **common** nouns, such as *man*, and **proper names**, such as *Plato*. Common nouns, again, are subdivided into **class-nouns**, such as *man*, and **material**-nouns, such as *iron*. **Collective** nouns, such as *crowd*, are a subdivision of class-nouns, all other class-nouns being included under the head of **individual** nouns:

$$
\text{concrete}
\begin{cases}
\text{common nouns}
\begin{cases}
\text{class-nouns}
\begin{cases}
\text{individual } (\textit{man}) \\
\text{collective } (\textit{crowd})
\end{cases} \\
\text{material nouns } (\textit{iron})
\end{cases} \\
\text{proper names } (\textit{Plato})
\end{cases}
$$

Class-Nouns.

151. We call such a word as *man* a class-word (class-noun) because it stands for a class or number of individual things having certain attributes in common by which they are distinguished from other classes of things, such as ' monkeys,' ' trees,' ' houses.' Hence *monkey, tree, house* are also class-words. All these words are **individual** class-words as distinguished from **collective** class-words such as *crowd* (153).

152. Class-nouns denoting only a single object are called **singular** class-nouns, or, more briefly, singular nouns. Thus in popular language *sun* and *moon* are singular nouns as opposed to **plural** nouns, such as *tree, man,* although in the scientific language of astronomy *sun* and *moon* are as much plural nouns as the other two. Singular nouns are just as much class-nouns as plural nouns are : even if astronomy had not revealed the existence of other suns and moons, we should still regard *sun* and *moon* as class-words on the ground that *if* we had occasion to speak of other bodies— either real or imaginary—resembling our sun and moon, we should unhesitatingly extend the old names to these new objects.

Singular and plural nouns must, of course, not be confounded with nouns in the singular or plural inflection.

Collective Nouns.

153. Collective nouns express a number of things collected together so that they may be regarded as a single object. *Crowd, fleet, nation* are collective words. *Crowd* means a number of human beings so close together that at a distance they seem to form a solid mass. So also *fleet* means a number of ships sailing together under one command; and *nation* means a number of people bound together by a common language, government, habits of life, etc.

154. Collective nouns are as much class-words as individual nouns such as *man* are : we can think of a number of crowds or fleets or of different nations as well as of a single crowd, fleet, etc. *Crowd* etc. are, therefore, at the same time plural nouns. *Universe* may be regarded as a singular collective noun.

Material Nouns.

155. Such words as *iron, glass, bread, water* do not express any definite thing, as the class-words *tree* etc. do, but each of them includes the whole mass of matter possessing the attributes implied by the word. Thus *iron* means not only the nails and the hammer I may have in my hands at this present moment, but all the iron in the universe, whatever may be the form or quantity of each portion of it. Material words thus make us think more of the attributes they suggest than of the thing itself. Thus *iron* makes us think of hardness, weight, liability to rust, etc., associated together in a substance of indefinite form. Hence material words approach very near in meaning to pure attribute words.

When a material noun is used to express an individual object of definite shape, it is no longer a material noun, but a class-noun. Thus *iron* in the sense of 'implement to smooth cloth with,' or *glass* in the sense of 'vessel to drink out of' are pure class-nouns.

Proper Names.

156. Such words as *man* and *crowd* suggest an indefinite number of separate objects, and such a word as *iron* suggests part of an indefinite mass of matter. We include class-nouns and material nouns under the term **common nouns**, meaning that such a designation as *man* is shared—or may be shared—in common by an indefinite number of individual men, and that such a designation as *iron* is shared in common by portions of an indefinitely large mass. None of these words by themselves suggest a definite individual or a definite portion of matter.

157. One way of making an indefinite class-noun definite is by qualifying it with a mark-word (**35**), such as *this* or *the*, as when we make the indefinite *man, river* into the definite *this man, the man, the river.* But mark-words define only relatively, not absolutely : *the man*, or its equivalent *he*, by itself does not enable me to identify the person till I know exactly who is referred to ; and *the river* may mean the Thames, but it may also mean the Rhine, or the Nile, or any other river which is uppermost in the thoughts of the speaker —generally, of course, the river which is nearest to the place where he lives. **Name-words** or **proper names**, such as *Plato, London, Thames* also mark off individuals of a class, and exclude other individuals of the same class, but they are absolute or permanent, not relative and shifting marks: we can shift the designation *the river* from the Thames to the Rhine, and from the Rhine to the Nile, but we cannot do this with the designation *the Thames*, etc.

158. A proper name need not be confined to a single individual, but may include a definite group of individuals, as we see in family names (surnames), such as *Collins* : a surname by itself does not tell us which individual of the family is meant, although it marks off all the members of the family from the members of other families. Surnames are, there-fore, **collective name-words**, as opposed to **individual name-words**, such as the christian name *John*, and the names *Plato, London*, etc. *The United States* is also a collec-tive name-word, as opposed to the state-names *Maine, Virginia*, etc., which are individual name-words.

159. It often happens that the same name is applied to a number of unconnected objects, simply because the number of objects that we have to name is so great that it is impos-sible to find a perfectly distinctive name for each, and to be certain that the name we use has not been used before ; and this applies to proper as well as common names. Thus there is a *Boston* in England and another in the United States of North America, and such a name as *John* is given every year to a large number of children. Even such a name as *John Collins* may be ambiguous; whence the practice of giving more than one christian name, as in *John Stuart Mill.* But however imperfect the result may be, the intention is the same in all proper names, that is, to exclude ordinary individuals of the same class, and it is this intention which puts the ambiguous *John* on a level with the unambiguous *Plato.* Conversely, the fact that such a word as *sun* in popular language expresses only a single object, does not make it a proper name, because in the word *sun* there is no intention of excluding other possible suns.

160. As regards their relation to common words, proper names fall under two well-defined classes, according as they are connected or unconnected with common words in the same language. Such christian names as *Patience*, *Violet*, and such surnames as *Brown*, *Smith* may be called **connected names,** because all these sound-groups express not only name-nouns but also a variety of common words, *patience* being an abstract noun, *brown* an adjective, *smith* a class-noun, and so on. So also such place-names as *New-castle*, *The Strand* are connected names. Such proper names as *Philip*, *John*, *London*, *Thames*, on the other hand, are un-connected. The history of language shows however that all unconnected names were originally connected; that is to say, that all proper names have arisen from limiting the application of some common word to one particular object. Just as the first man who was called *Brown* was so called because of his brown hair or brown complexion, so also the first man who was called *Philip* was so called because of his love of horses or skill in driving or riding; for in Greek—the language in which this name was first formed—it was origi-nally an adjective (*philippos*) meaning 'fond of horses.'

Proper names are thus never arbitrary in their origin : we can be certain that there was always a reason for a name when it was first given, however fanciful this reason may have been, and however much the meaning and use of the name may have changed afterwards.

161. As regards their form, proper names may consist of a single word or a word-group, which, again, may be made up of proper names. as in *John Stuart Mill*, or of common words, as in *High Street*, or of a mixture of proper names and common words, as in *John the Baptist, Edward the First*. Proper names may also consist of phrases or even sentences.

162. As regards their meaning, proper names fall under a great variety of heads, such as **personal names**, which, again, include christian names, surnames, **patronymics**, or names formed from the father's name, such as *Williamson* ' son of William '; **geographical** names, including place-names, such as *England, London, Islington*, river-names, mountain-names, etc. ; **names of natural objects**, horses, dogs, or animals, trees (as in *Burnham beeches*), stars, con-stellations ; **names of artificial objects**, such as ships, steam-engines, guns, bells (*Big Ben*).

163. Such classifications evidently give part of the meaning of a proper name. Thus it is part of the meaning of such proper names as *John* and *Plato* that they denote persons, and not places, etc. But they mean more than this : they imply ' male human being,' just as *Mary* implies ' female human being.' Each name has besides a vast number of special meanings. Thus the name *Plato* implies all the charac-teristics—personal attributes, actions, feelings, thoughts, writings, etc.—that distinguish the man Plato from all other men.

It is, therefore, incorrect to say that proper names are devoid of meaning. On the contrary, they have more meaning than common words through being more highly specialized (39). The mistake has arisen from confusing unmeaning with uncon-nected (160).

164. Proper names are always liable to change into common words. One way in which this change may begin is by the metaphorical use of a proper name to express other persons who possess some attribute or attributes implied by the proper name. Thus, as Plato was a philosopher, we may say of any other philosopher that he is *a second Plato*, or, more briefly, *a Plato*. In the same way a strong man may be called *a Hercules*. Another way in which proper names may be made into common words is seen in such a word as *china*, which means a particular kind of earthenware which was originally brought from China. In such cases as these, a proper name is made into a noun. Proper names are also made into verbs, either indirectly as in *to hector*, or directly, as in *to boycott*. Proper names are often used in a more or less arbitrary way to form names of newly invented articles of trade, as in *Wellington boot*, shortened to *wellington*, *Gladstone bag*; or of new plants, trees, minerals, etc., as in *fuchsia* (so called from the German botanist *Fuchs*, which, again, means 'fox,' from the slyness attributed to some one of his ancestors), *Blenheim orange* (a kind of apple shaped like an orange, and first grown at Blenheim, the seat of the duke of Marlborough, so called from the victory won by the duke of Marlborough at Blenheim), *Prussian blue*.

It must be borne in mind that every name is not a proper name. *Blenheim orange* is a name that was given arbitrarily—though less arbitrarily than such a name as *Wellington boots*—to a new kind of apple, but as it includes all individual apples or apple-trees of the same kind, instead of excluding them, it is a common, not a proper name. So also such a nickname as *Tory* is applied indiscriminately to all men of certain political views, and is therefore an ordinary class-word. But when king Edward the First was called *Longshanks*, this nickname was used to distinguish him from the other Englishmen of the time, whether longlegged or shortlegged, and consequently was a true proper name.

Such an epithet as *the discoverer of the circulation of the blood* or *the first Christian emperor of Rome* is not a proper name, for, although it almost necessarily denotes one single, definite individual, it does so by virtue of its meaning and grammatical construction, and not by any arbitrary restriction. Such an epithet as *the man with the iron mask*, on the other hand, approaches very near to a proper name, because there might be several men who have worn iron masks, and we use this epithet to denote one particular man in history whose identity is still disputed.

Abstract Nouns.

165. The secondary use of nouns as regards their meaning is to express attributes and phenomena, attribute-nouns and phenomenon-nouns being included under the common designation **abstract nouns.**

166. Permanent attributes being primarily expressed by adjectives, most attribute-nouns are formed from adjectives by various derivative processes : thus the attribute-nouns *redness, length, height, stupidity, prudence* are formed from the adjectives *red, long, high, stupid, prudent.* Changing attributes or phenomena being primarily expressed by verbs, most phenomenon-words are derivatives of verbs ; thus the phenomenon-nouns *reading, action, conversation, proof, speech* are formed from the verbs *read, act, converse, prove, speak.* Many abstract nouns are also formed by the direct conversion of a verb into a noun ; thus from the verbs *to run, to ride, to sound* are formed the nouns in such collocations as *a good run, to go for a ride, a loud sound.* When an adjective is converted into a noun, it generally becomes concrete, and often undergoes further changes of meaning, as in the noun *goods* from the adjective *good*, the *reds and yellows in a picture*, which means the yellow and red portions of the picture, *redness* and *yellowness* being purely abstract.

167. But there are many abstract nouns which are neither derived nor converted from adjectives or verbs. Such abstract nouns are—*beauty*; *lightning, thunder, shadow*; *day, night,*

summer, winter ; disease, fever ; joy, hope ; ease, energy.
Most of the ideas expressed by these words are so indispensable and familiar that nouns were framed to express them
directly (**57**).   The adjectives and nouns corresponding to
these independent abstract nouns are either distinct words,
such as *to burn* corresponding to *fire*, or are derivatives from
them, such as *easy, beautiful* from *ease, beauty*.

168. Some nouns, especially those of complex meaning,
may be regarded as half-abstract, or intermediate between
abstract and concrete.   Thus *north* and *south* are abstract if
regarded from the point of view of the rising and setting of
the sun, while they are concrete if we regard them merely
as parts of the earth or points on the horizon or in the sky.

169. Particles and interjections are occasionally converted
into nouns.   Thus we say, ' there is an *if* in that,' meaning
some reservation or condition.   So also in

Leave Now to dogs and apes! Man has Forever.

(BROWNING)

170. Words belonging to all parts of speech may be used
as nouns to express the word itself apart from its meaning, as
when we say ' *if* is a conjunction,' ' the objective case of *I*
is *me*.'

FUNCTION.

171. The primary grammatical function of nouns is to
serve as **head-words**.   A head-word may be modified by
having something either implied or stated about it.   Hence
a noun may be modified either by an assumptive (attributive)
word or a predicate.   Thus the nouns *snow, height, action,
ride* are modified by assumptive words in *melting snow, a
great height, a generous action, a long ride*, and by predicative
words and word-groups in *the snow has melted, the height is
enormous, such an action is not justifiable, the ride was too long.*
The assumptive or predicative word may be a mere qualifier,
as in *all men, the men are here.*

172. The secondary function of nouns is to serve as **adjunct-words**, by modifying other nouns or verbs.

173. When a noun is put before the noun it modifies it is called an **assumptive** (attributive) noun. Thus in *king Alfred* the first noun is assumptive. When a material noun is used assumptively it resembles an adjective, as in *stone wall, gold chain.* But we can see the general difference between an assumptive noun and an assumptive adjective by comparing *gold chain* with *golden hair. Golden* is a pure attribute-word, expressing one only of the attributes of gold, namely its colour; while the assumptive noun *gold* in *gold chain* implies all the attributes of gold, a gold chain having not only the colour of gold, but also its weight, hardness, etc. There is the same distinction between *silken hair* or *silky hair* and *silk thread.* As thinking of all the attributes of a substance is practically the same thing as thinking of the substance itself, it really does not matter much whether we regard *stone* and *gold* in *stone wall, gold chain* as concrete or abstract words.

In noun-compounds such as *man-servant, cattle-market, cannon-ball,* the first noun is an adjunct to the second exactly as in *stone wall,* etc. It is in fact difficult to decide whether to regard *stone* in *stone wall* as an element of a compound or not. It certainly has something of the fixity of a compound : we cannot separate its elements as we can separate those of *a green tree* in *so green a tree*; we can hardly even make *stone wall* into *the wall is stone.* But as both elements of such groups keep their strong stress, and as there is not marked isolation of meaning, it is equally justifiable to regard them as mere word-groups analogous to the combination of an assumptive adjective with its noun. In fact, in older English *a gold chain* was called *a golden chain,* and we can still write *silken thread* instead of *silk thread* without any change of meaning.

This has led some people to regard *stone, gold* in *stone wall, gold chain*—and even *cannon* in *cannon-ball*—as adjectives. There can, indeed, be no question that the combination *gold chain* bears a close resemblance to *golden hair,* not only logi-

cally, but also grammatically, which we need not be surprised
at when we consider that *gold*, etc. are material nouns, and that
these material nouns approach very near in meaning to pure
attribute-words (155).   Material nouns resemble adjectives
formally in not taking any articles, so that while *man-servant*
etc. are clearly shown to be compounds by the want of the
articles *a* or *the* which *man* would require if it were independent,
the absence of the articles from the material nouns *stone*, etc.
not only does not make *stone wall* a compound, but increases
the difficulty of distinguishing these nouns from adjectives.
But as the most marked formal characteristic of adjectives is
comparison, and as comparison of *stone* in *stone wall* is impossible, even if the meaning of the combination allowed it,
while there would be no grammatical objection to making *stony
road, golden hair* into *stonier road, the most golden hair,* we
must refuse to admit that assumptive nouns have any of the
really distinctive features of adjectives.

174. A noun following a verb may serve as adjunct to the
verb alone, as in *I saw the man,* or the verb may be only a
link to connect the adjunct noun with the subject noun-word,
as in *he became a lawyer, he is a lawyer* (**131**).   Of the relations in which a verb-modifying noun stands to its verb the
most important are those of the direct and indirect object,
which have been already explained (**131, 132**).   But there are
a variety of other relations in which an adjunct noun can
stand to its verb, most of which make the adjunct noun
grammatically equivalent to an adverb, as in *he stopped the
night* compared with *he stopped long, he walked all day. he ran
a race* (**252, 253**).   For the use of a noun as complement to
a noun-word governed by a verb, as in *they made him king,*
see § **267.**

175. A noun in an oblique case—or oblique case relation—
or governed by a preposition is always an adjunct word.
Thus *day's* and *of honour* in *a day's work, a man of honour,*
are adjunct words or word-groups, as also *boy* in *he beat the
boy* compared with *boy-beating.*   In fact, the only nouns that
are not adjunct words are those that are in the subject rela-

tion, as in *the earth is round.* Even a nominatival noun is
an adjunct-word when it is not a subject-word, as in *the earth
is a globe,* where *globe* is an adjunct to *earth.*

Adjectives.

FORM.

176. The only regular inflections of adjectives in English
are those of **comparison,** which, however, may be regarded
as being almost as much a process of derivation as of inflection (**79**). There are two degrees of comparison, the **comparative** and **superlative,** in contrast to which the uncom-
pared adjective is said to be in the **positive** degree. The
comparative is formed by adding -*er,* or prefixing the form-
word *more,* the superlative by adding -*est* or prefixing the form-
word *most.* Thus from the positives *big, beautiful* are formed
the comparatives *bigger, more beautiful,* and the superlatives
biggest, most beautiful.

177. In concord-languages, such as Latin, adjectives have
inflections corresponding to those of nouns—though generally not exactly the same in form. The general rule in such
languages is that adjectives agree with their nouns—that is,
the nouns to which they serve as adjuncts, whether assumptively or predicatively—in case, number, and gender. Thus
in such a sentence as *he has beautiful daughters, beautiful*
would take the same inflections as *daughters,* namely the
accusative case, plural number, and feminine gender. English still has a trace of adjective-concord in the adjective-
pronouns *this* and *that,* which have plurals *these, those,* as in
these men compared with *this man.* Otherwise English
adjectives have no inflections of case, number, or gender.

178. In languages which inflect their adjectives, the
accompanying noun is often dropped when it can be easily
supplied from the context, the adjective inflections being
enough to show the gender, number, and grammatical relations of the resulting **free adjective.** Thus in such lan-

guages *the good* in the masculine singular would be understood to mean 'the good man,' and in the feminine plural it would mean 'the good women,' while *good* in the neuter plural would be understood to mean 'good things.' In such instances as these there is no conversion of the adjective into a noun : the noun is simply dropped, and the adjective keeps its own inflections unchanged. Thus in German *die gute* 'the good (woman)' forms its genitive singular *der guten* 'of the good (woman)' with an exclusively adjective inflection ; for if *gute* were a noun, it would remain unchanged in the genitive singular, like the feminine noun *die tante* 'the aunt,' genitive singular *der tante.*

179. But in English such free adjectives could not be used without ambiguity because of the want of adjective inflections ; hence in English an ordinary adjective [for adjective pronouns see § **193**] cannot be used as a noun without being converted —either wholly or partially—into a noun, and even then its use is often much restricted. When we talk of *goods and chattels* or *the reds and yellows in a picture, good, red, yellow* are pure nouns, as much so as *chattels* and *picture* themselves. These are therefore cases of complete conversion, which is frequently accompanied by considerable changes of meaning, as in the case of *goods.* But when we speak of *the true and the beautiful,* meaning 'what is true,' 'what is beautiful,' or say that *the good are happy,* meaning 'good people are happy,' the conversion is only partial, for although *the good* in this sentence has exactly the same grammatical function as *men* or any other noun in the plural, it does not take the plural inflection which it would require if it were a real noun ; and in it as well as in *the true and the beautiful,* the form-word *the* has a different function from what it would have with a noun ; for we could not say *the men* in the sense of 'men in general.'

180. Another way of using an adjective without its noun in English is to substitute the unmeaning noun-pronoun *one* for the noun, the inflection of the noun being transferred to this **prop-word**, as we may call it.   In this way we can distinguish between the singular *a good one* and the plural *good ones*, as in *give me a book, an interesting one—one tall man and two short ones*.   In such cases a concord-language would of course employ the inflected adjective without any noun or prop-word.   These prop-forms are generally used in English only when the adjective is absolute, that is, when its noun can be supplied grammatically from the context : we cannot use *good ones* in the general sense of *the good*, but only with reference to a preceding noun.

Meaning.

181. The primary use of adjectives as regards their meaning is to express the attributes of substance-words.   Such adjectives as *big, green, good* are pure **attribute-adjectives** : they express simple attributes apart from the substances in which these attributes are found.   These adjectives are also formally independent of nouns.   Adjectives formed from nouns also often express simple attributes, as in *golden hair*.

182. When an adjective expresses a group of attributes, it approaches near in meaning to a substance-word, and when an adjective formed from a substance-noun expresses all the attributes belonging to that noun, it is practically identical with it in meaning.   Thus *the English climate* means exactly the same as *the climate of England*, and *a silken thread* means exactly the same as *a thread of silk*.   We call such adjectives substance-adjectives or **concrete** adjectives.   It is evident that these adjectives fall under the same classes as the nouns to which they correspond in meaning.   Thus *human* in *the human mind* is a class-adjective, *silken* in *silken thread* and *wooden* in *wooden spoon* are material adjectives, and *English* is a name-adjective, as also *Crimean* in *Crimean war* = ' the War in the Crimea.'

183. In such a combination as *Foreign Office* = ' office for transacting the business of the nation with foreign countries,' the adjective may be called a **condensed** adjective, for it implies adjective + noun.

184. In considering the meaning of adjectives, we must carefully distinguish between attributive adjectives, such as we have hitherto been considering, and **qualifying** adjectives, which do not imply or state attributes, but merely limit or define the noun they are associated with **(34)**. Some of these qualifying adjectives have perfectly definite meanings, such as *many*, while others, such as the articles *a* and *the*, have only more or less vague grammatical functions, most of them belonging to the class of adjective-pronouns.

185. The only words of which attributes can be implied or stated are substance-words, that is, concrete nouns. Hence every adjective which is associated with an abstract noun must be regarded as a qualifying, not as an attribute-adjective. Thus, while *great* in *great man* is a true attribute-adjective, it is only a qualifier in *a great height, great stupidity*. So also *quick* and *rash* are qualifying adjectives in *quick motion, rash actions*.

FUNCTION.

186. The grammatical function of adjectives is to serve as adjuncts to noun-words. We distinguish adjectives as **assumptive** (attributive) and **predicative** according as they imply or state an attribute or qualification of the noun-word. Thus we have assumptive adjectives in *good men, many men, great goodness, quick motion*, and predicative adjectives in *he is good, his goodness is great, riding is healthy, to err is human*. In *riding is a healthy exercise, healthy* is, of course, an assumptive adjective, although it forms part of the predicate-group.

187. An adjective following a verb logically modifies the noun-word which is the subject of the verb, as in *he is ready*, where *ready* modifies *he*. If the verb has an independent meaning, the adjective may be said to modify it to a certain extent, although even then it is an adjunct mainly to the subject-word, as in *he turned red*. Here *red* not only tells us that 'he' is red, but may also be said to tell us *how* he turned. In these instances the adjective follows a link-verb (262). If a word having the form of an adjective follows an independent verb, as in *he breathed hard*, it must be regarded as converted into an adverb. For the use of an adjective as complement to a preceding noun-word governed by a verb, as in *to paint a house white*, see § 267.

188. When an adjective serves as adjunct to another adjective which follows it, it must be regarded as an adverb, as in *dark red, deep red, greenish yellow*, unless we prefer to regard these groups as compounds. But such groups as *much greater, little better* cannot well be regarded as compounds, so it is better to regard *dark* in *dark red* also as an adverb, especially as both elements in such groups retain their strong stress, and there is no special isolation in meaning.

Such a group as *quick-revolving*, with its predominant stress on the first element, makes more the impression of a compound.

Pronouns.

189. Every pronoun is either a noun—**noun-pronoun** or simply **pronoun,** or an adjective—**adjective-pronoun.** Many pronouns are used both as nouns and as adjectives, in which case the adjective use is generally the primary and the more important; thus *that* is a noun-pronoun in *I know that*, an adjective-pronoun in *that man, that fact*.

Form.

190. Pronouns are distinguished from ordinary nouns and adjectives by various formal characteristics.

191. Some of the noun-pronouns have special inflections (*he, him*), and special distinctions of gender (*he, she, it*).

192. When an adjective-pronoun is made into a noun, it sometimes takes the ordinary noun-inflections, as in *the other*, plural *the others* (*the others have come* compared with *the other men*), and sometimes keeps its adjective form, that is, remains indeclinable, as in *some think differently* = *some men think differently*.

193. The adjective-pronouns differ from ordinary adjectives in the following features :—

(*a*) Many of them can be used absolutely without any prop-word (**180**) : *he has some bread, I have some too.* Some of them have special absolute forms : *he has no books, I have none either.*

(*b*) Most of them can be converted into noun-pronouns without the restrictions that apply to ordinary adjectives (**179**) : *much remains to be done, many think differently.* Some of them, however, cannot be converted into nouns or used absolutely without the addition of some prop-word, such as *one, body, thing* : *has anyone come? has anybody come? everything went wrong.*

(*c*) They are often peculiar in their use of the articles. Some of them never take them at all, such as *this, that*, and, of course, the articles *a* and *the* themselves ; others only with some change of meaning or function, as in *to take a little trouble, the whole day*, compared with *to take little trouble, whole loaves* ; while others, again, take them in peculiar positions, as in *all the day* compared with *the longest day*.

It is often difficult to draw the line between adjective-pronouns and ordinary adjectives. But if an adjective does not show any of the above formal peculiarities, it cannot be regarded as a pronoun, however much it may resemble an adjective-pronoun in meaning. Thus *several* is a pronoun because it can be used absolutely, as in *I have several* ; but although *divers* has the same meaning as *several*, we cannot say **I have divers* any more than we can say **I have good* in the sense of *I have good books* ; so *divers* can be regarded only as an ordinary adjective.

MEANING.

194. If we compare pronouns with ordinary nouns and adjectives, we shall find that pronouns always have a very general meaning. Thus the noun-pronoun *you* means 'anyone that I am speaking to,' and the adjective-pronoun *the* can be prefixed to any noun to single it out from other nouns. We might therefore from a purely logical point of view define pronouns as **general nouns** and **adjectives**, as opposed to the ordinary special nouns and adjectives, bearing in mind that some nouns and adjectives are more general in their meaning than others. Hence a noun of general meaning is often almost equivalent to a pronoun. Thus *men say, people say* mean much the same as *they say*, and in a book it does not matter much whether the author speaks of himself as *I* or *the author, the writer*, or whether he speaks of his reader as *you* or *the reader*. In fact the distinction between *men say* and *they say* is purely formal: we restrict the name pronoun to *they* because it has formal peculiarities of its own which keep it apart from such nouns as *man*, however general the latter may be in meaning. We have also seen (**193.** 1) that it is sometimes difficult to draw the line between ordinary qualifying adjectives—which always have a more or less general meaning—and adjective-pronouns.

FUNCTION.

195. The grammatical function of pronouns is to serve as **mark-words** (35). When a man says of himself *I think* instead of *William Smith thinks*—or whatever his name may be—or when he speaks of some other man as *he*, instead of calling him by his name, or saying *the man who was here yesterday*, etc., he does much the same as the man who makes a cross instead of signing his name, or puts a block of wood on his library shelf to show where a book has been taken out. Just as the cross or the block may stand for any one name or any one book, so also the pronouns *I*, *he* may stand for any one noun whose meaning allows of these pronouns being applied to it, and they may be transferred from one noun to another : *he* may point to *William Smith* at one time, and to *John Collins* at another. They are thus **shifting** or **moveable mark-words**, name-words (proper names), such as *William Smith*, being permanent or fixed mark-words (**157**).

196. A noun-pronoun is at the same time a **substitute** for a noun or group of nouns. Pronouns are used partly for the sake of brevity, as when we say *you* instead of 'the person I am speaking to now,' partly to avoid the repetition of a noun, and partly to avoid the necessity of definite statement.

197. As the cross at the end of a receipt or similar document only tells us that a name is meant, without telling us what the name is, so also a pronoun has no independent meaning of its own: it conveys only enough information to let us know what noun it refers to. It is true that *he* generally means 'male being' and *she* generally means 'female being,' but the distinction of sex in these pronouns is made only for the sake of more distinct reference ; and when we refer to a ship as *she*, the word *she* is as devoid of independent meaning as the cross which stands for a name.

198. Adding an adjective-pronoun to a noun is equivalent to putting a mark on the noun. Thus, to single out one particular book in a library catalogue by calling it *the book* or *this book*, or to single out one particular house in a row by calling it *the house*, is equivalent to ticking off the name of the book in the catalogue or chalking a cross on the door of the house. Adjective-pronouns can be shifted from one noun to another in the same way as a pencil tick can be shifted from the title of one book to that of another in the catalogue. The difference between noun-pronouns and adjective-pronouns is, of course, that while a noun-pronoun takes the place of a noun, an adjective-pronoun can only qualify it :

the difference is the same as that between making a cross stand for a name, and simply adding it to a name. Thus when we talk of a man or a woman as *the man, the woman,* we only put a mark on the nouns; but when we talk of a man as *he* or a woman as *she,* we substitute the mark-words *he, she* for the nouns *man, woman.* So also when we talk of *William Smith* as *he,* we substitute a moveable general mark-word for a fixed, special designation. As *man* and *woman* are nouns of comparatively general meaning, the groups *the man, the woman* approach very near in meaning and function to the noun-pronouns *he, she.*

Classes of Pronouns.

199. As regards their function in the sentence, pronouns fall under two main divisions, **independent** and **dependent**. A sentence or clause introduced by a dependent pronoun cannot stand alone, but makes us expect another (independent) sentence, called the principal sentence or clause, without which the dependent clause is incomplete. Thus the dependent pronoun in *who was here yesterday* makes us expect some such principal clause as *I know the man—I know the man who was here yesterday,* while a sentence introduced by the corresponding independent pronoun *he* can stand alone—*he was here yesterday.* Dependent pronouns are subdivided into **relative** and **conjunctive**. All pronouns also fall under the heads of **definite** and **indefinite**. The more special divisions are **personal, possessive, emphatic, reflexive, reciprocal, interrogative, negative, quantitative.** These divisions cross one another in various ways. Thus an emphatic pronoun may be either personal or possessive, besides necessarily being either dependent or independent, and definite or indefinite.

Personal Pronouns.

200. The personal pronouns are all noun-pronouns. They have plural- and case-inflections, and some of them

distinguish gender.   They are distinguished by **person,**
as first, second, third person pronouns. The pronoun of
the **first person** singular, *I,* means 'the speaker,' that is,
from the point of view of the speaker himself.   The first
person plural *we* is not really the plural of *I,* whose meaning
does not admit of plurality: *we* means either 'I + you'
(*you* itself meaning either one or more than one person), or
'I + he, she, it, or they'; that is, the only way of making
a plural to *I* is by associating with it the idea of the second
or third person pronouns.   The pronoun of the **second
person** is *you,* which is both singular = 'you man,' 'you
woman,' etc., and plural = 'you people,' the old singular *thou*
being preserved only in the higher literary language.   But
in combination with the emphatic pronoun *self* (**205**) we
make a distinction between the singular *yourself* and the
plural *yourselves.*   The pronouns of the **third person** distinguish gender in the singular, but not in the plural :
singular masculine *he,* feminine *she,* neuter *it,* plural for all
genders *they.*   The reason of the gender not being marked
in the plural is that a number of persons may be of different
sexes, and it is not worth while stopping to consider whether
they means 'the men ' or 'the women' or 'the men and the
women together.'

Gender is to some extent distinguished in the plural of the
interrogative pronoun *who,* which is really a special kind of
personal pronoun (**201.** 1).

201. Most of the personal pronouns are **definite** pronouns : they point to some definite person or thing.   The
French *on* in *on dit* 'they say' is, on the other hand, an
indefinite pronoun of the third person singular.   This
indefinite personal pronoun is represented in English sometimes by *one,* sometimes by the definite personal pronouns
you and *they: one would think so, you would think so, they say.*

Although the designation 'personal pronoun' is generally
confined to the above pronouns, there are several other pro-

nouns which for convenience are classed under different heads, and yet are really personal pronouns. Such pronouns are the interrogative and relative *who, what* (**211**).

202. It must be observed that the neuter pronoun *it* does not always refer to a definite thing, but is often entirely unmeaning. Thus in *it rains* the *it* is a mere prop-word, the logical subject of the sentence being contained in *rains* itself (**57**).

Possessive Pronouns.

203. The possessive pronouns are exactly parallel to the personal pronouns, each personal pronoun having its own possessive, so that the possessive pronouns make the same distinctions of number and person as the personal pronouns. Thus to the personal pronoun *he* corresponds the possessive third person *his* in *his book*. The possessive pronouns may be regarded either as noun-pronouns in the genitive, or as personal noun-pronouns made into adjectives. That is, we may regard *his* in *his book* either as standing in the same relation to *of him* as *John s* does to *of John*, or as *he* made into an adjective. It must be observed that a possessive pronoun does not necessarily imply possession any more than a genitive case does: when a slave talks of *his master*, or the master of *his headache*, it does not mean that the slave possesses the master, or the master possesses the headache. Some of the possessives, such as *his* and *its*, certainly have the inflections of genitives—although the vowel of *his* is not the same as that of *he*; but others, such as *my*—the possessive of *I*—have not; for the regular genitive of *I* would be **I's*. Some of the possessives make a distinction between **conjoint** and **absolute** forms. Thus *my* in *my book, my own book* is the conjoint form corresponding to the absolute *mine*. The conjoint form is used when the possessive pronoun comes before its noun. The absolute form is used when there is no accompanying noun, being itself equivalent either to an adjective, as in *the book is mine*, or to a pure noun : *he does not seem to know the distinction between mine and thine.* Those pronouns which have the genitive ending *s* in the conjoint form, such as *his* and *its*, do not make any distinction between conjoint and absolute : *his book, it is his.* Some of the others, such as *her*, take the genitive *s* in the absolute form : *her book, it is hers.* As there is not a trace of genitive inflection in such possessives as *my*, *mine*, and as the distinction between conjoint and absolute is more charac-teristic of adjectives than of nouns, we can have no hesitation in regarding possessive pronouns, taken as a whole, as adjec-tives rather than as genitive cases of noun-pronouns.

204. The possessive pronouns in English are : first person singular *my* (absolute *mine*), plural *our* (absolute *ours*) ; second person singular *thy* (absolute *thine*), plural *your* (absolute *yours*) ; third person singular masculine *his*, feminine *her* (absolute *hers*), neuter *its*, plural *their* (absolute *theirs*).

Thy, thine occurs only in the higher literary language, *your(s)* being substituted for it in ordinary language.

The genitives *one's* and *whose* of the indefinite *one* and the interrogative and relative *who* may also be regarded as pos-sessive pronouns.

Emphatic Pronouns.

205. The personal pronouns are made emphatic by adding the noun-pronoun *self*, plural *selves*, as in *I did it myself, we did it ourselves*, where the personal pronoun is put in the possessive form, as before an ordinary noun ; while in other combinations, such as *himself, themselves*, the personal pronoun is in the objective case, *self, selves* being in a kind of apposition to it.

206. The possessive pronouns are made emphatic by add-ing the adjective-pronoun *own* : *my own book, it is my own.*

From these emphatic possessive pronouns, new, doubly emphatic noun-pronouns are formed by adding *self: my own self.*

Reflexive Pronouns.

207. The compounds of the personal pronouns with *self* are also used as reflexive pronouns, as in *we should try to see ourselves as others see us,* 'where *ourselves* is the reflexive pronoun corresponding to the ordinary personal pronoun *us.* A reflexive pronoun is a personal pronoun standing in the object-relation to a verb, or else joined to it by a preposition, as in *he thinks too much of himself,* being at the same time a repetition of the logical subject of the verb. In *we see ourselves* the reflexive pronoun stands in the direct object-relation to the verb *see,* and refers us back to *we,* which is the subject of the verb. In *John told him to give himself plenty of time,* the reflexive pronoun *himself* stands in the indirect object-relation to the verbal (verb-equivalent) *to give,* and refers us back to the logical subject of *give,* namely *him, told him to give himself* being equivalent to *told him that he should give himself* (**445**).

208. It will be observed that in the last sentence the reflexive pronoun refers back to the logical subject of the verb-equivalent it follows, which logical subject is in this sentence not the grammatical subject in the sentence. In English a reflexive pronoun always refers back in this way to the nearest logical subject of the preceding verb or verbal. But in some languages, such as Latin, a reflexive pronoun necessarily refers back to the grammatical subject of the sentence, so that in Latin the above sentence would imply that John himself was to have plenty of time given him. So also in such a sentence as *he begged me to defend him, him* would take the reflexive form in Latin—*oravit ut se defenderem*—which would be impossible in English, because the logical subject of the verbal *to defend* is *me,* which is not of the same person as *him,* and cannot therefore be repeated by it. The Latin reflexives are therefore **grammatical reflexives,** the English **logical reflexives.**

In English we sometimes use the simple personal pronouns in a reflexive sense, as in *he looked about him.*

209. The emphatic forms of the possessive pronouns are used also as reflexives, as in *he goes in his own carriage* ; but when it is not necessary to emphasize the reflexive meaning, we generally use the simple possessives in a reflexive sense, as in *he has sold his carriage, he drives his carriage himself.* In all these sentences such a language as Latin would employ the reflexive forms.

Reciprocal Pronouns.

210. The group-pronouns *each other, one another*, in such sentences as *they help each other, they would not speak to each other, he told the three children to help one another*, are called reciprocal pronouns. Reciprocal pronouns, like reflexives, stand as adjuncts to a verb or verbal, and at the same time refer back to the logical subject of the verb or verbal. But this subject, as well as the reciprocal pronouns themselves, must always be in the plural. *Each other* generally implies only two, *one another* more than two persons, though this distinction is not always strictly observed. Reciprocal pronouns are necessarily plural, because there is always a cross-relation between the subjects and the reciprocal pronouns. Thus *they help each other* means ' A helps B, and B helps A.'

Interrogative Pronouns.

211. The interrogative or questioning pronouns in English are *who, what, which. Who* is used only as a noun. It has two genders, the **personal**, including masculine and feminine, expressed by *who*, and the **neuter**, expressed by *what : who is that man ?, who is that woman?, what is that thing ?* These forms are plural as well as singular : *who are those men ?, who are those women ?, what are those things ?* We see that the distinctions made in the interrogative pronouns are much vaguer than in the personal pronouns, the distinctions made in *he, she, they* being levelled in *who*, although, on the other hand, the retention of the singular forms of the interrogative pronoun in the plural enables it to distinguish the neuter from the personal gender in the plural as well as the singular. The reason of this greater vagueness of the interrogative pronouns is, of course, that a question is naturally vaguer than a statement, for all questions imply a certain amount of ignorance. *Who* and *what* also differ from *he, she* and *it* in having a common genitive or possessive form *whose*. *Who* has an objective case *whom*, parallel to *him*, from which, however, the uninflected *who* is substituted in the spoken language, as in *who(m) do you mean?*

212. *What* differs from *who* in being used as an adjective as well as a noun. In both functions it can be used in a personal sense, but in a meaning different from that of *who*: *what is he?, what woman is that?*

213. *Which*, like *what*, is mainly neuter in meaning, though it is used personally as well. It is both a noun and an adjective, and is indeclinable, not having even a possessive form, as *what* has : *which (of those things) do you want?, which boy do you mean?*

214. When an interrogative pronoun is used to introduce an independent sentence (199), the interrogation is said to be **direct**. When it introduces a clause dependent on a principal clause containing a statement or question, the interrogation is said to be **indirect**. Thus we have indirect interrogation in such a sentence as *I asked him who he was and what he wanted*, contrasting with the direct interrogation sentences *who are you?, who is he?, what does he want?*

215. It must be borne in mind that an interrogative pronoun is always the predicate of the sentence it introduces, whether the sentence is independent or dependent. Thus the questions *who is he?, (I asked) who he was* correspond to the statement *he is somebody*.

Relative and Conjunctive Pronouns.

216. In English the interrogative pronouns *who, what, which* and the definite pronoun *that* are used also as relative (and conjunctive) pronouns.   *That* when used as a relative is indeclinable, as in *the men that were here yesterday* compared with *those men*, being used also only as a noun, not as an adjective.   The use of *who, what, which* as relatives is parallel to their use as interrogatives : the relative *who* is used only as a noun, the relatives *what* and *which* both as nouns and as adjectives, the use of these three pronouns as regards inflection being much the same when they are relative as when they are interrogative.   The English relative pronouns also agree with the interrogative pronouns in making no distinctions of person ; thus *who* can refer to *I* as well as to *he* or to a noun : *I, who know all about it—he who knows— the man who knows.*

217. The relative pronoun makes the clause it introduces —the relative clause—into an adjunct to some noun-word— called the **antecedent**—in the principal clause.   Thus in *I know the man who was here yesterday*, the clause *who was here yesterday* is an adjunct to the antecedent *man* in the principal clause *I know the man* ; and in *I say it who know it*, the antecedent is the pronoun *I*.   It is easy to see that a relative clause is an adjunct, because we can often substitute an adjunct-word—generally a participle (adjective-verbal)— for the relative clause without change of meaning, as in *the window looking on the garden, the lost child = the window which looks on the garden, the child that was lost* or *the child which was lost*.   Sometimes the whole of the principal sentence constitutes the antecedent, which is then a **sentence-antece- dent**, as in *I said nothing, which made him still more angry*, where *I said nothing* is equivalent to such a word-group (noun group) as *my saying nothing* or *my silence*.

218. In the above examples the relative clause is logically, as well as formally, an adjunct, subordinate to its antecedent. But in some cases a relative pronoun is used to join on a clause which is logically coordinate (**45**) to the principal clause. Thus in the sentence *I told John, who told his brother, and he told his wife*, the relative pronoun *who* has exactly the same meaning as *and he* in the following sentence. We call such relatives—which are equivalent to *and* + personal pronoun, being thus relatives in form only—**progressive relative** noun-pronouns.   ·

In spoken English relative noun-pronouns are omitted in certain constructions, as in *the man I saw yesterday* = the literary *the man whom I saw yesterday*.

219. The function of a relative adjective-pronoun is to make the noun it qualifies relative, the combination relative adjective + noun being thus equivalent to a relative noun-pronoun. Thus in the last example in § **217** we might refer to *I said nothing* by the relative group *which proceeding* instead of the simple noun-relative *which*: *I said nothing, which proceeding of mine made him still more angry*. So also we might refer to *Plato* as *which philosopher* instead of simply as *who*.

220. It sometimes happens that the antecedent to a relative noun-pronoun is not expressed either by a noun-word or a sentence, the relative itself doing duty for the antecedent as well. Such a relative is called a **condensed relative** (**112**). Only *who* and *what* are used as condensed relatives, *what* being the more frequent of the two in this use. The clause introduced by a condensed relative precedes, instead of following, the principal clause: *what you say is quite true*; *what I say I mean*: *what is done cannot be undone*; *who(ever) said that was mistaken*. In the first of these sentences the condensed relative *what* is the object of the verb *say* in the relative clause, and is at the same time the subject of the verb *is* in the principal clause, while in the second sentence it is the object in both clauses, and in the third sentence it is the subject in both clauses. If we alter the construction of such sentences, the missing antecedent is often restored: *it is quite true what you say; if I say a thing, I mean it.* Nevertheless, in such a sentence as *what you say is quite true* we are not sensible of any omission, because we feel that *what* unites in itself relative and antecedent : it is relative by virtue of its form, while its prominent position at the beginning of the clause-group seems to make it belong to the principal clause also.

221. The interrogative pronouns are also used as **conjunctive pronouns** in English. A conjunctive pronoun makes the clause it introduces—the conjunctive clause—into an adjunct to the verb in the principal clause, which we may call the **antecedent verb**. Thus in *I know who you are*, the conjunctive pronoun *who* is the subject of the verb *are* in the conjunctive clause *who you are*, and this conjunctive clause is an adjunct to the verb *know* in the principal clause, standing in the same direct object relation to this verb as the noun-word *you* in *I know you*. In *I wonder what he meant, I asked what he meant, what* is the object of the verb of the conjunctive clause, and this clause is the object of the verb of the principal clause. In such a sentence as *this is what I mean*, the conjunctive *what* is the object of the verb of the conjunctive clause, and this clause stands in apposition to the subject of the principal clause, being therefore in the nominative relation.

222. Such a sentence as *this is what I mean* may be changed into *what I mean is this* with a condensed relative instead of a conjunctive. So also *I say what I mean=what I say I mean*. If we confined ourselves to such sentences as these, we might be inclined to regard a conjunctive pronoun as condensed or contracted: *this is what I mean* = *this is that which I mean*. But we do not feel such a sentence as *I know who you are* to be equivalent to *I know him who you are* or *I know the man who you are*; and even *I say what I mean* has not exactly the same meaning as *what I say I mean*.

223. So far from identifying conjunctive with condensed relative pronouns, we do not feel them to be relative at all, but rather associate them with the interrogative pronouns. Not only do we use the same pronouns conjunctively which we use interrogatively, but the form of a conjunctive sentence is identical with that of an indirect interrogation. Thus *I asked what he meant* is both an indirect interrogation sentence and a conjunctive sentence. All indirect interrogation sentences are necessarily conjunctive, although all conjunctive sentences are not interrogative. But even in an affirmative conjunctive sentence such as *I know what he means*, the *what* is felt to introduce a sort of answer to the implied question *what does he mean?* The affinity between conjunctive and interrogative sentences is also shown in such sentences as *I know who you are*, where the grammatical predicate in the conjunctive clause is the unmeaning form-word *are*, the real logical predicate being *who*, exactly as in the interrogative sentence *who are you?* (215).

Definite Pronouns.

224. The definite pronouns *this, that, the* are primarily adjectives. Such definite pronouns as *the* and *yonder* are used only as adjectives, and although *this* and *that* are used as nouns as well as adjectives, yet we generally think of them as qualifying some noun.

225. Definite pronouns fall under various subdivisions. **Demonstrative pronouns** point to something in space or time, as in *this house, that day*. **Reference pronouns** (generally included under demonstratives) point to something in thought. When we talk of *this man, that man*, or *the man*, meaning a man that has just been mentioned, *this*, *that* and *the* are reference pronouns. *The*, which is the typical reference adjective-pronoun, is called the **definite article**. As we see, *this* and *that* are both demonstrative and reference pronouns, while *the* is a reference pronoun only. Reference pronouns are distinguished as **back-pointing** and **forwards-pointing**, according as they refer to something that has been said or to something that is to follow. Thus *that* in *I know that* is back-pointing, while *this* in *this is what I mean* is forwards-pointing.

226. The distinction between definite and indefinite applies also to personal pronouns. Thus *he* is definite, *they* in *they say* indefinite. The distinction between demonstrative and reference pronouns applies also to the definite personal pronoun ; thus in *who is he?* meaning 'who is the man standing there? *he* is a place-demonstrative. The main difference between the personal and the definite pronouns is that the former are primarily nouns, while the definite pronouns are primarily adjectives.

227. *Such* is a definite pronoun of quantity and quality when used as an adjective, as in *such a quantity*, *I never heard such nonsense*. In its rarer use as a noun it approaches very near in meaning to an ordinary personal pronoun, as in *of such is the kingdom of heaven*.

228. *The same*, as in *the same day*, *I will do the same*, may be regarded as a definite pronoun of identity.

Indefinite Pronouns.

229. The most important of the indefinite pronouns is the **indefinite article** *a*, *an*, which, like the definite article, is used only as an adjective. The indefinite article puts a mark on a noun, but without identifying or defining it, having thus a function exactly contrary to that of the definite article: *a man wants to speak to you ; I do not know who he is ; he is not the man who was here yesterday*. The noun-pronoun most nearly corresponding to the indefinite article is the indefinite personal pronoun *one, they* = French *on*. The indefinite *one* must be distinguished from the numeral *one* (237); it is used both as an indefinite personal pronoun and as a prop-word (180).

230. Other indefinite pronouns are *some* in *some bread, any* in *any knife will do*, the corresponding negative *no* (absolute *none*), for which *not any* is substituted in spoken English, as in *I have not any bread, I have not any* = the literary *I have no bread, I have none*. The nouns corresponding to these adjective-pronouns are formed with prop-words : *someone, somebody, something ; anyone, anybody, anything ; no one, nobody, nothing*.

231. *Other (the other, another)*, in the sense of ' different,' as in *give me another plate, this one is not clean ; I like the other (book) best*, is an indefinite pronoun of quality. In the sense of 'additional,' 'another of the same kind,' as in *give me another piece of bread*, it is a quantitative pronoun (235). The group-pronoun *one another* is used as a reciprocal (210).

Quantitative Pronouns.

232. Quantity is of two kinds, (*a*) continuous quantity, expressed by such words as *size, big, long. much. less*, and (*b*) discrete or broken quantity, called ' number.' expressed by such words as *number, numerous, count, three, both, many*. Many quantitative nouns and adjectives, such as *size, number, big, long, numerous*, have nothing to distinguish them grammatically from ordinary nouns and adjectives, while others, such as *much, less, both, many*, have more or less of the formal characteristics of pronouns.

233. Many of the pronouns included under the other classes imply quantity. Thus the indefinite *some* in *some bread* implies ' not much,' *I* implies 'one.' etc. But these words only *imply* quantity, the expression of distinctions of

quantity not being their main function, and therefore it is not necessary to class them as specially quantitative.

234. The chief pronouns of continuous quantity are *much*, *more*, as in *more bread*, *most* [*more* and *most* are also pronouns of number], *a little*, as in *a little bread* [*little* by itself is an ordinary adjective, as also in *a little loaf*, etc.], *less*, *least*, *all the*, *the whole*, as in *all the day*, *the whole day* [*all* by itself is a pronoun of number, and *whole* by itself is an ordinary adjective], *enough*.

235. The pronouns of number are distinguished as **collective** and **separative**. A collective pronoun, such as *all*, makes us think of a number of objects in a mass ; a separative pronoun, such as *each*, makes us think of them one by one. The collective pronouns are : the emphatic *some*, as in *some people think so* [the unemphatic *some* in *some bread, I saw some people there*, is an indefinite pronoun], *several*, *few*, *many*, *more*, as in *more men than women*, *most, all* ; *both, other* in the sense of 'additional' **(231)**. The separative pronouns are : *every*, *each*, the alternative *either* = 'one of two' with its negative *neither*, *several* in *they went their several ways*. There are also nouns formed with prop-words : *everyone*, *everybody*, *everything*, *each one*. The group pronoun *each other* is used as a reciprocal **(210)**.

Negative Pronouns.

236. The pronouns beginning with *n-* are negative or not-pronouns. *Neither* is the negative corresponding to the positive *either*. *No* and its absolute form *none* are in form negatives of *one*, though in meaning they are negatives of *any*, *not any* being indeed substituted for *no*, *none* in spoken English **(230)**. From *no* are formed the noun-pronouns *no one*, *nobody*, *nothing*.

Numerals.

237. The numerals *one, two, three,* etc. differ from the pronouns of number, such as *some, many, all,* in expressing distinctions of discrete, quantity definitely instead of indefinitely. The difference between *one* the numeral and *one* the pronoun (**229**) is that the numeral *one* makes us think of 'one' as opposed to 'two' etc., while *one* the pronoun makes us think only of a vague singling out from an indefinite number of objects, the meaning 'oneness' being so much forgotten that we use *one* as a prop-word in the plural—*some good ones.*

238. Numerals, being intended to give definite information, have nothing of the character of mark-words about them. In form, however, they have all the characteristics of pronouns. They can be used freely both as adjectives, as in *three men. we are seven,* and as nouns: *the three, all three. three of us, by twos and threes.*

239. The above remarks apply mainly to **cardinal** numerals—*one, two, three, ten, hundred,* etc. **Ordinal** numerals —*first, second, third, tenth, hundredth,* etc.—are primarily adjectives, their use as nouns being limited like that of the other adjectives.

Verbs.

Form.

240. The ordinary inflections of an English verb—including the verbals—are as follows:—

(*a*) Third person, singular number, present tense, indicative mood: *calls, sees.*

(*b*) Preterite tense: *called, saw.*

(*c*) Present participle and gerund: *calling, seeing.*

(*d*) Preterite participle: *called, seen.*

In most verbs the finite preterite and the preterite participle have the same form—*called.*

241. The common form *call* expresses four grammatical categories : (*a*) present indicative, with the exception of the third person singular (*calls*), as in *I call, they call*; (*b*) present subjunctive, as in *if he call*; (*c*) imperative mood, as in *call!*; (*d*) infinitive, as in *let him call*.

242. In English, verbs are modified partly by inflection, partly by form-words—particles and verbs—which latter constitute the **periphrastic** forms of the verb. Inflections and periphrastic forms together make up the **conjugation** of a verb.

243. The form-particle *to* (preposition or adverb) is prefixed to the common form of the verb, this combination constituting the **supine** or periphrastic infinitive, as in *I wish to see*, which has the same grammatical function as the infinitive in *I will see*. Hence we often include the supine under the term infinitive. The adverb *not* also enters into the periphrastic forms of the verb, especially in the spoken language, as in *I don't know*, which is the negative form of *I know*.

244. The form-verbs used to modify the English verb are called **auxiliary** verbs, or auxiliaries. The chief auxiliaries are *be, have, do, will, shall, may.* When a full verb is associated with an auxiliary, it is always made into a verbal, so that the function of predication is transferred to the auxiliary. Thus the finite inflected verb in the present indicative *he sees* becomes an infinitive in the future tense *he will see*, a present participle in the definite indicative *he is seeing*, and a preterite participle in the perfect tense *he has seen*. If, as is often the case, a periphrastic form is made up of more than one auxiliary, only one of these keeps its finite form, all the others being made into verbals, as in *he has been seeing, he will have seen*, where *has* and *will* are the only finite verbs.

Many of the auxiliaries are used also as full verbs. Thus *will* in *I will do it, whether you like it or not* is not a form-word, but a full word meaning 'I am determined to.' Such combinations do not form part of the verb-conjugation.

We have seen that inflecting a noun and putting a preposition before it express the same grammatical function (78), so that *of men* stands to *men's* in the same relation as *he has seen* to *he saw*, although the two verb-forms differ slightly in meaning. But while it is most convenient to treat of noun-inflections and the use of prepositions separately, the inflectional and peri-phrastic forms of the verb are so mixed up that in treating of the meanings of verb-forms it is impossible to separate them. Thus *I see* and *I do see* differ only in the latter being more emphatic.

245. In English the finite verb must always be preceded by a subject-word, except in the imperative (*see!*). If no other noun-word comes before it, a personal pronoun must be used: *the man came*; *I know who came*; *he came*.

Hence the addition of the unmeaning *it* in *it rains* (**202**).

The pronouns are omitted only in colloquial, elliptical phrases, such as *don't know — I don't know*.

MEANING.

246. The primary use of verbs as regards their meaning is to express phenomena (changing attributes), as in *come, fall, grow, die* [compare the permanent attribute-word *dead*], *walk, strike, see, live, think*. In other verbs the idea of phenomenality is less predominant, as in *live, shine* — compared with *flash, twinkle*; *stand* — compared with *fall, rise*; *lie, sleep*. In *exist*, which is the most abstract and general of all verbs that have an independent meaning, we can realise the sense of phenomenality only by the contrast with non-existence.

247. Verbs are classed according to their meaning as **transitive** and **intransitive, reflexive, reciprocal, im-personal.**

Transitive and Intransitive Verbs.

248. Transitive verbs, such as *strike, see, like*, require a noun-word or noun-equivalent in the direct object relation to serve as complement to them, that is, complete their mean-ing, as in *he struck him*; *the man saw the boy*; *boys like jam*;

I do not like having my hair cut.   Verbs which do not take a direct-object noun-word after them are called **intransitive**, such as *come, fall, live.*   It is easier to form a complete sentence with an intransitive than with a transitive verb, as in *he fell, the tree lives.*   But transitive verbs can also stand without any object-noun, not only when the object-noun may be understood from the context, as in *I see,* meaning 'I see what you mean,' but also when the object idea is so vague or uncertain that it is not necessary or easy so to express it, as in *blind men saw,* where *saw* means 'saw things in general,' that is, 'received the power of sight.'   In *I see=* 'I see what you mean,' the verb is fully transitive—the omission of the object-word or word-group being only an ellipse — while in *blind men saw* it may be regarded as half intransitive.

249.   Transitive verbs are sometimes used without an object-word for a different reason, namely, that their grammatical subject is logically their direct object, as in *the book sells well, meat will not keep in hot weather,* which mean 'they are selling the book well,' 'we cannot keep meat in hot weather,' the subject not being expressed because of its indefiniteness, just as the object is not expressed in *blind men saw* for the same reason.   We call *sells* and *keep* in such constructions **passival** verbs.

This inversion of the relations between subject and object is also expressed by a definite grammatical form called the **passive voice** (311).

250. Intransitive verbs can often be converted into transitives by a slight change of meaning, as in *the groom walks the horse about,* where *walk* means 'cause to walk,' 'make walk.'   So also in *I ran a thorn into my finger* compared with *a thorn ran into my finger.*   Such transitives are called **causative** verbs.

For the converse change of a transitive verb into an intransitive, as in *to stop short,* see § **255**.

251. When an intransitive verb requires a noun-word to complete its meaning, the noun-word is joined to it by a preposition, forming a **prepositional complement**, as in *he came to London ; he looked at the house ; I thought of that ; he thinks of going abroad.* ꞌ We can see from these examples that the distinction between transitive and intransitive is mainly formal, for *think of* and the transitive verb *consider* in *I considered that* have practically the same meaning, and *think* itself is used transitively in some phrases, as *I thought as much.* So also the slight difference in meaning between *he looked at the house* and *he saw the house* has nothing to do with one verb being intransitive, the other transitive. The meaning of a transitive as well as an intransitive verb may be extended or defined by a preposition-group, as in *to fill a glass with water, to accuse a person of dishonesty.* When the combination of an intransitive verb with a preposition is logically equivalent to a transitive verb, we call the combination a **group-verb**. Thus *think of* is the group-verb corresponding to the transitive verb *consider*.

252. When an intransitive verb takes a noun in the common form after it, as in *to run a mile, to stop the night*, these nouns are not ordinary complement-nouns, as in *to stop a horse, to stop in the house*, but are equivalent to adverbs. Thus *the night* in *to stop the night* stands in the same relation to *stop* as the adverb or adverb-group in *to stop long, to stop for a short time.* We call *a mile* and *the night* in such constructions **adverbial objects** of the verb.

253. Sometimes an intransitive verb is followed by a noun in the common form which repeats the meaning of the verb, as in *sleep the sleep of the just, fight a good fight*, where the noun is simply the verb converted into a noun, and in *fight a battle, run a race*, where the noun repeats the meaning, but not the form, of the verb. Such object-nouns are called **cognate objects**. A cognate object-noun must necessarily be an abstract noun.

Reflexive Verbs.

254. In such a sentence as *he contradicts himself*, we have a transitive verb followed by a reflexive pronoun in the object-relation. So also in *to wash oneself, to keep oneself in the background.* But in *to wash in cold water, to keep in the background, to keep quiet,* the reflexivity is not expressed by any pronoun, but is implied in the verb itself, which is thus changed from a transitive into an intransitive **reflexive** verb.

Some languages have special inflections or other formal marks to show when a verb is used in a reflexive sense, such as the Greek 'middle voice' (**316**).

255. It often happens that after a verb has been changed in this way, the reflexive meaning is lost sight of, so that all we feel is the change from transitive to intransitive. Thus, while such intransitives as *to wash and dress* have a definitively reflexive meaning, *to keep* in *to keep quiet* is hardly felt to be equivalent to *keep oneself,* but rather to 'remain,' 'stay,' etc. So also there is nothing specially reflexive in *to stop the night,* although in *he stopped short=*'he pulled himself up,' the reflexive meaning still lingers. We may call these verbs **converted intransitives.** The greater the change of meaning in a converted intransitive, the less there remains of the reflexive meaning. Thus the intransitive *stole* in *he stole away* is so detached in meaning from the transitive *steal* that we do not now regard the former as reflexive.

In some languages the combination of a transitive verb with a reflexive pronoun is used passively. Thus in French, *se vend,* literally 'sells itself,' is used to mean 'is sold,' being thus equivalent to *sells* in *the book sells well.*

Reciprocal Verbs.

256. In such sentences as *they fought each other, they fought one another, we quarrelled with each other,* we have the combination of a verb with a reciprocal pronoun. If these pronouns are dropped, and the idea of reciprocity is implied in the verb itself, it becomes a **reciprocal** verb, a transitive verb becoming intransitive at the same time. *Fight* and *quarrel* are reciprocal verbs in such sentences as *those two dogs always fight when they meet*; *we quarrelled, and made it up again.* In such a verb as *meet* in *we shall meet again soon,* the reciprocal meaning is less prominent.

Impersonal Verbs.

257. Impersonal verbs, such as *to rain, to freeze, to snow, to thunder,* are words expressing natural phenomena, and uniting logical subject and predicate in one word, *raining,* for instance, being equivalent to ' drops of water falling from the sky,' or, more briefly, 'falling water.' So also *to freeze* means that the temperature of the air is below freezing-point, while in *it thunders* ' sky ' might be regarded as the logical subject. Hence, when such a noun as *rain* is made into a verb, it not only does not require, but cannot take, a logical subject, whether expressed by a noun or a pronoun. But as in English a finite verb must be preceded by a noun-word of some kind, the unmeaning *it* is prefixed as a prop-word—a purely grammatical empty subject-word. These verbs are called ' impersonal ' because they allow of no variations of person. Nor can they be used in the plural.

Of course there is nothing to prevent these verbs from being made into personal verbs by a metaphorical change of meaning, as when we speak of *thundering out a command.*

FUNCTION.

258. The grammatical function of a finite verb is to serve as a predicate-word, that is, in an ordinary affirmative sentence to state something about the subject of the sentence, which is expressed by a noun-word or noun-equivalent word-group : *the sun shines : he sleeps ; to stand all day tires one ; standing tires me ; that you should think so surprises me.*

259. Although in English the verb must have a subject-word before it, except in the imperative (309), it must be observed that the inflectional *s* in *comes* is equivalent to a pronoun, for it tells us that the verb must refer to *he*, *she* or *it* as subject if it does not refer to some other noun-word. Hence in *he comes* the subject is really expressed twice over = ' he come-he.'

260. In highly inflected languages, such as Latin, where each person of the verb has a distinct ending, the personal pronouns are superfluous, and are therefore prefixed only for emphasis, so that in Latin *venio* 'come-I' can stand alone as a sentence-word. Even in English the imperative *come !* does not require a pronoun, because it would be superfluous, command being necessarily in the second person.

261. But although the Latin *venio* and the English *come !* are sentence-words, the predicative element predominates in them. In such a Latin sentence as *Caesar venit* 'Caesar comes,' where the subject is a noun of very definite and special meaning, the inflection of the verb becomes a mere mark of concord, like the *s* of *comes*. In English, too, we can expand *come !* into *come thou !*, making *come* into an exclusively predicative word.

262. Although verbs are necessary for predication, there are many verbs which are incapable of forming logical predicates by themselves, and require the help of some other part of speech—generally an adjective-word or noun-word. There is one verb, indeed—the verb *to be*—which is absolutely unmeaning by itself. Thus *he is* conveys no sense whatever. It tells us that predication is intended, but we cannot tell what that predication is till some other word is added —*he is ready*, *he is a lawyer*, *he is here*. We call such verbs **link-verbs**, because they serve to connect the predicate with its subject. *To be* is a pure link-verb, that is, a pure form-word, devoid of independent meaning, although having the inflections of a verb enables it to express distinctions of time

and other shades of meaning, as in *he was here* compared with *he is here.*

263. Other link-words, while having the same grammatical function of connecting subject and predicate, have also definite meanings of their own. ͵ Thus *turn* and *become* in *he turned red, he became a Methodist,* while connecting subject and predicate in the same way as *to be* does, have also the meaning 'change.' Thus *he turned red* combines the meanings 'he changed' and 'he is red' or 'he was red.' So also *look. seem* in *he looks pleased, he seems pleased.* But although these verbs have some independent meaning of their own, none of them can stand alone : we cannot say *he became, he seems* without a predicative complement, and we can make *he turns* stand alone only by changing its meaning and function so that it is no longer a link-verb.

264. All link-verbs are necessarily intransitive. Many intransitive verbs which are not regular link-verbs—that is to say, which can stand alone without any predicative complement —are occasionally used as such. We call such verbs **half link-verbs.** Examples are : *the tree grew tall; he lived a saint, and died a martyr.* We feel that the first of these sentences is equivalent to 'the tree grew, and became tall,' *tall* being not merely a predicate to *tree,* but serving also to modify *grew.* In such a sentence as *the invalid grew strong again, grew* is a pure link-verb, being equivalent to *became.*

265. Verbs are often followed by more than one noun-word standing to them in different relations.

266. The most frequent case is when a transitive verb is followed by a direct and an indirect object, as in *give it me,* where *it* is the direct object of the verb, and *me* its indirect object, standing in the interest-relation. In such combinations the two objects do not stand in any special relation to one another, being connected together only indirectly by being objects to the same verb.

267. But in such combinations as *they made him king, they elected Sir Isaac Newton president,* the first noun-word after the transitive verb is its direct object, and the second noun-word is a complement to the other one : *they made him* makes us ask ' made him what ?', and this question is answered by the noun *king,* which we call the **object-complement.** But these object-complements are also connected with the verb itself, as we see by changing these sentences into *they made a king of him*; *they elected a president, namely Sir Isaac Newton. King,* therefore, in *they made him king* is at the same time the direct object of *make* and the complement to *him.* So also in *they called him a fool*; *they called him bad names*; *the examiners asked me three questions.* The object complement can be an infinitive or supine, that is, a nounverbal : *I saw him come*; *I want him to come*; *I like boys to be quiet.* It can also be an adjective or adjective-verbal (participle) : *to paint a house white*; *they made him angry*; *I saw him coming*; *I saw it done.*

FORM-CLASSES.

268. The forms which make up the conjugation of a finite verb are classed under the grammatical categories of **number, person, tense, mood,** and **voice.** There are also some other miscellaneous categories included under the head of ' forms.'

Number.

269. The only grammatical category that verbs have in common with nouns is that of **number,** although it is expressed in totally different ways in these two parts of speech. In the regular English verbs the only distinction between singular and plural is that the third person present indicative ends in *s* in the singular, as in *he sees, they see,* all the other persons having the common form in the singular as well as the plural, so that there is no inflectional distinction between

I see and *we see*, etc. There is no distinction made in the preterite : *he saw, they saw.* More distinctions are made in some of the irregular verbs: *I am, we are; he was, they were.*

There are no distinctions of **gender** in the English verb, as there are in the Arabic verb, and in such Latin periphrastic forms as *miratus est* ' he wondered,' *mirata est* ' she wondered.'

Person.

270. There are three persons of verbs. first, second, and third, corresponding to the three persons of the personal pronouns. The only personal inflection of the English regular verbs is the *s* of the third person singular present indicative —*he sees.* In the other forms of the regular verb there are no distinctions of person. Some of the irregular verbs make further distinctions : *I am, you are, he is, we are.*

Tense.

271. The only tense which is expressed by inflection in English is the preterite (*I called, I saw*), the absence of the preterite inflection constituting the present tense (*I call, I see*). The other tenses are formed by means of auxiliaries, thus the future (*I shall see, he will see*) is formed by the combination of the auxiliary *shall* or *will* with the infinitive, the perfect tense (*I have seen*) consists of *have* + the preterite participle, the definite tenses (*I am seeing, I was seeing*) consist of *be* + the present participle.

272. Tense is primarily the grammatical expression of distinctions of time.

273. Every occurrence, considered from the point of view of time, must be either past, as in *I was here yesterday*, present, as in *he is here today*, *he is here now*, or future, as in *he will be here tomorrow.* We call *was* the **preterite** tense of the verb *to be*—using ' past ' as a general term to include other varieties of past time besides the preterite—*is* the **present**, and *will be* the **future** tense of the same verb.

Simple and Compound Tenses.

274. The present, preterite, and future are **simple** tenses. But there are also **compound** tenses, the most important of which belong to the perfect-group, comprising the perfect, pluperfect, and future perfect. These compound tenses combine present, past and future respectively with a time anterior to each of these periods : perfect (present perfect)= preterite + present, pluperfect (past perfect)=pre-preterite + preterite, and future perfect = pre-future + future.

275. The **perfect** (*I have seen*) combines past and present time. Thus *I have come* in the sentence *I have come to see you* combines the two ideas 'I came here' and 'I am here now.' So also *he has lived here a good many years* means that he lived here in the past, and lives here in the present. The perfect therefore expresses an occurrence which began in the past and is connected with the present, either by actual continuance up to the present time, as in the latter example, or in its results, as in the former example, where although the action of coming is completed, its result—namely 'being here'—is felt to belong to the present. The simple preterite, on the other hand, expresses a past occurrence without any reference to the present. Often, indeed, the preterite entirely cuts away an occurrence from the present ; thus the preterite *he lived here for some time* implies that 'he' is dead, or has gone to live somewhere else. Although the preterite in *I came to see you* does not necessarily imply 'I went away again,' it certainly detaches the coming from the present, or, at any rate, throws more emphasis on the coming here in the past than on the being here in present. Hence *I came to see you* and *I have come to see you* really express the same relations of time, but from different points of view.

276. The **pluperfect** (*I had seen*) stands in the same relation to the simple preterite as the perfect does to the present, that is, it expresses an occurrence which took place before the time denoted by a preterite tense, and yet continuing into the latter; thus in the sentence *when I had seen everything in Edinburgh, I went on to Glasgow*, the action expressed by *had seen* is shown to have taken place before that expressed by *went*, and yet the two actions are felt to be connected together.

277. The **future perfect** (*I shall have seen*) stands in the same relation to the simple future; that is, it expresses an occurrence taking place in the future, and yet before the occurrence expressed by the accompanying simple future, the two occurrences being regarded as connected together in the same way as in the perfect and pluperfect, as in *I shall have finished my letter by the time you come back*, where *come*, though a present in form, is logically a future, and would be expressed by a future tense in many languages.

278. The future-group of compound tenses is represented by the future preterite. If we regard an occurrence as impending in the past instead of in the present, we have the **future preterite** tense (*I should see, he would see*), as in *I knew how it would turn out*, compared with *I know how it will turn out*, where *will turn* is simple future.

Primary and Secondary Tenses.

279. When we speak of an occurrence as past, etc., we must have some point of time from which to measure it. When we measure the time of an occurrence from the time when we are speaking, that is, from the present, the tense which expresses the time of the occurrence is called a **primary** tense. The present, preterite, future, and perfect are primary tenses. A **secondary** tense, on the other hand, is measured, not from the time *when* we are speaking, but from some past or future time *of which* we are speaking, and consequently a sentence containing a secondary tense makes us expect another sentence containing a verb in a primary tense to show the time from which that of the secondary tense is to be measured. The pluperfect and future perfect are both secondary tenses. Thus such a sentence as *I had finished writing my letter* makes us expect another sentence containing a preterite, such as *when he came—I had finished writing my letter when he came.* The definite preterite (*I was seeing*) is also a secondary tense, as in *I was writing a letter when he came.* These two tenses are both measured from a past primary tense. The future perfect (*I shall have seen*) is measured from a future primary tense.

280. The primary tense required to supplement a secondary tense need not always be expressed if it is clear from the context. Thus we can shorten *I am glad you have come at last: I have been waiting for you a long time* into *I have been waiting for you a long time.*

When a secondary tense is freely used without being referred to an expressed primary tense, it is called an **independent secondary** tense. The Latin 'imperfect' (*videbam*), which otherwise corresponds to the English definite preterite (*was seeing*) is an independent secondary preterite : *Verres inflammatus furore in forum venit* (preterite) ; *ardebant* (imperfect) *oculi, toto ex ore crudelitas eminebat* (imperfect), 'Verres, inflamed with passion, came into the forum ; his eyes gleamed, in his whole countenance ferocity was conspicuous.' Here the gleaming of Verres' eyes is stated as an independent fact, but not as an isolated one, being put in the imperfect to show that it was going on while something else happened, namely his coming into the forum. In English, on the other hand, we cannot indicate this subordination without associating the primary and secondary tense more closely together: *when Verres came into the forum, his eyes were gleaming.*

Complete and Incomplete Tenses.

281. It is evident that an occurrence of which we speak in the present must be incomplete at the time, for if it were completed, it would no longer belong to the present. Thus *the clock is striking twelve* implies that it is in the middle of striking, and that we know beforehand that there ought to be, and probably will be, twelve strokes. As soon as the last stroke has sounded, we are obliged to use the perfect, and say *the clock has (just) struck twelve.* Here the perfect denotes completion in the present : it is a **complete** perfect. So also in *I have lived my life* meaning ' the active part of my life is over,' *I have lived* is a complete perfect. But in *I have lived here a good many years, I have lived* is an **incomplete** perfect, for the speaker is necessarily implied to be still living in the place referred to.

In Latin the tense called ' perfect ' (*vidī*) corresponds not only to the English perfect (*I have seen*), but also to the English preterite (*I saw*), so that the idea of past time is more prominent in it than in the English perfect. Hence it is used only as a complete perfect, the English incomplete perfect being expressed in Latin by the present, as in *jam diu hic habito* ' I have lived here a long time,' literally ' I live here already long.'

282. When we distinguish between complete and incomplete secondary tenses, we mean, of course, complete or incomplete with reference to the accompanying primary tenses. Thus in *I had written my letter when he came,* the action of writing is represented as being finished at the time denoted by the preterite *came,* so that *I had written* is here a complete (pluperfect) tense. In *I was writing a letter when he came,* on the other hand, the action of writing is represented as going on at the time shown by the preterite *came,* so that *I was writing* is here an incomplete (definite preterite) tense.

Tense-aspects: Duration, etc.

283. By tense-aspect we understand distinctions of time independent of any reference to past, present, or future. Thus the duration of an occurrence is independent of the relation of the time of the occurrence to the time when we are speaking or of which we are speaking. The distinction of duration between *fell* and *lay* in *he fell down,* and *he lay* *there nearly an hour*, or between *to laugh* and *to burst out laughing* has, of course, nothing to do with grammar, because it is not shown by any grammatical forms, but by the meaning of the words themselves. But in some languages such distinctions of meaning are shown by inflection. Thus in Greek the present infinitive *gelán* means 'to laugh,' the 'aorist' infinitive *gelásai* means 'to burst out laughing.' We may call the former of these a **long tense**, the latter a **short tense**. In English the definite perfect *I have been seeing* generally expresses duration, as in *I have been writing letters all day* compared with *I have written only one letter to-day. I have been writing* is, therefore, a long tense. *I have written*, on the other hand, is neutral as regards duration, being sometimes a short, sometimes a long tense. Long tenses may be either **continuous** or **recurrent**, denoting repetition, habit, etc. Thus we have a continuous present in *he lives in the country*, a recurrent present in *he goes to Germany twice a year*. The absolute duration of an occurrence is often disregarded in language, an occurrence of considerable length being often put on a level with one that is quite short or even instantaneous. This is generally the case when a succession of occurrences are narrated. Thus in describing a journey, *we passed through . . , we stopped a minute . . , we stopped three days . . , we set out for . .* are all regarded simply as points in a series. When tenses are used in this way, without regard to their absolute duration, we may call them **point-tenses**.

284. There are many other tense-aspects of more special meaning. Thus futurity may be regarded from various points of view, according to the certainty or uncertainty of the impending occurrence, or its nearness or remoteness. In English we have an **immediate future** formed with the auxiliary *go*, as in *I am afraid it is going to rain*, compared with *I am afraid it will rain to-morrow.*

285. Some languages have special **inchoative** tenses to express an occurrence as only just beginning, or an action as only attempted. Those languages which have not special forms for this purpose sometimes use various incomplete tenses instead. Thus in Latin the imperfect (**280. 1**) is used to express attempt, as in *consulēs sēdabant tumultum* 'the consuls tried to put down the disturbance,' compared with *consulēs sedaverunt* (perfect) *tumultum* 'the consuls put down the disturbance.'

286. We can see from this last example that a tense which was originally meant only to express distinctions of time may come to imply a variety of special meanings. Thus, as present time is necessarily incomplete (**281**), past time naturally—though not necessarily—suggests completion. Future time suggests uncertainty. When an occurrence expressed by a secondary tense is thought of as going on when something else, expressed by a primary tense, happens, we connect the former with the idea of long duration, the latter with that of short duration (**283**).

287. It is these implied meanings which make it often difficult to compare the tenses of one language with those of another, or to define their exact meanings.

Definite and Indefinite Tenses.

288. Tenses differ greatly in definiteness. The shorter a tense is, the more **definite** it generally is both in duration and in its relation to the distinctions of past, present, and future. Long tenses—whether continuous or recurrent— are generally more **indefinite**. The difference between a definite and an indefinite tense is seen by comparing the English definite present in *I am writing a letter* with the indefinite *I write my letters in the evening*; the former means 'I am writing at this present moment,' the latter means 'when I write letters, I write them in the evening.' So also the shorter the interval between present and future, the more definite the time of the future occurrence is, and the more likely it is to come off ; hence the immediate future (**284**) is more definite than the ordinary future.

289. We see that the indefinite present (*I write*) includes, to some extent, past and future as well as present. This is especially the case in such statements as *the sun rises in the east, platinum is the heaviest metal.* The verbs in such sentences do not express any distinctions of time at all, and it is only because predication and tense-distinctions are associated together in verbs that we are obliged to put verbs in such sentences in some one tense. For the purpose of such statements the present is best suited, as being in itself the most indefinite of the tenses. When the present is used in this way without implying any real distinctions of time, we call it the **neutral** present. Other tenses may be used as neutral tenses. In Latin the perfect ('gnomic perfect') is employed as a neutral tense as well as the present.

290. Although we have confined ourselves hitherto to the meanings of tenses, it must not be forgotten that 'tense' always implies grammatical form. There are many ways of expressing distinctions of time which have nothing to do with tense. Thus in *I start tomorrow* futurity is expressed by the adverb *tomorrow*, the verb itself being in the present tense. We call *I start* present, because this form generally expresses present time, and when a form has once received a definite name, it keeps it through every variety of meaning. Again, distinctions analogous to those expressed by tenses may be expressed lexically by the use of distinct words (**283**), or by grammatical forms distinct from tense-inflections. Thus distinctions of time may be expressed by derivation, as in the Latin inchoative verbs in -*sco*, such as *albesco* 'begin to grow white,' where the inchoative meaning is part of the verb itself, and has nothing to do with tense.

In French, however, the derivative ending of the Latin inchoatives was first extended to a variety of verbs which did not take it in Latin, and was then restricted to certain tenses of these verbs, and so came to be part of pure tense-inflections, as in the imperfect *il finissait* 'he finished,' which would answer to a Latin **finiscebat* 'began to finish,' the real Latin imperfect being *finiebat*.

291. After seeing how tenses develop all kinds of special meanings out of what were originally only distinctions of time, we need not be surprised to find tenses sometimes used to express ideas which have no connection at all with distinctions of time. Thus the preterite *knew* in *if I knew his address I would write to him*, expresses present time just as much as *know* in *I know his address now, so I shall write to him*, the change of the present *know* into the preterite *knew* expressing hypothesis as opposed to a statement of fact.

292. The following are the chief tenses used in English in simple statements :—

	Indefinite.	*Definite.*
Present.	I see.	I am seeing.
Preterite.	I saw.	I was seeing.
Perfect.	I have seen.	I have been seeing.
Pluperfect.	I had seen.	I had been seeing.
Future.	I shall see.	I shall be seeing.
Future Perfect.	I shall have seen.	I shall have been seeing.
Preterite Future.	I should see.	I should be seeing.

Mood.

293. By the moods of a verb we understand grammatical forms expressing different relations between subject and predicate. Thus, if a language has special forms to express commands as distinguished from statements, we include the forms that express command under the term 'imperative mood.' Thus in English *come !* is in the imperative mood, while the statement *he comes* is in the 'indicative' mood.

In many grammars the term 'mood' is still applied to the infinitive, which is accordingly called 'the infinitive mood,' although the infinitive, which is a noun-verbal, has nothing in common with the moods of finite verbs.

294. From the point of view of mood-distinctions state-ments fall under two main divisions, according as they state something as a fact or only as a thought. Thus *it is true, it is not true, I think so*, are all meant to imply statement of facts as opposed to mere thoughts. Whether such statements are really true—really statements of facts—is no concern of grammar, which deals only with the meaning of the form itself. From a grammatical point of view, moreover, doubt-ful statements, such as *perhaps it is true*, are just as much statements of fact as the most positive assertions.

295. There are various ways of stating in the form of a thought as opposed to a fact. The most unmistakeable one is by stating in the form of a hypothesis, as when the fact-statements *it is true, it is not true*, are made into the hypothe-tical clauses *if it is true, if it is not true*. Here both pairs of sentences offer us a subject and a predicate standing to one another in the opposite relations of affirmation and negation, but while the first two sentences express the affirmation and negation as facts, the last two merely suggest them as objects of thought. In fact, we often say *supposing* (that is, 'think-ing') *it is true* instead of *if it is true*. A hypothetical clause requires a principal clause to complete the sense, the whole combination being called a **conditional** sentence. Thus *if you are right, I am wrong* is a conditional sentence, *I am wrong* being the principal clause. **Concessive** clauses, such as *even if it is true, although it is true*, are a variety of hypo-thetical clauses.

296. Another way of stating something as a thought is by stating it as a **wish**, as in *God save the queen!* and *I wish it were true*, where *I wish* states a fact, *it were true* expresses a wish. Clauses of **purpose** are a special class of wish-sen-tences : *I wrote to him that he might know I was at home ; they took away the knife lest he should cut himself.*

297. When we repeat a statement made by another person, we can do so in different ways. We can quote his very words, as in *John said, 'I am sorry.'* Here the speaker makes his own statement, namely, that John said something, and then lets John, as it were, make his own statement in his own words, so that the whole sentence contains two separate statements of facts. This way of repeating statements is called **direct narration.** When the speaker repeats what was said to him in his own words we have **indirect narration,** as in *John said (that) he was sorry.* Here John's being sorry is not stated by John himself at all. Nor is it stated as a fact even by the speaker, who mentions it only as an idea suggested to him by some one else. Hence the subject of all indirect narration is a statement not of facts but of thoughts.

298. We will now consider the expression of these different kinds of statement in language. When there are only two moods in a language to express statements, a fact-mood and a thought-mood, as is the case in Latin, French, German, and Old English, these moods are distinguished as **indicative** (fact-mood) and **subjunctive** (thought-mood). Some languages have special moods to distinguish different kinds of thought-statements. Thus Greek has, in addition to the indicative and subjunctive moods, an **optative** mood, used primarily to express wish, which in such languages as Latin is expressed by the subjunctive.

299. In English the only inflectional moods are the indicative and subjunctive. But the inflections of the English verb are so scanty that we need not be surprised to find that the distinction between indicative and subjunctive is very slight. The only regular inflection by which the subjunctive is distinguished from the indicative in English is that of the third person singular present, which drops the *s* of the indicative (*he sees*) in the subjunctive (*he see*). In the verb *to be*, however, further distinctions are made : indicative *I am, he is, he was,* subjunctive *I be, he be, he were,* although in the

spoken language the only distinction that is still kept up is
that between *was* and *were*. Consequently the sense of the
distinction in function between subjunctive and indicative has
almost died out in English, and we use the subjunctive *were*
only in combination with other mood-forms (**301**), the other
subjunctive inflections surviving only in a few special phrases
and constructions, such as *God save the queen !*, where the
subjunctive expresses wish, being thus equivalent to the Greek
optative.

300. The few distinctions that English makes between
fact-statements and thought-statements are mainly expressed,
not by inflections, but by auxiliaries (periphrastic moods),
and by peculiar uses of tense-distinctions. The following are
the auxiliary forms:

(*a*) The combination of *should* and *would* with the infinitive
(*should see, would see*), when used in the principal clause of
conditional sentences (**295**), is called the **conditional mood**.
The conditional mood has the same form as the future preterite tense (**278**).

(*b*) The combination of *may* and its preterite *might* with
the infinitive (*may see, might see*) is called the **permissive
mood**, as in *may you be happy !* where it expresses wish, *let
the dog loose that he may run about a little* ; *we let the dog
loose that he might run about a little*, where it expresses
purpose.

(*c*) The combination of the finite forms of the verb *to be*
with the supine (*is to see, was to see, were to see*) is called the
compulsive mood. This combination is so called because
it primarily expresses compulsion or obligation, as in *what
am I to do ?, what is to be done ?* In this sense it can hardly
be considered a mood. But it is used as a pure mood in
conditional sentences, as in *if it were to rain, I do not know
what we shall do.*

301. We use tenses to express thought-statements in the
hypothetical clauses of conditional sentences, as in *if I knew*

his address, I would write to him (291); *if it were possible I would do it.*   In the latter example (as also in *if it were to* § 300) the hypothesis is shown not only by the preterite tense, but also by the subjunctive inflection, which is really superfluous.   When a thought-statement is expressed by a tense in this way, we call it a **tense-mood**.   *Were* in *if it were* is a **subjunctive tense-mood**.

302. As we see, in some conditional sentences all three ways of expressing thought-statements are used—inflectional mood (subjunctive), auxiliary mood (conditional), and tense-mood (preterite).   For convenience we will include all these methods of expression under the term **thought-form**.   We understand, then, by thought-form any grammatical form meant to show that a statement is of a thought as opposed to a fact.

303. As might be expected, we find that in language the correspondence between fact-statements and thought-statements on the one hand, and fact-forms and thought-forms on the other, is not always perfectly logical.   That is to say, in such languages as Latin, we do not always find fact-statements expressed by the indicative mood and thought statements expressed by the subjunctive mood, other languages showing divergences of their own, so that the details of the use of the subjunctive in different languages never entirely agree, in spite of the agreement in general principles.

304. The mere stating of an occurrence as a thought and not as a fact need not necessarily throw any doubt on the truth of the statement.   Thus when I repeat a statement made to me by someone else, and repeat it in indirect instead of direct narration (297), I may do so because I doubt the truth of the statement, but I may also do so merely because I do not remember the exact words of the statement, or because I want to shorten it.   Nevertheless in some cases thought-statement does almost necessarily imply that the

statement is false. Thus in Latin, while a true reason is put in the indicative because the reason stated is a fact, a reason which the speaker believes to be false must necessarily be put in the subjunctive, because to him it is a statement of a thought, not of a fact. Hence the rule of Latin grammar that the subjunctive in a causal clause states a rejected reason, as in the sentence *pugiles ingemiscunt, non quod doleant* (subj.), *sed quia profundendā voce omne corpus intenditur* (indic)., ' boxers groan, not because they are in pain, but because in uttering the sound the whole body is braced up.'

305. Hence there is in all languages a tendency to use the subjunctive—or whatever thought-forms the language may possess—to imply doubt or denial as opposed to certainty or affirmation. This is especially noticeable in conditional sentences. Conditional sentences are of two kinds : (*a*) those which do not imply anything as to the fulfilment of the condition, such as *if you are right, I am wrong*, where the speaker does not let us know whether he thinks the other one to be in the right or not; (*b*) those which imply the rejection of the hypothesis, such as *if you were right, I should be wrong*, which may be expanded into *if you were right— which is not the case—I should be wrong*. We distinguish these two kinds of sentences as sentences of **open condition** and of **rejected condition**. Now although all conditional sentences express thought-statements as opposed to fact-statements—for even a sentence of open condition does nothing more than leave the truth of the statement open without in any way confirming it—yet as it is just as important to distinguish between open and rejected conditions as to distinguish between accepted and rejected reasons, most languages use the indicative in sentences of open condition—not to imply that the condition will be fulfilled, but merely to show that it is not rejected.

306. In English the distinctions between thought-form and

fact-form are to a great extent levelled.   Thus the English verb makes no distinction between true and false reasons, or between direct and indirect narration.   In fact, the whole distinction between indicative and subjunctive, as carried out by such languages as Latin, French, and German, offers great difficulties to English-speakers who have not been trained in general principles of grammar and the study of inflected languages.

307. The general principle in English is not to mark the distinction between fact-statements and thought-statements where it is superfluous, that is, where it is clearly shown by the context.   Thus English does not mark the distinction between true and false reasons by any change of mood simply because the rejected reason is always unmistakeably marked by the negative form of the clause (*not because* . . ,).   For the same reason English finds it unnecessary to mark the distinction between direct and indirect narration by any modification of mood.   Such a distinction, on the other hand, as that between open and rejected condition is not shown by the context, and being a useful one is accordingly marked by grammatical form.

Imperative Mood.

308. In the imperative mood the relation between subject and predicate is not that of statement, as in the indicative, subjunctive, optative, etc., but of **hortation**, that is, command, request, etc.   The imperative does not state a command, but addresses it directly to another person.   Hence the statement of a command in the indicative (*I tell you to go!*) or of a wish in the optative or subjunctive (*God save the queen!*) are quite distinct from the imperative, which does not imply statement of any kind.

309. As the imperative can be used only in addressing someone, the subject of an imperative sentence must always be in the second person, and so an English verb in the im-

perative does not require a pronoun to mark distinctions of person, as it would in a mood of statement, but can form a sentence by itself, any defining or additional words that may be required either for clearness or emphasis—including the personal pronouns—being added separately: *come!*; *come, John!*; *come, you boys!* The inflection of the imperative is, then, a purely negative one (**77**), being merely the common form of the verb used as a sentence-word in the second person, no distinction being made between singular and plural, any more than in the indicative (*you see*).

310. Although there cannot be any imperative of the first person singular or third person singular or plural, there can be an imperative of the first person plural when it is equivalent to *I* or *we+you*, the hortation being addressed to the implied *you*. In English this form of the imperative is expressed by the auxiliary verb *let* with the infinitive: *let us go!*

Voice.

311. By voice we mean different grammatical ways of expressing the relation between a transitive verb and its subject and object. The two chief voices are the **active** (*he saw*) and the **passive** (*he was seen*).

312. In English the passive is formed by combining the finite forms of the auxiliary verb *to be* with the preterite participle of the verb. Thus the active forms *I see, I saw, I have seen, I shall see* become in the passive *I am seen, I was seen, I have been seen, I shall be seen.*

313. In a sentence with a fully expressed transitive verb, such as *the dog killed the rat*, although there is only one subject, namely, *dog*, yet from a logical point of view the statement about killing applies to the object-word *rat* as well as to the subject-word *dog*; and it may happen that we wish to state the killing rather with reference to the rat than the dog. It may also happen that all we know is that the rat was killed, without knowing how it was killed. In short, we may wish

to make the object-word *rat* into the subject-word of the
sentence. This we do by changing the active form *killed* into
the corresponding passive form *was killed* : *the rat was killed.*
The original subject is added, if necessary, by means of the
preposition *by* : *the rat was killed by the dog.* In this sentence *rat* is the **inverted object** and *by the dog* is the **inverted subject.** The passive voice is, therefore, a grammatical device for (*a*) bringing the object of a transitive verb
into prominence by making it the subject of the sentence,
and (*b*) getting rid of the necessity of naming the subject of
a transitive verb.

314. When the active sentence *they made him king* (**267**) is
changed into the passive form *he was made king*, both the
nouns stand in the nominative instead of the accusative relation, one of them (*he*) being the subject-word, and the other
(*king*) being in apposition to the subject. Both of them are,
therefore, inverted objects. In such sentences only one of
the object-words can be made into the subject of the passive
sentence.

315. But when such a sentence as *the examiner asked me
three questions* is made passive, either of the object-words
may be made the subject of the passive sentence : *I was
asked three questions by the examiner* ; *three questions were
asked me by the examiner.* It will be observed that in the last
sentence the object-word *me* is kept unchanged, and in the
preceding sentence. although there is nothing in the form of
questions to tell us what grammatical relation it stands in, yet
we certainly feel it to be parallel with *me* in the other sentence, that is to say, it remains in the object relation. We
call *me* and *questions* in such constructions **retained objects,**
distinguishing them, if necessary, as retained indirect and
retained direct objects respectively.

For the passive construction *I was spoken to*, see § 390.

316. Some languages, such as Greek, have a **reflexive,**

or **middle voice**, as it is also called, in which the action of the verb is referred back to the subject in various ways. In the **direct reflexive** the implied pronoun stands in the direct object relation, by which the necessarily transitive verb becomes intransitive ; thus in Greek from the transitive *loúō* 'I wash' is formed the direct middle intransitive *loúomai* ('I wash myself'). In the indirect reflexive a pronoun standing in the indirect object relation is implied, as in the Greek *práttomai* 'I make for myself,' 'gain,' from the active *prátto* 'I make.' In Greek the change from active to middle is often accompanied by further changes of meaning. Thus the active *peítho* 'I persuade' becomes in the middle *peíthomai* 'I let myself be persuaded,' 'I obey.' Latin also has **deponent** verbs, as they are called, which unite passive inflection with active meaning, such as *loqvor* 'I speak,' these verbs being remains of an older middle voice. In Greek also the inflections of the middle and passive voices are nearly identical.

We can see from this last example that reflexivity and passivity often approach in meaning, for *I persuade myself* and *I am persuaded* mean much the same thing. It will be observed that when a transitive verb is made passive, it becomes equivalent to an intransitive verb, *it is seen*, for instance, being equivalent to *it appears*. So also, as we have seen, when a transitive verb is made into a direct reflexive, it becomes intransitive. Lastly, we have seen that it is often difficult to decide whether a transitive verb that has become intransitive is to be regarded as reflexive or not (**255**). All this shows the close connection there is between intransitive, reflexive, and passive verbs. Historically, passive verbs seem generally to have developed out of middle verbs (compare **255**, 1).

Miscellaneous Forms.

317. The English verb has special auxiliary forms to express **negation, emphasis and interrogation**, as in the negative *I do not see* (ai dount sij) compared with the unemphatic positive *I see*, the emphatic positive *I do see*, and the interrogative *do I see?*

318. These different forms are combined in various ways. Thus *do not I see ?* (dount ai sij) is negative interrogative.

Verbals.

319. The verbals are intermediate between finite verbs on the one hand and nouns and adjectives on the other. They are incapable of expressing predication, and lose several of the formal distinctions that characterize verbs, namely number, person, and mood. But they preserve the distinctions of tense and voice, though often more vaguely than in the finite verb. They preserve the special functions and meanings of the verbs from which they are formed, a transitive verb remaining transitive as a verbal, one that is joined to its complement by means of a preposition keeping that preposition when it becomes a verbal, and so on. Thus the verbs and the corresponding verbals have the same constructions in such sentences as *when I saw him I thought of you* and *seeing* (gerund) *him made me think* (infin.) *of you.*

320. In treating of the verbals apart from the finite verb, we exclude the verbals used in the periphrastic forms *I shall see, I have seen,* etc., where the verbals are, from a logical point of view, predicates (**120**). Even from a purely grammatical point of view, these periphrastic forms may be regarded as verb-groups in which the original function of the verbals is lost sight of. No one, for instance, realizes that *seen* in the active form *I have seen* is a passive participle, or can understand without historical investigation how it came to be used in such a construction. We must therefore distinguish between **periphrase-verbals** and **independent verbals**, the latter only being real noun-words and adjective-words. It is with these latter that we have now to deal.

INFINITIVE AND SUPINE.

321. The infinitive, as in *I can see it,* and the supine, as in *I wish to see it,* are noun-verbals.

The infinitive is sometimes called the 'infinitive mood' (293. 1).

322. The simple infinitive and supine are primarily active, but there is also a **passival supine**, as in *this house is to let*.

323. There are also periphrastic tenses, both active and passive, of the supine, such as the perfect active *to have seen* and the present passive in *this house is to be let or sold*.

GERUND.

324. The gerund, as in *I remember seeing him*, is a noun-verbal, the present participle, which has the same form, being an adjective-verbal, as in *running water*. The gerund also differs from the present participle in not entering into the periphrastic forms of the finite verb.

325. The gerund has periphrastic forms to express distinctions of tense and voice, as in *I remember having seen him, I do not like being asked to make a speech*.

326. The gerund is less of a verb than the infinitive inasmuch as it does not join in the conjugation of the finite verb, and more of a noun, inasmuch as it can be joined to another noun by means of a preposition. as in *I had not the pleasure of knowing him*, which cannot be done with the infinitive or supine.

327. But in many cases the gerund and the infinitive can be used almost indifferently ; thus *seeing is believing* could also be expressed by *to see is to believe*.

328. In *seeing is believing* the two gerunds are nearly equivalent to abstract nouns such as *sight, inspection, belief, credence*, although the two classes of words are kept apart by difference of grammatical construction : compare *seeing a thing* with *the sight of a thing; believing a person* with *belief in a person*.

329. But when an abstract word in *-ing* is inflected like a noun and is associated with adjectives and other noun-modifiers without keeping any verb constructions, it must be regarded as a noun, as in *I never saw such doings.* But until a verbal has been isolated from its verb by change of meaning—especially by taking a concrete meaning, as in *wire netting*—it is not entirely on the same footing as ordinary nouns.

PARTICIPLES.

330. Participles are adjective-verbals.

331. The simple participles are the **present active participle**, such as *seeing, running* in *seeing a crowd, I stopped* and *I saw him running to catch the train,* and the **preterite passive participle**, such as *called, thrown* in *a boy called John, I saw him thrown out of his trap.*

332. The present participle is sometimes used passivally, as in *there is an answer waiting,* where *waiting* = 'being waited for.' The preterite participle, on the other hand, has an actival meaning in some isolated constructions, as in *a learned man* = 'a man who has learnt much.'

333. There are periphrastic participles, such as the perfect active participle *having seen* in *having seen all that was to. be seen at Rome, we went on to Naples,* and the present passive participle *being seen* in *not being seen by any one, he escaped.*

334. Participles retain the meanings and constructions of the verbs they are formed from when they are equivalent to clauses, as in the examples just given, where, for instance, *having seen* is equivalent to *when we had seen.*

335. On the other hand, in such combinations as *running water, a charming view, a ruined man, an ill-built house* the participles are pure adjectives, being put before nouns like ordinary adjectives, and several of them being capable of comparison (*more, most charming*), while they are all isolated from their verbs in meaning—except perhaps in the first instance—and in the case of *ill-built* in construction also, for there is no verb *to ill-build.* But many passive participles used as adjectives retain traces of their verb origin in preferring *much* to *very* as a modifier ; thus *much pleased* sounds better than *very pleased*, just as we say *it pleased me much*.

Adverbs.

336. There are two main classes of adverbs corresponding to the distinction between adjective-pronouns and ordinary or 'special' adjectives (**194**). **General adverbs**, such as *here, there, where, now, then, soon, quite, very, not*, resemble adjective-pronouns in function and meaning. Thus the general adverbs *here, there*, modify the verb *stand* in *stand here! stand there!* in the same way as the adjective-pronouns ('general adjectives') *this* and *that* modify the noun *position* in *take this position !, take that position !*, all four words having the same demonstrative meaning. The adverbs *now* and *then* have a similar meaning, only applied to time instead of place ; *quite* and *very* express general qualifications of quantity; and *not* expresses the most abstract and general of all qualifications, namely negation.

337. Most general adverbs are at the same time **primary** adverbs, showing no connection with the other parts of speech, except the other particles—prepositions and conjunctions. Thus the adverbs *in* and *up* in *come in! come up!* are used also as prepositions, as in *to stay in the house, he came up the road*, but they are not related to ordinary nouns, adjectives, or verbs.

338. Special adverbs, on the other hand, show their likeness to adjectives as opposed to adjective-pronouns by the fact that most of them are formed directly from adjectives by adding *-ly* ; thus from the adjectives *bright, quick* are formed the special adverbs *brightly, quickly*. These adverbs are, therefore, at the same time **secondary** adverbs—formed from other parts of speech. Some adverbs are formed from adjectives by direct conversion, such as *full* in *full many* —

'very many,' *hard* in *work hard.* Other secondary adverbs are formed from nouns, and occasionally from verbs, such as *home* in *go home, bang* in *go bang,* formed from *home, to bang.*

339. **Adverb-groups**—that is, word-groups having the grammatical function of adverbs—are formed in various ways, sometimes by joining a preposition to a noun or an adjective used as a noun, as in *today, upstairs, in short*; sometimes by other combinations, into which adverbs themselves often enter, such as *nevertheless, however.* Such combinations as the above may be regarded as compound adverbs because of their isolation of meaning, although some of them are written as two words. But it is difficult to draw the line between adverb-groups and compound adverbs.

340. It will be seen that some secondary adverbs are more general in their meaning than others, although not so general as the primary adverbs. The adverb *full* has, however, the same general meaning as *very,* although it is much more restricted in its application. It must be observed that *very* itself was once a secondary adverb formed by conversion from the adjective *very* 'true'—which is still preserved in the superlative *veriest*—so that it had originally the same meaning as the derived adverb *verily.* But the adverb *very* has diverged so much in meaning from its adjective that the connection between them is no longer felt.

FORM.

341. The only adverbs that can be recognized by their form are the special adverbs in *-ly,* such as *brightly, quickly*; but it must be borne in mind that this test is not decisive, for there are several adjectives in *-ly,* such as *goodly, manly.*

342. Most primary adverbs are indeclinable. But secondary adverbs formed from adjectives are compared like

adjectives: *quick, quicker, quickest,* as in *come quick* (or *quickly*), *we will see who is done quickest, usefully, more usefully, most usefully,* as in *more usefully employed.* A few primary adverbs are also capable of comparison: *soon, sooner, soonest.*

MEANING.

343. Adverbs are classed according to their meaning under the main heads of place, time, order, quantity, manner, cause, and assertion. Some adverbs have a variety of meanings, which necessitates putting the same adverb into several classes :— -

344. (*a*) **Adverbs of place**, such as *here, there, where, away, up, down, in, out, inside, outside, above, below, together.* Many of these are used also as prepositions, such as *up, down, in, inside, outside, above, below.* Most of the adverbs of place express **motion** as well as **rest**, as in *he came here, he went away, he went in, they flocked together* compared with *he stood here, he is away on a holiday, he is in, they stood together.* In the literary language there is a group of adverbs expressing **motion to**, namely *hither, thither, whither,* with a corresponding group expressing **motion from**— *hence, thence, whence,* which in the ordinary language are expressed by *from here,* etc. When these adverbs are used, the corresponding *here, there, where* are restricted to the meaning of rest.

There is often used as a pure form-word without any meaning of its own. When used in this way it loses its stress and is weakened to (ðər), which we call 'the weak *there*' as distinguished from 'the strong *there*'= (ðeə). Thus in the sentence *there is no one there* (ðə z nou wɛn ðeə), the first *there* is weak and a mere form-word, while the second *there* is strong and keeps its full meaning as an adverb of place.

345. (*b*) **Adverbs of time** admit various other subdivisions: *now, today, at once, immediately* are adverbs of **present time**, *then, yesterday, lately, formerly, once,* in *I* *thought so once,* are adverbs of **past time**, *afterwards, to-morrow, soon, presently* are adverbs of **future time**. Some adverbs of time, such as *henceforth,* combine present and future time, = now + in the future. Such adverbs as *at once, immediately* might also be regarded as adverbs of immediate futurity, as compared with *presently,* which implies delay. *Ever, never, always, continuously* are adverbs of continuous time or **duration**, while *often, frequently, occasionally, seldom, rarely, once, again, twice, daily, yearly, annually, periodically* are adverbs of discrete time or **repetition**, the distinction between continuous and discrete time being analogous to that between continuous and discrete quantity (**232**).

It must be observed that some adverbs which would seem to express continuous time, such as *continually, incessantly, perpetually,* are not really equivalent to 'continuously,' but express **very frequent repetition** : *he comes here continually—every other day ; it rains incessantly—almost without ceasing.*

346. (*c*) Place and time both fall under the head of **order**. Hence the analogy in meaning between such place-adverbs as *here, there, where* and the time-adverbs *now, then, when.* Hence also the use of some adverbs of place in a temporal meaning, as in *here he stopped short in his speech,* where *here* means 'at this point of time,' *all these events came together* meaning that they happened at the same time.

347. (*d*) **Adverbs of quantity.** Of adverbs of quantity, degree, measure, some express **definite measure**, such as *equally, less, least, more, most,* as in *equally happy, less happy, most happy,* some **indefinite measure**, such as *little, a little, slightly, much, very, greatly, excessively,* as in *little the worse, a little better, much pleased, very glad. Rather* in *I would rather* is an adverb of definite, in *rather good* of indefinite measure. Others express **causal quantity**, that is, quantity in its relation to purpose or result, such as *enough, sufficiently, too, too much, too little.* Others, again, express quantity in its relation to **unity** (part and whole), such as *wholly, quite,* *completely, perfectly, exactly, almost, nearly, hardly, scarcely.* To these are allied adverbs of **addition**, such as *also, besides, too* (which is also used to express excess), and **exclusion**, such as *only, merely.* *So* and *as* in *not so good as, than* in *better than, the* in *the more the merrier* are adverbs of **comparison**, *the* expressing double comparison or **proportion**.   Most adverbs of quantity express continuous quantity.   Of those that express discrete quantity, such as *twice* in *twice as many,* some are used also as adverbs of time.

It will be observed that many adverbs of time are also adjective-pronouns of quantity, such as *less, least, more, most, enough.*

348. (*e*) **Adverbs of manner**, such as *how, thus, so, as, like.* *So* and *as* are adverbs of manner in *it is done so, do as you are told! like* is an adverb of manner in *sing like a bird.* These are general adverbs of manner. There is also an unlimited number of special adverbs of manner, such as *well* and *ill* in *well done, ill done,* most of them formed from adjectives by adding -*ly,* such as *quickly, wisely, knowingly, avowedly.* Many of these are used as adverbs of quantity, being practically equivalent to *very,* as in *remarkably clever, horribly dull, awfully tired, piercingly cold.*

349. (*f*) **Adverbs of cause**, such as *therefore, wherefore, why, because, accordingly.* Adverbs which belong to the other classes are also used to express cause, such as the place-adverbs *hence, whence,* the time-adverb *then,* as in *will you do it then?,* and the adverb of manner *so,* which in the spoken language takes the place of *therefore,* as in *so you will not do it?*

350. (*g*) **Adverbs of assertion** express **affirmation**, such as *yes, yea;* denial or **negation**, such as *no, nay, not;* **asseveration**, including certainty, doubt, etc., such as *surely, certainly, assuredly, truly, undoubtedly, indeed, perhaps, possibly.*

Of these *yes, yea, no, nay* are sentence-adverbs (**368**).

351. Adverbs are also used metaphorically to express a variety of occasional meanings. Thus *together* in *they conspired together* expresses the idea of co-operation, derived metaphorically from the idea of proximity in place.

352. General adverbs also fall under other classes similar to those under which pronouns fall. Thus we have definite adverbs, such as *here, there* (of place), *now, then* (of time), *so, thus* (of manner), corresponding to the definite pronouns *this, that; here* being equivalent to *in this place, now* to *at this time, then* to *at that time, thus* to *in this way, so* to *in that way*.

353. Indefinite adverbs are formed by combining the indefinite pronouns *any* and *some* with interrogative adverbs, and by combining interrogative pronouns with the adverbs *ever* and *-soever* : *anywhere, somewhere, wherever, wheresoever, whenever, whensoever, anyhow, somehow, however, howsoever*.

354. **Negative** adverbs are formed, like negative pronouns, by prefixing *n-* and *no-* : *n-ever, nowhere, nohow*. It will be observed that *no* is compounded with the interrogative form of the adverbs.

355. Most of the **interrogative** pronouns begin with *wh*, like the interrogative pronouns : *where* (of place), *when* (of time), *why* (of cause) ; *how* (of manner).

FUNCTION.

356. General adverbs, like pronouns, admit of a division into **independent** and **dependent**. An independent adverb, such as *very* in *he is very tall*, simply modifies some word (or sentence), while a dependent adverb not only modifies some word, but at the same time makes us expect something more to complete the sense. Thus the dependent adverb *as* in *he is as tall* makes us expect *as I* (*am*) or some such completion of the sense. **Correlative** adverbs are a special class of dependent adverbs.

357. All adverbs fall under the two heads of **word-modi-**

fying and **sentence-modifying**, although it is often difficult to distinguish between the two classes.

All special adverbs are independent word-modifiers.

Independent Adverbs.

Word-Modifying.

358. The grammatical function of independent word-modifying adverbs is to modify adjectives, adverbs, verbs, and occasionally nouns. Their most important function is in connection with verbs, adverbs standing in the same relation to verbs as adjectives do to nouns, as we see by comparing *he walks quickly* with *he is a quick walker, he has a quick step.* The great majority of adverbs indeed—especially secondary adverbs in -*ly*—are used only in connection with verbs.

359. The adverbs which modify adjectives and adverbs are all general adverbs of degree (quantity), as in *quite right, very good, most beautiful, most beautifully, fearfully ugly.* Most of these adverbs cannot be used with verbs. These adverbs can modify a group-adverb, as in *he is quite in the wrong, I am half through my work,* where the adverbs *quite, half* do not modify the prepositions *in* and *through,* but modify the whole group in each case.

360. Adverbs follow their verbs, as in *he came quickly, he came home yesterday,* and precede adjectives and adverbs, as in *very quick, quickly :* *enough,* however, follows, as in *good enough, not quickly enough.*

361. When an adverb modifies a noun, the noun is generally felt to be equivalent to an adjective or verb, as in *he is quite a gentleman, he is quite the gentleman* = 'he is a complete or perfect gentleman,' *he is fully master of the subject,* compared with *he is quite gentlemanly, he has fully mastered the subject.*

362. A noun-modifying adverb evidently approaches very near in function to an adjective. In such a construction as *he is quite a gentleman* we feel that *quite* is not an adjective, because, if it were, it would come after, instead of before the article *a*, as in *he is a perfect gentleman.* But in such constructions as *you are the very man I want, he is an only son,* we must regard *very* and *only* as adjectives, *only* being of course an adverb in such a construction as *he is only a child.* Hence we see that although the adverb *well* is used as an adjective and felt to be such in *he is quite well,* the conversion is not complete, for we cannot talk of **a well man.*

363. In such constructions as *the house here, the man there,* the adverb follows its noun instead of preceding it, because these combinations are felt to be contractions of such sentences as *the house is here, the man stands there,* etc.

Sentence-Modifying.

364. As assertion, denial, etc., consist in stating a certain relation between the subject and predicate of a sentence, it follows that adverbs of assertion (**350**) cannot modify either subject or predicate exclusively, but modify the relation between them, that is, modify the general meaning of the sentence. Thus *certainly* in *I certainly think so* does not modify *think* alone, as if the sentence were equivalent to *I think with certainty* or *I think correctly*, but the whole sentence is equivalent to *it is certain that I think so.* That such is the meaning of the adverb is confirmed by the form of the sentence, for if *certainly* modified *think* only, it would follow it, as the adverb *so* does in *I think so.* Nor can it modify *I*, because adverbs precede the noun-words they modify. Lastly, the freedom with which *certainly* can be moved about in the sentence seems to show that it does not belong specially to any one word in it: *certainly I think so, I certainly think so, I think so certainly.*

365. In the same way the adverb *not* in *I do not think so* is a sentence-modifier serving to deny or negative the connection between the subject *I* and the predicate *think so.* Here also the grammatical form confirms the grammatical analysis, for *not* is joined on to the unmeaning form-word *do*, which serves only as a prop for the negative particle, so that by attaching *not* to the one unmeaning word in the sentence, we seem, as it were, to distribute the negation over the whole sentence.

366. But in such a sentence as *he is not a fool*, the *not* might formally be associated with the noun as well as with the verb, being in a position which would enable it to modify either. In fact such sentences have in the spoken language two forms (hij iznt ə fuwl) and (hijz not ə fuwl). In the former the negation being attached specially to an unmeaning form-word must necessarily logically modify the whole sentence, just as in *I do not think so* (ai dount pink sou), so that the sentence is equivalent to ' I deny that he is a fool.' In the other form of the sentence the *not* is detached from the verb, and is thus at liberty to modify the following noun, so that the sentence is felt to be equivalent to *he is no fool*, where there can be no doubt that the negative adjective-pronoun *no* modifies the noun, so that (hijz not ə fuwl) is almost equivalent to ' I assert that he is the opposite of a fool.' Again, in such a sentence as *he gave his money not from benevolence but from ostentation*, *not* cannot be regarded as a sentence-modifier, for if so, the sentence would imply ' he does not give money' while it means the exact opposite.

We see from these examples not only that the same adverb may be sometimes a sentence-modifier, sometimes an ordinary word-modifier, but that there is often great difficulty in distinguishing between word-modification and sentence-modification generally. This is especially the case when a verb is the word that seems to be modified. If the verb has no meaning of its own, it cannot of course be logically—though it may be grammatically—modified by the adverb. But if the verb has a distinct meaning of its own, its importance in the sentence makes any modification of it almost logically equivalent to modification of the whole sentence. Thus there can be no doubt that an adverb of motion such as *home* in its regular position after a verb of motion such as *go* must be regarded as specially modifying that verb, and yet in such a sentence as *John came home yesterday*, *home* practically modifies not *came* only, but the whole sentence, for it is not any one at any time that came home, but it is *John* that came home, and he came home *yesterday*.

In grammar we are, of course, bound to consider such questions as much as possible from a purely grammatical point of view, and from the grammatical point of view there can be no doubt that *home* in *John came home* modifies *came*, and *came* only.

367. Some sentence-modifying adverbs single out one particular word, although they still modify the sentence as a whole. *even* and *only* in *even Homer sometimes nods*, where *even Homer = Homer himself*, *only a fool would do that*, are examples of such 'word-sentence-modifying,' word-emphasizing adverbs. In such a sentence as *he is only a common soldier*, *only* is a word-modifying adverb.

Sentence-Adverbs.

368. The answer to the question *is he here?* can be either the affirmative *yes* or the negative *no*. It is evident that *yes* and *no* are sentence-modifying adverbs and at the same time sentence-words like *come!, John!, alas!. no* in the above example is equivalent to *he is not here*; it is, therefore, at the same time the absolute form corresponding to the conjoint *not*. There is no conjoint adverb corresponding to *yes*, because the ordinary form of the sentence (*he is here*) is taken to imply affirmation. The nearest approach to such a conjoint affirmative adverb is the emphatic assertive *certainly* (*he is certainly here*), which, like many other adverbs, can also be used absolutely—though without any change of form—as in the answer to the question *will you come too?*

Dependent Adverbs.

369. Dependent adverbs are of two kinds, **word-introducing** and **sentence-introducing**. A sentence containing a word-introducing adverb can be supplemented by a word or word-group as well as a sentence, as in *he is taller than you, he is taller than you are*; while a sentence-introducing adverb requires a full sentence, as in *I know how it is done.*

Correlative Adverbs.

370. These are a special class of word-introducing dependent adverbs. By correlation we understand the use of two or more form-words of similar meaning and function belonging to the same part of speech, and standing to one another in a relation of mutual dependence. *as . . as* in *he is nearly as tall as you (are), so . . as* in *he is not so tall as you (are), the . . the* in *the more the merrier, the more you beat them the better they be* are examples of correlation-pairs. The distinction between *as tall as you* and *as tall as you are* is, of course, parallel to that between *than you* and *than you are* (**369**). It will be observed that although correlation-pairs often consist in the repetition of the same word, they may be made up of two different words, provided these words are parallel in function and meaning. In correlation-pairs the second correlative refers back to the first something in the same way as a relative refers back to its antecedent, *he is as tall as you* being equivalent to 'he is tall in the degree in which you are tall.' Correlation consists therefore in mutual logical dependence and parallelism of the members of the correlation-pair.

371. Adverbs of more independent meaning may also form correlation-pairs, such as *partly . . partly, sometimes . . sometimes, now . . now,* as in *he did it partly from benevolence, partly from ostentation; sometimes grave, sometimes gay, (now grave, now gay).*

372. The members of a correlation-pair sometimes become fixed so as to form **correlation-groups** or correlation compounds, such as *to and fro; up and down; here, there, and everywhere.*

No pair of related words can be regarded as a correlation-pair unless in addition to the characteristics of mutual logical dependence it shows grammatical parallelism. Thus an antecedent noun and its relative pronoun (*men . . who*) cannot be regarded as correlative, because they belong to different parts of speech, the pronoun being also markedly subordinated to the noun; and even when the antecedent is a personal pronoun (*I who . .*) we do not feel the two to be grammatically parallel and on a footing of equality. But if we could expand *what I say I mean* into **what I say, that I mean* we might call *what . . that* in such a construction correlatives.

More . . than in *he is more industrious than his brother* cannot be regarded as a correlation-pair for another reason, namely, that the analogy of *he is stronger than his brother* shows that it is simpler to regard *than* as joined on to the group *more-industrious*, *more* itself being too closely connected with its adjective to be able to enter into a correlation-pair by itself. *So . . that* in *I was so tired that I could not go any further* cannot be regarded as a correlation-pair for the same reason.

Relative and Conjunctive Adverbs.

373. Dependent sentence-introducing adverbs are subdivided into **relative** and **conjunctive** adverbs, corresponding to relative and conjunctive pronouns. Thus the place-adverb *there* in *we stopped there a week* is an independent adverb corresponding to the independent pronoun *that* in *we stopped in that place*. In *we went on to Rome, where we stopped a week*, *where* is a relative (progressive) adverb corresponding to the relative pronoun *which* in *we went on to Rome, in which place we stopped a week*. In *I know where he is, where* is a conjunctive adverb answering to the conjunctive pronouns *who* or *what* in *I know who he is, I know in what place he is*. All the interrogative adverbs are used relatively and conjunctively as well. Thus *why* is relative in *the reason why, how* is conjunctive in *I know how it is done*. In *I asked how it was done, how* is both a conjunctive and an indirect interrogation adverb. just as the pronoun *what* is both conjunctive and indirectly interrogative in *I asked what it was.*

374. The conjunctive adverb of affirmation *that*, as in *I know that it is true, that it is true is a fact*, and the conjunctive adverbs of doubt *if* and *whether*, as in *I wonder if it is true, I do not know whether it is true or not*, have no corresponding interrogative adverb, because such an adverb would be superfluous in such a sentence as *is it true?* where the form of the sentence by itself shows that it is interrogative.

Compare the analogous want of a conjoint adverb of affirmation (**368**).

The conjunctive *that* is often dropped in Spoken English, as in *I know it is true*.

375. In the cases we have hitherto been considering, the dependent adverb, where it introduces a word, a word-group, or a sentence, does so in order to modify some one word—it is a word-modifying, not a sentence-modifying adverb; but in some cases definite formal criteria fail us. In clauses which contain relative pronouns it is easy to distinguish between reference to a single word (*the man . . who*) and reference to a whole sentence (*I said nothing, which . .*), because the antecedent to a relative pronoun has definite formal characteristics by which we can recognize it to some extent independently of its meaning; but when we have to deal with relative and other connective adverbs, there are often no formal criteria by which we can tell whether they modify single words or whole sentences. In such a sentence as *I know when he came* we do not hesitate to regard *when he came* as associated specially with the verb *know*. In *he came to the house when I was out, he came while I was out* we are also inclined to regard *when I was out, while I was out* as adjuncts to *came*. But in *he came yesterday because he knew I was out* we are inclined to regard *because he knew I was out* as an adjunct to the whole sentence *he came yesterday*, or, in other words, as connecting the two sentences together as wholes, instead of merely joining the second clause to a single word in the first. If so, we must regard *because* as a conjunction, not an adverb. But *he came while I was out* may imply that he came because I was out, so that we should have to regard *while* as an adverb in one shade of meaning and a conjunction in the other.

This is why it is most practical to class all sentence-connecting adverbs as conjunctions without stopping to enquire into the exact way in which the connection is effected (381).

Connection between Adverbs and other Parts of Speech.

Connection between Adverbs and Adjectives.

376. An adjective after a link-verb often approaches in meaning to an adverb, especially when the link-verb has some independent meaning, as in *he looks very angry*, *he stood firm*, compared with *he stared at him angrily*, *to stand firmly on his feet*. In *to stare angrily*, *stare* has so full and independent a meaning that its adjunct *angrily* is felt to be a pure adverb in meaning as well as form; but *looks* in *he looks angry*, although it has enough independent meaning to take an adjunct-word of its own, is, on the other hand, almost equivalent to the pure link-verb *is*, so that *angry* from this point of view is felt to be logically as well as grammatically an adjective. In some cases adjectives are used as complete adverbs without any change of form, as in *to drink deep, to work hard*, especially when compared, as in *he works harder than ever, I know where it can be done cheapest.*

Connection between Adverbs and Pronouns.

377. We have already seen that general adverbs resemble pronouns (336). In some cases the similarity of adverbs to pronouns in grammatical function is so great that we can hardly tell which part of speech the word belongs to. In such combinations as *I think so, I told you so*, the adverb *so*

does not merely modify its verb like an adverb—as if *I think
so* meant 'I think in that way'—but answers the question
'think what?', so that it is logically equivalent to a pronoun
in the direct object relation, and we might change the above
sentences into *I think that, I told you that* without any per-
ceptible change of meaning. In *he likes it, and so do I ; he
is fond of it, and so am I, so* is felt to be equivalent partly to
a pronoun of reference—'he likes it, and that (i.e. liking)
do I'—partly to 'also.'

378. In *who else?, what else?* the adverb *else* has no
longer the sense of 'otherwise,' but is almost felt to be equivalent to the pronoun *another*, although it is most convenient
to regard *who else*, etc. as group-compounds like *whoever,
whosoever*. The adverb *yonder* in *look yonder, the man yonder*
(compare *the man there*, § **363**) has been converted into a
pure pronoun in *yonder man*.

379. In Old English and Modern German such combinations as *in it, in what, in which*, are made into *here-in,
there-in, where-in*; such a combination as *the house in which
he lives* being expressed by *the house wherein he lives*, the
adverbs *here, there, where* being substituted for the neuter
pronouns *it (this, that), what, which*. The reason of this is
that lifeless objects are generally stationary, and hence often
come to be looked at from a purely local point of view.
Hence instead of saying 'he is in it,' meaning 'he is in the
house' or 'he is in that (this) room,' we may say *he is in there*
or *he is in here*, as the case may be ; and instead of
saying *the book is on it*, meaning 'on the shelf,' we say *it is up
there*. The difference between this Modern English and the
Old English usage is that in the latter they said *here in =*
'here inside,' instead of *in here*, and then ran the two
adverbs together so as to form a single word.

Connection between Adverbs and Prepositions.

380. In such a sentence as *John is stronger than Thomas,* the adverb *than* has an evident similarity to a preposition : it makes the noun *Thomas* into an adjunct to *stronger*, just as the preposition *beyond* might do in such a sentence as **John is strong beyond Thomas*. In fact *than* governs an objective case like a preposition in such a construction as

> *Beelzebub, than whom,*
> *Satan except none higher sat.* (MILTON.)

Than and *as* may also be regarded as case-governing adverbs in such constructions as *he is taller than me, he is as strong as me*, although it is simpler to regard them here as absolute pronouns, as in *it is me*.

Connection between Adverbs and Conjunctions.

381. When an adverb introduces a sentence as a modifier, not of a word in the preceding sentence, but of the whole sentence, the adverb becomes indistinguishable from a conjunction (375); and as it is often difficult to distinguish between word-modification and sentence-modification (366. 1), it is for ordinary grammatical purposes most convenient to regard all sentence-introducing adverbs as conjunctions (408). Thus, although it is not strictly correct to call the sentence-introducing *like* in *do like I do!* a conjunction as opposed to the 'adverb' *like* in *she sings like a bird*, yet the rule ' *like* is an adverb, not a conjunction in standard English,' or ' it is vulgar to use *like* as a conjunction,' cannot be expressed so shortly and conveniently if we refuse to call the sentence-connecting *like* a conjunction.

382. Word-connecting adverbs such as *than* and the correlative *as . . . as* bear an equally close resemblance to word-connecting conjunctions such as *and* (403). But as sentence-connecting is regarded as the most characteristic function of conjunctions, it is not usual to extend the designation ' conjunction ' to such adverbs.

Prepositions.

Form.

383. Prepositions, like adverbs, are of two kinds, primary and secondary. **Primary** prepositions, such as *of, in, on, to, till, for, with, by,* are connected only with the two other classes of particles—adverbs and conjunctions. Most prepositions are used also as adverbs; thus *by* is a preposition in *he passed by the house,* an adverb in *he passed by.* A few are used also as conjunctions (or conjunctional adverbs), such as *till* in *wait till he comes, for* in the sense of 'because.' Some prepositions are not used as adverbs, such as *of, to, for.*

Originally, however, *off* was the adverb corresponding to *of,* and *too* was the adverb corresponding to *to.* But now *off* and *too* have diverged so much from the corresponding prepositions that there is no longer any association between them.

384. Secondary prepositions are formed from the declinable parts of speech. Thus *across* is formed from the noun *cross; round* in *walk round the garden, along* are formed from the adjectives *round, long;* and *excepting, except, during, past* in *half past one,* are formed from the verbs *except, dure* = *endure, pass.*

385. There are also **compound** prepositions, some primary, formed from other prepositions and from adverbs, such as *into, upon, throughout,* and some secondary, formed partly at least from declinable words, such as *notwithstanding.*

386. There is also an important class of **group-prepositions,** such as *by means of, for the sake of, with regard to,* consisting of a noun governed by a preceding preposition and followed by another preposition, which grammatically governs the following noun, although logically the noun is governed by the whole group. Thus in *I will do it for the* *sake of peace*, the noun *peace* is governed grammatically by *of*, but logically by the group *for-the-sake-of*.

The group-preposition *because of* contains only one distinct independent preposition, but the *be-* is really a weakening of the preposition *by*.

387. Prepositions are put before noun-words. They govern personal pronouns in the objective case : *to me, of him*. In more highly inflected languages, prepositions generally govern a variety of cases, the same preposition often governing several cases with corresponding differences of meaning. Thus in Latin and German such a preposition as *in* governs the accusative case when associated with verbs of motion or a noun-word expressing the end or goal of the motion expressed by the verb; while it governs some case equivalent to the locative (in Latin the ablative, in German the dative) when rest is expressed, the same distinction being made with *on* and other prepositions. Through want of the necessary inflections English has lost this distinction, so that a new compound preposition *into* has been formed to denote motion, as in *he came into the house*—where Latin would have *in the house* with *house* the accusative—compared with *he is in the house*, where Latin would have the ablative. But we still use the adverb *in* to express motion, as in *he came in*. A preposition need not be prefixed immediately to its noun, but may be separated from it by intervening adjuncts to the noun, as in *on a very high hill*. In a concord-language the declinable adjuncts *a* and *high* would of course be put in the same case as *hill*. We may call the combination of a preposition with the words it governs a **preposition-group**.

In some languages prepositions follow, instead of preceding the noun-words they govern, either generally or only in special cases. Even in English *therein* is equivalent to *in there, in it*

(379), although *in* in *therein* is not a true preposition but an adverb.

388. Prepositions sometimes govern adjectives, especially in adverbial groups such as *in short, after all.* They also govern adverbs, as in *till now, since then, from here.* In such constructions the adjectives and adverbs must be regarded as converted nouns, being also logically equivalent to nouns: *in short* = 'in a short statement,' 'in few words'; *till now* = 'till the present time.'

FUNCTION.

389. The grammatical function of a preposition is to make the noun-word it governs into an adjunct-word. A preposition-group may serve as adjunct to—

(*a*) A noun-word, as in *a man of honour, a widow with three children, freedom from care.*

(*b*) An adjective, as in *black in the face, free from care, good for nothing.*

(*c*) A verb, as in *climb up a tree, I thought of it, he did it with the greatest ease.*

(*d*) A sentence, as in *I stopped at home because of the rain, he caught cold through getting wet.*

It will be observed that in such constructions the adjunct-group is generally a sentence-equivalent, *rain*, for instance, being a subject-predicate word (**257**), and *through getting wet* being equivalent to the clause *because he got wet.* Even if the preposition-group is made up with a concrete noun-word, as in *I caught cold through you* or *it was all through you that I caught cold*, we can mentally expand the preposition-group into a phrase such as 'through your persuading me to go out in the rain.' Prepositions in such constructions are, therefore, logically equivalent to conjunctions, and we can make the first sentence into *I stopped at home because it rained* — with the conjunction *because* instead of the group-preposition *because of*—without any change of meaning. Conversely, we can express *we saw the lightning before we heard the thunder*, where *before* is a conjunction, in the form of *we saw the lightning before hearing the thunder*, where *before* is a pre-position.

In such a sentence as *after the old king's death his son came to the throne* the way of expression makes it necessary to put the preposition-group first, which makes the preposition resemble a conjunction still more. The normal order may be restored by a slight change : *the son came to the throne after the old king's death*.

390. A preposition-group qualifying a noun is often equivalent to an adjective ; thus *of honour* in *man of honour* is equivalent to *honourable* ; and *a man with a red nose* means the same as *a red-nosed man*.

391. As adjectives and verbs are generally qualified by adverbs, a preposition-group qualifying an adjective or verb is generally equivalent to an adverb. Thus *blind of one eye* means much the same as *partially blind*, and *with ease* means exactly the same as *easily*.

392. Adding a preposition to a noun-word has the same function as inflection. Thus the preposition-group *of John* means exactly the same as the genitive *John's*, and *with ease* is equivalent to the instrumental case of those languages which have that inflection.

393. Prepositions serve also to express a variety of more general grammatical relations. Thus in *the town of Birmingham* the *of* denotes apposition, the group being equivalent to *Birmingham the town*. In *the rat was killed by the dog*, the *by* is the sign of the inverted subject, the group *by-the-dog* being logically equivalent to a nominative case.

394. Although a preposition is grammatically associated with the noun-word it governs, it is in meaning associated quite as closely with the word modified by the preposition-group—in some cases even more so, especially when the

head-word is a verb. Thus in such sentences as *I saw him pass by the window* and *run across the road and tell him to come here*, the prepositions are so closely associated with the preceding verbs that we can omit the nouns that follow them without altering the meaning, except that we make it vaguer: *I saw him pass by, run across and tell him to come here.* So we may regard *pass-by* and *run-across* in such constructions as **group-verbs**, logically equivalent to such simple transitive verbs as *pass* and *cross* in *he passed the house, he crossed the road*, just as *look-at, think-of, attend-to* are logically equivalent to *survey, consider*, etc.

395. In English such group-verbs can be put in the passive voice in imitation of the transitive verbs which they resemble in meaning, as in *it has been thought of, he shall be attended to*.

396. In such group-verbs the preposition follows the verb so closely that it is often completely detached from the noun-word it originally governed. When a preposition is used in this way we call it a **detached** preposition. Detached prepositions are liable to be disassociated from their noun-words not only in position, but also in grammatical construction, as in *he was thought of*, where the detached preposition is no longer able to govern the pronoun in the objective case because the passive construction necessitates putting the pronoun in the nominative. Prepositions are also detached in some constructions in connection with interrogative and dependent pronouns and adverbs, as in *who are you speaking of?, I do not know what he is thinking of, where is he going to?, I wonder where he came from*; such constructions as *of whom are you speaking?* being confined to the literary language. It will be observed that here too the detached preposition loses the power of governing the pronoun in the objective case, the *who* in *who are you speaking of?* being felt to be the logical nominative in the sentence. In such sentences as *you are the very man we were speaking of, that is the place he came from*, which in the literary language would become *you are the very man of whom we were speaking, that is the place from which he came* (*whence he came*), the dependent pronoun or adverb is omitted, so that the detached preposition is grammatically isolated or absolute, being referred back logically to *who* and *place*—the logical subjects of the independent clause.   Although detached prepositions approach very near to adverbs, yet they cannot be regarded as full adverbs for the simple reason that those prepositions which are otherwise never used as adverbs, such as *of*, can be detached with perfect freedom.

Meaning.

397. The meanings expressed by prepositions are very numerous, but they may be classed under the three heads of (*a*) **space**, including place, rest, and motion, (*b*) **time**, and (*c*) other **abstract** relations, such as quantity, manner, cause, deprivation.

398. All three classes of meanings are often expressed by the same preposition.   Each preposition generally has some one fundamental meaning which runs through one or more of the above classes.   Thus *to* and *from* as prepositions of space have exactly opposite meanings, as in *the road from London to York, he went from London to York*.   As the space preposition *from* expresses the beginning of a sequence or direction and the starting-point of motion, so also as a preposition of time it expresses the beginning of a period—*from that time*—and as an abstract preposition it expresses the beginning of change, while *to* in accordance with its primary meaning expresses the end or result of a change, as in *to change from black to red, from* also expressing metaphorically the various causal relations of origin, inference, etc., as in *to result from, to infer from*.

Conjunctions.

FORM.

399. Of the **primary** conjunctions the most unmistakeable
are those words which are used as conjunctions, and as conjunctions only, such as *and* and *or.* Some English conjunctions are also prepositions. such as *for, since.* As the prepositional use of these words is the original one, they may be
regarded as **secondary** conjunctions. The connection between conjunctions and adverbs has been already treated
of (**381**).

400. Some conjunctions are **simple**, such as *and* and *or.*
some **compound**, such as *although.* There are also **group-
conjunctions**, such as *in order that, as soon as, as if,* most
of which contain either a simple conjunction, such as *if,* or
one or more adverbs.

401. Conjunctions are often used correlatively (**370**).
Both . . and, though . . yet are examples of correlative
conjunction-pairs.

402. Conjunctions generally precede the word or sentence
they modify.

FUNCTION.

403. The grammatical function of conjunctions is to connect words with words and sentences with sentences. Conjunctions are therefore of two kinds. **word-connecting** and
sentence-connecting. A sentence introduced by a conjunction (or any particle equivalent to a conjunction) is called
a **prepared sentence**, sentences which are not introduced
in this way being called **unprepared** (**458**). The same
conjunction is often used both as a word-connecter and as a
sentence-connecter. Thus *and* is a word-connecter in *two
and three make five,* and a sentence-connecter in *he went one
way and I went another (way).* By 'connect' we mean the
statement of any kind of relation ; hence such a conjunction

as *or* in *answer yes or no!*, which, in one sense, separates instead of joining together the two words it comes between, is as much a conjunction as *and* itself.

404. Conjunctions are purely connective words: they connect without governing; and this is what distinguishes word-connecting conjunctions from prepositions. These two classes of words resemble each other closely, as we see by comparing *John and I went there* with *John went there with me*. But in *John with me*, the preposition connects the two noun-words only indirectly, by combining with the pronoun to form an adjunct-group which modifies *John*, the preposition at the same time governing the pronoun in the objective case. *and* in *John and I*, on the other hand, not only has no governing relation to either word, but can hardly be said to modify either of them even logically, or to subordinate one to the other, except in as far as the unavoidable necessity of putting one word after the other necessarily leads to putting the less important word last, and so making it appear to be subordinated. In *two and three make five* there cannot be any logical subordination—*three* being, indeed, a more important factor than *two*—although from a grammatical point of view we are obliged to regard *three* as joined on to the other word, and so subordinated to it.

405. Such a sentence as *he is tall but not strong* might be expanded into *he is tall, but he is not strong* without any change of form except the repetition of *he is*, so that we might regard *but not strong* as an elliptical or contracted sentence (**488**), and *but*, accordingly, as a sentence-connecting instead of a word-connecting conjunction. So also such a sentence as *Mr. Smith and Professor Green called while you were out* might be expanded into *Mr. Smith called first, and then Professor Green called by himself*, but it would generally be taken to mean that they called together— that Mr. Smith brought Professor Green with him. In *Mr. and Mrs. Smith called to take leave*, the *and* would almost necessarily have the latter function ; and it would evidently be absurd to expand *he ate three pieces of bread and butter* into *he ate three pieces of bread, and he ate three pieces of butter* ; while to expand *two and three make five* into *two makes five and three makes five* would result in nonsense.   Again, the grammatical structure of such a sentence as *Caesar and Pompey were both great men* makes it impossible to expand it into two full sentences without completely recasting it. It is evident, therefore, that from a grammatical point of view it is not only simplest and easiest, but also most correct to regard *but* in *he is tall but not strong, he is tall but weak* as a word-connecter, *tall-but-not-strong, tall-but-weak* being group-predicates logically equivalent to such a group as *tallness-with-weakness* in such a sentence as *he combines tallness with weakness.*

406. But the main function of conjunctions is to connect sentences.   The most unmistakeable conjunctions are those which connect sentences as wholes, without entering into any special relations with any of the separate words of which the sentences are made up.   Thus in the sentence-combination *he went one way and I went another*, we cannot say that *and* is associated with or modifies either logically or grammatically any one word in either sentence.

407. But it sometimes happens that the form of a sentence is modified by a conjunction.   Thus in German the verb of a clause introduced by such a conjunction as *if* is always put at the end of the clause, so that such a clause as *if it is true* appears in German as *if it true is, the verb having the same position as in English in an independent sentence such as *it is true.*   Sometimes the addition of a conjunction is attended, in English as in other languages, by changes in the individual words composing the sentence, as in *if I knew it, if it were true*, compared with *I know it, it is true.*   But such changes are quite different from the mechanical change of *with I into *with me* : we feel that the change of *know* into *knew* is only an imperfect method of modifying the whole sentence. In fact, the change in *if it were true* is really independent of the conjunction *if*, which may be dropped altogether without altering the sense, *were it true* having exactly the same meaning as *if it were true*.

408. We have already seen (375) that the distinction between pure conjunctions and dependent adverbs is that while the former join sentences together as wholes, the latter join the sentence they introduce to some word in the other sentence, so that their sentence-joining function is, to some extent, a secondary one. Strictly speaking, if we call *when* in *I know when he came* a conjunction. we ought to call the pronoun *who* in *I know who came* a conjunction also, specially when we observe that in such a sentence as *why consult John, who knows nothing about it* it has the full causal meaning of the conjunction *because*, this sentence being equivalent to *it is no use consulting John, because he knows nothing about it*. In fact it is only the difficulty of distinguishing between dependent adverbs and conjunctions that makes us include them all under the latter head.

409. There is also a class of **independent adverbs** which closely resemble conjunctions. such as *still* and *nevertheless*, as in *your arguments are strong : still (nevertheless) they do not convince me*, compared with *your arguments are strong, but they do not convince me*. For convenience we may call such adverbs **half-conjunctions**. The difference between half- and full conjunctions is that half-conjunctions connect logically only, not formally also, as full conjunctions do. Two clauses connected by a full conjunction run on without a pause and constitute a single complex sentence, while two sentences connected by a half-conjunction may be—and often are—separated by a pause, and the whole group is felt to be a logical not a formal group. Hence, in writing, sentences connected by full conjunctions are generally separated by a comma, or not at all, while sentences connected by half-conjunctions are separated by a semicolon or full stop. The difference between these two classes of particles is analogous to that between an independent pronoun such as *he* and the corresponding dependent pronoun *who*: just as *he* refers to a preceding sentence telling us who 'he' is, so also *still* and *nevertheless* refer us back to a sentence which the one they introduce seems to contradict; and yet the sentences introduced by these three words are all formally independent of the preceding ones.

410. It will be observed that half-conjunctions are in one respect more closely allied to full conjunctions than dependent adverbs are, namely that they never refer back grammatically to any one word in the preceding sentence.

411. Half-conjunctions are necessarily sentence-modifying adverbs. Many of them do not necessarily stand at the beginning of the sentence, as is always the case with pure conjunctions in English. Thus the half-conjunction *however* can stand at the beginning, in the middle, or at the end of a sentence : *however, I told him it would not do—I told him, however, it would not do—I told him it would not do, however.* So also *nevertheless* stands at the end of the sentence in *he did it nevertheless.* In this way half-conjunctions are often used concurrently with full ones, as in *if, however, . .* = *but if . .*

412. But half-conjunctions often single out one particular word in the sentence they introduce. *Also, too,* which are the half-conjunctions corresponding to *and*, often have this function, as in *I also will go, I will go too*, where they single out *I*, although *too* is put at the other end of the sentence.

Compare the similar use of *even* in *even Homer sometimes nods* (**367**).

MEANING.

413. The conjunctions (including dependent adverbs) and

half-conjunctions are classed according to their meaning as affirmative (copulative), alternative, negative, adversative, concessive, hypothetical, temporal, and causal.

414. The chief **affirmative** or copulative conjunction is *and*, which simply connects without implying any special kind of connection. It is thus the most abstract and general in meaning of all the pure conjunctions. The correlative pairs *both . . and*, *not only . . but* have the same meaning as *and*, but are more emphatic. The half-conjunction corresponding to *and* is *also*, for which *too* is substituted in the spoken language. *Likewise* and *as well as* have the same function, but are more emphatic. There are besides a large number of affirmative half-conjunctions with various shades of meaning, such as *further, moreover, now, well*. Thus *now* in *not this man, but Barabbas ; now Barabbas was a thief*, adds an explanatory circumstance ; the other words show a step in an argument, etc.

415. The chief **alternative** conjunction is *or*, whose emphatic form is the correlative *either . . or*. Alternative conjunctions imply that one only of two or more words, word-groups, or sentences joined together by them is to be taken into consideration, it being left open which is to be selected. Thus *answer yes or no !, answer either yes or no !* implies the expectation of one of these answers, and one only, the speaker not knowing which answer will be given. These are examples of **strong alternatives**. When *or* implies indifference, as in *give me two or three nails*, it is a **weak alternative**, and is often used to express a mere verbal alternative, as in *Christ or the Messiah, Canute or Cnut*. which is also expressed by the adverb *alias*. It is to be observed that the emphatic *either . . or* always has the strong meaning.

416. The chief **negative** conjunctions are the correlative *neither . . nor*, the simple *nor* being in less frequent use. They are of course formed from the alternatives *either, or* by prefixing the negative *n-*, and may therefore be included under the alternative conjunctions. It is evident that negativing an alternative—that is, forbidding us to select any of the members of it—is equivalent to negativing all of them. Thus *he has neither relations, nor friends, nor money* = *he has not either relations, or friends, or money* is equivalent to *he has not any relations, he has not any friends, he has not any money*. Hence the negation of an alternative simply amounts to the negation of an affirmative, so that *nor* is equivalent to *and not*, as in *I remained silent, nor did he speak a single word*.

417. The chief **adversative** conjunction is *but*. Adversatives add something which is unexpected, or, at any rate, does not follow naturally from what has just been said, or seems to check the natural progress of a narration, argument, etc. Thus the idea of 'trying' naturally suggests that of 'succeeding,' and hence words or word-groups expressing these two ideas in their natural sequence are joined together by *and* : *he tried several times, and at last succeeded.* Failure, on the other hand, though a frequent result of trying, is felt to check this natural sequence, and so a statement of failure is joined on to a statement of attempt by means of *but* : *he tried hard, but did not succeed.* But if there is anything in the foregoing context which prepares us for the idea of unsuccessful attempt, then the statement of failure is joined on by *and* : *he is very unlucky ; he is always trying new things, and always failing.* *But* most frequently connects the contrasts of affirmation and negation, as in *he is rich, but not happy.* There are several half-conjunctions used adversatively, such as *still, nevertheless, however, only*, and several half-conjunction groups, such as *at the same time, for all that, in spite of that.*

418. The **concessive** conjunctions are closely allied to the adversative. The most important of them are *though, although*, and the correlative *though . . yet*. *Though* and *although* imply that the statement they introduce will be followed by one with an adversative meaning. Thus in *although I dislike the man, I have not anything to say against him*, the concessive conjunction states the speaker's dislike of another man, but at the same time warns us against inferring that he will speak ill of that man. So also in *though deep yet clear* (said of the Thames as it once was) the deepness of the river is admitted, but we are warned against inferring that the river is therefore wanting in clearness. The difference between an adversative and a concessive conjunction is that the former refers back, the latter forwards. Hence the correlative *though . . yet* is really equivalent to *although . . but*, so that if we drop the *though*, the remaining *yet* is almost identical in meaning with *but* : *deep yet clear = deep but clear*.

419. The chief **hypothetical** conjunction is *if*. *Unless* is a **negative hypothetical** conjunction = *if not* : *unless I am mistaken = if I am not mistaken*. There are also a variety of hypothetical group-conjunctions, such as *in case, supposing that, provided that*, which are often shortened into *supposing, suppose, provided*.

420. There are some conjunctions which express hypothesis with other meanings. *Otherwise*, for which *or* is substituted in the spoken language, has the meaning ' if otherwise,' and expresses **hypothetical difference**, as in *we must make haste, otherwise (or) we shall be too late*, where *otherwise* means ' if we act differently,' that is, ' if we do not make haste,' the negation implied referring back, so that *otherwise* is quite distinct in meaning from *unless*, in which the negation refers forwards. The correlative pair *whether . . . or* expresses **alternative hypothesis**, as in *he will have to do it whether he likes it or not*. **Hypothetical concession** is expressed by *even if*: *even if he is mistaken, you need not tell him so*. **Hypothetical comparison** is expressed by *as if*: *he started as if he had been shot*.

The hypothetical *if* and *whether*, which are pure conjunctions, must be distinguished from the dependent adverbs *if* and *whether* (**374**).

421. The **temporal** conjunctions, or conjunctions of time, are connected partly with adverbs, such as *when* and *as*, partly with prepositions, such as *before, after, since, until, till*. *While* is associated with *when* through beginning with the same consonant, which is, however, a mere chance, *while* being originally a noun meaning 'time' quite unconnected with *when*. The most markedly adverbial of these is *when*, which is used (*a*) as an independent interrogative adverb, as in *when did he come?*; (*b*) as a relative adverb, as in *he remembers the time when there were no railways*; (*c*) a conjunctive adverb, as in *I know when he came*; and (*d*) less distinctly as an adverb, though hardly as a pure conjunction: *he came when I was out; I had scarcely begun, when I was interrupted again; when he came, I was not at home*. *While*, *as*, and the conjunctions formed from prepositions are used only in constructions similar to those given above under (*d*): *he came while I was out; as he passed by, he looked in at the window; he came before I had finished breakfast; wait till I have finished my letter*. There are many secondary and group-conjunctions of time, most of which express **immediateness**, such as *directly* in *directly he came*; *immediately, as soon as, just as, just after*, etc.

Adverbs of **place** are not regarded as conjunctions even when they are used in the same constructions as *while*, etc., as in *I will stay where I am*.

422. Causal conjunctions are subdivided into four classes, conjunctions of cause, of effect, of result, and of purpose.

423. The two chief conjunctions of **cause** are *because*, which states an immediate and direct cause, and *for*, which adds an explanation or reason, often as a kind of afterthought: *we took our umbrellas, because we were afraid it would rain; for the barometer had been falling for some time*. *For* is, accordingly, freely used after a pause, and is therefore only a half-conjunction. *Since* and *as*, which are primarily conjunctions of time, are used also as pure conjunctions of cause.

424. The chief conjunction of **effect** is *therefore*, for which *so* is substituted in the spoken language : *it is getting late, so I will go home.* The temporal *then* is also used as a conjunction of effect : *then you had better go home. Accordingly* and *consequently* are secondary conjunctions of effect. All conjunctions of effect are half-conjunctions, because they introduce what are logically independent clauses, as we see by comparing *it is getting late, so I will go home* with *as it is getting late, I will go home.* In each of these two sentences only one clause is prepared : in the first sentence only the independent clause is prepared, in the second it is left unprepared. In languages which favour correlation, such as Old English, both clauses in such sentences are often prepared, so that the two sentences appear in the form of *because it is getting late therefore I will go home* or *therefore I will go home because it is getting late.*

425. The chief conjunction of **purpose** is *that* together with the more emphatic *in order that* : *we sow (in order) that we may reap.* **Negative purpose** or avoidance is expressed by *lest*, for which *so that . . not* is generally substituted in the spoken language : *they took away the knife lest he should cut himself = they took away the knife so that he should not cut himself.*

Coordinative and Subordinative Conjunctions.

426. We have seen (**404**) that such a conjunction as *and* does not logically subordinate the word or sentence it introduces to what goes before. Thus in such a sentence as *he is tall and strong, strong* is as much a predication-element as *tall*, neither adjective being, from a logical point of view, subordinated to the other, so that we can transpose them without affecting the sense : *he is strong and tall.* We call such conjunctions **coordinative** conjunctions, or, more shortly, **co-conjunctions**.

427. A **subordinative** conjunction, or **sub-conjunction**, on the other hand, makes the word or sentence it introduces into a logical adjunct to what precedes. Thus the sub-conjunction *if* in *if it is fine, I will go* makes *it is fine* into an adjunct to *I will go*, and we cannot shift *if* from one clause to the other, as we could *and*, without altering the sense or making nonsense.

428. Of the pure conjunctions the following are coordinative : *and, both . . and* ; *or, either . . or* ; *nor, neither . . nor* ; *but.* The half-conjunctions belonging to the same classes as these are also coordinative, such as *also, nevertheless, however.*

429. All the other pure conjunctions and all dependent adverbs are subordinative : *though, although, though . . yet* ; *if, unless, whether . . or* ; *because, since, as, that* ; *when, as, while, before, after, since* in their various meanings.

The half-conjunctions belonging to the same classes as the above are often regarded as sub-conjunctions, especially those of cause —*for, therefore, accordingly.*

430. If we take the word conjunction in its widest sense, we may say that *and* and *that* in *I know that it is true* represent the two extremes of abstract coordination and abstract subordination.

Detached Conjunctions.

431. The co-conjunctions *and, or, nor, but*, are often so detached from what precedes them that they are almost equivalent to half-conjunctions, as in the following passage, where the detached conjunctions are in Roman letters :—

If any artist, I do not say had executed, but had merely conceived in his mind the system of the sun, and the stars, and planets, they not existing, and had painted to us in words, or upon canvas, the spectacle now afforded by the nightly cope of heaven, great would be our admiration. Or *had he imagined the scenery of this earth, the mountains, the seas, and the rivers ; the grass, and the flowers, and the colours which attend the setting and the rising sun, and the hues of the atmosphere, these things not before existing, truly we should have been astonished.* But *now these things are looked on with little wonder, and to be conscious of them with intense delight is esteemed to be the distinguishing mark of a refined and extraordinary person.* (SHELLEY : *On Life.*)

432. It is evident that the detached *or* and *but* in this passage have a function different from and vaguer than that of the same conjunctions as they occur undetached in the first paragraph of it. Detached conjunctions are often marked by strong stress, especially when they are followed, as is often the case, by an adverb or half-conjunction or a parenthetic word-group or sentence, as when the paragraphs of a long argument begin with *and, indeed, . .* ; *nor, on the other hand, . .* ; *but, if we consider . . , . .* etc.

A detached conjunction stands in the same relation to an undetached one as a progressive relative (218) does to an ordinary relative.

Interjections.

433. Interjections are sentence-words expressing various emotions, such as—

surprise : *o !, oh !, ah !, ha !, aha !,* the first often expressing mere attention or interest (real or affected) in what is said.

joy : *hurrah !, huzza !*

approbation : *bravo !*

grief : *ah !, alas !, heigho !*

dislike, vexation, etc. : *pah !, ugh !, pshaw !, tut !, fie !*

These are all **emotional interjections**.

434. There is also a class of interjections of more definite meaning, which, instead of merely expressing an emotion of the speaker, are equivalent to imperative sentences, and may therefore be called **imperative interjections**.   Thus instead of the imperatives *look!*, *behold!* we may in writing use the interjection *lo!*   Another imperative interjection is *hush!* from which a verb *to hush* has been formed.

435. **Expletives** and oaths, of which there is a large number in English, are a class of interjections intermediate in function between the two former classes, being used partly to express emotion, partly to influence the actions of other human beings and animals.

436. Of the above interjections some are primary, some secondary.   **Primary** interjections are mostly reproductions of the sounds we make involuntarily when under the influence of various emotions.   It will be observed that many of the written interjections—such as *tut!*—are imperfect attempts to express sounds which do not occur in the non-interjectional words of the language.

Thus *tut!* represents one of that class of sounds known as 'clicks,' which form part of the regular non-interjectional sound-system of many barbarous languages, such as Zulu and the native languages of California.   It represents the 'point-click,' formed by putting the point of the tongue in the t-position, and sucking the air from under it, so that when the contact is loosened, a smacking sound is produced.   Some written interjections represent a familiar sound in an unfamiliar occurrence.   Thus *hush!* represents the consonant (ʃ) uttered without a vowel.

437. **Secondary** interjections are ordinary words which have come to be used as interjections by various processes of isolation.   Thus the old-fashioned expletive *marry!* is simply the name of the Virgin Mary with the vowel shortened. *Bravo!* is an Italian adjective or adverb meaning 'good,' 'well done,' which in Italian itself came to be used as an interjection, and was then imported into English.

438. If an ordinary word is used as an interjection without being isolated either in form—as in *marry!*—or in meaning —as in the case of *bravo!*—we cannot regard it as a full

interjection, but only as an **exclamation-word**. *Good !,
shame !* are examples of exclamation-words, one being an
exclamation-adjective, the other an exclamation-noun. *For
shame !* is an example of an **exclamation-group**.

439. Interjections occasionally imitate the constructions
of the other parts of speech. Thus *ah !* governs an objective
case in *ah me !*; *alas !* takes a noun-adjunct by means of the
preposition *for*, as in *alas for the deed !*, or without any preposition, as in *alas the heavy day !*

WORD-GROUPS.

440. Word-groups differ greatly in the closeness with
which their elements—that is, the words of which they are
made up—are associated together. Many word-groups
resemble sentences in the freedom with which they allow one
word to be substituted for another of like grammatical function, or a new word to be introduced. We call such word-
groups **free groups**. Thus the free group *for my sake* can
be made into *for his sake, for his own sake*, and the skeleton
for . . sake can be transposed into *for the sake of*. But in
such groups as *son-in-law, man-of-war, bread-and-butter, cup
and saucer*, no such variations are possible, the order of the
elements of these groups being as rigidly fixed as in a compound word. We call such combinations **group-compounds**,
to distinguish them from full compounds such as *blackbird*.
The essential difference between the two kinds of compounds
is seen in the plurals *sons-in-law*, etc., where the first element
is independent enough to take an inflection of its own. We
have another kind of group-compounds in *no use = useless,
whatsoever, moreover*, etc.

Most of these resemble true compounds in having one predominant stress : *'son-in-law, bread and 'butter, whatso'ever.*

441. Word-groups (and group-compounds) can be put

before a single noun so as to form a kind of compound with it, by which the members of the group are often logically united together more closely than when the group is detached, although for convenience they are separated in writing. Thus *cat and dog life* is analogous to *home-life, good all round man* to *prizeman*, etc.

These compounds also have one predominant stress: *cat and ·dog life, good all ·round man.*

442. Even in derivation, word-groups are treated like single words, a derivative ending being added to the last member of the group, while it modifies the meaning of the whole group, by which it binds them together more closely than they are connected in the underived group. Thus from the free group *old maid* is formed the fixed derivative group *old-maidish.*

We have a peculiar kind of group-derivation in *artificial florist* corresponding to *artificial flower*, in which *florist* is felt to be equivalent to **flower-ist*, the whole group meaning not 'a florist who is artificial,' but 'artificial-flower-maker.'

443. In inflection it is quite common in English to treat a word-group like a single word. Not only group-compounds such as *son-in-law* form their genitives *son-in-law's*, etc., but also free groups, as in *the man I saw yesterday's father*, where it would make nonsense to regard *yesterday* as the genitive of the single word *yesterday*. Here, as in *old-maidish*. it is the final modification which binds the elements of the group closely together.

444. In this way a word-group may be grammatically equivalent to a part of speech: in the example just given the word-group not only has the meanings and grammatical functions of a single noun, but takes the inflection of a noun. So also the group *no use* in *it is no use* is an adjective equivalent; and the combination preposition + noun-word is equivalent to an adverb, as in *with ease = easily*.

445. Word-groups often approach very near in grammatical function to sentences. If we take a simple sentence and change its finite verb into a verbal, the resulting **verbal-group** has really as much meaning in it as the corresponding sentence, as we see by comparing the sentence *he came home* with the verbal-group *his coming home*. In a verbal-group containing an infinitive, a noun-word in the objective relation may be a logical subject, as in *I want him to go home = I wish he would go home*.

SENTENCES.

446. Sentences—like word-groups—consist of significant elements, or words.

447. A sentence is a word or group of words capable of expressing a complete thought or meaning. Whether or not a given word or group of words is capable of doing this in any one language depends on the way in which that language constructs its sentences—that is, on their form. Thus in Latin *comes* would be a complete sentence, but not in English, although in itself *comes* is as intelligible as the complete sentence *some one comes* or *some one is coming*. A sentence is, therefore, 'a word or group of words whose form makes us expect it to express a full meaning.' We say 'expect,' because it depends on the context whether or not any one sentence expresses a complete meaning. Thus, such a sentence as *he is coming*, though complete in form, shows on the face of it that it is incomplete in meaning, for *he* means 'some one who has been mentioned before,' and makes us ask 'who is he?' Nevertheless *he is coming* is a complete sentence because it has the same form as *John is coming, I am coming*, etc., which are complete in meaning as well as form—as far, at least, as any one sentence can be said to be complete.

448. As regards the relation between the meaning of the

sentence and the meanings of its elements, sentences are of two kinds, general and special. A **general sentence** is one whose meaning is the necessary result of the meanings of the separate words of which it is made up and the principles on which words are joined together grammatically. Thus any one who knows the meanings of such words as *have, book, dog, uncle*, etc., and the rules of English grammar can form any number of ' Ollendorffian ' sentences such as *I have a book ; my uncle has the big dog, but I have the good book*, and so on. In **special sentences** or **idioms**, on the other hand, such as *how do you do?, I cannot help it*, the meaning of the whole cannot be inferred from the meanings of its elements. In fact, in *I cannot help it, help* may be said to be used in the sense of ' hinder,' ' prevent,' which is the opposite of its ordinary meaning. In idioms, therefore, the meaning of the whole is isolated against that of the parts, just as in compound words (**68**). But many idioms, though irregular in meaning, are quite regular and normal in form, *I cannot help it*, for instance, being formally on a level with such a general sentence *I cannot see him* : just as the latter can be made into *we cannot see him, they cannot see him*, etc., so also *I cannot help it* can be made into *we could not help being late*, etc. Such an idiom as *how do you do?* is more fossilized, being capable of very little variation : we could hardly say *how did you do yesterday?*

449. Hence we can make *how do you do* into a word with plural inflection, as in *how-do-you-do's were exchanged. Forgetmenot*, the name of a flower, is an example of a group compound—with isolation of meaning—formed directly from a sentence.

450. Sentences—like words—differ in fulness of meaning. Just as there are empty words, so also there are **empty sentences** (or clauses), as opposed to full ones. Thus in the complex sentence *is it me (that) you want?* the first clause *is it me?*, though grammatically an independent clause, is logically superfluous, and the same meaning might be expressed by getting rid of it, and putting the *me* into the dependent clause, which then becomes an independent sentence—*do you want me?* The clause *is it me?* is evidently made up solely in order to make the *me* more prominent by bringing it nearer the beginning of the sentence and making it the logical subject. Hence, although such empty clauses are, as clauses, devoid of meaning, they necessarily contain an emphatic full-word.

451. As every sentence is the expression of a thought, and as thought consists in joining together subject and predicate, and as the idea of predication is expressed in English by a (finite) verb, it follows that every normal English sentence ought to contain at least two words—a subject-word and a predicative verb. Hence also every group of words which contains a verb is, grammatically speaking, a sentence.

452. In some cases, however, a complete meaning is expressed by a single word—a **sentence-word**—such as *come!* = 'I command you to come,' where the subject being self-evident, the predicate-word by itself is enough to constitute a sentence. In *John!* = 'I ask John to come—to attend to me,' etc., the subject-word does duty for the predicate as well, which is omitted because of its vagueness. In *yes* = 'I agree with you,' 'I will do so,' etc., *no, alas!* = 'I am sorry for it,' etc., the distinction between subject and predicate is felt only vaguely. We see, then, that these 'one-word-sentences' are of two kinds, consisting (*a*) of a definite subject or predicate standing alone, and (*b*) of a word which is in itself neither definite subject nor definite predicate—in which the ideas of subject and predicate are not differentiated, but are 'condensed,' as it were, in one word. From a grammatical point of view these condensed sentences are hardly sentences at all, but rather something intermediate between word and sentence. A group of words without a finite verb (or verbal) may also be equivalent to a sentence—may constitute a

sentence-group.   *The more the merrier* is an example of a
sentence-group which is equivalent to a combination of two
clauses.   Many other examples are afforded by proverbs,
sayings, titles of books, etc., such as *better late than never*,
Measure for Measure.

453.   A sentence is not only a logical but a phonetic unity.
A continuous discourse from a phonetic point of view consists of a succession of sounds divided into **breath-groups**
by the pauses required for taking breath.   Within these
breath-groups there is no separation of the individual words
(**51**).   For the sake of clearness we generally wait to take
breath till we come to the end of a statement, question, etc.,
so that a breath-group is generally equivalent to a **sense-
group**, that is, a sentence.   In a dialogue, which is the
simplest and most natural way of using language, the short
sentences of which it mostly consists are marked off by a
complete cessation of the speaker's voice.   The end of a
sentence may be marked phonetically in other ways, especially by intonation.   Thus in English we mark the close of a
statement by a falling tone, while a rising tone shows that
the statement is incomplete, or that a question is intended.
In writing we mark off the end of a complete statement by
various marks of punctuation, especially the full stop (.).

454.   A long sense-group or sentence is often divided into
smaller sense-groups by change of intonation, etc., or by a
slight pause.   The slower or the more emphatically we speak,
the more pauses we make.   In writing, these smaller divisions
are generally marked by a comma (,), showing the rise of
the voice which tells us that though we have arrived at the
end of a sentence, yet the sense is not complete till we come
to the falling tone indicated by the full stop, semicolon, etc.
Thus in *when I came back, I found no one at home* we have
two simple sentences or clauses united in this way into a
complex sentence.

455.   The form and function of a sentence may be regarded from two points of view, internal and external. The **internal** structure of a sentence is determined by the relations between the words of which it is made up (**81**), in English especially by their order. The most important distinctions in the internal structure of sentences are those by which they express the different relations between subject and predicate in statement, question, etc. (**43**).

456. But we must also consider the **external** relations of sentences, by which we regard each sentence as a whole or unit, without troubling ourselves about the relations between the words of which it is made up. When we look at sentences from this point of view, we find that they can stand in the same relations to other sentences and to single words as words do to one another. Thus in *I see you are mistaken,* the clause *you are mistaken* stands in the same grammatical relation to the verb *see* as the noun-word *that* does in *I know that.*

457. There are two ways of showing the external relations of sentences. One is by their order. Just as words in sentences have a more or less fixed order, so also in groups of sentences the sentences or clauses follow each other in a certain fixed order. Thus in the above example the adjunct-clause follows the head-clause, while in other combinations the order is reversed, as in *if you are ready, we will start at once.*

458. Another way of showing the external relations of sentences is by the help of form-words, such as relative and conjunctive pronouns, adverbs, and conjunctions, all of which generally come at the beginning of the sentence. A sentence modified by a form-word is called a **prepared** sentence. Thus in *I see that you are mistaken, that you are mistaken* is a prepared sentence or clause, as compared with the unprepared clause *you are mistaken* in *I see you are mistaken.*

The external relations of sentences cannot be shown by inflection, because an inflected sentence is necessarily converted into a word (449). For the same reason they are incapable of derivation. Sentences are also incapable of composition in the way words are compounded: in a complex sentence there is no isolation of the meaning of the whole against that of the clauses of which it is made up.

RELATIONS BETWEEN SENTENCES.

459. Simple sentences are of two kinds, independent and dependent [cp. 199]. An **independent** sentence is one whose grammatical structure allows it to stand alone. A **dependent** sentence is one that cannot stand alone, but makes us expect another—generally an independent —sentence to complete its meaning. Thus in the complex sentence *when I came back, I found no one at home*, the first sentence is dependent, the second independent. All prepared sentences introduced by dependent words, whether pronouns, adverbs, or conjunctions, are necessarily dependent. Thus in the above example the dependent sentence *when I came back* is introduced by the dependent adverb or conjunction *when*. Unprepared dependent sentences may generally be expanded into prepared sentences. Thus the unprepared sentences in *you are the man I want, I see you are mistaken* may be expanded into *whom I want, that you are mistaken*.

460. Sentences are also distinguished as **coordinate** and **subordinate,** according as they are introduced by a coordinative or a subordinative conjunction (426).

Sentences introduced by a progressive relative pronoun or adverb must be regarded as coordinate (218, 373).

461. The distinction between independent and dependent does not always exactly agree with that between coordinate and subordinate, because the former is a purely grammatical distinction, the latter a logical one. Hence although all independent sentences are necessarily coordinate, it does not follow that all coordinate sentences are necessarily independent. In fact all sentences introduced by conjunctions are grammatically dependent.   Thus such a coordinate sentence as *and I will ride* can no more stand alone than a subordinate one such as *while I ride,* both equally requiring a preceding independent sentence to complete their meaning : *you shall walk and I will ride ; you shall walk, while I ride.* So also it makes nonsense to introduce a sentence with *or* without telling us what the other alternative is.

A sentence introduced by a detached conjunction (**431**) must, of course, be regarded as independent.

Clauses and Complexes.

462. Two or more sentences may be joined together to form a single complex sentence, or **complex**, as we may call it for the sake of brevity.   When simple sentences are joined together in this way we call them **clauses**.

463. In every complex there is one independent clause, called the **principal clause**, together with at least one dependent clause, which stands in the relation of adjunct to the principal clause.   The dependent clause may be either co-ordinate or subordinate.   We call a coordinate clause a **co-clause**, a subordinate clause a **sub-clause**.   Thus in *you shall walk, and I will ride,* the first clause is the principal clause, and the second is a co-clause.   In *you are the man I want,* the second clause—*I want*—is a sub-clause.   So also in *you shall walk while I ride.*

464. When a principal clause is followed by one or more co-clauses—as in the first of the examples given above—it may itself be called a co-clause, as being coordinate with the clauses that follow it.

In such a sentence as *the more you beat them, the better they be,* the two clauses are so mutually dependent on each other that it is difficult to decide which is the principal clause, and whether they are not both dependent.   For grammatical purposes we may regard the first as the principal clause simply on the ground of its coming first.

465. A complex in which the principal clause is modified by a co-clause is called, for the sake of brevity, a **co-complex**, and one in which it is modified by a sub-clause is called a **sub-complex**. Thus the first complex in § 463 is a co-complex, the other two are sub-complexes.

466. As it is most natural to put the principal clause first in a complex, it is not generally necessary to call attention to the order of the clauses except when the adjunct-clause is put before the head-clause. This is impossible with co-complexes, but is frequent with sub-complexes. When a sub-clause comes before its principal clause, the former is called the **front-clause**, the latter the **after-clause**. Thus in the sub-complex *if I can, I will do it*, the hypothetical sub-clause *if I can* is called the front-clause, and the principal clause *I will do it* is called the after-clause.

Inserted, Parenthetic, and Appended Clauses.

467. When a sub-clause is put inside another clause. so as to cut it in two, it is called an **inserted clause** ; thus in *I hope, if all goes well, to finish it tomorrow*, the sub-clause *if all goes well* is inserted in the principal clause *I hope to finish it tomorrow.*

468. If we expand this complex into *I hope, if all goes well, that I shall finish it tomorrow*, we have a three-clause instead of a two-clause complex, and the inserted clause, instead of interrupting a simple sentence, only breaks the continuity between a principal clause and a sub-clause which is more intimately connected with the principal clause than the inserted clause is. When a clause is inserted in this way it may be called a **middle clause**.

469. A clause may be inserted into a dependent clause, as in *he is a man, who, if he chose, might do great things.* Here the inserted clause *if he chose* is put immediately after the sentence-link *who*, which is a frequent position of an inserted clause.

470. When an inserted clause contains an inserted clause in itself—which last may again contain an inserted clause—the process is called **incapsulation,** and the whole group is called an incapsulation-complex.

471. When an independent sentence is inserted, it is called a **parenthetic sentence** or a parenthesis. Thus in *I shall finish it, I hope, by the end of the week, I hope* is a parenthesis. In this example the parenthetic sentence contains a transitive verb without an object-word, the logical object of *hope* being really expressed by the sentence into which the parenthesis is inserted, so that *I hope* is logically the principal clause, the whole sentence being equivalent to *I hope I shall finish it by the end of the week.* So also with the frequent parenthetic use of verbs of saying, etc., as in *this, I say, is the place.* Sometimes a parenthesis—especially when its verb does not require to be supplemented by an object-word, etc. —is logically equivalent to a sub-clause, as in *the two brothers —they were twins—were exactly alike,* where the parenthesis explains why they were alike, and is thus equivalent to a causal clause. So also in the frequent parentheses containing the verb *mean* : *he says—I mean John Smith—that . . .* In the above examples the parentheses are unprepared. But co-clauses and sentences introduced by half-conjunctions can also be used parenthetically, as in *if you are in the wrong — and I am sure you are in the wrong—you must apologize,* where we may substitute the half-conjunction *for* for the co-conjunction *and.* In this we have an example of what may be called a **middle parenthesis** (cp. **468**), and, at the same time, of a parenthesis which is a complex instead of being a simple sentence.

472. In such a sentence as *I am a doctor, you know,* the second clause is exactly analogous to a parenthesis, except that it comes at the end. We may call such a clause an **appended clause.**

Extended Complexes.

473. A complex which consists of more than two clauses is called an **extended complex**.

474. The simplest kind of extended complex is one which consists of a principal clause followed by two or more co-clauses: *I read the paper, and then I wrote a letter, and then I went for a walk.* In such complexes the clauses stand in no special relation to one another, being connected only by forming part of the same complex.

475. But if an extended complex contains a sub-clause, the sub-clause must necessarily be specially connected with some other clause which acts as principal clause to it, forming with it a lesser complex within the extended complex. Thus in such an extended complex as *I began to write a letter, but I could not finish it, because I was interrupted*, the sub-clause *because I was interrupted* is inseparably connected with the preceding clause, forming with it the sub-complex *I could not finish it, because I was interrupted.* The sub-clause cannot therefore enter into special relations with any other clause but this in the extended complex, so that it has no direct connection with the clause *I began to write a letter*; but the combination of which it forms part—the lesser complex—can do so: in the above example the lesser complex is put in a coordinate relation to the clause *I began to write a letter* by means of the conjunction *but*, so that the whole extended complex consists of a principal clause followed by a coordinate sub-complex, which we may express briefly thus: principal + coordinate sub-complex. It will be seen that such extended complexes contain two principal clauses. We call the principal clause of the lesser complex—*I could not finish it*—the **secondary principal clause**, as opposed to the **primary** principal clause *I began to write a letter*, which is the principal clause of the whole extended complex.

476. It is evident that extended complexes containing

sub-clauses admit of a great variety of form, for the lesser complexes contained in them may be co-complexes as well as sub-complexes, and they may be joined to the primary principal clause subordinately as well as coordinately. Thus in the extended complex *it is a book which I have read once, and which I hope to read again*, we have the combination principal + subordinate co-complex. In *I am anxious because the letter I expected has not arrived* we have principal + subordinate sub-complex, *I expected* being an inserted clause (467).

477. We can also have a principal complex instead of a principal clause, as in *the earth is a big ball that is always spinning round like a top, and at the same time it moves round the sun in a circle* = principal sub-complex + co-clause. This scheme can of course be varied by substituting a co-complex or a sub-clause.

478. But an arrangement consisting entirely of co-complexes and co-clauses in any order is indistinguishable from an extended complex made by adding on separate co-clauses to a principal clause. Thus such an extended complex as *I have written a letter, but I wrote it in a hurry, and it is very badly written* can be analysed only into separate clauses, and does not contain any lesser complexes, as it would if a sub-clause were substituted for one of the co-clauses. thus *I have written a letter, but it is very badly written, because I was in a hurry* = principal + coordinate sub-complex.

479. In the examples given above, the principal clause precedes, but its place may be taken by a front-clause or front complex : *if it is a mistake, you are responsible for it, and so am I* = front clause + co-complex.

480. Four-clause complexes containing sub-clauses are of two kinds. (*a*) Some of them consist of two complexes : *I have always thought, and I always shall think that it was a mistake which could have been avoided* = co-complex + subordinate sub-complex ; *if we watch a ship* *when she is sailing out to sea, we can see that the earth is round* = front sub-complex + sub-complex. (*b*) The other class of four-clause complexes consist of a principal clause and a clause-group consisting of a secondary principal clause combined with a lesser complex : *I meant to call on you yesterday, but a friend of yours told me he had heard you were not at home* = principal + coordinate (principal + subordinate sub-complex).

481. Extended complexes consisting of more than four clauses often contain groups of two complexes, as in the following six-clause complex : *there is not generally much dew, if the sky is not clear ; because, if the sky is cloudy, the clouds prevent the earth from giving out its heat ; and if the earth is not cold enough, the dew will not settle on it* = sub-complex + subordinate (sub-complex + coordinate sub-complex). It will be observed that in this example there are two secondary principal clauses—*the clouds prevent the earth . . .* , and *the dew will not settle on it.*

Sequences.

482. In a complex the clauses must be joined together by conjunctions, or else the adjunct-clauses must be dependent, as in *you are the man I want.* When two or more independent sentences are associated together logically in the same way as in a complex, the combination is called a **sequence**. Thus we have an adversative sequence in *am I right, am I wrong?* which is logically equivalent to the complex *am I right, or am I wrong?* Such a sequence is therefore equivalent to a co-complex. Such a causal sequence as *I am sure of it : I saw it myself* is, on the other hand, equivalent to the sub-complex *I am sure of it, because I saw it myself.* In both of these examples the adjunct-sentence is unprepared. We call such sequences **unprepared sequences**.

483. The only prepared sentences that can form part of a sequence are those which are introduced by a half-conjunction, as in the prepared sequence *I was tired; so I went to bed*, compared with the unprepared sequence *I am tired: I cannot go any further*, and the complex *I was so tired that I could not go any further.*

484. When a sequence is made up partly of prepared, partly of unprepared sentences, it is called a **partially prepared sequence.**

Relations between Sentences, Complexes, and Sequences.

485. Although the distinction between sentence and complex is generally quite clear, there are some simple sentences which approach very near to complexes.

486. A word-group containing a verbal often differs only grammatically from the same group with the verbal made into a finite verb, that is, from a sentence (**445**). Hence such a simple sentence as *I heard of his coming home* can be expanded into the complex *I heard that he had come home.* So also *I wish him to come back* may be expanded into I *wish he would come back.* Such sentences as *I heard of his coming home, I wish him to come back*, which contain in themselves the germs of dependent sentences, are called **extended sentences.**

487. Extended complexes can often be simplified by substituting an extended sentence for a lesser complex. Thus in *we can see that the earth is round, if we watch a ship when she is sailing out to sea*, the sub-complex can be shortened into *if we watch a ship sailing out to sea*, and this extended sentence itself can be further reduced to the verbal-group *by watching a ship sailing out to sea.* A complex can sometimes be shortened into an ordinary unextended sentence by a slight change : thus the principal clause in the above extended complex could be shortened into *we can see the roundness of the earth.* Indeed, the whole four-clause complex can be shortened into the simple sentence *we can see the roundness of the earth by watching a ship sailing out to sea.*

488. Another way in which complexes are shortened is by making sentence-connecting into word-connecting conjunctions, as when the complex *he is tall, but he is not strong* is made into a simple sentence with a group predicate— *he is tall, but not strong.* Such sentences may be regarded as a kind of extended sentences, but it is better to distinguish them from the extended sentences we have just been considering by calling them **contracted sentences.** When a complex is shortened merely by omitting to repeat a personal pronoun, as in *I wrote a letter, and then went out for a walk; he went away, but soon came back again,* the contraction is so slight that we can hardly regard *wrote a letter and then went for a walk* as a group-predicate, and it is therefore better to call such complexes **contracted complexes**, and so distinguish them from contracted sentences, such as *he is tall but not strong*, which are really distinct in form and, to some extent, even in meaning—from complexes.

We must distinguish between contraction and ellipse. In such a sentence as *the first month is called January, the second February,* the second clause is not merely contracted, it is elliptical, both meaning and grammatical construction requiring the repetition of *is called*; for if we regarded *the second February* as anything but a sentence, it would imply that there were two Februarys in the year. So also in *if possible, I will come tomorrow,* we must assume ellipse in the front clause.

489. As co-complexes are more easily shortened than sub-complexes, most extended complexes contain more of the latter than of the former, especially in the spoken language, which always avoids unnecessarily long complexes.

490. A sentence containing a parenthesis is not grammatically a complex, for any connection there may be between the two is logical, not grammatical : it remains a simple sentence. So also if a parenthesis is introduced into a complex it does not in any way alter the grammatical relations between the clauses of the complex.

491. It sometimes happens that a sub-clause stands alone, as if it were an independent sentence—is **detached.** The principal clause to such a detached clause is understood from the context. Detached clauses are most frequent in answers, where the principal clause is inferred from the question : *why do not you do it ? because I can not.* Here the detached clause *because I can not* stands for the complex *I do not do it, because I can not*—where the sub-clause is elliptical— the principal clause not being expressed because it has been already expressed in a slightly different form by the question itself.

492. The distinction between complex and sequence is often very slight. When the sentences of which a sequence is made up are uttered with a rising tone, and are run together with little or no pause—being separated in writing only by commas—they are practically equivalent to clauses, as in the unprepared sequence *I came, I saw, I conquered,* and the prepared sequence *there was no one there, so I went away.*

493. An extended group of sentences is often composed partly of dependent clauses, partly of sentences either unprepared or introduced by half-conjunctions, so that the whole group is partly a complex, partly a sequence. We call such groups **mixed complexes** or **mixed sequences**, according to which element is predominant. In the two following examples we have mixed complexes consisting of a complex followed in one instance by an unprepared sentence, in the other by one introduced by a half-conjunction : *I would not do it if I were you : you are sure to repent it some time or other*

we went out for a walk, but it came on to rain, so we soon came back. Mixed sequences are generally coordinate : *he came, he saw, and he conquered.*

CLASSES OF SENTENCES.

494. The most obvious way of classifying sentences is according to the form-words by which they are introduced. Thus a sentence beginning with *but* is necessarily an adversative sentence (or clause). A clause beginning with *because* is a causal clause, and the complex of which it forms part is a causal complex. Sentences beginning with affirmative conjunctions such as *and* are called copulative sentences. Those beginning with negative conjunctions such as *nor* are generally included under alternative sentences. Clauses introduced by dependent pronouns and adverbs are either relative or conjunctive clauses.

495. Unprepared sentences are classed according to the nature of the form-word required to make them into prepared sentences. Thus *I want = whom I want* in *you are the man I want* is an unprepared relative clause, *it is true = that it is true* in *I think it is true* is an unprepared conjunctive clause. So also *I came, I saw, I conquered* is a copulative unprepared sequence.

The principal clause in *we took our umbrellas because we were afraid it would rain* may be regarded as an unprepared clause of effect (**424**).

Part of Speech Relations.

496. We have already seen (**456**) that dependent clauses stand to their principal clauses in relations similar to those in which single words stand. From this point of view clauses fall under the three main heads of **noun-clauses, adjective-clauses,** and **adverb-clauses**.

When we call a clause a noun- etc. clause, we do not mean to imply that it partakes of the inflections or any other formal characteristics of a noun ; for it is evident that it would thereby cease to be a sentence, and would be converted into a noun. We use the terms noun-clause, etc. only because of their convenience and because they cannot cause misunderstanding.

497. A noun-clause may stand to its principal clause in the relation of (*a*) subject, (*b*) predicate, (*c*) direct object, (*d*) apposition :—

(*a*) subject noun-clause : *what you say is true—that you should think so is quite natural.*

(*b*) predicate noun-clause : *this is what I mean—my opinion is that he is mistaken.*

(*c*) object noun-clause : *I know what he means—what he wants I cannot make out—I think you are mistaken.*

(*d*) apposition noun-clause : *the wish that he may succeed is very general—the fact that he is a foreigner does not excuse him.*

498. Adjective-clauses always modify a noun, as in *the door which leads into the garden = the door leading into the garden, the man I saw yesterday, the house where I was born, the town he lives in, the reason why I did not do it, the way in which it is done, the way it is done.*

The difference in meaning between a noun-clause and an adjective-clause is often very slight, as we see by comparing the noun-clause in *I know where he lives* with the adjective-clause in *I know the place where he lives.*

The distinction between apposition noun-clauses and adjective-clauses is, of course, analogous to that between a noun in apposition and an adjective : an apposition noun-clause is more independent of its noun than an adjective-clause is, so that it is more difficult to shorten the former.

499. An adverb-clause stands to its principal clause in the same relation as an adverb. Thus the adverb-clauses in *he came while I was out, he came before I had gone out* are equivalent to the adverb *then* in *he came then.* Adverb-clauses are classed according to their meaning as adverb-clauses of time, place, cause, etc. Thus the adverb-clauses given above are adverb-clauses of time, a clause beginning with *because* is an adverb-clause of cause, etc.

Hence a clause introduced by a relative expressing cause

(408) may be regarded as partly an adverb-, partly an adjective-clause.

Relations between Subject and Predicate.

500. In thought, subject and predicate stand to one another in a variety of relations, and these relations are indicated in language more or less imperfectly by changes in the form of sentences. In their function of expressing the relations between subject and predicate sentences fall under the four main groups—(*a*) sentences of statement, or **declarative** sentences, (*b*) sentences of exclamation, or **exclamative** sentences, (*c*) sentences of question, or **interrogative** sentences, and (*d*) sentences of hortation or **imperative** sentences.

501. (*a*) **Declarative** sentences are of two kinds, (a) sentences of positive statement, or **affirmative** sentences, such as *the moon is full tonight,* and (β) **negative** sentences, such as *the moon is not full tonight.* But sentences containing a negation are often equivalent to affirmative sentences with a negative predicate (**366**). The word-order of a normal declarative sentence in English is that the subject precedes the predicate.

502. (*b*) **Exclamative** sentences, such as *how bright the moon is tonight!, how well he rides!, what a fool he looks!,* may be regarded as emphatic affirmative sentences: they express wonder, joy, grief, indignation, and other kinds of excitement, either intellectual or emotional. In English the grammatical predicate of an exclamative sentence comes after the subject, as in a declarative sentence—*the moon is . .* —but the word which is emphasized by the exclamation is put at the beginning of the sentence preceded by an interrogative word such as *how* or *what—how bright . . , what a fool . .* In these two examples the emphasized word is the logical, as opposed to the grammatical, predicate; in *how well he rides!* it is only an adjunct to the verb, the verb being in this case the logical as well as the grammatical predicate. Exclamative sentences approach closely in form to interrogative sentences (503). In writing we mark exclamative sentences with the mark of exclamation or admiration (!), with which we also mark the imperative sentences.

503. (c) **Interrogative** sentences imply ignorance about the predicate, and express the desire of enlightenment about it. They are of two kinds, general and special. **General interrogative** sentences, such as *is the moon full tonight?*, state a subject and predicate, and enquire whether the relation between them is affirmative or negative, that is, they expect the answers *yes* or *no, it is* or *it is not, yes it is, no it is not*, etc. General interrogative are formally distinguished from declarative sentences by having the grammatical predicate at the beginning of the sentence, so as to indicate that the speaker is mainly interested in the predicate. **Negative (general) interrogative** sentences, such as *is not the moon full tonight?*, imply the expectation of an affirmative answer, the *not* seeming to forbid or challenge denial='if the moon is *not* full—which I believe it is—say so.' General interrogative sentences are uttered with a rising tone (*is the moon full tonight'*) instead of the falling tone which characterizes not only declarative and exclamatory sentences, but also special interrogative sentences.

504. **Special interrogative** sentences, such as *who is he?, what is his name?, where does he live?, when did he come?, how did he come?*, begin with an interrogative word, whose meaning indicates what kind of information is sought. Thus, if the sentence begins with *who*, we know that the speaker wishes to be informed about the identity of the person indicated by the subject-word ; if the sentence begins with *where*, we know that information about the place of some thing or occurrence is sought, and so on. Hence these questions are answered, not by *yes* or *no*, but by some word which specializes the meaning indicated by the interrogative

word.   Thus the answer to *where does he live?* may be *not far from here, in London, in the north of London,* etc., with various degrees of definiteness, or the answer may be evaded by the other speaker saying *I do not know,* etc.   Special interrogative sentences are distinguished from general interrogative sentences by being uttered with a falling tone (*who is he`),* like declarative and imperative sentences, because they are felt to be equivalent to imperative sentences, *when did he come?,* for instance, being equivalent to 'I know he came some time or other ; I want to know when.'

When a special interrogative sentence is uttered with a rising tone, it implies that the speaker wishes for the repetition of an answer, thus *what is his name'?* means 'tell me his name again.'

505. There is another class of special interrogative questions which are still more definite than those introduced by interrogative words, namely, **alternative questions,** such as *is he an Oxford or a Cambridge man?,* which are characterized by the presence of the strong alternative conjunction **(415),** and do not differ from general questions in form, except that they are uttered with a falling tone, being, like the other class of special questions, equivalent to a command = 'I know he is one or the other ; tell me which he is.'   But the answers to these questions are defined even more definitely than in the other class, being, in fact, given in the question itself.   If a weak is substituted for a strong alternative conjunction in these sentences, the question becomes a general one, is uttered with a rising tone, and is answered with *yes* or *no ; is he an Oxford or Cambridge man'?* meaning really 'has he studied at Oxford or Cambridge—I do not care which—as opposed to the University of London, the German universities, etc.'   As already remarked, alternative questions require very definite answers ; thus in the example given, the answer must be either *Oxford* or *Cambridge.*   But there is a class of **alternative general** questions, such as *are you* *ready, or are you not?* uttered with a falling tone, which are, however, answered in the same way as general questions : although, being emphatic, they generally receive an emphatic answer—*yes, I am ready*, etc.   In writing, all kinds of questions are marked by the note of interrogation (?).

506. (*d*) **Imperative** sentences are those which contain a verb in the imperative mood, expressing hortation, by which we understand any appeal to others by which we endeavour to influence their actions, especially entreaty, request, and command, as in *come!, you do it at once!, do come!, do not do that!, do not you do that!*   Imperative sentences are uttered with a falling tone.   In writing they are generally marked by the note of exclamation (!)

507. It must be understood that the above divisions are grammatical, and therefore mainly formal.   Thus, although imperative sentences serve to express certain meanings, yet we call a sentence 'imperative' primarily because it has a certain form which distinguishes it from declarative etc. sentences.   And although imperative sentences are the most convenient means we have of expressing hortation, we can also express it by purely declarative sentences, such as *I beg you to come, I insist on your doing it at once.*

508. The meaning of an imperative sentence may also be expressed by a sentence in the general interrogative form, such as *will you be quiet!—be quiet!*   But as such sentences are uttered with a falling tone—being accordingly written with the note of exclamation—they are formally intermediate between the two classes, and may therefore be called **imperative-interrogative** sentences.

509. So also a declarative sentence may imply a question, as in the doubtful *you will soon be ready'*, which has the rising tone of a true question, and the more decided *you will be there at six, then`*, which takes the answer *yes* for granted, and is accordingly uttered with a falling tone.

510. The above divisions apply to independent sentences. For dependent declarative clauses (indirect narration) see § **297**, and for dependent interrogative clauses (indirect interrogation) see § **214.**

HISTORY OF LANGUAGE.

Changes in Language.

511. The most important fact in the history of language is that it is **always changing.** Words, parts of words—inflections, derivative elements, etc.—word-groups, and sentences are always changing, both in form and meaning : the pronunciation of words changes, and their meaning changes ; inflections change both in form and meaning : word-groups and sentences change their form in various ways—by altering the order of their words, by changes of stress and intonation —and are liable to change their meaning also, so that the meaning of the word-group or sentence can no longer be inferred from that of the words of which it is made up. These changes are **inevitable.**

512. Sound-changes (phonetic changes, changes of pronunciation) are inevitable, because all speech-sounds are the result of certain definite actions or positions of the organs of speech—tongue, lips, etc. ; and the slightest deviation from the position which produces a sound alters that sound. Thus the vowel-sound expressed by *o* in *no* is produced by drawing back the tongue and narrowing the lip-opening ; and if we draw back the tongue still more and raise it so as to make the mouth-passage narrower, and at the same time narrow the lip-opening by bringing the lips closer together, the sound passes by degrees into the *u* in *rule* ; while if we open the lips and widen the mouth-passage, the sound of *o* passes into that of the *a* in *father.* Now in uttering a sound it is as impossible always to hit exactly the same position of the organs of speech as it would be always to hit the mark exactly in shooting with a bow or a gun. For this reason children never reproduce exactly the sounds they learn by imitation from their parents; and even when this deviation is so slight as to escape notice, it is liable to be increased in after life by carelessness and laziness of pronunciation. But the initial deviation is often so marked that it can be expressed in writing, as when children in trying to imitate the sound of (þ) in *thin* make it into (f). We call sound-changes due to the tendencies of the organs of speech—such as the change of (o) into (u) or (a)—**organic** sound-changes; and we call changes due to defective imitation—such as that of (b) into (f)—**imitative** sound-changes. Organic and imitative sound-changes are both the result of something *in* the sound itself, and are therefore included under the common designation **internal** sound-changes. **External** sound-changes, on the other hand, have nothing to do with the nature of the sound changed, but are the result of the influence of other words associated in some way—generally by similarity of meaning —with the words containing that sound, as in the change of *spake* into *spoke* by the influence of *spoken* (**539**).

513. The **meanings** of words change because the meaning of a word is always more or less vague, and we are always **extending** or **narrowing** (generalizing or specializing) the meanings of the words we use—often quite unconsciously. Thus in the present English the meaning of the word *morning* has been extended so as to include what in Scotland is still called the *forenoon*, the word *morning* originally denoting the time of day just after sunrise; but as the sun rises at different times at different seasons of the year, the distinction between *morning* and *forenoon* was always liable to be confused. We have an example of narrowing the meaning of a word in the modern English use of *deer* to signify one special kind of wild animal, while in Old English the word— in the form of *deor*—meant 'wild animal in general,' being applied to foxes, wolves, etc., as well as deer ; Shakespere still uses the word in its older and more general meaning—

> *But mice, and rats, and such small deer*
> *Have been Tom's food for seven long year.*   (King Lear.)

514. Of these processes, extension is the more important, especially that kind of extension known as **metaphor**, by which we use the name of a material object or an attribute to express some more abstract idea suggested by the original meaning of the word, as when we call a sly man a *fox*, or say that the sun is the *source of light and heat* on the analogy of *source of a river*, thus using the familiar word *source* to express the more abstract idea of ' cause ' or ' origin.' So also when we speak of a *bright idea* or *dark schemes.*   It was mainly by the help of metaphor that primitive man was able to enlarge his originally scanty stock of words so as to find an expression for each new idea as it arose in his mind.

515. The use and meaning of inflections changes in the same way.   Thus the genitive case in Modern English has not the same functions as in Old English.   So also with derivative elements, etc.

516. Linguistic changes often take the form of the **loss** of sounds, sound-groups, parts of words, and complete words. By phonetic change a sound may be so weakened as to become almost inaudible, so that its dropping is almost in- evitable.   Sounds and syllables may be dropped because they are superfluous—because the word is intelligible without them, as when *examination* is shortened to *exam.*   Words may drop out of sentences for the same reason.

517. The **addition** of a sound is generally only apparent when it is the result of organic change.   Thus the change of (nr) into (ndr) in Modern English *thunder* from Old English *þunor,* genitive *þunres,* is really a change of the second half of the (n) into (d).

But sounds may be added to words, and words added to sentences by external influences.

518. Most of these changes of form and meaning are **gradual** in their operation—especially the internal sound-changes—so that most of them are carried out **unconsciously** by those who speak the language, and are therefore beyond their control. The speakers of a language cannot prevent it from changing; all they can do is to retard the changes (**532**). These changes are the result of natural tendencies of the organs of speech and of the human mind, and are therefore to a great extent **uniform** in their operation. Thus if one child in a community says (fruu) instead of *through*, we expect other children to do the same, because if one child finds it easier to pronounce (f) than (p), other children will probably find it easier too. So also if one man gets into the habit of using a word which originally meant ' wild animal ' in the sense of ' deer,' because deer are the most important wild animals in the place where he lives, it is natural to expect that most of his neighbours will get into the same habit. Even when different changes of the same sound, etc. are made by different speakers of the community, one change will generally get the upper hand, either from having the majority of speakers on its side, or because it is more convenient or easier to carry out.

519. Each linguistic change is **regular** in its operation. If the meaning of a word is changed in one sentence, we expect to find it changed in all the other sentences in which it occurs. So also if a sound is changed in one word, we expect to find it changed in all other words. Thus, if we find that a child learning to speak makes (p) into (f) in the words *think* and *three*, we can assume with tolerable certainty that it carries out the change in all the other words that contain a (p). If—as is generally the case—the change is the result of inability to form the sound (p), it is evident that it must be carried out with no exception. But one sound-change may be less general than another. One child may change all (p)'s into (f) s, while another may pronounce such words as *think* and *thing* correctly, while substituting (f) in *through* and *three*, that is, in the combination (pr). Again, a third child might change *th* in *think* into one sound, and *th* in *through* into a different sound, carrying out these changes in all the words containing (p). We see then that the same sound may undergo different changes under different circumstances—different combinations with other sounds, different positions in the word (initial, etc.) Thus, to take an example from changes which have actually occurred in English, we find that (k) has been dropped in the special combination *kn*, as in *know* (nou), *knowledge*, but only when initial, the old *k* being kept in such a word as *acknowledge*, where it is preceded by a vowel.

520. It sometimes happens that the same word changes in two or more different ways, according to its surroundings. Thus in English the indefinite article *an* drops its *n* before another word beginning with a consonant, as in *a man* compared with *an enemy*. When a word splits up in this way, the resulting forms are called **doublets (54)**.

521. Stress has a great influence on sound-change, and often gives rise to doublets. Thus in the Middle English of Chaucer *with* and *of* were pronounced with final voiceless consonants (wip, of), but in the transition to Early Modern English the final consonants of these words became voiced when they were uttered with weak stress, the original sounds being preserved when they were uttered with strong stress, so that, for instance, *with* was pronounced (wið) in such a sentence as ' I will go with you, not with him,' and was pronounced (wip) in such a sentence as ' not *with* him, but *against* him.' We call such pairs as (wip, wið) **stress-doublets**. In the case of *an*, *a* and of strong and weak *with* the differentiation of form is not accompanied by any differentiation of meaning and function, but in the case of Middle English *of* there has been differentiation in both ways. In Old and Middle English *of* was used in the sense of ' of ' and ' off,' but in

Early Modern English the weak (ov) was gradually restricted to the less emphatic meaning, while the more marked adverbial meaning was appropriated by the strong (of), which was written *off* to distinguish it from the preposition *of* = (ov). In the present English (of) has become (ɔf), and the two words—the adverb and the preposition—have diverged so completely in form and meaning that the connection between them is forgotten. In fact *of* itself has split up into stress-doublets in the present English—the strong (ov) and the weak (əv, ə).

Such pairs as *whole* and *hale*—both from Old English *hal* 'complete, healthy'—are not organic doublets, but dialectal doublets, *whole* being the regular Standard English descendant of *hal*, while *hale* is an importation from the Northern dialect of English, in which Old English *a* appears regularly as *a*, instead of becoming *o*, as in the standard dialect.

Effects of Change on the Relations between Words.

522. It is evident that when two or more words resemble each other in form or meaning, or stand in any other relation to one another, these relations are liable to be modified by linguistic changes, which must further modify them in the direction either of **convergence** or **divergence**. If convergent changes are carried far enough, the result is the **levelling** of distinctions between the words. Thus in Modern English the two words *no* and *know* have been brought closer and closer together by convergent sound-change till at last they have been phonetically levelled under the common form (nou). We call such phonetically levelled pairs **homonyms**. Such homonyms as *bear* (the animal) and *to bear* show levelling in spelling as well as sound. Convergent change of meaning, if carried out as far as possible—to the point of levelling—results in a **synonym**. Thus *to buy* and *to purchase* are synonyms.   Divergent change is most noticeable in doublets. Thus we have divergent sound-change in the Modern English *of, off.*

523. Linguistic changes have a great effect on **association-groups (20)**. Convergent and divergent changes
have directly opposite effects. Convergent changes form
new association-groups, by bringing words into connection
with one another which originally had little or nothing in
common. Thus *buy* and *purchase* now form an association-
group of a very intimate kind through having exactly the
same meaning, but *purchase* originally meant 'to pursue,'
and only gradually passed into its present meaning through
that of 'attain,' 'acquire,' so that the two words were
originally quite disassociated from one another in meaning
as well as form.

524. Divergent changes tend to break up association-
groups and to isolate the members of a group from one
another. Thus in English words of foreign origin the
addition of a derivative element often causes shifting of
stress, as we see by comparing *photograph, photographer,
photographic*, where the stress falls on a different syllable in
each word, so that a vowel which is strong in one word is
weak in another; and as weak vowels are often weakened to
(ə) in English, the spoken forms of these words differ much
more than their written forms would lead us to expect:
(·foutəgræf, fətogrəfə, foutəgræfik). As the consonant
skeleton of these words remains unaltered together with
their meaning, the shifting stress and the great difference
in the vowels is not enough to break up the association-
group, but merely loosens the connection between its
members. In the case of *of* and *off* (**521**), where there
has been change not only of form but of meaning, the
association has been not only loosened, but completely
broken, so that the two words are isolated from one
another.

525. Isolation often leads to the creation of new grammatical categories. As we have seen (**68**), isolation is the
essence of composition as opposed to mere word-grouping.

So also the distinction between an idiom and an ordinary 'general' sentence is that in the former the meaning of the whole is isolated from that of its elements (448). The development of proper names out of common nouns and adjectives is also a process of isolation : when the nickname or surname *Brown* or *Smith* was specially assigned to one particular man in a community, although there were perhaps other brown men and other smiths in it, isolation had begun ; and when these appellations had become fixed family names, being given to the descendants of these men without regard to their complexion or trade, the isolation was complete as far as the meaning was concerned, so that the proper names *Brown* and *Smith* no longer had anything in common with the words *brown* and *smith* except in form, being partially isolated from them in form as well by the divergent use of the article, etc. (148). The change of full-words into form-words, the use of nouns and adjectives as particles, etc. all go hand in hand with isolation. Thus the conjunction *because* appears in Middle English in the form of the group *bī cause þat* 'by the cause that,' 'through the cause that,' but in Modern English it has been completely isolated from its elements *by* and *cause* not only by change of grammatical function, but also by the weakening of *bī* into *be* and the shortening of the vowel in the second syllable, formal isolation being carried still further in the careless colloquial pronunciation (koz).

526. Linguistic changes give rise to grammatical **irregularities.** The two main classes of changes that produce irregularities are convergent changes of meaning, and divergent sound-changes. What we call an 'inflection' often consists of a number of different forms having distinct though similar meanings, which gradually converged so that they came to be identical in meaning and grammatical function. Thus the original reduplication in the preterite *held*, the vowel-change in *saw*, and the addition of *d* in *called*, all express the same grammatical function, although there can be no doubt that they each had a distinct meaning originally.

527. We can observe the effect of divergent sound-change in the variations of the preterite-ending *d* in *called, stopped* (stopt), and the accompanying vowel- and consonant-changes in such preterites as *kept, taught* from *keep, teach.* Here the original unity has been broken up by purely phonetic changes.

Effects of Change on Language as a Means of Expression.

528. We can see from what has been said that linguistic changes have two opposite effects on language considered as a means of expressing ideas. They have a **constructive** and a **destructive** effect : sometimes they help to build up the language, and make it better fitted to express ideas; sometimes, on the other hand, they tend to break up its structure, and make it unfit for the expression of ideas.

529. It is evident that many of the changes we have been considering are mainly constructive. Thus the differentiation of Old English *of* into the Modern English doublets *of* and *off* enables us to express two distinct sets of ideas by distinct words instead of having only one word for both. The language has therefore gained in precision by such a change. So also such a process of isolation as that by which we are able to introduce a causal sentence by means of the monosyllable (koz) instead of the cumbrous word-group *by the cause that* has not only made the language more precise but has also made it more concise.

530. But it is equally evident that many changes result only in the multiplication of superfluous distinctions. Thus the distinction between strong (wiþ) and weak (wið) is a superfluous one, for the sentence-stress by itself is enough to tell us whether the word is emphatic or not. The distinction between *a* and *an* is equally superfluous. In fact doublets are always superfluous, except when they develop useful distinctions of meaning, which, in the nature of things, they do only occasionally. When convergent changes result in the formation of synonyms, such as *begin, commence*, they evidently make one member of the pair superfluous. So also of the various ways of forming the plural in English, all except one —that is, of course, the regular ending *s*—are superfluous.

531. Many changes are not only superfluous but injurious. The formation of homonyms, such as *a bear, to bear*, although not positively destructive, always tends to make the language ambiguous. And although change of meaning—especially metaphor—is an essential factor in building up the vocabulary of a language, yet the great variety of often almost contradictory meanings which may be thereby developed in the same word often tend to obscure clearness of expression. Among purely destructive changes, the most important are those which affect inflectional elements. When inflections consist —as they often do—mainly of final weak vowels, they are peculiarly liable to be shortened, obscured, and finally dropped altogether. Thus in the popular Latin of the Empire weak inflectional endings soon began to shorten their vowels and drop their final consonants, so that, for instance. the nominative singular *mensa* 'table,' the accusative *mensam*. and the ablative *mensa* were levelled under the common form *mesa*, the distinction between nominative *dominus* 'lord' and accusative *dominum*, between accusative, dative, genitive, ablative *hominem* 'man,' *homini, hominis, homine* were by degrees entirely lost, the inevitable consequence being that the feeling for the grammatical distinctions of case was first weakened, and then lost. so that even those case-endings which from their greater fullness—such as the genitive plural ending in *mensarum, dominorum*—were less liable to phonetic decay, were also discarded, so that in Italian the nouns have entirely lost the old case-inflections.

Logical Control of Changes.

532. Now although the speakers of a language have no power of absolutely preventing changes in it—for we have no evidence of a language ever having been preserved absolutely unchanged even for a few centuries—yet they have considerable control over it. In the first place, they can **resist** change, and retard it. When parents correct the mispronunciations of their children, and when boys at school ridicule the pronunciations and expressions of those boys who do not conform to the pronunciations and expressions of the majority, they are all doing their best to prevent change. In fact, if they did not, the languages of two successive generations would become mutually unintelligible. Hence every generation can tolerate only a certain amount of change, so that if a language changes much in one direction, it has to make up for it by being conservative in another direction. Thus English obscures and shortens its vowels, but is on the whole very conservative in its consonants. Modern French, on the other hand, drops consonants freely, as we see by comparing Modern French *bete* with Old French *beste*, which was imported into Middle English, and still keeps its consonants unimpaired in the Modern English *beast*, although the vowel has undergone considerable changes. Again, in Modern French many of the Old French final consonants which are preserved in writing are not pronounced, as in *mais* (me). Now the tendency to drop final consonants is as natural to English people as to French, but as consonant-dropping and vowel-weakening together would have made English unintelligible and unfit for the communication of ideas, it was necessary to check one or other of these changes. From a variety of complicated causes it was found more necessary to check consonant-weakening than vowel-weakening in English. Whether the attempt to arrest a certain change is successful or not depends, of course, partly on the ease with which it is controlled.   Thus the change of (þ) into (f) is easily observed and easily corrected, so although it is begun by thousands of children in every generation, it has never been able to get a permanent footing, while other changes which were less easy of control have established themselves firmly, some of which have been more injurious than that of (þ) into (f) would have been.

533. The speakers of a language always have the power of discarding superfluous forms, especially one of a pair of synonyms and doublets.   Hence English has now got rid of the superfluous distinction between (wið) and (wiþ) by simply discarding the latter form.

Ellipse.

534. When a language drops words in groups and sentences because these words are not absolutely required to make sense, we have the phenomenon of ellipse (**111**).   We must distinguish between logical and historical ellipse. **Logical ellipse** implies only that some word is wanting to complete the grammatical construction, as in *at my uncle's*. **Historical ellipse** implies that a word is missing which at an earlier period of the language actually formed part of the sentence, and it does not matter whether the missing word is grammatically necessary or superfluous.   In the example just given the ellipse is historical as well as grammatical.   But in such a phrase as *go to sea* compared with *go down to the river*, there is no historical ellipse, because such phrases were framed at a period when there was no definite article at all in English, and a few of them becoming isolated from the rest, were able to resist the introduction of the article and so have kept the shorter form to the present day.

Analogy.

535. The main factor in getting rid of irregularities is **group-influence**, or **analogy**—the influence exercised by

the members of an association-group on one another. We
have already seen (23) that irregularity consists in partial
isolation from an association-group through some formal
difference. Thus the irregular plurals *men* etc. belong to the
same group as the regular plurals *trees* etc., but stand outside
it to some extent through not having the same ending. The
irregularity and isolation of such plurals as *men* is the more
conspicuous because of the small number of irregular plurals
in English, and the overwhelmingly large number of nouns
that have their plural in -*s*. This preponderance of the
s-plurals is itself the result of group-influence. In Old English
there were a variety of regular noun-plurals, and the ending
-*as*, from which the Modern English -(*e*)*s* is descended, was
only one of several endings, all of which were added to a
considerable number of nouns, the ending -*as* itself being
confined to certain masculine nouns, such as *stān* 'stone,'
plural *stanas*. Other plural endings in frequent use were -*a*,
-*u*, -*an*. Many neuter nouns were unchanged in the plural,
and we still preserve this formation in *sheep*. In Middle
English the distinctions of grammatical gender were soon
lost, and as it was found inconvenient not to distinguish
between singular and plural, such neuter nouns as *hūs*
'house' instead of remaining unchanged in the plural were
allowed to take the ending -*es*=Old English -*as* of the corresponding masculine nouns, whence the Modern English
plural *houses*=Old English *hus*; and this ending was by
degrees extended to all nouns except a few such as *man, ox*,
so that the ending -*en* in *oxen*=Old English *oxan*, instead
of being on an equal footing with the ending -*es*, as it originally was, came to be an isolated—that is, an irregular—
inflection. The change therefore of such an Old English
plural as *naman* (singular *nama*) into the Modern English
names is not a phonetic change of *n* into *s*—which would
be impossible—but is an external, analogical change due to
the influence of the Old English inflection in *stanas* etc.

536. Which form in an association-group gets the upper hand in cases of analogy, depends partly on its natural preponderance in the group, partly on its efficiency as a means of expression. A form may preponderate either by being used in the greatest number of words, or by being used in those words which are in most frequent use, so that a form which is used in a comparatively small number of very important words may preponderate over one which is used in a greater number of words. The efficiency of a form depends partly on its phonetic distinctness—a hissing consonant such | as *s* being, for instance, preferable to an obscure vowel— partly on its logical distinctness, that is, its freedom from ambiguity and liability to be confused with other forms. From this point of view the English plural -*s* is objectionable, because it has the same form as the genitive singular (*man's*).

537. Analogy is not only an instrument of change, but is | a part of the daily life of language. In speaking a language we learn only a few of the grammatically modified words ready-made ; all the others we form on the pattern of those already learnt. Thus when we first have to speak of an unfamiliar animal, such as a zebra, in the plural, we do not stop to think whether we have heard the word used in the plural before, but we form a plural *zebras* without hesitation on the pattern of such familiar plurals as *horses, donkeys,* etc.

538. Now it is evident that this method of inflecting or otherwise modifying words by pattern or analogy may lead us into mistakes when we have to deal with irregularities which are not in very frequent use. Thus an uneducated speaker who | had to form the plural of *fungus* would naturally make it **funguses* on the analogy of *mushrooms, mosses,* etc., instead of *fungi.* But if an irregular form is so frequent in the language that we not only learn it ready-made, but hear and repeat it incessantly, it fixes itself so firmly in the memory that we have no occasion to form it by pattern, and it remains unaffected by the influence of the regular forms. Thus we are so used to such an irregular plural as *men* that it is only by an effort that we could make it into *mans. But if by any chance such a word became rare or partially obsolete, it would certainly and inevitably take the plural -*s*, at least in the vulgar and colloquial language. This is why in all languages — at least in their natural colloquial form — the irregularities always occur in the commonest words, irregular forms of rarer words being confined to the higher literary language.

539. No one would mistake the change of *n* into *s* in the plural *names* = Old English *naman* for an organic sound-change, but would at once recognize it as an analogical, external change. In some cases, however, analogical sound-change might be mistaken for internal — organic or imitative sound-change by anyone who was not acquainted with the internal sound-changes of the language in question. Thus the change of *a* into *o* in *spoke* = the earlier *spake*, *broke* = *brake*, etc., although at first sight it looks like an organic sound-change — the organic change of *a* into *o* being frequent in many languages — is in Modern English confined entirely to these verb-preterites, there being no such change in *take*, *name*, etc. This change is not only confined to preterites of verbs, but is further confined to those verbs which have *o* in their preterite participles, so there can be no doubt that the change of *spake* into *spoke* is the result of the influence of the preterite participle *spoken*, through the similarity in meaning between *he spake* and *he has spoken*.

540. In the cases we have hitherto been considering, the analogy is logical, that is, associations of meaning or grammatical function lead to the change of a sound into another one which may be totally different. But there is also a purely formal or **phonetic analogy**, by which the meaning of a word is modified by that of another word because the latter is similar in form to the other. Thus the word *parboil* was originally formed by prefixing *per-* 'through,' so that it originally meant 'to boil thoroughly.' But now the meaning of the prefix has been forgotten through its change of form, and it has been associated with the noun *part*, so that the word has now taken the exactly opposite meaning of 'boil imperfectly.'

541. We can also see phonetic analogy in the **familiariza-tion** of unfamiliar words, commonly known as 'popular etymology,' as in the change of *asparagus* into *sparrow-grass* —a form which, though now vulgar, was in general use in the last century. Familiarization consists simply in substituting familiar for unfamiliar sounds or syllables, without regard to the meaning, although the process is often helped by some chance coincidence, as in the present example, where the fact of *asparagus* being a vegetable has helped to fix the change of the unfamilar *gus* into the familiar and significant *grass*.

542. Although analogy works most vigorously when a few forms are brought under the influence of a large association-group, or one which contains words in very frequent use, yet --as we see from the examples just given of phonetic analogy—it can also work in groups of only two words. When the groups are so small, it often happens that the forms or words influence each other partially and mutually, instead of one only being influenced, the result being a **blending**.

The effect of blending on grammatical constructions has been already treated of (125).

543. Analogy not only helps to get rid of irregularities, but helps also to bring grammatical categories into harmony with the logical ones (26). In primitive languages they are generally in harmony, but in more advanced languages they frequently disagree, as in the contrast of grammatical to natural gender (146). Thus in Old English and in German words denoting young children and young of animals are neuter. Hence also diminutive words were made neuter, such as Old English *mægd-en*, German *mad-chen*, which originally meant 'little maid,' 'little girl,' but afterwards came to be applied to full-grown women, still having their neuter gender, though it had become unmeaning. But in both languages such words came to be referred to as 'she' as well as 'it' on the analogy of other words which were grammatically feminine and also denoted female beings. German has not gone any further than this : although in German *mädchen* is referred to as 'she,' it always takes a neuter article and adjective. But in Middle English we find such grammatical neuters as *meiden* 'girl' and *wīf* 'woman' made into regular feminine nouns.

Origin and Development of Language.

544. Language begins with associations between sounds and ideas. These associations may be of various kinds. The most obvious kind is that seen in **imitative** words, such as *cuckoo, buzz, hiss*. We have another kind of association in **symbolical** words, such as the Latin *bibere* 'to drink,' where the lip-consonant *b* symbolizes the action of the lips in drinking. We have also **interjectional** words, such as the Old English *feond* 'enemy'—whence the Modern English *fiend*—which was originally formed from an interjection of dislike similar to *pah!* or *fie!* So also the pronoun *me* and the words *mamma, mother*, all seem to be made up with the consonant *m* because it is easiest, and the one first uttered by infants. But there is so little natural connection or resemblance between sounds and ideas that we may be sure that when language first arose, the names given to things, attributes, etc., often had very little connection with what they meant, and that the connection was often almost a matter of chance. But there must always have been *some* connection —some association.

545. At first each sound or sound-group expressed rather a thought than an idea. Thus when men first said *cuckoo!*

in order to communicate an idea to other men, they meant to express some such thought as 'there is the cuckoo or 'I hear the cuckoo.' If the speaker pointed somewhere at the same time, it meant, of course, ' there is the cuckoo.' There can be no doubt that primitive speech was thus partly made up of **gesture**. Such a sound-group as *cuckoo* was, therefore, not a true word, but something between a word and a sentence—a kind of **sentence-word**.

546. When people began to join such a significant sound-group as *cuckoo* to other significant sound-groups—as, for instance, to a sound-group meaning ' sing ' or ' song '—so that the meaning of the one might be taken in connection with that of the other—so that, for instance, *cuckoo sing* or *cuckoo song* meant 'the cuckoo sings' or ' the cuckoo sang,' then *cuckoo*, etc., instead of being sentences, came to be parts of sentences or **words**.

547. Language thus arose spontaneously in individuals through the habit of associating sounds with ideas through mimicry, etc. This was done at first merely for amusement : the idea of using these sounds to communicate wishes, information, etc., to others was an after-thought. This after-thought was the result of community of impression among different individuals : the sound-group *cuckoo* naturally suggested the idea of the bird that makes the sound to all who were familiar with it.

548. Of course, when the connection was fanciful, or vague—as if, for instance, *hiss* were used to signify not only ' hiss,' but also ' serpent,' ' cat,' and ' steam '—it became necessary to make it more definite ; and this could only be done by a number of individuals constantly meeting together and settling definitely what meaning to give to each sound-group. Of course this process of selection came about of itself, unconsciously, and was not the result of deliberate choice and consultation, which would, indeed, have been impossible at a time when language was not yet evolved.

549. When language had reached this stage, the connection between words and the ideas they expressed was no longer self-evident, except in a few cases, and the details of the language had to be learnt one by one by the infants of the community and by strangers.

550. Language thus begins spontaneously in the individual, but is developed and preserved by the community.

DEVELOPMENT OF GRAMMATICAL CATEGORIES.

551. As we have seen, language implies the power of joining words together into sentences, just as ideas are joined together to form thoughts (16).

552. At first words were joined together without any definite order—it did not matter whether people said *cuckoo sing* or *sing cuckoo*; in other words, the sentence had no form.

553. After a while people began to put the words in sentences in a more definite order. Even before the logical significance of word-order had dawned on their minds, some sentences which had become familiar by incessant repetition would naturally settle down to a fixed word-order; and when this had been carried out in a number of separate sentences, some general principle of word-order could not fail to be evolved. There are various principles of word-order. The natural **logical** word-order is to put the subject first and the adjunct-word after it, so that, for instance, *cuckoo song* or *cuckoo sing* would mean 'the cuckoo sings' or 'the singing cuckoo,' and *sing* (or *song*) *cuckoo* would mean 'the song (or singing) of the cuckoo.'

554. But there are other principles of word-order, which sometimes contradict this purely logical order. **Emphatic** word-order consists in putting first that word which is most prominent in the speaker's mind. Thus in such a sentence as *that man is a good man* or *he is a good man*, it is evident that *good* is a more important word than the accompanying *man*, because the idea expressed by the

latter word has been already expressed by *that man* or *he*. Hence many languages which generally put an assumptive adjective after its noun often put the adjective first when it is emphatic.   It is evident that in a language which admits emphatic word-order, the same sentence may appear in a variety of forms, as far as the order of its words is concerned. Even such a simple sentence as *the cat caught a mouse* or *the cat killed a mouse* may admit of a variety of natural word-orders.   If the speaker sees, or thinks of, the mouse coming out of its hole and running about before the cat appears, the natural order is *mouse cat catch* ; if he sees a dead mouse and the cat running away, the natural order is *mouse kill cat*, which we express more accurately by the passive construction *a mouse has been killed by the cat*.   We need not therefore be surprised to find that different languages have different principles of word-order.

555. But whatever the word-order of each primitive language may have been, it must at first have been a fixed one. for not only is a fixed word-order necessary in an uninflected language—as we see by comparing the comparatively fixed word-order of English with the free word-order of Latin —but without fixed word-order inflections could never have developed themselves.   And not only inflection, but composition. derivation, the development of form-words, are all the result of fixed word-order, aided, as we shall see. by differences of stress.

556. Primitive language consisted, then, of series of fullwords in fixed orders.   At first sentences were formed with an effort, each word being uttered with strong stress and followed by a slight pause—just as we are still apt to speak a foreign language.   In time, however, certain combinations which occurred frequently were run over more rapidly. and joined together without any pause.   In this way logical wordgroups were formed, such as *big man* or *man big, little man, old brother, young brother, sharp stone* = ' flint,' *yellow stone* = ' gold,' *white stone* = ' silver,' etc.   Then words forming part

of such groups which were felt to be subordinate to the other word or words, came to be uttered with diminished stress, so that a distinction could be made, for instance, between *·me ·here* = 'I am here,' and *·man -here* = 'the man here' or 'this man.' In this way logical groups developed into formal stress-groups, the diminished stress of subordinate words serving not only to show that they were logically subordinate, but also to bind the two members of the group together and mark them off from the other words and word-groups in the sentence. When this formal isolation was accompanied by isolation of meaning, these groups developed into **compounds**, so that it was now possible to make such distinctions as that between *black bird* and *blackbird* in English.

557. It is evident that of the words thus subordinated in stress and meaning some would be in more general use than others. Such an adjective as *white* would be specially subordinated to but few substance-words ; but such an adjunct as *here* or *this* would be connected with almost all such words. All primitive languages show a great variety of such demonstrative words, whose meanings become more and more definite and fixed as the language develops. When a word which originally pointed to an object in space came to be used as a mere reference-word, so that, for instance, *man-here* meant simply 'the man,' it became a **form-word**. So also when some such distinction was made as between *top hill* — 'the top of the hill' and *hill-top* = 'on the hill,' *top* in the latter collocation was on its way to become a mere form-word — in this case, a preposition — and if the full-word *top* became obsolete through being supplanted by a different word of similar meaning, such as *summit*, the isolation of the form-word would be complete.

558. When a word is always subordinated to other words both in meaning and stress, it is natural to slur it over, and obscure its sound in various ways. Such obscurations of subordinate words as we can observe in the English (dʒonz hiə, dʒonl kɛm, hijl kɛm) = *John is here, John will come, he will come*, have occurred in all primitive languages.

559. If a form-word is obscured so much that it becomes an inseparable part of the word it modifies, and is at the same time isolated from the full-word of which it is a weakening, it ceases to be a word, and becomes part of a word ; and if it forms part of a number of words, so as to be easily recognized as a general modifier, it becomes either a derivative or an inflectional element. If it makes the words it modifies into new words—as when in English the addition of (-mən) to *shop* makes it into the new word *shopman*—it is a **derivative**, or at least a composition-element on its way to become a derivative ; if it leaves the special meaning of the words it modifies unaltered, and merely adds some general qualification, and shows that they stand in certain grammatical relations to other words in the sentence, it is an **inflection**. Mere obscuration without isolation is not enough to constitute a derivative or inflection. Thus the (l) in (hijl) = *he will*, does not constitute an inflection, because it is added indifferently to all words, and because we can change the unemphatic (hijl) into the emphatic (hij wil), and so break up the connection between the two words and restore the original full form of the (l). (-mən) in *shopman*, on the other hand, though only a weakening of the full word (mæn), cannot be used anywhere in a sentence as the unemphatic form of *man*, and is inseparably connected with the word it modifies. We can see how form-words develop into true inflections in the French future *aimerai*, 'I shall love,' which comes from the late Latin *amare habeo*, 'I have to love.' We can still divide *aimerai* into the French words *aimer ai*, 'to-love (I) have,' but the plural *aimerons*, 'we shall love,' is isolated from *aimer* and *avons*, 'we have.' *Aimerai* itself is really isolated, though to a less degree ; for *aimer ai* is as impossible a construction in French as *to love have* would be in English. The English (nt) in *won t, shan't* may be regarded as on the way to become an inflectional element, for it is isolated from the full form *not* grammatically as well as phonetically, for this contraction never occurs except after certain verbs, which are themselves isolated in the contracted form, as in (wount) compared with (wil not) *will not*.

ORIGIN OF THE PARTS OF SPEECH.

560. It is evident that the relations between full-words in sentences are dependent to some extent on the meaning of the full words. Thus in a primitive language there would be a tendency to use substance-words, such as *tree, man, snow*, and personal pronouns, such as *I. he*, mainly as subject-words, and to use permanent attribute-words, such as *white, big*, assumptively in connection with the above substance-words, as in distinguishing between *the big man* and *the little man*.

561. These permanent attribute-words would not be used much as predicates because the whiteness of snow, etc. would be taken for granted, and not require to be stated expressly. The words most frequently used as predicates would be phenomenon-words, such as *fall, melt, come*, which cannot so easily be taken for granted in connection with their head-words, and must therefore be stated expressly.

562. Substance-words and phenomenon-words would therefore have different positions in the sentence, and by degrees different form-words would cluster round them. Substance-words would be naturally modified by words expressing distinctions of place and number; thus the idea of 'tree' would excite the ideas of 'one tree,' 'more than one tree,' 'by the tree,' 'behind the tree,' etc. Phenomenon-words, on the other hand, would not require these modifiers, but would be modified by other words expressing distinctions of time and other accompaniments of phenomena ; thus the idea 'come' would excite the idea of 'come in the past,' 'come in the future,' etc.

563. But the necessity of using permanent attribute-words, and qualifiers, such as *here, there*, as predicates, would be very soon felt; it would soon be necessary—or, at least, convenient—to distinguish between *the man here* and *the man is here*; and after a time it would even be desirable to distinguish between *melting snow* and *the snow melts*. Some languages began by making the distinction entirely by means of position. Thus in Chinese *green tree* means 'a green tree' or 'the green tree,' and *tree green* means 'the tree is green,' etc.

564. Many primitive languages marked the predicate formally by joining on to it a personal pronoun, 'the cuckoo sings' being expressed by *cuckoo song-him, cuckoo its-song*, or something equivalent. This clumsy device is found in languages all over the world. We can still see the primitive first person pronoun in the English *a-m*, which originally meant 'existence of-me' or 'my being.'

565. Such a thought as 'the tree is green' could be expressed similarly by *the tree its-green(ness)*, but such a thought as 'the man is there' would be more naturally expressed by a construction equivalent to *the man stands there* or *the man stays there*. So also 'the tree is green' could be expressed by *the tree grows green*. In course of time some of the verbs used in this way lost all independent meaning and became pure link-verbs. We can easily see how this happens by thinking of such Modern English phrases as *he stood convicted, to rest content*, etc., where *stood* does not imply standing or *rest* resting, these verbs being equivalent to *was* and *to be*. We need not therefore be surprised to find that *was* itself originally meant 'dwelt' or 'remained,' and that *be* originally meant 'grow.'

566. In this way verbs that were originally phenomenon-words came to have the purely grammatical function of predication. So also form-words or inflections which marked original substance-words gradually came to suggest the grammatical conception of 'subject-word'; and when it became necessary to make statements about attributes or phenomena — to make statements about 'whiteness,' 'falling,' etc.—the formal marks which at first belonged only to substance-words were transferred to abstract words, so that the inflections and other formal characteristics of such words as *tree* no longer necessarily marked them off as substance-words, but only denoted those grammatical functions which we conveniently sum up by calling *tree* a 'noun'—functions which it has in common with many purely abstract words, such as *whiteness* and *falling*.

567. The further development of the parts of speech is the result of the various processes of sound-change, change of meaning and grammatical function, differentiation, isolation, analogy, etc., which have been already described. Thus analogy brought about concord (**91**), by which declinable adjectives are distinguished from indeclinable adverbs ; sound-change and isolation made nouns and adjectives into particles.

Relations of Languages to one another.

568. It is evident from what has been said about the origin of language that wherever human beings are gathered together in a community, however small, there was a probability of that community developing a language of its own. Hence, as the number of such communities must have been indefinitely great in the early periods of man's history, there must have been an indefinite number of separate, unconnected languages. But as civilization increased, and it became necessary to use single languages over wider areas, an immense number of languages spoken only by small and obscure communities became extinct—a process which we can observe going on still.

569. The difference between languages is not always the

result of differences of origin. On the contrary, almost every language bears a more or less close resemblance to certain other languages—a resemblance which cannot be explained except on the supposition that all these languages are modifications of one and the same language. We call such languages **cognate** languages, belonging to the same **family** of languages, and descended from a common **parent** language. Thus English, Latin, and Greek are cognate languages belonging to the Arian family, and descended from Parent Arian. We have no direct records of this parent language, and can only reconstruct it hypothetically by comparing its extant descendants together, and so finding out what original features of the parent language are preserved in them. In other cases, however, the parent language has been preserved—though, of course, only in a ' dead,' written form—so that we do not require to construct it hypothetically. Thus French, Italian, Spanish, and Portuguese are all Romance languages, descended from Latin in its spoken form.

Linguistic Separation : Origin of Dialects and Cognate Languages.

570. The unity of a language can be kept up only by free and uniform intercourse between all the members of the community which speaks the language. If the community is too large or unwieldy to admit of this intercourse, the language begins to split up into an infinite number of dialects, each dialect differing but slightly from the dialect nearest to it, but differing considerably—in course of time—from those farthest away from it.

571. If a dialect or group of dialects which has arisen in this way is separated by natural boundaries, such as a river or mountain-chain, from the other dialects, or by a different government, or if communication is checked in any other way, there will be a corresponding linguistic divergence : the dialects thus cut off from the rest will diverge rapidly and develop many features of their own.

572. But when a nation thus speaking a variety of dialects attains a high degree of civilization, that unity and centralization which results in one town becoming the capital, results also in one definite dialect—generally, of course, that of the capital itself—being used as the general means of communication throughout the whole territory, especially if, as is generally the case, the dialects have already diverged so much from each other that some at least of them are mutually unintelligible.

573. If this centralization goes on long enough, this common or **standard** dialect swallows up the local dialects, although before that happens it is generally considerably influenced by them, every standard dialect importing a certain number of words from its cognate dialects. Thus in modern English we find the dialectal *hale* by the side of the standard *whole* (**521.** 1).

574. There is no definite distinction between **dialect** and **language**. Dialects develop into languages by further divergent changes, so that a group of dialects becomes a family of cognate languages. When we describe two or more forms of speech as 'distinct but cognate languages,' we generally imply that they are mutually unintelligible and that they are spoken by distinct nationalities.

575. Uniformity of intercourse between the speakers of a language may be checked in various ways besides separation in space. Even in only moderately civilized communities class separation leads to the distinction between aristocratic, **refined**, or educated speech on the one hand, and **vulgar** speech on the other. So also each trade, profession, coterie, etc. tends to develop its own technical language or slang. We may call these non-local dialects the **strata** of language.

576. Again, religion and literature tend to keep up words, grammatical forms, and expressions that have ceased to be part of the language of everyday life. Hence we get sacred or **liturgical** strata, such as the language of the English Prayer-book, and various **literary** strata. For in literature itself we must distinguish between the language of **poetry** and of **prose**, and again, between the higher and the lower prose, the latter approaching most to the spoken language. Hence also we make a distinction between the literary and the **spoken** or colloquial language. Although this distinction is not dependent on writing—being found in the languages of illiterate savages—yet the preservation of an archaic literary language is greatly helped by its being at the same time a written language.

577. It is important to observe that the literary language is always colloquial in its origin : all literary forms which differ from the contemporary spoken language are really fossilized colloquialisms of an earlier period. Thus such forms as *thou hast, he hath*, which are now used only in the liturgical and poetical strata, were once in common colloquial use. Literary languages are therefore to some extent anachronisms, being a mixture of the contemporary spoken language with the spoken languages of earlier periods. For this reason the study of a language should always be based—as far as possible—on the spoken language of the period which is being dealt with.

Influence of one language on another.

578. Not only dialects influence each other, but also distinct languages, whether cognate or not, the degree of influence depending entirely on the intimacy of intercourse between the speakers of the two languages. There is, indeed, no limit to the mixture of languages in sounds, inflections, and grammar generally, as well as in vocabulary. But a very strong influence of one language on another generally ends in the complete extinction of the weaker one, so that a great many of these strongly mixed languages have perished without leaving any permanent record.

DIVISIONS AND METHODS OF GRAMMAR.

579. We have seen (2) that a grammar may be either **descriptive** or **explanatory**, the latter falling under the heads of **historical, comparative**, and **general** grammar.

580. It is evident that all study of grammar must begin with being purely descriptive. Thus it is no use attempting to study the history of inflections in different periods of a language or in a group of cognate languages, if we have not previously got a clear idea of what inflections really are ; and it is neither profitable nor interesting to compare languages or periods of languages of which we have no practical descriptive knowledge. Nor can we enter on the study of general grammar till we have learnt to analyse at least one special language grammatically.

ACCIDENCE AND SYNTAX.

581. The business of grammar is to state and explain those relations between forms and meanings which can be brought under general rules (18). Theoretically speaking, these two—form and meaning—are inseparable, and in a perfect language they would be so ; but in languages as they actually are, form is never in complete harmony with meaning—there is always a divergence between the two (26). This divergence makes it not only possible, but desirable, to treat form and meaning separately—at least, to some extent. That part of grammar which concerns itself specially with forms, and ignores their meaning as much as possible, is called **accidence**. That part of grammar which ignores distinctions of form as much as possible, and concentrates itself on their meaning, is called **syntax**. Thus an English grammar in dealing with the plurals of nouns would under accidence state briefly the meaning of plural-inflections in general, but would give this information solely in order to identify them—so as, for instance, to distinguish between the plural *trees*, the genitive *John s*, and the verb-inflection in *comes*. Having once given this information, accidence does not concern itself further with the shades of meaning expressed by the plural-inflection of nouns, but, on the other hand, carefully describes all the details of its form—how some nouns take final *s*, while others add *-en*, etc. Syntax, on the other hand, ignores such formal distinctions as those between the plurals *trees*, *oxen*, etc., or rather takes for granted that the student is acquainted with them, and considers only the different meanings and grammatical functions of noun-plurals in general, especially as opposed to the singular. The business of syntax is, therefore, to explain the meaning and function of grammatical forms, especially the various ways in which words are joined together in sentences.

In some grammars syntax is regarded entirely from the latter point of view, so that it is identified with the analysis of sentences, the meaning of grammatical forms being included under accidence. Although this is narrowing the scope of syntax too much, it is no doubt sometimes most convenient to treat of the meaning of grammatical forms under accidence, especially when the variations of meaning are either very slight, or else so great that they cannot be brought under general rules.

582. Syntax may be studied from two points of view. We can either start from the grammatical forms, and explain their uses, as when we describe the meanings and functions of the genitive case or the subjunctive mood; or we may take a grammatical category, and describe the different forms by which it is expressed, as when we give an account of the different ways in which predication is expressed—by a single verb, by the verb *to be* with an adjective or noun-word, etc. We distinguish these as **formal** and **logical** syntax respectively. It is evident that the first business of syntax is to deal with the phenomena of language formally, reserving logical

statements—which are often very useful and instructive—till all the grammatical forms of the language have had their functions explained. It is evident that logical syntax belongs more to general grammar than to the special grammar of one language.

GRAMMAR AND DICTIONARY.

583. We have seen (**18**) that the grammar is distinguished from the dictionary by dealing mainly with those phenomena of language which can be brought under general rules, while the dictionary deals with isolated phenomena. On this principle it is easy to see that such phenomena as word-order must belong exclusively to the grammar, while such isolated phenomena as the meanings of primary full-words must belong as exclusively to the dictionary. It is also easy to see that inflections belong to the grammar. In fact, the grammar of such a highly inflected language as Latin consists mainly of a description of the forms and functions of inflections, and the ways in which they join words together in sentences.

584. But when a language makes an extensive use of form-words, many difficulties arise ; for the distinction between form-word and full-word is often uncertain and fluctuating. Even in dealing with Latin it is a question whether or not prepositions should be included in the grammar ; but as in Latin the prepositions are only a kind of auxiliaries to the cases, the treatment of prepositions is regarded rather as an appendix to the grammar than as an integral part of it. In English, on the other hand, the prepositions play so important a grammatical part that they are really of more weight than the scanty remains of case-inflection, so that they can no more be excluded from English grammar than such periphrastic verb-forms as *mīratus est* 'he wondered,' compared with *vīdit* 'he saw,' can be excluded from Latin grammar. But the number of prepositions and other form-words is so great, and their meanings are so various, that in a grammar of limited length it is necessary to select a part of the facts, and omit details which do not bear directly on grammatical questions.

585. Nor is historical grammar concerned with the etymologies of isolated words, for which it refers the student to an etymological dictionary.

DESCRIPTIVE AND HISTORICAL GRAMMAR.

586. In studying grammar it is important to keep the descriptive and the historical view apart. The first object in studying grammar is to learn to observe linguistic facts as they *are*, not as they *ought* to be, or as they were in an earlier stage of the language. When the historical view of language gets the upper hand, it is apt to degenerate into one-sided antiquarian philology, which regards living languages merely as stepping-stones to earlier periods, and studies a family of languages solely in order to reconstruct their parent language, ignoring as much as possible the characteristic independent developments in the separate languages.

587. The first thing in studying a language is to learn to look at its phenomena from the point of view of the speakers of the language—to understand what is called ' the genius of the language,' that is, the general principles on which its grammatical categories are unconsciously framed by the speakers of the language. In every language the feeling for certain logical and grammatical categories is more highly developed than for others. Thus English has no forms to express clearly (except in a few special cases) the distinction between fact-statements and thought-statements (294), which in Latin are most carefully distinguished by means of the subjunctive mood; nor has English any distinct and unambiguous way of marking the direct object relation and distinguishing it from the nominative relation, while in Latin, again, these two relations are sharply distinguished by the accusative and nominative inflections.   Hence it is against the genius of English to set up an accusative case in imitation of Latin grammar; and although English still preserves traces of a subjunctive mood, we have to acknowledge that the language has entirely lost the feeling for the original function of the mood as an expression of thought-statements, so that the few constructions in which we still keep the old inflection are only fossilized archaisms.   Distinctions of verb-tense, and the use of prepositions and of verbal-groups instead of dependent sentences are, on the other hand, highly developed in English, and are part of the genius of the language.   The faculty by which we instinctively know whether a certain form or construction is in accordance with the genius of the language or not, is called 'the linguistic sense.'   This faculty is naturally more highly developed in some people than in others; but it can always be strengthened by training, and the first business of grammar is to cultivate it as far as possible.

588. From the descriptive point of view grammatical phenomena are of two kinds, **living** and **dead**.   In English such forms as the plural -*s* and the derivative ending -*ness* are living (or productive) forms, because they are still used freely to form new inflected and derived words on the pattern of those already existing in the language : when a new noun is introduced into the language, we can give it a plural in -*s*, and when a new adjective is formed, we can generally form a derivative in -*ness* from it.   Dead (or sterile) forms, on the other hand, cannot be reproduced by pattern or analogy, but are preserved only in certain words which have to be learnt one by one.   Most irregular forms— such as the plural *men* —are dead, being only exceptionally reproduced by analogy.   In English this form is so dead that even such a noun as *Norman* forms its plural *Normans*. So also such derivatives as *for-* in *forgive* are dead.   Dead forms tend to become fossilized in meaning and isolated from one another; thus *forgive* and *forbid* have nothing in common except the form of their prefix.

Dead forms are sometimes reproduced by analogy for the sake of amusement in colloquial language, as when in English *wink, collide, pipeclay* form their preterites **wunk, *collode, *popeclew* on the analogy of *sunk, rode, slew,* forms which have been taken seriously by some learned foreigners.

We can, of course, distinguish between dead and living forms in a 'dead' language—that is, a language which is no longer spoken, such as Latin, as well as in a 'living' language such as French. Thus the Latin genitive in *pater-familias* is a dead form, the living genitive being *familiae.*

Grammatical Difficulties.

589. It is evident that the linguistic sense can be based only on living forms and constructions which occur frequently and in a variety of circumstances. Hence if a form or construction survives only in a few isolated sentences, or if its meaning has become fossilized, our linguistic sense may be at a loss with regard to it, because we have learnt it ready-made and therefore mechanically, without having had occasion either to form it afresh on the pattern of similar forms or constructions, or to form other constructions in imitation of it. *I had rather,* in such sentences as *I had rather not do it now,* is an example of such an isolated construction, in regard to which our grammatical instinct leaves us at fault. In this construction we hardly know whether to regard *had* as a full verb or an auxiliary: we ask ourselves, If it is a full verb, what is its direct object—*rather* or *not*?; either supposition goes against our linguistic sense; and, on the other hand, such a construction as **I had do it* is grammatically impossible. In the more colloquial form *I would rather . .* these difficulties disappear. From a purely logical and descriptive point of view such difficulties as those presented by *I had rather* are simply insurmountable; and it is better to take such constructions as wholes, without grammatical analysis—just as we take such a word as *man* as a whole, without attempting to explain how its meaning results from the sounds of which it is made up. Blendings, such as *themselves*, and elliptical constructions also offer special grammatical difficulties.

590. All such difficulties require the help of historical grammar. Sometimes, indeed, the historical explanation is self-evident, as in the case of the blending *these kind of things* and the ellipse in *he is at Mr. Smith's*. The difficulty of such forms and constructions as *themselves* and *I had rather*, on the other hand, can be cleared up only by detailed historical investigation. Even in cases where the explanation seems self-evident, historical investigation is necessary as a corrective (7). Thus, as the colloquial *I'd rather* may be a contraction either of *I had rather* or *I would rather*, we might get rid of the difficulty by assuming the latter to be the original form, and supposing *I had* to be an erroneous expansion of *I'd*. But historical investigation shows *I had rather* to be the original form.

Grammatical Analysis.

591. Before analysing a sentence or other passage grammatically, it should generally be analysed from a logical point of view, especially if it involves any divergence between logical and grammatical categories. Thus in analysing such a complex as *it is you that I mean*, we should understand clearly that it expresses a simple thought, and is logically equivalent to a single sentence, the principal clause *it is you* being only an empty sentence (**450**).

592. Analysis from a purely descriptive point of view should then follow. The most elementary step in this analysis is to settle what parts of speech the separate words belong to, an operation generally known as **parsing**. The relations between the words should then be analysed, and lastly the relations of the whole sentence to other sentences should be analysed, if necessary. If any construction does not admit of grammatical analysis from the descriptive point of view, the fact should be acknowledged, and the construction designated as ' isolated ' or abnormal.

593. Any historical or comparative questions that may arise should then be considered ; and when it seems advisable, special constructions may be examined in the light of general grammar, and compared with parallel constructions in other languages whether cognate or not.

Historical and general grammar should be admitted only when they do not confuse the learner. In learning a foreign language they should be used sparingly and cautiously.

HISTORY OF ENGLISH.

PERIODS.

594. The name ' English language' in its widest sense comprehends the language of the English people from their first settlement in Britain to the present time.   For the sake of convenience we distinguish three main stages in the history of the language, namely **Old English** (OE), **Middle English** (ME), and **Modern English** (MnE).   OE may be defined as the period of *full* endings (*mona, sunne, sunu, stānas*), ME as the period of *levelled* endings (*mone, sunne, sune, stones*), MnE as the period of *lost* endings (*moon, sun, son, stones* = stounz).   We further distinguish periods of transition between these main stages, each of which latter is further divided into an **early** and a **late** period.   The dates of these periods are, roughly, as follows :—

Early Old English (E. of Alfred)   .   .   .   700–900
Late Old English (E. of Ælfric)   .   .   .   900–1100
Transition Old English (E. of Layamon)   .   .   1100–1200
Early Middle English (E. of the Ancren Riwle) .   1200–1300
Late Middle English (E. of Chaucer) .   .   .   1300–1400
Transition Middle English (Caxton E.)   .   .   1400–1500
Early Modern English (Tudor E.; E. of Shake-
   spere)   1500–1650
Late Modern English   1650–

to which may be added **Present English**, by which we understand the English of the present time as spoken, written, and understood by educated people, that is, roughly speaking, 19th-century English.

COGNATE LANGUAGES.

595. English belongs to the **Arian** (or Aryan) family of languages, descended from a hypothetical Parent Arian language, the chief of which are given in the following table, different periods of their development being separated by dashes.

(A) **East-Arian**, or Asiatic :

(*a*) Sanskrit, the sacred language of India—Pali—Bengali and the other **Gaurian** languages of India.

(*b*) **Iranian** languages : Zend or Old Bactrian. Old Persian, which is the language of the Cuneiform inscriptions— Modern Persian.

(*c*) Armenian, which is really half-way between East- and West-Arian.

(B) **West-Arian** or European :

(*d*) Greek—Romaic or Modern Greek.

(*e*) Latin—the **Romance** languages : Italian, Provencal, French (Old French, Modern French), Spanish, Portuguese, Roumanian.

(*f*) **Celtic** languages. Gaulish. The **Goidelic** group : Irish, Manx, Gaelic. The **Cymric** group : Welsh, Cornish, Breton (introduced from Britain).

(*g*) **Slavonic** languages. Old Bulgarian — Russian, Polish, Bohemian, Servian, Bulgarian.

(*h*) **Baltic** languages. Lithuanian, Lettish.

(*i*) **Germanic** languages.

596. The Germanic group, to which English belongs, consists of the following languages :—

(A) **East-Germanic** :

(*a*) Gothic.

(*b*) **Scandinavian** languages. **West-Scandinavian** group :

Norwegian, Icelandic.   **East**-Scandinavian group : Danish, Swedish.

(B) **West-Germanic** :

(*c*) **Low German** languages. Old Saxon—Dutch, Flemish. **Anglo-Frisian** group : English, Frisian.

(*d*) High German, or German.

597. English is then a member of the Anglo-Frisian group of the Low German languages.

Old English.

598. In the fifth century—or perhaps earlier—Britain was partially conquered by a variety of Germanic tribes from the other side of the German Ocean, the chief of which were—

(*a*) **Saxons** (OE *Seaxan*), from the country between the Elbe and the Rhine.

(*b*) **Angles** (OE *Engle*), from the district still called Angeln (OE *Angel*) in the South of Schleswig.

(*c*) **Jutes** (OE *Geotas*) from the North of Schleswig.

599. The first settlement is said to have been that of the Jutes, who took Kent and the Isle of Wight.

600. The Saxons occupied the country south of the Thames ; except Cornwall, where the Britons still kept their nationality. Some of the Saxons settled in Sussex, which means 'South-Saxons' (OE *Suþ-seaxan*); some north of the Thames in Middlesex, which means 'Middle-Saxons' (OE *Middel-seaxan*), and Essex, which means 'East-Saxons' (OE *East-seaxan*); the remaining portion of the tribe being called 'West-Saxons' (OE *West-seaxan, Wes-seaxan*), whence their state is called Wessex.

601. The rest of England was occupied by the Angles. Suffolk (OE *Suþ-folc*='South-people') and Norfolk (OE *Norþ-folc*='North-people') were included under the name of East-Anglia (OE *East-engle*='East-anglians'). Another tribe of Anglians occupied what are now the Midland Counties, between the Thames and the Humber. These were called **Mercians** (OE *Mierce*), which means 'borderers,' from OE *mearc* 'mark,' 'boundary.' Mercia was so called because it bordered on Wales, the country of the Welsh or 'foreigners' (OE *Wealas, Welisce menn*), the name given by the English to the native Britons. The country north of the Humber was occupied by a variety of Anglian tribes included under the name of **Northumbrians** (OE *Norþ-hymbre*). Ancient Northumbria extended up to the Firth of Forth, and thus included the greater part of what is now the Lowlands of Scotland.

602. All these tribes spoke the same Anglo-Frisian language with slight differences of dialect. These differences increased by degrees, so that already in the 8th century we can distinguish four main dialects: **Northumbrian** and **Mercian**, which together constitute the **Anglian** group; and **West-Saxon** and **Kentish**, which together constitute the **Southern** group.

Kentish was originally more akin to the Anglian than the Saxon dialects, but in course of time it was strongly influenced by West-Saxon.

603. All these tribes agreed in calling their common language **English** (OE *Englisc*), that is, 'Anglish,' because the Angles were for a long time the dominant tribe. The supremacy afterwards passed to the West-Saxons, and their capital, Winchester, became the capital of England; and West-Saxon became the official and, to a great extent, the literary language all over England. The West-Saxons still continued to call their language English, the name Anglo-Saxon (OE *Angel-seaxan*) being used only as a collective name for the people, not the language.

604. In this book OE words are always given—unless the contrary is stated—in their Early West-Saxon forms; that is, in the dialect of King Alfred.

CHARACTERISTICS OF OLD ENGLISH.

605. The characteristics of OE are those of the other Low German languages. It was, as compared with MnE, a highly inflected language, being in this respect intermediate between Latin and Modern German. In its syntax it closely resembled Modern German. It also resembled Modern German in having an unlimited power of forming new words by derivation and composition, as when it made *Scribes and Pharisees* into 'bookers and separation-saints' (OE *boceras and sundor-hālgan*).

LATIN INFLUENCE.

606. Nevertheless it adopted many Latin words, some of which it brought with it from the Continent—such words as *strǣt* 'high road,' 'street,' *mīl* 'mile,' *casere* 'emperor' from Latin (*via*) *strata, mīlia* (*passuum*), *Caesar*——while others were learnt from the Romanized Britons, such as *ceaster* 'city,' *lǣden* 'language' from *castra,* (*lingva*) *Latīna.* These are all popular words. There is another layer of learned words which came in after the introduction of Christianity in 597. Such words are *deofol* 'devil,' *mynster* 'monastery,' *fers* 'verse,' from *diabolus, monasterium, versus.*

CELTIC INFLUENCE.

607. Very few Celtic words came into OE, because the Britons themselves were to a great extent Romanized, especially the inhabitants of the cities, who were mainly the descendants of the Roman legionary soldiers. *Dry* 'sorcerer' is an example of a Celtic word in OE.

SCANDINAVIAN INFLUENCE.

608. Towards the end of the 8th century Scandinavian pirates—chiefly from Norway, but also from Denmark, all being indiscriminately called 'Danes' by the Anglo-Saxons—began to harass the coasts of England. By the end of the next century they had conquered and settled East-Anglia (in 870), Mercia (in 874), and Northumbria (in 876); although in the next century they were forced to acknowledge the supremacy of the West-Saxon kings. In 1016 the whole of England was conquered by the Danes, and England was ruled by Danish kings till 1042, when the Anglo-Saxon royal line was restored in the person of Edward the Confessor.

609. It is not till the close of the OE period that Scandinavian words appear. Even Late Northumbrian (of about 970) is entirely free from Scandinavian influence.

French Influence.

610. With the accession of Edward the Confessor in 1042 Norman influence begins; and in 1066 the battle of Hastings made the Norman duke William king of England, although the actual conquest was not completed till 1071.

611. The Normans were Scandinavian by race, but their language was a dialect of Old French.

612. The influence of Norman French on OE was of course even slighter than that of Scandinavian, so that it does not become a factor of importance till the ME period. Nevertheless several French words passed into literary OE even before the Conquest, such as *castel* 'castle,' *capun* 'fowl.'

Middle English.

613. In its Middle period English went through much the same changes as the other Germanic languages, though at a quicker rate. Many of the sounds were changed, most of the old inflections were lost, their place being supplied by form-words—prepositions, auxiliary verbs, etc.—and many words became obsolete.

Dialects of Middle English.

614. The Norman Conquest, by depriving the old West-Saxon of its literary and political supremacy, gave free play

to the development of the dialects.   Although the ME dialects
are continuations of the OE ones, it is convenient to call
most of them by different names.   The main divisions are
Northern, corresponding to the Old Northumbrian, **Midland**, corresponding to the Old Mercian, **Southern**, corresponding to the old West-Saxon, and **Kentish**.   We include
the first two under the term 'North-Thames English,' the
last two under 'South-Thames English.'

615. Of these dialects the Midland was the predominating
one.   Its commanding position in the heart of England
enabled it to exercise a direct influence on all the other
dialects, while Southern and Northern were completely cut
off from one another.   Hence even the earliest Southern of
about 1200 shows considerable influence of the Midland—or
Old Mercian—dialect.

616. It is to be observed that the changes which distinguish one period of English from another went on much
faster in the North of England than in the South.   In fact,
the Old Northumbrian dialect of the 10th century had already
entered on its transition period—characterized by a general
confusion in the use of inflections, and was thus almost on a
level with the Early Southern Middle English of about 1200.
Again, the Northern dialect in its Early Middle period had
got rid of nearly all the inflections that are not preserved in
MnE, being thus several centuries ahead of the South-Thames
dialects.   The Midland dialects were more conservative than
the Northern, though less so than the South-Thames dialects.
It will be seen, then, that the criteria of full, levelled, and lost
endings by which we distinguish the periods of English (**594**)
apply only to the South-Thames dialects.

Struggle between French and English.

617. For a long time the two languages, French and
English, kept almost entirely apart.   The English of 1200 is
almost as free from French words as the English of 1050;

and it was not till after 1300 that French words began to be adopted wholesale into English.

618. Meanwhile English was steadily gaining the upper hand. In 1258 we find it officially employed in the Proclamation of Henry III. In the next century French gradually fell into disuse even among the aristocracy. In 1362 English was introduced in the courts of law instead of French. About the same time English took the place of French as the vehicle of instruction in schools.

RISE OF THE LONDON DIALECT.

619. In the ME period the dialects had diverged so much that speakers of the extreme Northern and extreme Southern dialects were no longer able to understand one another, and the need of a common dialect became pressing. Such a common dialect can be formed only in a centre of intercourse where speakers from all parts of the country meet constantly. Such a centre was London, which now was not only the capital of England, but also a place of great and growing commercial importance.

620. The London dialect, as we find it in its earliest document, the Proclamation of Henry III, shows such a mixture of Midland and Southern forms as we might expect from its position on the border-line between these two dialects. The Midland dialect was intermediate between the two extremes, Northern and Southern, not only geographically but also linguistically; so that speakers of Midland could understand both Northern and Southern much better than Northerners and Southerners could understand one another. Hence the Midland element in the London dialect made the latter peculiarly fitted to serve as a means of general communication. Hence also the Midland element in the London dialect became stronger and stronger in the course of the ME period, till at last even Northern forms

passed into it through the medium of the Midland dialect, while Southern influence became weaker and weaker.

Scandinavian Influence.

621. Of the Scandinavian settlers in England the Norwegians spoke a West-Scandinavian, the Danes an East-Scandinavian dialect, the difference between these dialects being however very slight. The Scandinavian words imported into English seem to be mostly Danish. Although the Scandinavian dialects were not intelligible to the Anglo-Saxons, yet the cognate languages English and Scandinavian were so similar in structure and had so many words in common—*hus* 'house,' *land* 'land,' for instance, being both English and Scandinavian—that the languages blended together with the same facility as the races that spoke them. English got the upper hand, but Scandinavian nevertheless left its mark on every English dialect, especially the East-Midland and Northern dialects, where the population was half Scandinavian. *Ill, fro* in 'to and fro,' *bound* in 'bound for a place,' are examples of Scandinavian words in England (Icelandic *ill-r* ' bad,' *fra* ' from,' *buinn* ' ready ').

French Influence.

622. The Norman French introduced into England was not a uniform dialect, but was itself split up into local varieties or sub-dialects, which in the Norman spoken in England— the 'Anglo-Norman' or 'Anglo-French' language —were mixed together indiscriminately. The accession of Henry of Anjou in 1154 brought in the influence of another French dialect—the Angevin. The loss of Normandy in 1204 put an end to the influence of Continental Norman ; and henceforth Anglo-French was influenced only by the literary French of Paris, this Parisian French having the same predominance among the French dialects as London English had among the English dialects. At the time when the influence of Anglo-

French on English begins to be important—that is, in the late ME period—it was, therefore, a mixture of Old French of different periods and different dialects, modified by changes of its own, and also by the influence of English itself, especially in its pronunciation.

623. Old French was a language standing in the same relation to its parent language Latin as MnE to OE, and Modern Danish to Old Icelandic. It was therefore not only remotely cognate with ME—both languages being of West-Arian origin—but was also in much the same stage of development. This similarity in general character between . the two languages greatly increased their influence on one another.

624. French influence on English is most marked in the vocabulary. Soon after the Conquest English ceased for several centuries to be the language of the higher purposes of life, and sank almost to a mere peasant's dialect. So when English came again into general use, it had lost a great part of its higher vocabulary, for which it had to use French words, such as *sir, duke* ; *captain, army, battle* ; *sermon, preach*. Even when the English word was kept, the same idea was often expressed by a French word, whence numerous synonyms such as *work* and *labour*, *weak* and *feeble*.

LATIN INFLUENCE.

625. In Old French itself we must distinguish between **popular** and **learned** words. The popular words in Old French, such as *sire* 'lord,' from Latin *senior* 'older,' are simply Latin words which have undergone those changes which take place in every language whose development is natural and unimpeded. But as Latin was kept up as an independent—we might almost say a living—language throughout the Middle Ages, Latin words were imported into Old French as well as the other Romance languages, being used first in books, then in ordinary speech. These learned words were kept as much as possible unchanged, being pronounced as they were written. It often happened that a Latin word which had assumed a popular form in French, was re-imported direct from Latin, so that chronological doublets were formed, such as *caitif* 'wretched' and *captif*, both from Latin *capñvus*, whence the English *caitiff* and *captive*.

626. These learned French words were introduced into ME in great numbers. Hence when Latin words came to be imported directly into English, they were put into a French shape on the analogy of those Latin words which had really been brought in through French. Thus when a word in -*tio*, such as *nominatio*, was taken direct from Latin, it was made into -*tion* (MnE *nomination*) on the analogy of the older importations, such as *nation* (ME *nācioun*).

627. French had also some influence on English syntax, and many French idioms and phrases were adopted into spoken English through imitation of the aristocracy.

628. On the whole, however, the influence of French on the grammatical structure of English was not great, the numerous agreements between the two languages being the result of independent development.

Modern English.

629. In the Middle period literary English was still distinctly an inflectional language. In the Modern period it became mainly uninflectional, with only scanty remains of the older inflections.

630. The Modern period is that of the complete ascendency of the London dialect, which henceforth is the only one used in writing throughout England. Henceforth the other dialects of England continued to exist only as illiterate forms of speech confined within narrow areas.

631. The Northern dialect of Scotland was more independent of the influence of the London dialect; but long before the union of the crowns of the two countries in 1603 literary Scotch showed strong English influence, and by the time of the union of the Scotch and English parliaments in 1707, literary Scotch was wholly assimilated to literary English. Literary English had indeed been the liturgical language of Scotland ever since the Reformation, when the English trans- lation of the Bible was adopted without any attempt to adapt it to the Northern dialect of Scotland. But the pure 'Broad Scotch' continued to be the spoken language of the upper as well as the lower classes both in town and country up to the end of the last century.

632. In England, on the contrary, London English was not only a literary, but also a spoken language, which every educated man acquired more or less perfectly, whatever his native dialect might be; although, of course, it was always liable to be influenced by the local dialects in various degrees, according to the education of the speaker and other circum- stances. This influence is still very strong in Scotland, whose educated speech, though almost pure English in vocabulary and grammar, is in its sounds strongly dialectal.

633. The spread of Modern London English—or 'Stan- dard English,' as we may now call it—was greatly aided by the introduction of printing in 1476. The publication of Tindal's translation of the New Testament in 1525 paved the way for the Authorized Version of 1611, which made Early Modern London English what it has ever since been— the sacred or liturgical language of the whole English-speaking race.

INFLUENCE OF OTHER LANGUAGES.

634. In the Early Modern period, the Renascence—the revival of the study of the classical authors of Greece and Rome—led to the adoption of an immense number of Greek as well as Latin words, the Greek words being generally Latinized, just as the Latin words imported into Middle English were Frenchified.

635. As the first prose writings were mostly either translations from Latin, or else the work of scholars to whom Latin was in some respects a more natural means of expression than English, it was inevitable that Early MnE prose was greatly influenced by Latin, not only in vocabulary, but also in grammatical structure and idioms. In a few generations many Latin—and some Greek—words and expressions which were at first purely learned and technical passed into the language of everyday life; while, on the other hand, many others became obsolete.

636. As the relations of England with other countries became more extended, many words were imported into English from almost every European language, especially Dutch, French, Italian, Spanish, and Portuguese, and from many other languages besides, such as Arabic, Persian, and Turkish, and the native languages of America.

637. Standard English has always been influenced by the different English dialects. The literary revival of Broad Scotch at the end of the last century by Scott and Burns has introduced many Scotch words into literary English.

PERIODS.

638. The main general difference between Early and Late MnE is that the former is the period of experiment and comparative licence both in the importation and in the formation of new words, idioms, and grammatical constructions. The Late MnE period is, on the other hand, one of selection and organization. The most marked differences in detail are the great sound-changes undergone by the spoken language—changes which have been completely disguised by the fixity of the orthography.

Present English.

639. In the second half of the present century the old local dialects had begun to die out, especially in

England, where they are gradually giving way to Standard English.

640. But on the other hand new local dialects are developing themselves by cleavage of the common London dialect in the Modern period—especially the Late Modern period—mainly through colonization.

641. The English colonization of Ireland in the Early Modern period made Early Modern Standard English the general language of culture throughout the island.   Hence the present vulgar Irish-English is really an independent dialect of Standard English, which is in many cases more archaic than the present London dialect, although many of its peculiarities are the result of the influence of Celtic Irish.   The speech of the educated Irish is Present Standard English mixed in various degrees with vulgar Irish-English.

642. Through the colonization of British North America in the 16th and 17th centuries, the American English of the United States and Canada is another independent modification of Standard English, though much less archaic than Irish-English.   Educated American English is now almost entirely independent of British influence, and differs from it considerably, though as yet not enough to make the two dialects—American English and British English—mutually unintelligible.   American English itself is beginning to split up into dialects.

643. Australia and New Zealand were colonized during the present century, and their educated speech differs but slightly from British English, except that the influence of the vulgar London or 'Cockney' dialect is stronger in Australasian than in British English.

644. These new dialectal differences are mainly observable in the spoken language.   Literary English still maintains its unity everywhere, a few 'Americanisms' excepted, the differences of the spoken dialects being utilized in literature only for comic purposes, or to give what is called 'local colour,' the reproduction of the real dialect being generally only partial and often inaccurate.

645. This grammar deals mainly with educated British English, the standard for which is the educated speech of London and the South of England generally.

STRATA.

646. Of this Standard English we must distinguish 'strata,' or non-local dialects.

647. The main division is that between the spoken or colloquial, and the written or literary language. The spoken language is again distinguished as educated or polite colloquial, and vulgar colloquial. The vulgar speech of London and the district immediately round London is called **Cockney.** There are also varieties of literary English. The language of prose often approaches very closely to that of ordinary conversation ; while that of poetry—and, to some extent, of higher, imaginative prose as well—is characterised by many peculiar words and forms, many of which are Early Modern colloquialisms which have become obsolete in the spoken language. The liturgical language of the Bible and the Church Services is still pure Early MnE ; it has strongly influenced the spoken as well as the written English of the present day. The language of proverbs and other sayings also contains many archaisms.

PHONOLOGY.

PHONETICS.

648. Phonetics is the science of speech-sounds.

649. As the ordinary or Nomic spelling does not always show the real pronunciation, it is necessary to use a **phonetic** spelling, which, to prevent confusion, we enclose in ( ). Thus (səəkl) is the phonetic spelling of Nomic *circle*.

Analysis.

650. The foundation of speech-sounds is breath expelled from the lungs, and variously modified by the vocal organs— throat, nose, mouth, lips. Each sound is the result of certain definite actions or positions of the vocal organs, by which the sound-passage assumes a certain definite shape.

THROAT-SOUNDS: BREATH AND VOICE.

651. The first modification the breath undergoes is in the throat. If the vocal chords, which are stretched across the inside of the throat, are kept apart so that the air can pass through with but little hindrance, we have **breath**, as in ordinary breathing or sighing, and in the consonant (h), as in *high*. If the chords are brought together so as to vibrate, we have **voice**, as in murmuring or in the word *err*.

NASAL SOUNDS.

652. If the passage into the nose is left open, we have a **nasal** sound, such as (m) in *am*. In the formation of all sounds that are not nasal—non-nasal sounds—such as the (b) in *amber*, the nose-passage is closed by pressing back the uvula or soft palate.

Consonants.

653. If the mouth-passage is narrowed so as to cause audible friction—that is, a hissing or buzzing sound—a **consonant** is produced. Thus if we bring the lower lip against the upper teeth, and send out breath, we form the ' lip-teeth-breath,' or, more briefly, the ' lip-teeth' consonant (f). If we form an (f) with throat-vibration, we get the corresponding ' lip-teeth-voice' consonant (v). Breath or voiceless consonants are sometimes expressed by adding (*h*) to the symbol of the corresponding voice consonant, thus (w*h*) as in *why*, is the breath consonant corresponding to the voice consonant (w) as in *wine*. ' Stopped' consonants are formed with complete stoppage of the mouth-passage. Thus the ' lip-stop' consonant (p) is formed by bringing the lips together so as completely to stop the passage of air.

Vowels.

654. If the mouth-passage is left so open as not to cause audible friction, and voiced breath is sent through it, we have a vowel, such as (aa) in *father*. Every alteration in the shape of the mouth produces a different vowel. Thus a slight alteration of the (aa)-position produces the vowel (æ) in *man*.

Vowel-like Consonants.

655. Some consonants have hardly any friction when voiced, and are called **vowel-like** consonants. Such consonants are (l), as in *little* (litl), and (m).

Synthesis.

656. We have now to consider the **synthesis** of sounds, that is, the different ways in which they are joined together in speech.

657. When sounds are joined together we have to consider their relative **quantity, stress,** and **intonation.**

Quantity.

658. By quantity, sounds are distinguished as **long, half-long** or medium, and **short,** 'long' being often used to include half-long as well. In phonetic notation long and half-long vowels are doubled, short vowels being written single, as in (məəmə) *murmur.* The length of consonants is only occasionally marked by doubling.

Stress.

659. There are three main degrees of stress or loudness : **strong, half-strong** or medium, and **weak.** Thus in *contradict* the last syllable is strong, the first half-strong, the next weak. We mark strong stress by (·), half-strong by (:), these marks being put before the sound on which the stressed syllable begins, weak or unstressed syllables being left unmarked : (:kontrə·dikt). Weak stress is marked when necessary by prefixing (-), as in (-it reinz) ' it rains.'

660. Sounds which occur only in unstressed syllables, such as the short (ə) in (məəmə) *murmur,* are called **weak.**

Intonation.

661. Intonation or tone is either **level, rising,** or **falling,** marked respectively (‾, ′, `). The level tone is not much used in speech. The rising tone is heard in questions, such as *what′,* the falling in answers, such as *no`.* Besides these **simple** tones, there are **compound** tones, formed by uniting a rising and a falling tone in one syllable. The **compound rise** or falling-rising tone (marked ˇ) may be heard in *take care!* when used warningly ; the **compound fall** or rising-falling tone (marked ˆ) may be heard in *oh!* when expressing sarcasm.

662. The level tone may be either **high** or **low** in pitch, and the other tones may begin either in a high or a low pitch. When excited, we speak in a high pitch or key; when depressed, in a low key.

663. The non-level tones can pass through different **intervals.** The greater the interval, the more emphatic the tone becomes. Thus *what'* with a slight rise expresses mere enquiry, but with a long rise—rising from a very low to a very high pitch—it expresses surprise or indignation.

GLIDES.

664. Glides are sounds produced during the transition from one sound to another. Thus in (kii) *key* we have the glide from the (k)-position to the (ii)-position, which does not, however, require to be written, as it is implied by the positions of (k) and (ii).

665. Consonants are often joined together without any glide, not only in such combinations as (nd) in *hand*, where the (d) is formed by continuing the (n), the nose-passage being closed at the same time, but also in such words as the English *act* (ækt).

SYLLABLES.

666. A syllable is a vowel, either alone or in combination with consonants, uttered with a single impulse of stress. Every fresh impulse of stress makes a new syllable, the beginning of the syllable corresponding with the beginning of the stress. Thus (ə·tæk) *attack* has two syllables, the first syllable consisting of the vowel (ə) uttered with weak stress, the second of (tæk) uttered with a new impulse of stress beginning on the (t). Vowel-like consonants often form syllables in the same way as vowels, as in *battle* = (bæt-l).

DIPHTHONGS.

667. If two vowels are uttered with one impulse of stress, so as to form a single syllable, the combination is called a diphthong, such as (oi) in *oil*. Most diphthongs have the stress on the first element. If three vowels are combined in this way, we have a **triphthong**, as in (faiə) *fire*. A simple long vowel, such as (əə), is called a **monophthong**.

We now have to consider sounds more in detail.

Vowels.

668. As every alteration in the shape of the mouth produces a different vowel, the number of vowels is infinite. Hence what we call the vowels, (a), (i) etc., are really **groups** of an indefinite number of vowels differing very slightly from one another.

Rounding.

669. The shape of the mouth-passage by which vowels are formed depends partly on the position of the tongue, partly on that of the lips. If the lip-opening is narrowed while the tongue is in a certain position, the resulting vowel is said to be **rounded**. Thus (y) in French *lune* is the round vowel corresponding to the unrounded (ii), which is nearly the sound in English *he*, both vowels having the same tongue-position.

Tongue-Retraction.

670. The tongue-positions depend partly on the degree of **retraction** of the tongue, partly on its **height** or distance from the palate.

671. If the root of the tongue is drawn back, we have a **back** vowel, such as the (aa) in *father*. If the fore part of the tongue is advanced, we have a **front** vowel, such as (ii). If the tongue is left in its neutral position, intermediate between back and front, we have a **mixed** vowel, such as (əə).

Tongue-Height.

672. If the tongue is raised as close to the palate as is possible without making the vowel into a consonant, a

high vowel is formed. Thus (i) is a high-front vowel, (u), as in *full*, a high-back-round vowel. There are two other degrees of height, **mid** and **low**. For convenience we may include mid and low vowels under the common name 'un-high' vowels, distinguishing them as **close** and **open**, according to the degree of openness of the mouth-passage. We denote open vowels, when necessary, by italics. French *é* in *été* is the mid-front-close vowel, or, more briefly, the front-close vowel, for when a vowel is not expressly called high. we assume it to be un-high. English (*e*) in *men* is the corresponding mid-front-open vowel. The Scotch vowel in *men* is more open than the English, being a low-front vowel; but these English and Scotch vowels are so similar that we include them under the common name 'front-open.' Very open vowels are called **broad**. (æ) in *man* is a broad front vowel. The distinction of close and open applies also to the high vowels. Thus French (i) in *fini* is the close high front vowel, English (*i*) in *finny* is the open high front vowel.

Acoustic Qualities of Vowels.

673. If we compare the acoustic qualities of the vowels—that is, the impression they make on the ear—we find that they differ in pitch and clearness, close (i) having the highest pitch and clearest sound, while (u) has the deepest sound. Tongue-retraction and lip-rounding both have the same effect of lowering the pitch and dulling the sound of the vowels. Thus the back and mixed vowels (aa. əə) are duller in sound than the front vowels (i, e, æ), and the front round vowel (y) is duller than the corresponding unrounded vowel (i). Hence vowels formed in quite different ways often have the same pitch, which makes them very similar in sound. Thus the English mixed vowel (əə) and the French front round vowel (œ) in *peur* are very similar in sound.

The Vowels in Detail.

The following are the most important vowels.

(A) Unrounded vowels.

674. (a) 'clear back.' This vowel occurs only long in English, in such words as (faaðə) *father, farther,* (aamz) *alms, arms.* Short (a) occurs in French and German, and in many English dialects, as in the Yorkshire *man.*

675. (ɐ) 'dull back.' The English vowel in *son, sun, courage* (kɐridʒ).

676. (ə) 'mixed' or 'neutral' vowel. (təən) *turn,* (bəəd) *bird.* The short (ə) in (məəmə) *murmur* is a weak vowel (660).

677. (i) 'high front.' Close (i) in French *fini,* the short E. *i* being always open. Weak open (i)—which, when necessary, we write (ɪ)—as in (petɪ) *petty* is opener than the strong (i) in *pit,* being really intermediate between (*i*) and (*e*). Long close (ii) is the older E. sound in such words as *see, sea, receive, machine,* and this sound is still preserved in Scotland and the North of England. In the South of England it is diphthongized into (*i*) followed by very close (i), which is nearly the sound of the consonant (j) in *you,* so we write (sij), etc.

678. (e) 'front.' French *é* is close front. The E. vowel in *men, bread, leopard* (lepəd) is open front (*e*). Before (ə)—with which it forms a diphthong—it is still opener, as in (feə) *fare, fair,* (ðeə) *there, their.* The long close front (ee) is still preserved in Scotch in such words as *name, day,* where Standard E. has the diphthong (ei).

679. (æ) 'broad front.' The E. vowel in *man, thresh.*

(B) Round vowels.

680. (u) 'high back round.' Close in French *sou,* the E. short (*u*) in *full, good* being always open. The older close (uu) in such words as *moon, move, you* (juu) is still kept in Scotland and the North of England, but in the South of England it becomes (uw) with a distinct (w). Weak open (u), as in *value*, is the high mixed round vowel, which, when necessary, we write (ü)—(vælju).

681. (o) 'back round.' Close in French *beau* (bo). Close (oo) in Scotch *no*, *know*, where Standard E. has the diphthong (ou). The (o) in the diphthong (oi), as in *boy*, is the same open sound. Weak (o), as in *October*, is the open mixed vowel, which, when necessary, we write (o)—(oktoubə). Weak (öu), as in *fellow*, is hardly to be distinguished from (ö).

682. (ɔ) 'broad back round.' This is the sound of the E. short vowels in *not*, *what*. The long broad vowel is heard in such words as *naught*, *fall*. For convenience we write the short vowel (o), the long (ɔ) in Standard E.—(not, nɔt).

683. (y) 'high front round'=rounded (i). French *une*. German *über*.

684. (œ) 'front-round.' Close in French *peu*, whose vowel is a rounded French *e*. Open in French *peur*.

Nasal Vowels.

685. If a vowel is formed with the nose-passage open, it is said to be **nasal**, which we mark by (*n*). Thus we have nasal (a, æ) in French *sang*, *sans* (sa*n*), *vin* (væ*n*).

Diphthongs.

686. We call (ei, ou ; ij, uw) **half diphthongs**, because they are not very distinct, their two elements differing only in height.

687. **Full diphthongs**, on the other hand, such as (ai, au, oi) are made up of vowels as distinct as possible from one another. But in E., as in many other languages, the elements of such diphthongs are not kept so distinct as they might be. Thus, while the diphthong in Italian *aura* is really a clear (a) followed by a high close (u), the corresponding E. diphthong in *house* begins with a mixed vowel resembling (æ), and ends with an indistinct mixed (o), the E. diphthong (ou) ending nearly in the same way. So also the E. diphthong in *why*, *time* begins with a mixed vowel and ends in a sound between (*i*) and (*e*). The E. (ei, oi) end in the same way. So by writing (haus, whai, taim) we merely indicate a movement from openness to closeness either of the mouth-passage or the lip-passage.

688. There is another class of **murmur diphthongs** ending in (ǝ), as in *hear, here* (hɪǝ), *fare, fair* (feǝ), *poor* (puǝ), *pure* (pjuǝ), *more* (mɔǝ). There are also murmur triphthongs, as in *fire* (faiǝ), *loyal* (loiǝl).

689. The following table will show the relations of the chief vowels more clearly. Those marked * do not occur in English : —

high back *ʌ	*high mixed* *ï	*high front* i
back a ; ɐ	*mixed* ǝ	*front* e ; æ
high back round u	*high mixed round* ü	*high front round* y
back round o, ɔ	*mixed round* ö	*front round* œ

690. The relations of the English vowels may be shown thus :

Short : . . . ɐ	ǝ	i	e, æ	u	o
Long : . . . aa	ǝǝ				ɔ
Half diphthongs : .		ij	ei	uw	ou
Full diphthongs : . ai, au					oi
Murmur diphthongs :		iǝ	eǝ	uǝ	ɔǝ

Consonants.

691. Consonants admit of a two-fold division (*a*) by form, (*b*) by place.

Form.

692. By form there are five classes :—

693. (*a*) **Open**, in which the passage is narrowed without stoppage, such as (s).

694. (*b*) **Side**, formed by stopping the middle of the passage and leaving it open at the sides, as in (l).

695. (*c*) **Stopped**, formed by complete closure. The voiceless stops (k, t, p) are in English followed by a breath glide or slight puff of breath, thus *cat* almost = (khæth).

696. (*d*) **Nasal** consonants are formed with complete closure of the mouth-passage, the nose-passage being left open, as in (m). When an unstopped (open or side) consonant is formed with the nose-passage open, it is said to be **nasalized.**

697. (*e*) **Trills** are the result of vibration of the flexible parts of the mouth. Thus in the trilled Scotch (r) the point of the tongue vibrates against the gums, the E. (r) in *red* being an open consonant without any trill.

Place.

698. By place there are also five classes :—

699. (*a*) **Back**, formed by the root of the tongue, such as (k, n) in *king* (kin). The back open consonant (x) is the sound of *ch* in the Scotch and German *loch*. The corresponding voice consonant (ʒ) is heard in German *sage*.

700. (*b*) **Front**, formed by the middle of the tongue, such as the front open voice consonant (j) in *you*, which is really a consonantal (i). The corresponding breath consonant (ç) is heard in German *ich* and Scotch *hue*, *Hugh* (cuu), which in Southern E. is pronounced (hjuw).

701. (*c*) **Point**, formed by the tip of the tongue. In the **point-gum** consonants, such as E. (t, d, n, l) the point of the tongue is brought against the gums just behind the teeth ; in the **point-teeth** consonants, such as the point-teeth-open

(b) in *thin*, it is brought against the teeth.   The voice consonant corresponding to (p) is (ð) in *then*.

702. (*d*) **Blade**, formed by the blade of the tongue—that part of it which is immediately behind the point.   (s, z) are blade consonants.   In the **blade-point** consonants, such as the blade-point open (ʃ) in *she*, the blade position is modified by raising the point of the tongue.   The corresponding voice consonant (ʒ) is heard in *measure* (meʒə).

703. The point and blade consonants are included under the name of **forward** consonants.

704. (*e*) **Lip**, formed by the lips, such as (p, m).   The lip-open consonant (ɸ) is the sound produced in blowing out a candle; the corresponding voice consonant occurs in German in such words as *quelle* (kβelə) ; (f, v) are **lip-teeth** consonants.   (wh), as in *why*, and (w) are **lip-back** consonants, formed by narrowing the lip-opening and raising the back of the tongue at the same time, (w) being a consonantal (u).   In Southern E. (wh) is often pronounced (w).

Compound Consonants : Rounding, Fronting.

705. (wh, w) are really **compound** consonants, formed in two places at once.   If instead of back-modifying the lip-open consonant, as in (wh), we lip-modify or **round** the back-open consonant (x), we get the back-round consonant (xw) in German *auch*.   Other consonants may be rounded in the same way, which we express by adding (*w*); thus (rwed) is *red* pronounced with a rounded (r).

706. When a consonant is modified by raising the front of the tongue, it is said to be **front-modified** or fronted, which we express by adding (*j*).   Thus the lip-open front-modified consonant is the sound in French *huit* (βjit) ; it is almost a consonantal (y).

Intermediate Positions.

707. Besides the main positions known as back, front, etc., there are an indefinite number of intermediate positions, which we distinguish roughly as **inner** or nearer the throat, and **outer** or nearer the lips. Thus we have inner (k) before back vowels, as in *caw*, outer (k) before front vowels, as in *key*. E. (r), as in *red*, is an inner point consonant.

THE ASPIRATE.

708. The aspirate (h) is partly an open throat consonant, partly a breath vowel-glide. Thus (h) in *hook* is mainly formed by unvoicing the beginning of the (u), almost as if we were to write the word (w*h*uk). So also the (h) in *he* resembles a weakened (c). (h) also occurs before the consonant (j), as in *hue* (hjuw).

---

709. The following is a table of the chief consonants. Those marked * do not occur in E.

	BREATH.								
	Throat.	*Back.*	*Front.*	*Pcint.*	*Blade.*	*Blade-Point.*	*Lip.*	*Lip-Back.*	*Lip-Teeth.*
Open	h	*x	*ç	*r*h*, þ	s	ʃ	*φ	w*h*	f
Side .	—			*l*h*					
Stop .		k	*c	t			p		
Nasal	—	*ŋ*h*	*ñ*h*	*n*h*			*m*h*		
	VOICE.								
Open	—	*ʒ	j	r, ð	z	ʒ	*β	w	v
Side .	—			l					
Stop .	—	g	*q	d			b		
Nasal	—	ŋ	*ñ	n			m		

710. We generally write (rh), etc., instead of (r*h*) for the sake of convenience.

R IN ENGLISH.

711. (r) in E. occurs only before a vowel following it without any pause, as in *here he is* (hiər ij iz); before a consonant or a pause it is dropped, leaving only the preceding (ə), as in *here she is, he is here* (hiə ʃij iz, hij z hiə). This (ə) is absorbed by a preceding (əə, aa), as in *err, erring, far, far away* (əə, əəriŋ, faa, faar əwei). After (ɔ) the (ə) is kept finally, but dropped before the (r), as in *pour, pouring* (pɔə, pɔriŋ), being also dropped before a consonant in the same word, as in *poured* (pɔd).

712. Short strong vowel + (r) occurs only medially, as in *spirit, merit, courage* (kʊridʒ), *sorry*.

713. Weak (ər, or), as in *after all, measuring* (aaftər ɔl, meʒəriŋ), *one or other* (wʊn or ʊðə), drop the (r) when not followed by a vowel, as in *afterwards* (aaftəwədz), *two or three* (tuw ŏ prij).

714. In Scotch and Irish E. and in many of the dialects of England (r) is kept as a consonant—often trilled—everywhere, in *far, far back*, as well as in *far away*.

LAWS OF SOUND-CHANGE.

715. Sound-changes fall under two main classes—internal and external.

716. **Internal** changes are either organic or acoustic. **Organic** changes are due to the natural tendencies of the organs of speech, as in the change of OE *stān* into MnE *stone* through the natural tendency to pronounce a back vowel without opening the mouth fully, and so to round it.

717. **Acoustic** changes are the result of the impressions which sounds make on the ear, as when one sound is substituted for another because of their likeness to the ear: thus children often make *through* (pruw) into (fruw), and point (r) is changed into back (ʒ) in French and other languages. These are **imitative** changes.

718. **External** changes are those which are independent of organic and acoustic tendencies. Thus the change of *spake* into *spoke* in MnE is not the result of any tendency to change *a* into *o* in MnE, but of the influence of the preterite participle *spoken* (539).

719. Internal changes are further distinguished as isolative and combinative. **Isolative** changes, such as that of OE *a* into MnE *o*, affect a sound without regard to its surroundings, while in **combinative** changes one sound is modified by another one close to it, as in the change of ME (au) in *saw* into MnE (sɔɔ) through (sɔu) or (sou). Here we have two distinct combinative changes : first the rounding of the (a) by the influence of the following (u), and then the lowering of the high (u) till it is merged into the (ɔ). We see that the influence of one sound on another is either **backwards**, as in the change of (au) into (ɔu), or **forwards**, as in the change of (ɔu) into (ɔɔ).

720. All combinative changes are, besides, either conver-gent or divergent. **Convergent** changes, as of (au) into (ɔu) are organic, being due to the tendency to save trouble by making the passage from one sound to another as short and easy as possible.

Complete convergence or **assimilation** in diphthongs makes them into monophthongs, as when (ɔu) becomes (ɔɔ), and in this case is called **smoothing**.

721. Divergent changes are often partly acoustic, being due to the striving for distinctness, as when the half diphthong (ou) in *no* is made into full (au) in Cockney E. But **cleaving**, by which a long vowel is made into a diphthong, is an isolative organic change; it consists generally in forming the first half of the vowel with greater openness—either of the mouth- or the lip-passage—than the second. We see the beginning of cleaving in the E. change of (ii, uu) into (ij, uw), which by divergence could easily become (ei, ou) or (əi, ou) and then (ai, au).

722. We see from all these changes that even the most violent changes—such as that of (ii) into (ai)—are the result of a number of very slight changes—that sound-changes, like all other changes in language, are **gradual.** Organic sound-changes are mainly the result of carelessness, by which the speaker fails to hit the exact position for forming a sound, or laziness, as in combinative changes.

723. The **loss** of sounds or sound-dropping is the result partly of laziness, partly of the sound's indistinctness, as in the frequent dropping of weak vowels, or even syllables, as in the familiar (koz)=*because*; partly of economy, or the tendency to get rid of superfluous distinctions. Thus *sing* was pronounced (sing) in ME, but as (ŋ) occurs only before (g) and (k), the (g) could be dropped without confusing (sin) with (sink) *sink*, and so the superfluous (g) has been dropped in MnE.

OLD-ENGLISH SOUNDS.

Orthography.

724. The Anglo-Saxons brought with them to England their national Runic alphabet, which was founded on one of the Old Greek alphabets or possibly the Latin. On their conversion to Christianity they adopted the Latin alphabet in its British form, to which they afterwards added the two Runic letters þ=*th* and p=*w*. In the British-Latin alphabet—and consequently in the OE alphabet as well—several of the letters had peculiar forms, *g* for instance being written ȝ.

725. Each letter of the Latin alphabet was used to denote the OE sound nearest to that which the letter had in the pronunciation of British Latin, which was more archaic than that of the Continental Latin.

726. Spelling in OE was purely phonetic : the OE scribes wrote as they spoke, as far as the defects of their alphabet would allow them to do so.

727. In this book we supplement the defective distinctions of the OE orthography by adding diacritics, which gives the following new letters—*ę, ǫ, c, g, a,* etc., (ˉ) denoting vowel-length.

Pronunciation.

728. The vowels had the same sounds as in our phonetic notation, the unmodified vowels being all close except *a*. *a* = (a), as in *faran* 'go,' 'travel'; long in *stan* 'stone.' *e* = close (e), as in *etan* 'eat'; long in *me* 'me.' There was also an open *e*, which we write *ę*. as in *męte* 'food.' *i* = close (i), as in *witan* 'know'; long in *win* 'wine.' *o* = close (o), as in *God* 'God'; long in *god* 'good.' There was also an open broad *o*, which we write *ǫ*, as in *lǫng* 'long.' *u* = close (u), as in *sunu* 'son'; long in *hus* 'house.' *y* = close (y) as in *synn* 'sin'; long in *fȳr* 'fire.' The letter *y* thus preserved in OE its original Latin and Greek sound of French *u*; thus the Greek word *humnos* 'hymn' was imported into Latin in the form of *hymnus*—the *y* being simply a tailed Greek *u*—which, again, was imported into OE in the form of *ymen*, the first vowel having the same sound in all three languages. *æ* = (æ), as in *fædęr* 'father'; long in *hælan* 'heal.' *œ* had the sound of close (œ), as in *blœtsian* 'bless'; long in *fœt* 'feet.' The diphthongs *ea. eo* had the stress on the first element, which was open— = (æ)—in *ea. ea* (·æa, ·ǽæa), close in *eo. eo* (·eo, ·eeo) : *hęard* 'hard,' *dęad* 'dead'; *eorþe* 'earth,' *deop* 'deep.' In *ie* the two elements were originally pronounced separately, but in ordinary West-Saxon the diphthong was smoothed into open (*i*), as in *ieldra* 'older,' 'elder'; long in *hieran* 'hear.'

729. The following consonants require notice. *c* = (k), as in *cene* 'bold.' *c* = (c). resembling in sound our *ch* = (tʃ), as in *cirice* 'church.' These two sounds are sometimes distinguished in the manuscripts by writing *k* for the back-consonant. as in *kene*, and keeping *c* to denote the front sound. *g* when not initial was pronounced (ȝ), as in *dagas* 'days,' *burg* 'city,' *halga* 'saint,' except in the combination *ng*, which was pronounced (ng), as in *lang* 'long,' *singan* 'sing.' *g* in the combination *ng* was a front stop, this combination having the sound (ñq), as in *sengan* 'singe,' where the OE *g* has a sound very similar to that of the MnE *g* in *singe*. *cg* had the sound (qq), as in *brycg* 'bridge,' where, again, the OE sound closely resembles the (ʤ) of *bridge*; the *c* in this digraph is intended to indicate the front sound, the less frequent (gg) being generally written *gg*, as in *frogga* 'frog.' Initial *g* also had the sound (q), but seems also to have been pronounced (j): *geard* 'yard,' 'court,' *genumen* 'taken.' Non-initial *g* had the sound (j), except in the combinations *ng*, *cg*; *dæg* (day), *seggep* 'says,' *hergian* 'ravage.'

730. *x* = (ks), but in many words it was originally pronounced (xs), as in *weaxan* 'grow.'

731. *f, s, p* had the voice sounds (v, z, ð) between vowels and between *r, l* and vowels, as in *drīfan* 'drive,' *freosan* 'freeze,' *eorpe* 'earth.'

732. Initial *h* had the same sound as in E. *hw*, as in *hwīt* 'white,' = (wh). So also *hl, hr, hn* represented the voiceless sounds of (l, r, n) respectively, as in *hlud* 'loud,' *hring* 'ring,' *hnutu* 'nut.' In *hw* etc. the *h* and the *w* were originally pronounced separately. Non-initial *h*—'strong *h*'—had the sound of (x) in Scotch *loch*, as in *purh* 'through'; in some words it had the sound of (c) in German *ich*, especially after a front vowel, as in *gesihp* 'sight.'

733. *r* was always trilled, as in Scotch. *c, g, w* were pronounced clearly before consonants in such words as *cnawan* 'know,' *gnagan* 'gnaw,' *wrītan* 'write,' *wlac* 'lukewarm.'

734. Double consonants were pronounced double, or long, as in *mann* 'man'—distinct from *geman* 'I remember,' where the *n* was quite short—*sunne* 'sun' (the *nn* as in *penknife*) distinct from *sunu* 'son.'

Stress.

735. In OE the general principle of word-stress is to put the strong stress on the first syllable of a word, as in *·fiscas* ' fishes,' *·fiscere* ' fisher,' *·ryhtwis* ' rightly wise,' ' righteous,' *·misdǣd* ' misdeed.'

736. In sentences, form-words and words of subordinate meaning generally had weak stress, as in MnE; conjunctions, such as *and* ' and,' prepositions, such as *of* ' of,' ' off,' *on* ' on, and many other particles had weak stress, as also many of the pronouns, such as *ic* ' I,' including the definite article *se* ' the.' So also in separate words the inflectional and derivative elements were subordinated in stress to the body of the word.

737. The stress of full-words themselves was often subordinated to that of other full-words. In OE an adjunct-word is generally put before the noun it modifies, and takes a stronger stress than its head-word, as in the combination adjective or genitive + noun: *·god .mann* 'a good man,' *·gode :dǣda* ' good deeds,' *-þæs ·cyninges :sunu* ' the king's son.'

738. In compounds the same principle was followed: the modifying word came first, and took the chief stress, as in *ryhtwis.* So also the compound *dōmdæg* ' judgment-day' had the same stress as *domes dæg* ' day of judgment,' ' doomsday.'

But there are some exceptions to this rule of putting the stress on the first element of compounds :—

739. Group-compounds of preposition + noun, such as the adverbs *ofdune* ' down,' literally ' off-the-hill,' as in *he eode ofdune* ' he went down,' *onbæc* ' back,' literally ' on-the-back,' *tōdæg* ' today,' were of course originally independent word-groups in which the prepositions were without stress in accordance with the general rule, so that the stress necessarily fell on the succeeding noun.

740. Adverbs of full and distinct meaning are treated like adjectives as regards stress, taking strong stress when followed

by another word with which they form a group, as in *wīde
ge:siene* 'widely seen,' 'seen far and wide' [compare the
compound *wīdcūþ* 'widely known']. So also when a verb
follows, as in *·inn :gan* 'go in,' *·bī :standan* 'stand by,' 'help.'
But if the verb precedes, it takes the principal stress: *he ·eode
:inn* 'he went in,' *he ·stōd him bī* 'he helped him.' When
these particles precede their verbs, they are felt to form compounds with them through the group having the same stress as
compounds in general, so that we may write these groups as
single words—*inngān, bistandan.* But as these particles are, as
we see, liable to be separated from their verbs in other constructions, we call them **separable** particles.

741. But if these particles are compounded with nouns or
adjectives instead of verbs, they cannot be shifted, as in
·inngang 'going in,' 'entrance,' *bīspell* 'by-tale,' 'parable,'
whose elements can no more be separated than those of
ryhtwīs, etc.

742. In OE there is also a class of **inseparable** particles,
such as *for-* in *forgiefan* 'forgive,' which has no connection
with the preposition *for* 'for,' never occurring as an independent word. These inseparable particles ought strictly
speaking to be regarded as derivative elements, like the *un-* in
·uncūþ 'unknown,' but as many of them lost their independence only at a comparatively recent period in OE, it is
allowable to regard *forgiefan,* etc., as compounds. The inseparable prefix *be-* in *be·settan* 'beset' is, indeed, the same
word as the preposition *be* 'by,' although they have diverged
in meaning.

743. While abstract nouns compounded with inseparable
particles throw the stress on to the particle in the usual way,
as in *·forwyrd* 'destruction,' parallel to *inngang,* the corresponding verbs take the stress on the verb itself, as in *for-
·weorþan* 'perish,' *forgiefan.* This shifting of stress is
often accompanied by phonetic weakening of the particle;
thus to the strong form of the prefix in *·bigang* 'going

round,' 'cultivation,' 'worship' corresponds the weak *be-* in *began* 'go round,' 'cultivate,' etc., *besettan.*

The explanation of this is that *forwyrd, bīgang, inngang,* etc., were inseparable compounds already in Parent Germanic, at a time when *forweorþan,* etc. were still separable compounds like *inn-gan.* At that time the two elements of *forweorþan* etc. could stand in any order, and the principal stress could fall either on the particle or the verb, according as the one or the other was the more emphatic. After a time, some of the prefixes, such as *for-,* became vague in meaning, so that they lost not only their stress but their independence.

Quantity.

744. Long vowels in weak syllables were shortened in OE, as in *began* (**743**).

745. On the other hand short final strong vowels were lengthened, as in *hwa* 'who,' *þu* 'thou' = Germanic *hwa, þu.* Hence the short vowel of the unstressed article *se* in *-se mann* 'the man' is lengthened when the word is used in the sense of 'he,' as in *se -þe* 'he who.'

746. In Anglian, short vowels were lengthened before vowel-like consonants followed by another consonant— 'group-lengthening'—as in *ald* 'old,' *lǫng* 'long,' *blīnd* 'blind,' *dumb* 'dumb' = Early West-Saxon *eald, lǫng, lang, blind, dumb.* These lengthenings appear also in Late West-Saxon.

Vowels.

747. a (o), **æ, ea.** These vowels all correspond to Germanic *a,* still preserved in Modern German; thus OE *mann, fæder, heard* = German *mann, vater, hart.* Germanic *a* in the Oldest E. was kept only before nasals, as in *mann, hand, lang.* Everywhere else it was fronted to *æ,* as in *wæs* 'was,' *æcer* 'field,' *fæder.* Before 'group *r* and *l*,' that is, before *r* and *l* followed by a consonant, and before strong *h* the voice-glide (ə) was developed, as in E. (hiəriŋ) § **711**, which afterwards by phonetic divergence developed into full (a), as in *heard, earm* 'arm'; *eall, eald* 'old'; *geseah* 'saw,' *eahta* 'eight,' *weaxan* (**730**). Before a back vowel in the next syllable *æ* became the back vowel *a*, as in *dagas* 'days,' *dagum* 'to days' dat., compared with *dæg* 'day,' gen. *dæges.* These are the West-Saxon forms. In Anglian *a* before nasals became *ǫ*—as also often in Early West-Saxon—and *æ* before group *l* became *a*, so that the Anglian forms are *mǫnn, hǫnd* (**746**), *lǫng*; *heard,* etc.; *all, ald* (**746**).

748. i, e, eo. In Germanic, *e* before group-nasals became *i*, whence OE *bindan* 'bind,' *singan* 'sing' compared with *helpan* 'help.' In OE itself *e* also became *i* before single nasals, as in *niman* 'take' compared with *stelan* 'steal.' The vowel in such words as *witan* 'know' is Germanic and Arian *i*. In OE *e* before group *r* became *eo* much in the same way as *æ* became *ea* (**747**), as in *steorra* 'star,' *eorþe. e, i* became *eo, io* before a back—especially a back round—vowel in the next syllable, as in *heofon* 'heaven,' *cliopian* 'call,' the forms *hefon, clipian* also occurring.

For the change of weak *eo* into *ea, a,* as in *(e)am = eom* 'am,' see § **1067**.

749. u, o. In Germanic, *o* became *u* before group-nasals, and in OE itself *o* became *u* before single nasals, whence OE *gebunden* 'bound' compared with *geholpen* 'helped,' *genumen* 'taken' compared with *gestolen* 'stolen.' In such a word as *sunu* 'son,' the *u*s are Germanic and Arian.

750. The Germanic vowel *æ* is preserved in West-Saxon, as in *fær* 'danger,' *æfen* 'evening,' being narrowed to *e* in Anglian and Kentish—*fer, efen.*

MUTATION.

751. Mutation is the influence exercised by a vowel on the vowel of a preceding syllable, by which the first vowel is modified in the direction of the second one. Thus in OE *gecoren* 'chosen' = Old High German *gikoran,* compared with

OE *curun* later *curon* 'they chose,' *u* has been lowered to *o* by the influence of the *a*. This is therefore an *a*-mutation of *u*.

752. But the most important mutations in OE are the front mutations, caused by Germanic *i* and *j*, which after they had caused the mutation were generally lost or modified in OE. In these mutations the influence of the *i* or *j* on the vowel was not direct; the *i* or *j* first front-modified the preceding consonant, which in its turn influenced the preceding vowel; thus OE *ęnde* 'end' from Germanic *andio* passed through the following stages: (anjdji, enjdji), ęndi, *ęnde*. In most cases these fronted consonants were unfronted after they had modified the preceding vowel, as we see in the case of *ęnde*. But the fronted *c* and *g*—which we write *c, g* —were kept, as in *wręcca* 'exiled man,' which is our MnE word *wretch*, compared with *wracu* 'state of exile,' *wrecan* 'drive,' *sęcgan* 'say' compared with *sagu* 'saying,' 'saw.'

753. The following are the mutations in their Early West-Saxon forms:—

e . . . i.   *beran* 'carry,' *birẹþ* (Oldest E. *biriþ*) 'carries'; *cwẹþan* 'say,' *cwide* (Oldest E. *cwidi*) 'saying,' 'speech.'

a (æ) . . . e.   *faran* 'go,' 'travel,' *fẹrian* 'convey'; *mann* 'man' *mẹnn* (Germanic *manni*) 'men.'

ā . . . æ.   *hal* 'whole,' 'sound,' *hǣlan* 'heal'; *an* 'one,' *ǣnig* 'any.' This 'mutation *æ*' remains in the non-West-Saxon dialects, which change Germanic *æ* into *e*. For convenience we will in future distinguish the West-Saxon Germanic *æ* by writing it *æ̣*, as in *ǣfen* contrasted with *hǣlan*. Mutated Germanic *æ* remains unchanged in West-Saxon, as in *lǣce* 'physician' (Oldest E. *lǣci*), *dǣd* 'deed' (Germanic *dædi*), and becomes *e* in the other dialects: *lece*, *dēd*.

ea, eo . . . ie.   *eald* 'old,' *ieldra* 'older,' *nieht* (Germanic *nahti*) 'night'; *heord* 'herd' *hierde* 'shepherd,' In Late

West-Saxon this *ie* becomes *y* or *i* : *yldra, niht, hyrde.* In Anglian the one *ie* appears as *ę*, the other as *i* : *ęldra, ęldra, nęht* ; *hirde* (Oldest Anglian *hirdi*).

ēa, ēo . . . ie. *geleafa* 'belief,' *gelīefan* 'believe,' *eaca* ' increase ' (noun), *eac* ' also,' *īecan* 'to increase ' ; *geseon* 'see,' *gesīene* 'visible.' *ie* in Late West-Saxon becomes *y̆, i* : *gelȳfan, īcan, gesȳne.* In the other dialects it becomes *e* : *gelēfan, ecan, ġesēne.*

u . . . y. *full* ' full,' *gefyllan* ' to fill,' *cyning* ' king.' *y* in Late Kentish becomes *e* by lowering and unrounding, as in *ġefellan.*

u . . . ȳ. *cuþ* ' known,' *cȳþan* 'proclaim,' *mus* ' mouse,' *mȳs* ' mice.' *y* becomes *e* in Late Kentish, as in *mes.*

o . . . œ. *dohtor* ' daughter,' dat. *dœhter.* *œ* was unrounded into *e* in Late OE, the change beginning already in Early West-Saxon : *dehter.* As Germanic *o* became *u* before *i* in the same way as *e* became *i* (**753**), *y* is the most usual OE mutation of *o*, as in *gold* ' gold,' *gylden* (older *guldīn*) ' golden,' *fox* ' fox,' *fyxen* ' vixen.'

ō . . . œ. *foda* ' food ' *fœdan* ' feed,' *fot* ' foot,' *fœt* ' feet.' *œ* afterwards became *e*, the change beginning in Early West-Saxon : *fedan, fet.*

Consonant Influence.

754. In West-Saxon the front glide between *c, g* and a following vowel often developed into a full *e* forming a diphthong with the vowel.

755. cæ-, gæ- passed through (cjæ, ce·æ, qjæ, qe·æ) and then by phonetic divergence and stress-shifting (ce·a, c·ea, etc.) into *cea-, gea-*, as in *sceal* ' shall,' *geaf* ' gave ' [compar *cwaþ* ' said '] = non-West-Saxon *scēal, gaf.* This *ea* was mutated into *ie* in West-Saxon in such words as the noun *ciele* ' chill ' compared with *calan* ' be cold,' *giest* ' stranger,' [compare German *gast*] = non-West-Saxon *cęle, gęst.*

756. cǣ-, gǣ- became *cea-, gea-*, as in *sceap* ' sheep,' *geafon*

' they gave ' [compare *cwǽdon* ' they said ']=non-West-Saxon *scep, gêfon.*

757. ce-, ge- became *cie-, gie-,* as in *scield* ' shield,' *giefan* ' give' [compare *cwepan*] = non-West-Saxon *sceld, sceld, gefan.*

758. Through similar changes *g* followed by a diphthong in West-Saxon often corresponds to Germanic *j,* which in OE seems to have been made into the stop consonant (q). as in *gear* ' year' Anglian *ger, geoc* ' yoke,' *geong* ' young,' compared with German *jahr* (=Germanic *jǽr*), *joch, jung.*

759. In Anglian, the back consonants *c. h, g* smooth a preceding diphthong. *ea* became *æ,* as in *gesæh, waxan=* non-Anglian (West-Saxon and Kentish) *gesæh, weaxan. eo* became *e,* as in *fehtan* ' fight,' *werc* ' work ' (noun)—where, as is often the case, the influence of the back consonant passes through an intervening vowel-like consonant— = West Saxon *feohtan. weorc. ea. eo* became *é,* as in *ec, ege* ' eye,' *heh* ' high,' *flegan* ' to fly '=West-Saxon *eac, eage, heah, fleogan.*

760. *w* often changes a following *eo* into *o* or *u,* especially in Late OE, as in *sweostor* 'sister,' later *swustor, sweord, sword, swurd* ' sword.'

Consonants.

761. In OE *h* between vowels or between vowel-like consonants and vowels was dropped, often with lengthening of the preceding vowel. as in *furh* ' furrow,' dat. plur. *fürum, Wealh* ' foreigner,' ' Welshman,' plur. *Wealas, Wéalas, Wielisc* ' Welsh.' When two vowels came together in this way. they were often made into a diphthong, as in *geseon* ' see ' from *seohan* [compare *geseah* ' saw '].

.62. Open *g, g* became *h* before a breath consonant, as in *byht* ' bending ' [*bugan* ' bend '].

763. Final open *g* was also unvoiced in Late West-Saxon, as in *troh* ' trough,' *genoh* ' enough,' *burh*=earlier *trog. genog, burg.*

764. *r* is often transposed, as in *iernan* ' run '—the original form being preserved in *gerinnan* 'run together,' 'coagulate' —especially in Late Northumbrian, as in *þirda* ' third' = West-Saxon *þridda* [compare *þreo* ' three '].

765. *s* is often transposed in the same way, as in Late West-Saxon *āxian* ' ask,' *cirps* ' curly '=earlier *āscian, crisp.*

766. *r* in some words does not correspond to Germanic *r* but to a Germanic modification of *s*, as in *wæron* 'were' compared with *wæs* ' was,' *gecoren* ' chosen,' *cyre* ' choice' compared with *ceosan* ' choose.'   So also *g* and *d* often represent Germanic modifications of *h* and *þ* respectively, as in *cwædon, cwide* compared with *cwcþan, slægen* ' struck,' *slaga* ' slayer ' compared with *slean* [from **sleahan*] ' strike,' ' kill.'   These changes are the result of weak stress of the syllable containing *s, þ, h* in Early Germanic.   Hence we call the resulting *r* 'weak *r* ' to distinguish it from *r* = Germanic *r*, and so with the other consonants.

767. *þ* in the combinations *tþ, dþ, sþ* becomes *t*, to which a preceding *d* is assimilated giving the combinations *tt, st*, as in Early West-Saxon *bitt = bīteþ* ' bites ' and *bideþ* 'waits,' *cīest* ' chooses ' from *ceosan*.   We occasionally find *þæt tæt* written instead of *þæt þæt*, showing that consonants in separate words were assimilated.   *þætte* ' that' (conjunction) is regularly written so, being equivalent to *þæt þe*.

768. Double consonants in OE often represent a Germanic single consonant + *j*, as in *sellan* ' give ' *sceþþan* ' injure,' *settan* ' set '=Gothic *saljan, skaþjan, satjan*, the single consonant appearing in such forms as *seleþ, sceþeþ, seteþ* ' he gives,' etc., which point to older **saliþ*, etc.   Germanic *kj, gj, fj* appear in OE respectively as *cc, cg* and *bb*, as in *wrecca* ' one exiled,' *lecgan* ' lay,' *hebban* ' raise ' compared with *wracu* ' state of exile,' *læg* ' he lay,' *hafen* ' raised.'   Germanic *rj*, on the other hand, appears as *ri* in OE, as in *derian* ' injure ' [cp. *daru* ' injury '].

769. In OE itself *c, t, þ* are often doubled before *r* and *l*, as in *biter*, *bitter* ' bitter ' [cp. *bitan* ' bite '], *æppel* ' apple ' [cp. *apulder* ' apple-tree '], *nædre*, *næ̂ddre* ' serpent,' *fod(d)or* ' food '; and in the later forms *miċċle* plur. of *micel* ' great,' *deoppra* adj., *deoppor* adv. ' deeper.'

Gradation.

770. By gradation we understand certain traditional con-nections between the vowels—most clearly shown in the conju-gation of the ' strong ' verbs—which enable us to classify them under the following **gradation-series** :—

a . . . ō. *faran* ' proceed,' *for* ' proceeded '; *for* ' journey,' *gefæra*, *gefera* ' companion.'

e (i, eo) . . . a (æ, ea) . . . u (o). *windan* ' wind,' *wand* ' he wound,' *wundon* ' they wound '; *wendan* ' turn.' *beran* ' carry,' *bær*, *boren* ; *byr-þen* ' burden.' *beorgan* ' protect,' *bearg*, *burgon*, *geborgen* ; *beorg* ' mountain,' *burg* ' fortress,' ' city,' *borg* ' pledge,' ' security,' *borgian* ' borrow.'

a (æ, ea) . . . æ. *bær* ' he carried,' *bæron* ' they carried '; *bær* ' bier.' *spræc* ' he spoke,' *spræ̂con* ' they spoke '; *spræc* ' speech.'

ī . . . a . . . i. *writan* ' write,' *wrāt* ' he wrote,' *writon* ' they wrote '; *gewrit* ' writing ' (noun). *belīfan* ' remain '; *lāf* ' residue,' ' remains,' whence by mutation *læfan* ' leave.'

eo (u) . . . ea . . . u (o). *ceosan* ' choose,' *ceas* ' he chose,' *curon* ' they chose,' *gecoren* ' chosen '; *cyre* ' choice.' *for-leosan* ' lose '; *leas* ' devoid of,' *ā-līesan* ' release '; *losian* ' be lost,' ' perish.' *bugan* ' bend,' ' bow,' *beag*, *bugon*, *gebogen* ; *beag*, ' ring '; *boga* ' bow ' (noun), *byht* ' bending.'

These vowel-relations are the result of a variety of compli-cated changes in Germanic and Arian, their ultimate cause being shifting of stress and variations of intonation in Parent Arian. Thus in the pret. pl. and past participles the root-vowels were without stress in Arian; hence the short vowels in *-writen*, *curon*, *-coren*, *-bogen*—and also in *gewrit*, *boga*, etc.—

are weakenings of the diphthongs and long vowels in *writan,* *ceosan, bugan,* where they had full stress.

Hence also the weakened vowels are associated with weak *r, g, d* (766), as in *curon* compared with *ceosan.*

MIDDLE ENGLISH.

Orthography.

771. In the ME period the OE was superseded by the Old French orthography—Norman at first, but afterwards Parisian.

772. Old French orthography was founded on the traditional pronunciation of Latin; but by the time French was first written down—probably in the 9th century—the tradition of the Old Latin pronunciation had been partially lost.

773. In the 9th century pronunciation of Latin, *y* had lost its old value, having been unrounded into (i), and so had come to be a mere orthographic variant of *i.* So when Latin *u* was fronted to (yy) in French, as in *lune* (lyynə) from Latin *luna,* the *u* was kept as the symbol of the new sound (y). And when the French orthography was introduced into England, the sound of OE *y* was represented by *u,* which we write *u* to distinguish it from ME *u* = OE *u.* Hence in early Southern ME *sunne* ' sun ' and *sünne* ' sin ' = OE *synn* were written alike. In Old French there was a diphthong *ui* = (yi), which in Anglo-French was smoothed into (yy), and so was used—together with simple *u*—to express (yy) not only in French words, such as *fruit, früt* ' fruit,' but also in E. words, such as *fuir, für* ' fire,' *builden* ' build ' = OE *fyr, byldan, byldan.*

774. *y,* being thus superfluous, was almost completely disused for a time in Early ME, but in Late ME—as in Late Old French—it was written in many cases instead of *i*; because *i* was written without any dot, and so was liable to be mistaken for a part of another letter, especially *n*, *m*, *u*.   Hence it became usual to write *y* in such words as *bynden*, *wyues* = OE *bindan*, *wifes*.   It also became usual to write *y* at the end of words, as in *many*, *day* = Early ME *mani*, *dai*.

775. In Early Norman French *o* in many words had a sound between close (o) and (u), and as *u* represented the sound (y) as well as (u) in ME as in French, it was found convenient to use *o* for the sound (u)—in which case we write it *o*—especially in combination with such letters as *n*, *m*, *u* (= *v*) where *u* would cause graphic confusion, as in *comen* ‘come.’ *loue* ‘love’ = OE *cuman*, *lufu*; also before single consonants followed by a vowel, as in *bote* ‘but,’ *corage* ‘courage,’ because the earlier ME spellings *bute*, *curage* seemed to suggest (yy).

776. In Late Parisian the older diphthong (ou) was smoothed into (uu), as in *douz* (duuts) ‘sweet,’ and so *ou* was introduced into Late ME as the symbol of (uu), as in *hous* = earlier *hus* = OE *hus* ‘house,’ the actual sound remaining unchanged.

777. In Late Latin *e* was written instead of *ae*, *oe*, which fell into disuse, the classical *caelum*, *poena*, for instance, being written *celum*, *pena*; and so in Old French *e* was used to express open as well as close (e), and this usage passed into ME.   We write the long ME open sound $\bar{e}$ to distinguish *dēd* ‘dead’ from *dēd* ‘deed,’ the latter having the close sound. So also we express the long open *o* by ϱ, as in *stǫn* ‘stone’ distinguished from *mone* ‘moon,’ the two sounds not being generally distinguished—any more than the two *e* s—in ME orthography.   The Old French diphthong *ie* was smoothed into close (ee) in Anglo-French, and so came to express the latter sound in such words as *meschief* ‘mischief,’ *lief* ‘dear.’

778. In Parisian French, Latin *c* = (k) before front vowels, as in *ciel*, passed through (ts) into (s).   In some cases it developed into (tʃ), which combination was expressed by

ch, as in *chien*.   Latin *g* = (g) became 'soft' (dʒ) before front
vowels, as in *geste* 'exploit' from Latin *gesta*.　　Latin *j* = (j)
also developed into (dʒ), as in *ja* — Latin *jam*.　　Latin *qv*, *gv*
= (kw, gw) soon dropped their (w) in Old French, so that *qu*,
gu came to be regarded as symbols of 'hard' (k, g) respectively, especially before front vowels, as in *qui*, *langue* from
Latin *qvī*, *lingva*, the former being also expressed by
k—*ki*.

779. Hence in ME the old *c* was written *k* before front
vowels, as in *king*, as also when doubled, as in *þikke* 'thick,'
cw being expressed by the Early Old French *qu*, as in *quene*
'queen' = OE *cwen*.　*c* was kept before back vowels and
generally before consonants, as in *cumen, comen, clęne* 'clean.'
The ME development of OE *c* having nearly the sound
of French *ch*, this digraph was used to express it, as in
chirche = OE *cirice*.　*c* = (s) was used only in French words,
such as *face*.

780. In ME the difference in form between the OE ʒ
(**724**) and the French *g* was utilized phonetically.　The
letter *g* was assigned to (g), as in *god* 'good,' and the soft
French *g*, as in *geste* 'exploit,' and also to the ME development of OE stopped *g*, which had nearly the sound of (dʒ),
as in *sengen* 'singe,' *brigge* 'bridge' = OE *sęngan, brycg*.
Hard *g* was also expressed by the French *gu*, as it still is in
tongue = OE *tunge*.　*j* = (dʒ) was written only in French
words, such as *juggen* 'judge.'　　　ʒ, on the other hand, was
restricted to the open sounds, both back and front, as in
daʒes, ʒung = OE *dagas, geong*, the latter sound being afterwards expressed by *y*, as in MnE: *yong, young*.　　　　.

781. After much fluctuation OE strong *h* was written *gh*,
as in *right, doghter*.　　　　　　　　　　　　　　　　.

782. Latin *z* still kept its sound (dz) in Early Old French
—where it was also used to express (ts), as in *douz* 'sweet'—
and did not become simple (z) till a later period.　Hence it is
not till the end of the ME period that they began to write *z*

instead of $s = (z)$ in E. words, as in *wezele* 'weazel,' generally written *wesele*.

783. The Latin sound (w), which was expressed indifferently by the angular v or the round u, became (v) in Old French, the old symbol being kept, so *u, v* became the symbol of voiced OE *f* in ME, as in *luve* = OE *lufu*. The sound (w) was introduced again into Old French from Old German in such words as *warde*, from Old Low German *warda* (= OE *weard* 'custody'), developing into (gw), later (g) in Parisian—*guarde*. In those Old French dialects which kept German (w) it was expressed by two angular *u*s joined together, whence we still call the ligature ' double *u.*' In ME *w* soon superseded the OE p (**724**). As *w* in OE *snaw* 'snow' was practically an (u), in ME *w* came into general use in diphthongs, as in *snow, how* = OE *hu*, the *ow* = (uu) in the latter being only a written diphthong.

784. The other Runic letter *þ* was used throughout the ME period, but the digraph *th* soon came into use to express the voice as well as the breath sound of *þ*, as in *brēþen, brethen* (breeðən) ' breathe,' *brēþ, breth* (breeb) ' breath.' In Old French *th* was written only in learned words, proper names, etc., and had the sound (t), which it often kept in ME as well; we still pronounce such words as *Thomas* with a (t), as in ME. Old French *ph* = (f) was also used only in learned words and names, *f* being often substituted for it ; it was used in ME in such learned words as *phisik* 'physic,' also written *fisik*.

Stress.

785. In ME the noun- and adjective-prefixes *al-, mis-, un-* throw the stress forward, as in *al·mihti, mis·ded, un·cuþ* ' unknown' = OE ·*ı 'mih·tiġ, ·nais·ᵈþ* ' ·*u ̣ ū,* .

786. In Old French the stress generally fell on the same syllable as in Latin, as in *na·ture* = Latin *nā·turam*. Through the dropping of final Latin syllables many French words thus came to have the stress on the last syllable, as in *o·nour* = *ho·norem, pi·te* = *pie·tātem.* When first introduced into ME French words kept their original stress : *nā·ture, o·nur, pi·te ;* but such words afterwards threw the stress back on to the first syllable by the analogy of the native E. words, such as *·fader, ·bodi,* becoming *·natūre,* etc.

787. In longer French words, where it would have been inconvenient to throw the stress back to the first syllable, it was drawn back from the end to the middle of the word, as in *sove·reynete, con·dicioun* (kon·disiuun) and the other words in *-ioun* = Latin *-ionem.*

788. Many words of French origin compounded with particles, such as *a·vow* (a·vuu), *de·fense, dis·ēse* (dis·cezə), keep their original stress by the analogy of native words such as *a·rīsen, be·cumen.*

Quantity.

789. The first quantity-change that took place in ME was the lengthening of OE short consonants after a short strong vowel, so that OE *in* 'in' and *inn* 'dwelling' were levelled under the latter form ; and as it was no longer necessary to mark the distinction, the OE double consonants were written single, as in *al, man* = OE *eall, mann.* But double consonants before vowels were kept in ME in pronunciation as well as spelling, so that, for instance, *sunne* 'sun' = OE *sunne* was kept distinct from *sune* 'son' = OE *sunu,* these two words never rhyming on one another in verse.

790. The OE group-lengthenings were kept up in ME, as in *eld, long, blīnd, dumb, doumb* = Old Anglian *ald, long, blīnd, dumb.* Otherwise OE long vowels were generally shortened before two consonants, as in *askien, wisdom* [compare ME *wīs* 'wise'], *kepte* 'kept' pret. = OE *āscian, wīsdom, cēpte.* But length was often preserved before *st,* as in *lēst* 'least,' *prēst* 'priest' = OE *lǣst, preost.*

In the transition from ME to MnE the long vowels before *ng* and *mb* were shortened, whence MnE *long, young* (jɛŋ), *dumb* compared with *old* (ould), *blind* (blaind). Hence also OE *-anc, -ǫnc* appears as *-ank* in MnE, while OE *-ang, -ǫng* appears as *-ong,* as in *lank*＝OE *hlanc* compared with *long*＝OE *lang.*

791. In Late ME short vowels before a single consonant followed by another vowel were lengthened, as in *name, mę̄te* ' meat,' *brǭken* 'broken'＝Early ME *name, mete, ibroken*＝OE *nama, męte, gebrocen.* We call these lengthened vowels ' new-longs ' as opposed to the ' old-longs ' in such words as *wīn* ' wine '＝OE *wīn.* But the high vowels *i, ü, u* were never lengthened, as in *writen* 'written,' *dude* ' did,' *sune* ＝ OE *gewriten, dyde, sunu.*

792. Vowels were not lengthened in final strong syllables, as in *smal, swan, yaf* ' gave,' *God*＝OE *smæl, swan, geaf, God,* because the final consonants had already been lengthened (**789**).

793. Short vowels are often preserved in Late as well as Early ME before a single consonant followed by the full vowel *i,* as in *mani, peni, bodi,* or weak *e* ＋ a vowel-like consonant (r, l, n, m), as in *hamer, feter, coper* ; *sadel, hovel; seven, troden,* all of which still have short vowels in Present English. This is called **back-shortening.** Originally long vowels are sometimes back-shortened in ME, as in *laþer* from OE *leaþor.* But there are several exceptions to the general principle of back-shortening, as in Late ME *āker, cradel, stǫlen*＝OE *æcer, cradel, gestolen.*

The explanation of back-shortening is that the lengthening is shifted from the strong vowel to the final *i* or the vowel-like consonant, just as in Present English *pity* is often lengthened into (píti) [**944**].

Vowels.

794. In ME the OE weak vowels are generally levelled under *e,* especially when final: ME *name, beren, sune*＝OE *nama, beran, sunu.*   There was a tendency to drop weak *e* altogether after another weak syllable, as in *ladi*, ' lady' from OE *hlǽfdige.*

795. Many words which in OE end in a consonant, take final *e* in ME, which they get from the OE inflected forms; thus ME *quene* ' queen' comes not from the OE nom. sing. *cwen*, but from the acc. sing. *cwene*, plur. nom. *cwena*, etc. Other examples are *sinne* ' sin,' *dale* ' valley,' *bede* ' prayer' = OE *synn, dæl, gebed*, plurals *synna, dalu, gebedu.* Such forms as *narwe* ' narrow,' *yelwe* ' yellow' = OE *nearu, geolu*, plurals *nearwe, geolwe* arose in the same way.

796. a. In the strong vowels the most marked and earliest change is the smoothing of the OE diphthongs, shown in Late ME *hard, sterre* ' star,' *bręd* ' bread,' *dęp* ' deep' = OE *heard, steorra, bread, deop.*

797. In Early ME *ea* became (æ), which was generally written *e*, as in *herd, wes* = OE *heard, wæs.* This broad (æ) was then still further broadened to (a), giving Late ME *hard, was.* OE *a* was kept throughout in such words as *man, faren* = OE *mann, faran.* ME *a* in such words as *all, half*, comes from Anglian *all, half*, not from West-Saxon *eall, healf.*

798. i, u. In North-Thames E. *i* corresponds not only to OE *i*, as in *smiþ* = OE *smiþ*, but also to OE *y*, as in *sinne, dide.* But (y) was still preserved in the Southern dialect, as in *sünne, dude*, being represented by *e* in Middle as well as Old Kentish, as in *senne.* The London dialect generally has *i* = OE *y*, but some words have the Southern, and the few the Kentish forms : *sinne, büsi, kernel* = OE *synn, bysig* 'occupied,' *cyrnel*,' kernel.' In some words (y) was broadened to (u), especially after lip-consonants, as in *worien* ' worry,' *moche* ' much' = OE *wyrgan, mycel, micel.*

799. e. OE close (e) became open (ę) in Early ME, so that OE *e* and *ę* were levelled under the latter sound, which we write simply *e* in ME, as in *helpen, eten, rest, mete* = OE *helpan, etan ; ręst, męte.* OE *eo* also became open *e* in Late

ME, as in *erþe, hevene*. All these *e*s are liable to be lengthened in Late ME (**791**), as in *ēlen, mēle*.

800. u. OE *u* was kept unchanged in ME, as in *sune*.

801. o. OE close *o* became open in Early ME, as in *folk, nose, bodien* 'proclaim'=OE *folc, nosu, bodian*, being liable to lengthening in Late ME, as in *nǫse, bǫdien*.

802. The OE long vowels *ī, e, æ, u, o* were generally preserved unchanged in ME. *e, æ* being also the representatives of OE *eo, ea* respectively (**796**): *win, kene* 'bold,' *dep, sē* 'sea,' *hēved* 'head,' *hūs, hous, god* 'good'=OE *win, cene, deop, sǣ, heafod, hus, god*. So also ME *finden, feld* 'field,' *hund* 'dog,' *word* 'word'=Anglian *findan, feld, hund, word* (**746**). *ı* is sometimes the result of raising Anglian *e* before open *g* and front *h*, as in *īe* 'eye,' *hīh* 'high'=Old Anglian *ege, heh*, West-Saxon *eage, heah*, the open *g*=(j) being absorbed. So also open *g* was absorbed in ME by a preceding *u* or *u*, as in *fuel* 'bird,' *buen* later *bowen* 'bend'=OE *fugol, bugan*. It is to be observed that ME *e* represents not only the common OE *e* in *cene*, but also the Anglian *e*=West-Saxon *æ* and *īe*, as in *even* 'evening,' *dēde* 'deed,' *heren* 'hear,' *isene* 'seen'=West-Saxon *āfen, dǣd, hīeran, gesīene*. But *ę*=*æ* is frequent before and after *r*, as in *drēden* 'dread,' *þęr* 'there,' *wēren* 'were'=West-Saxon *ondrǣdan, þǣr, wǣron*.

803. In South-Thames E. *æ* and *ā* when shortened pass through *æ* into *a*, while in Northern not only Anglian *e*=*æ* but also *æ* shorten to *e*, Midland generally showing the same tendency. Hence such words as OE *hlǣfdige* 'lady,' *lædde* 'led,' *næddre* 'serpent,' *ondrædde* 'feared' appear in Southern as *lavedi, ladi, ladde, naddre, dradde*, in Northern as *lefdi, ledi, ledde, neddre, dredde*. But Southern has *e* in some words, such as *flesh*=OE *flǣsc*.

804. OE *ā* remained unchanged in the Northern dialect, as in *gā* 'go,' *stān*=OE *gān, stan*. In South-Thames E., and to a great extent in Midland, it was rounded into broad *ǫ*: *gǫ, stǫn*. So also in *lǫng* = OE *lang*. This change took place before the introduction of such French words as *dame, corage*, which therefore kept their *a* in South-Thames E. as well as Northern.

805. OE *ȳ* became *ī* in North-Thames E., as also in the London dialect, but was preserved in the Southern dialect, as in *fur* 'fire,' *kūþen* 'make known' = OE *fȳr, cȳþan*, which also preserved Late West-Saxon *ȳ* = older *īe*, as in *hūren* 'hear,' *brūsen* 'bruise' = Early West-Saxon *hīeran, brīesan*. Kentish kept its *e*, as in *mes* 'mice.' *ü* was brought into London E. in French words containing *u, ui*, as in *duc, cūre, fruit, frut* ; when final or before a vowel it became *eu*, as is shown by such spellings as *vertew, crewel* = *vertu, cruel*.

806. Most of the ME diphthongs are the result of the weakening of OE *w* and open *g* and *ʒ* after vowels, *w* and open *g* becoming *u*, as in *dęu, dęw, drauen* = OE *deaw, dragan*, open *g* becoming *i*, as in *wei* ' way' = OE *weg*. The glide between a back vowel and a following *h* developed into diphthongic *u*, which was sometimes written, sometimes not, as in *broghte, broughte* ' brought ' = OE *brohte*. The following are the ME diphthongs :—

ai = OE *ag*, as in *dai, saide* 'said' = OE *dęg, sęgde*.

ei = OE *eg, ęg*, as in *wei, leide* 'laid' = OE *weg, lęgde*.

ei = OE *eg*, as in *hei* 'hay' = OE *hęg*. *grei* = Anglian *grēg*, West-Saxon *grǣg*. But OE *eg* generally becomes *i* in ME (802).

ęi = OE *ag*, as in *kęie* ' key ' = *cęg*.

oi occurs only in French words, such as *joie, vois*.

au = OE *ag*, as in *drauen*. In such words as *laughter* from Scandinavian *hlahtr* it is the result of glide-development. In words of French origin *au* corresponds sometimes to Old French *au*, as in *cause*, sometimes to Old French nasal *a* before a nasal consonant, as in *chaumbre, servaunt* = Old French *chambre* (tʃaammbrə), etc., the spellings *chambre*, etc.

without *u* occurring also in ME, where the pronunciation varied between pure (aa*n*) and (au), which was an E. imitation of the former.

eu = OE *ew, eow*, as in *newe* 'new' = Old Anglian *neowe*, West-Saxon *nīwe*. French *ü* had this sound in certain cases (**805**).

ēu = OE *aw, ēaw*, as in *dẹu*.

ou = OE *ow, og*, as in *tow, bowe* = OE *tow, boga*.

ōu = OE *ow*, as in *stou* 'place,' *blōwen* 'bloom' = OE *stow, blōwan*. In Early ME this diphthong also results from the development of a glide before *h*, as in *inōuh*—also written *inoh*—'enough,' from OE *genoh*, earlier *genog* (**763**); this *ou* becomes *uu* in late ME: *ynough* (rˑnuux).

ǫu = OE *aw, ag*, as in *blǫwen* 'blow' (wind), *ǫwen* 'own' = OE *blāwan, āgen*.

---

807. In the above description of the ME vowel-system, vowels of foreign origin have been referred to only when they offer peculiarities of their own. The other vowels which were introduced in foreign words were identified with the native vowels, and went through the same changes in the later periods of the language. Thus (uu) in ME *crune* 'crown,' where it is of French origin, and in *dun* 'feathers,' 'down,' where it is of Scandinavian origin, went through the same changes as the (uu) in *hus*. So also the ME diphthong (ei) in *obeien* 'obey,' where it is of French origin, and in *heilen* 'greet,' where it is of Scandinavian origin, is entirely on a level with the native diphthong in *wei*. These remarks apply also to the consonants.

Consonants.

808. In Old French *h* was silent in most words of Latin origin—being often dropped in writing as well as pronunciation—but was always pronounced in certain words—

mostly of German origin—which, of course, kept their *h* when imported into ME both in spelling and pronunciation, the silent French *h* being sometimes written, sometimes not, but never pronounced. ME had silent French *h* in such words as *onūr*, *honour*, *hour*, *horrible*.

809. OE *hr-*, *hl-*, *hn-* became voiced in ME, as in *ring*, *lūd*, *note*; *hw-* was kept, being written *wh*, as in *what*.

The change of *hr* to *r*, etc. was not a phonetic weakening, but was a process of levelling, the few words beginning with *hr*, etc. being absorbed, as it were, into the much larger group of words beginning with the voiced sounds. *hw* was preserved because of its occurrence in some very frequent words, such as *what*, *when*.

810. The hisses were voiced initially in all native words in South-Thames E., as shown by such spellings as *volk*, *zingen*, but not in French words, such as *fęste* 'feast,' *sauf* 'safe,' because this change had been carried out before the introduction of French words. Southern *v* was introduced into the London dialect in a few words, such as *vixen*=OE *fyxen*, feminine of *fox*, *vat*=OE *fæt*' vessel.'

811. OE *c* and stopped *g* developed into the compound consonants (cç, qj)—that is, nearly into their MnE sounds (tʃ, dʒ)—as in *child*, *sengen*, OE *cc*, *cg* being written *cch*, *gg*=(ccç, qqj), as in *wrecche*, *seggen* 'say'=OE *wręcca*, *sęcgan*.

812. Open OE *g* was rounded into (ȝw), which passed into (w) and then (u) (**806**). *w*=OE *g* was kept after a consonant, as in *folwen* 'follow'=OE *folgian*.

813. Strong *h* was rounded into (xw) in the same way, as shown by its influence on preceding vowels (**806**). As final *h* in ME often corresponded to medial *w* in such pairs as *inōh* sing., *inowe* plur.=Late OE *genoh*, *genoge*, OE final *h* was changed into *w* when an *e* was added—as was frequently the case (**795**): thus ME *furwe* 'furrow,' *holwe* 'hollow'=OE *furh*, *holh*. When final *e* was dropped at the end of the ME period, a resulting final *w* was changed to *u* : *folu, holu.*

814. Open *g* was generally weakened to *ı* after consonants as well as in diphthongs : *bürien* 'bury,' *beli* 'belly' = OE *byrġan, belġ.*

815. Final OE front *h* was voiced in ME when a vowel was added ; thus *hih* 'high' has pl. *hiȝe, hie* (802), from which a new uninflected form *hi* was formed.

816. In OE the Anglian dialects seem to have changed medial *c, g* to *c, g* before a back vowel, as in Anglian *secan* = West-Saxon *secan.* Hence in ME we often find North-Thames *k*, as in *seke*, corresponding to South-Thames *ch*, as in *seche*, MnE having the Northern form in *seek*, the Southern in *beseech.* So also MnE *cold, gall* point to Anglian *cāld, galle, chalk* to Southern *cealc.*

817. Scandinavian words keep their (k) and (g), as in *ketel* 'kettle,' *gerþ* 'girth.' The Northern forms *mikel* 'great,' *give*, etc., = Southern *müchel, yiven*, may also be due to Scandinavian influence.

818. In some cases the fluctuation between the two classes of consonants is due to change of vowel in inflection. Thus the Standard ME *gate* 'gate' points to the OE pl. *gatu*, the Northern *yate* to the sing. (Anglian) *gæt.* So also *beginnen* = OE *beginnan* owes its *g* to the pret. and past partic. *begann, begunnen.*

819. *ng* kept its (g) not only in such words as *finger, English*, but also in *sing, singer*, etc.

820. *sc* passed through (sj) into (ʃ), written *sch, ssh, sh*, as in *short, shrud, fish* = OE *scort, scrud, fisc.* Scandinavian *sk* was kept before all vowels, as in *skin, skī* = Icelandic *sky* 'cloud.'

821. The combinations *lr, nr* are made into *ldr, ndr* in ME by making the second half of the *l* and *n* into a stopped consonant, so as to facilitate the transition to the *r*, as in *alder* (the tree), *þunder* from OE *aler* genitive *alre, þunor*

genitive *punres.*   So also *ml* became *mbl* in *þimbel* 'thimble'
from OE *þym(e)le* 'thumbstall,' literally 'little thumb,' from
þuma 'thumb.'

822. Several of the consonants were liable to be dropped
in weak syllables.   Thus to the strong *ich* 'I' = OE *iċ* there
corresponded a weak *ī*, which in Late ME almost supplanted
the strong *ich*.   Weak final *n* was frequently dropped, as in
game, bīnde infin., *ibunde* past partic. = OE *gamen, bindan,
gebunden*.   So also the dropping of *l* in *muche* = OE *micel,
ęch* = OE *ǣlc* 'each,' of the *w* and *l* in *such* = OE *swelc,*
seems to have begun in weak (unstressed) forms of these
words.

ENGLISH VOWELS.

OE	ME	PE
mann	man	mæn
sæt	sat	sæt
heard	hard	haad
nama	nāme	neim
witan	witen	wit
helpan	helpen	help
heofon	hevene	hevn
stelan	stęlen	stijl
sęttan	setten	set
męte	mēte	mijt
sunu	sune	sɐn
synn	sinne	sin
oxa	oxe	oks
open	ǭpen	oupn
stān	stǭn	stoun
dǣl	dę̄l	dijl
drēam	drēm	drijm
wīn	wīn	wain
grēne	grēne	grijn
dēop	dēp	dijp
hūs	hūs	haus
mōd	mēd	muwd
fȳr	fīr	faiǝr

Modern English Vowels.

ME		fMn		sMn	thMn	PE
a {	*man*	æ, a		æ	æ	æ
	path	æ, a		ææ	ææ	aͣ
1	*wit*	i		i	i	i
e	*end*	e		e	e	e
u	*son*	u		ʌ	ɐ	ɐ
o	*ox*	o		ɔ	ɔ	ɔ
ā	*name*	ææ, aa		ee	ee	ei
ī	*wine*	əi		əi	əi	ai
ē	*green*	ii		ii	ii }	ij
ę̄	*deal*	ee		ee	ee, ii }	
ū	*house*	öu		əu	əu	au
ō	*moon*	uu		uu	uu	uw
ǭ	*stone*	oo		oo	oo	ou
ai	*day*	ai, ee		æi, ee }	ee	ei
ei	*they*	ei, ee		ee }		
oi	*boil*	oi, ui		oi, ʌi	oi, əi	oi
au	*saw*	au, ɔɔ		ɔɔ	ɔɔ	ɔɔ
ēu (ǖ)	*new*	yy(u), iu		yy, iu }	juu	juw
ę̇u	*few*	eu		eu, iu }		
ōu	*grow* }	ou		ou, oo	oo	ou
ǭu	*know* }					

MODERN ENGLISH SOUND-CHANGES.

823. The sound-changes in MnE are so great that their history requires a threefold division of the period into

First MnE	.	.	1500–1600
Second MnE	.	.	1600–1700
Third MnE	.	.	1700–

These divisions are necessarily somewhat arbitrary. In reality, First MnE extended some way into the following century.

Orthography.

824. In First MnE weak *e* was generally dropped—always when final—as in (naam, fal, stoonz)=ME *name, falle(n), stones.* At the same time double consonants between vowels were shortened, as in (ʃilin, fulər, sitin)=ME *shilling, fuller, sittinge.* But as the doubling served to show that the preceding vowel was short, the ME spellings were retained, and the doubling was extended to words which in ME had a single consonant, as in *penny, herring, copper*=ME *peni, hering, coper.* Final *e* being now silent was often omitted in writing, so that such words as ME *belle* were written *bell* with a final double consonant, which led to a frequent doubling of final ME consonants to show shortness of the preceding vowel, as in *all, small, glass*=ME *al, smal, glas.* But this doubling was not carried out uniformly. So as the dropping of final *e* in such words as *hate* (haat), *hope* (hoop)= ME *hātien, hopien* would have led to confusion with such words as *hat, hop*, final *e* was kept in them, and came at last to be regarded as a mark of the length of the preceding vowel; and accordingly was added to many words which had no final *e* in ME, as in *wine, stone, foe*=ME *wīn, stǫn, fǫ. e* was always kept after *v* whether the preceding vowel was long or short, because *v* was generally written *u*, and such a word as *loue* — ME *love* would have been mistaken for *low* if the *e* had been dropped.

825. The writing of *y* for *i* was carried to great lengths in Early MnE. *y* or *ie* was always written finally as in *many*, *manie*, *citie*, but otherwise the two letters were written almost at random.

This use of -*ie* is the result of the weakening of ME - *īe* in such words as *melodie* 'melody,' *chivalrie*, which at the end of the ME period drew back the stress from the ending (**787**), so that the final *e* was dropped and the *i* shortened, and the ending was written indifferently -*ie* or -*y*.

826. The close and open ME vowel-pairs *e*, *ę* and *o*, *ǫ* diverged more and more in sound in Early MnE, so that it became necessary to distinguish them in writing. In ME *ee*, *oo* were used to express the close and open sounds indiscriminately, but in Early MnE they were gradually restricted to the close sounds, as in *see*, *moon* = ME *se*, *mone*, OE *seo(n)*, *mona*, the open sounds being expressed by the addition of the open vowel *a*, as in *sea*, *boat* = ME *sę̄*, *bǫt*, OE *sǣ*, *bat*. The latter sound was, however, more frequently expressed by single *o* with length-*e* after the following consonant, as in *stone*. Single *e* + length-*e*, on the other hand, expressed the close sound, especially in less familiar words, such as *complete*, *extreme*, *ee* being rarely written in such words.

827. In Early MnE *i* and *j*, *u* and *v* were still written almost indifferently both as vowels and consonants, so that, for instance, *us*, *vine*, *join*, could be written *vs*, *uine*, *ioyne*; but an arbitrary distinction began to be made, by which descending *i* and angular *u* were used only as consonants, as at present. This reform came from Italy through France.

828. In First MnE the orthography was still quite unsettled, but after a time it was found more convenient to keep one spelling for each word, even when there were differences of pronunciation; and as the number of books and readers increased, the fixed orthography adopted by printers became more and more general, till in the Third MnE period it settled down into its present shape, except in a few isolated words such as *cloathes, tyger*, which in the beginning of the present century were made into *clothes, tiger*.

829. But as the sounds of the language went on changing with even greater rapidity than before, the difficulty of mastering the traditional spelling has increased year by year ; so that although a knowledge of the standard orthography is the main test of education and refinement, few even of the upper classes have a perfect mastery of it.

830. We express this divergence between spelling and pronunciation by calling the present English spelling **un-phonetic**. The orthography of Old English was, on the contrary, a **phonetic** one—in intention, at least, and as far as the defects of the Roman alphabet on which it was based would allow. Thus in OE the letter *i* was used to express the vowel (i) short and long, and was used to express that sound only, while in the unphonetic MnE orthography it expresses such distinct sounds as (i, ai, ij), as in *bit, bite, machine*. But as the Latin alphabet does not provide enough letters for the OE sounds, it was necessary to use the same letter to express a variety of sounds, as when *s* was used to express (z) as well as (s), *g*, especially, being used to express a considerable number of distinct sounds (**729**). Middle English orthography, being based on that of Old French, which was much worse than that of British Latin, was correspondingly defective. But even in the Early MnE period the spelling was still in intention mainly phonetic : people tried to make their spelling represent their actual pronunciation, whereas now we learn the spelling of each word mechanically, by eye, without paying much regard to its pronunciation.

831. The first beginnings of intentionally unphonetic spellings appear at the end of the Old French period, when **etymological spellings** were introduced, by which, for instance, French *dete, dette* was made into *debte* by the influence of its Latin original *debitum*, and *parfet, parfit* (Modern French *parfait*) was made into *parfaict* by the influence of Latin *perfectum.* So also Old French *autour* (Modern French *auteur*) came to be written *auctour* by the influence of its Latin original *auctorem.* This Latinizing often led to etymologically incorrect spellings. Thus the Latin *rhetor* 'orator' (from Greek *rhetor*) was written *rethor*, because *th* was a more familiar combination of letters than *rh*. By the influence of *rethor, autour* was made into *authour*, so as to give the word a more learned appearance. All these innovations made their way into English, where some of them were further developed. Thus the two spellings of *autour* were blended into the form *aucthour* by the side of *auctour, authour*, and ME *parfit* was latinized into *ferfit, perfect.* None of these spellings had, at first, any influence on the pronunciation either of French or English. Modern French has, indeed, discarded these 'silent' letters in most of the above words. This writing of silent consonants in French was probably first suggested by *s* having been dropped in pronunciation before another consonant in Old French itself in such words as *isle* 'island' from Latin *insula*, which in late Old French was pronounced (iilə)＝Early Old French (izlə), the vowel being lengthened, so that by degrees *s* was often inserted without regard to etymology as a sign of length, as in *pasle* 'pale'＝earlier *pale* from Latin *pallidum.* When the French *isle* was introduced into English, the silent *s* was introduced in the native word *iland*, which was written *island*, the two words having really nothing in common except their meaning. Other native English words were misspelt in this way. Thus *antem* from OE *antefn* (from Greek *antiphona* through some Low Latin form) was written *anthem*, to give it a more learned appearance.

832. In course of time these false spellings began to influence the pronunciation. Thus although in Early MnE

perfect was still pronounced (perfet), by degrees the pedantic pronunciation (perfekt) came into general use. So also with many other latinized words.

833. In Latin *th* occurs only in words of Greek origin, and in the popular language it was made into (t), so that both in OE and MnE *th* in Latin, and consequently in foreign, words generally was pronounced (t), being often written so. Even in Early MnE this pronunciation was still very frequent, not only in such words as *author*, but also where the *th* was etymological, especially in proper names, such as *Thomas*. Even in Second MnE we still find such pronunciations as *apothecary* (potikəri). *Catherine* (kætərn). We still keep (t) in *Thomas*, and even write it in the shortened forms *Tom*, *Kate*; but in most of the other words—including *author*, *anthem*, etc.—the influence of the spelling has introduced the (þ)-sound.

834. Ever since the beginning of the Third MnE period the influence of the spelling on pronunciation has been stronger and stronger, so that our pronunciation of many words is a pure matter of chance, and gives rise to forms which are against the genius of the language. Thus the ME *milne* 'mill,' *kilne* 'kiln' both passed through *miln*, *kiln* into (mil, kil) in Early MnE, the former word being spelt phonetically *mill*, while the latter, being less familiar, kept its old spelling, the result of which is that the purely artificial pronunciation (kiln) was afterwards introduced. For other examples of artificial 'spelling-pronunciations' see §§ 855, 859, 872. In Present English we learn so many new words—names of newly-imported articles of trade, new inventions and scientific discoveries, etc.—by reading them in newspapers and books long before we ever hear them pronounced, that each of us guesses at the pronunciation from the spelling, and when the word comes into general use the wrong pronunciation often prevails.

835. But there is now so much intercourse with foreign

countries, and foreign languages are so much studied, that foreign words often keep their pronunciation as far as is consistent with English habits of speech. Thus *a* keeps its (aa)-sound instead of the English (ei) in such words as *drama, vase, promenade*, the older pronunciations (dreimə) etc. being now almost extinct ; and *i* is pronounced (ij) instead of (ai) in imitation of the French pronunciation in such words as *pique, fatigue, machine*, and many other words in *-ine*. Even the French nasal vowels are imperfectly imitated in such words as *ennui* ('aanwij), often further Anglicised into (oŋwij). Among the consonants, *ch*, whose regular sound is (tʃ), is pronounced (k) in Greek words, such as *chaos*, in imitation of the popular Latin and French pronunciation, and (ʃ) in French words such as the partiall/ anglicized *champagne* (ʃæmˑpein). Again, *zz* = (ts) in the Italian *mezzotinto, j* = (j) in the Hebrew *hallelujah*, etc.

836. We are now able to answer the question, Why is English spelling unphonetic? The main reason is that it has not followed the changes of pronunciation. The present English spelling represents not the sounds of Present English, but those of Early MnE or rather Late ME. Such a spelling as *knight* is not in itself unphonetic; on the contrary, it is a phonetic representation—though an imperfect one—of the sound-group (knict), which in ME was the pronunciation of one of the words which we now pronounce (nait), the other one having been pronounced (nict) in ME, and written accordingly *night*. Such a spelling as *island* is, on the other hand, unphonetic from every point of view, because it inserts a letter which is not pronounced now, and never was pronounced. Such a spelling as *author* was also originally unphonetic, though it has now become phonetic—but only by corrupting the pronunciation and obscuring the etymology of the word.

837. Another reason why our spelling is imperfect is that it is founded on two orthographic bases: (*a*) the traditional

English basis, which, as we see, is mainly ME; and (*b*) a great variety of foreign bases, chiefly Modern French. We see the effect of this mixture of bases in the three pronunciations of *ch*.

838. A third reason why our spelling is imperfect, is that its bases are all imperfect. Such defects as writing the initial consonants in *get* and *gem* (dʒem) with the same letter are defects not of MnE spelling itself, but of the Old French basis of ME spelling.

839. When we call English spelling unphonetic, we do not mean that it is wholly unphonetic. A wholly unphonetic orthography—one in which none of the separate letters expressed any definite sound whatever—could not be mastered by the most retentive memory. What makes it possible to master our present spelling is that many of the words are still spelt phonetically; thus such spellings as *win, set, stop, put* are as phonetic as any in Latin itself.

840. English spelling has never been intentionally unphonetic—except in a few etymological spellings—but has been forced into being unphonetic by a variety of circumstances. We need not therefore be surprised that many attempts have been made to reform it. Already in the 16th century there were many spelling-reformers, some of them scholars of high reputation; but the systems they proposed were too cumbrous and intricate for practical use. Nevertheless they introduced many reforms, such as the separation of *v* and *u*, *ee* and *ea*, *oo* and *oa* (826), which were purely phonetic reforms.

841. Most of the reformed spellings that have been proposed are on the basis of the English values of the letters: they take the most frequent symbol for each sound in the traditional spelling, and use it consistently to express that sound, using, for instance, *ee* to denote the sound (ij) not only in *see*, but also in *seat, seize, pique*, keeping, of course, *i* for the corresponding short vowel in *sit*. But it is evidently

unphonetic to make *ee* the long of *i*, and to assign *e* itself to another distinct sound, namely that in *set*. Such a system is phonetic, but it is phonetic on an unphonetic basis.

842. As the attempt to get a phonetic basis practically necessitates a return in most cases to the original Roman values of the letters, especially in the vowels, such a system is said to be on the 'Romic' basis. The Broad Romic notation used in this book is an example of such a system. In all Romic systems the long vowels have the same signs as the short ones, with such modifications as are required to show the quantity, as in *sit, siit, sīt = sit, seat*; diphthongs and consonant-groups are expressed by combining the signs of the elements of which they are made up, as in $ks = x$, the superfluous Roman letters being used to denote sounds not properly symbolized before, as when x is used for the sound of Scotch *ch* in *loch*, and the defects of the Roman alphabet being supplemented by the use of new letters such as 'turned *e*' — ə.

Vowels.

843. The most convenient way of dealing with the MnE vowels is to take each Late ME. vowel separately, and trace its history down to the present time.

844. a was gradually advanced to the broad (æ), so that such words as *man, sat* had exactly their present pronunciation in Second MnE. But in First MnE the old (a)-sound was still kept by many speakers. Before *l* not followed by a vowel *a* kept its back sound, and the glide between it and the *l* developed into an (u), so that such words as *fall, calm* became (faul, kaulm), being sometimes written *faull* etc. (a) was also kept after (w, wh), as in *was, what*, where it was rounded in Second MnE, whence the present (woz, whot), although there was no rounding when a back consonant followed, as in *wax, wag*. In Second MnE (æ) was lengthened before (s, þ) and in some other cases, as in *glass, path* (glææs, pææþ).   At the end of the Third MnE period this (ææ) was broadened into (aa), which is the present sound—(glaas, paab). .

845. i, e have generally remained unchanged.   But in First MnE *er* final or before a consonant became (ar) as in *star, hart, heart* = ME *sterre, hert, herte.*   Not in the weak *her.*

846. u was preserved in First MnE, as in *full, come* (kum).   In Second MnE it was unrounded to (ʌ), which was afterwards lowered to its present sound (ɐ)—(fɐl, kɐm). But before this lowering took place the (ʌ) was generally rounded back again to (u) between a lip-consonant and (l), as in *full, wool* = ME *wolle,* and in other words after lip-consonants, as in *wood* = ME *wode, put.*

847.   ü generally appears as *i* in MnE, into which it had already been unrounded in the London dialect of ME.   Thus MnE has *fill, sin* = OE *gefyllan, synn.*   But (y) was preserved in First MnE in some words still written with the French *u,* such as *busy, bury* = OE *bysig, byrgan.*

848.   o kept its ME sound (o) in First MnE, as in *top, ox,* and was broadened to its present sound in Second MnE, being lengthened before the same consonants which lengthen (æ), as in *froth, cross, off.*   In Early MnE a glide-(u) developed between (o) and *l* not followed by a vowel, as in *bowl* (boul) = OE *bolla* — where it was expressed in writing—*folk* (foulk) where it was not written any more than in the parallel *fall* **(844).**

849.   a underwent the same changes as *a,* being gradually narrowed till it passed from (ææ) into (ee), as in *name, take,* this last change being completed before the Second MnE lengthening of (æ) in *path,* etc.   In Third MnE (ee) was further narrowed into close (ee), which in the present century was cleft into (ei, ei).

850.   ı was diphthongized in First MnE by lowering and retracting the tongue in the first half of the vowel **(721)** till it became (ǝi), as in *wine, vice,* with a very high close (ǝ), which was broadened in the next two periods, till the diphthong became almost (ai), as at present.

851. e, ę. Late ME *e* probably had a very close sound between (ee) and (ii), and when in First MnE the old *ı* had become (əi), the old *e* developed into full (ii), as in *see, field=* ME *se(n), feld*, ME *ę* keeping its open sound (*ee*), as in *sea, there*, this (*ee*) being narrowed to (ee) in Second MnE, which by the middle of the Third MnE period was further narrowed to (ii), ME *e* and *ę* being thus levelled, as in (sii)*=see, sea*. But the change into (ii) was arrested by a preceding *r* in *break, great* (breik, greit), which were, however, also pronounced (briik, griit) in the last century. In First MnE *ę* was often shortened to (e), especially before stops, as in *bread, heavy*.

852. u was diphthongized in the same way as *ī*, becoming (ou) with very close (ö), as in *house, crown*, the first element being gradually unrounded and broadened into its present sound—between (ə) and (æ).

In *room=*OE *rum, stoop, droop* ME *u* has been preserved from the change into (au) by the influence of the following lip-consonants.

853. ō, ǫ. When *u* had become (ou), ME *ō*—which was probably a very close sound between (oo) and (uu)—was moved up into the place of the old *u*, as in *too, moon* (tuu, muun). *ǫ* kept its open sound (*oo*) at first, as in *go, stone*, and was narrowed to close (oo) in Second MnE, which in the present century was cleft into (ou, ou). The older sound has been preserved in *broad* (brod) through the influence of the (r).   (uu)=ME *o* was shortened in some words in First MnE, as in *flood* (flud), *mother, gum=*OE *flod, moder, guma*, whence the present forms (flʊd) etc.   There was another shortening of (uu) in Second MnE, especially before stops, as in *good* (gud), *book, bosom*. These words did not change their (u) into (ʊ), because this change was already completed.

854. ai, ei. In MnE the ME diphthongs *ei*, *ęi* shortened their first elements, and so were levelled under *ei*. As *ai* became (æi) in First MnE by the regular change of (a) into (æ)—which in this case was hastened by the fronting influence of the (i)—*ai* and *ei* became very similar in sound, so that there was a tendency to level *ei* under *ai*, as in *way*, *hay*, *clay* = ME *wei, hei, clęi* = OE *clæg*. The weak *they, their* kept *ei*, as also several other words, especially before *gh*, as in *neighbour*, *eight*. In Second MnE these diphthongs were smoothed into (*ee*), so that *tail* and *tale* etc. had the same sound, and went through the same changes.

855. oi was sometimes kept in First MnE, but in some pronunciations the (i) raised the preceding (o) to (u), such words as *boil* having the two pronunciations (boil) and (buil). In Second MnE this (u) underwent its regular change into (ʌ, ɐ) ; and the resulting (ɐi) was so similar in sound to the (əi) of *wine*, etc., that it was levelled under it, and *boil* etc. was pronounced (bəil) and (boil), the former being the more usual pronunciation. In the next period (boil) etc. again got the upper hand by the help of the spelling, and the noun *bile* = OE *býle* 'ulcer' was mistakenly made into *boil*.

856. au was kept in First MnE, but soon passed into open (ɔɔ)—the long of our vowel in *not*—as in *saw, fall* (**844**), which in the Third period was narrowed to its present sound. In some words *au* lost its (u), as in *laugh*, which in Second MnE passed through (læf) into (lææf), whence the present (laaf). *half*—also written *haulf—halve*. *au* = French *a* before nasals (**806**) generally went through the same changes, as in *aunt, comma(u)nd, la(u)mp*.

857. eu, u ; ęu. At the end of the ME period the cleaving of final *ū* into *eu* (**805**) had been extended to non-final *ū* as well, so that this sound was completely levelled under *eu*, which in First MnE became (iiu, iu) by the regular change of *e* into (ii), as in *duke, fruit, new, true*—also written *trewe* = ME *dūc, frūt, newe, trewe*. ME *ęu* remained in

First MnE, but with the usual shortening of the first element, as in *few* (feu)=ME *f̣ẹwe*, and became (iu) in Second MnE, all the three ME sounds *ü, eu, ẹu* being thus levelled under (iu). In the Third period (iu) shifted the stress on to the second element, becoming (i·uu, juu). The (j) was afterwards dropped after (r, ʃ, ʒ) and often after (l), as in *true, chuse*— now written *choose – juice, lute*. In Cockney and New-England American it is dropped after all the other consonants as well, as in *new, duty*, being kept only initially, as in *union*.

858. ōu, ǫu both became (ọou) or (ou) in First MnE, as in *grow, know, soul*=ME *growen, knọwen, sǫule*, which in the Second period was smoothed into (ọọ) and then narrowed into (oo), as in *go* (**853**), so that *know* and *no* etc. had the same vowel.

Weak Vowels.

859. In First MnE long weak vowels were generally shortened, as in *honour* (onur), *image* (imadʒ, imædʒ), *nation* (naasjun, nææsjun)=ME *onur, image, naciun*. Weak diphthongs were kept, as in *nature* (naatiur)=ME *natüre, certain*. Short vowels were generally kept, as in *moral, person, sorrow* (soru), but *e* before *r* was obscured to (ə), as in *better*, and occasionally other vowels as well in such words as *scholar, honour, nature*. But there was also an artificial pronunciation which tried to follow the spelling, pronouncing not only (skolar) etc. but also (naasjon, kondisjon) etc., although the *o* in *nation* was only another way of spelling (u) as in *son*= OE *sunu*. *ou, ow*=ME (u, uu) was also often pronounced (o) or even (ou) in *honour, emperour, sorrow*, etc.

860. In Second MnE the natural pronunciation got the upper hand again. Weak (u) passed by regular change into (ɐ), as in (nẹẹʃɐn) *nation*, and such pronunciations as (piktər)=*picture*, which are now vulgarisms, were in general use. As (ɐ) was very similar in sound to (ə), there was a tendency to make (ə) the general weak vowel, although the

older clear weak vowels were still kept in many cases, as in
(næʃenæl, næʃonæl) *national*, now pronounced (næʃənəl).
In Second MnE weak initial vowels were often dropped,
especially in long words, as in *apprentice* (prentis) *estate*
(stæt), *opinion* (pinjən). We still keep the short form of
the first word in the expression *'prentice hand*, but the vowel
has generally been restored by the influence of the spelling.

Consonants.

861. During the transition from ME to MnE the hisses *þ*,
s, f, became voiced in weak syllables, especially in inflectional
-es, as in the gen. sing. *mannes* and the plur. *stǫnes*, whence
MnE (mænz, stounz), the breath sounds being preserved in
strong monosyllables such as *ges, pens* = MnE (gijs, pens)
contrasting with *penies* = MnE (peniz). The same change
was carried out in weak monosyllables, so that numerous
doublets were formed. Thus the emphatic adverb *of* = MnE
off preserved its (f), while the preposition *of* was weakened
to (ov). There were similar doublets of *wiþ, is, his*, etc.
Initial *þ* was voiced in the weak forms of some very
frequent—mostly pronominal words—such as *þe, þē, þin,*
þat, þouh = MnE (ði, oij, oain, ðæt, ðou), the strong forms
being now lost.

These changes probably began in collocations where the
hiss-consonant was flanked by voice sounds, as in *mannes mod,*
of a man, to þe man, where *of a, to þe* etc. would naturally become
(ova, tooðe) on the analogy of *wives* genitive of *wif*, where the
alternation of *f* and *v* is of OE origin.

862. The voicing of weak (tʃ) into (dʒ) in *knowledge* =
ME *knǫwlȩche* is quite parallel to the voicing of weak (s) in
stones. We have the same weakening in the Present English
pronunciation of such words as *ostrich* (ostridʒ) and the
ending *-wich* in *Greenwich, Norwich*.

863. Towards the end of the First MnE period (s)
preceded by a weak vowel and followed by a strong vowel

became (z), whence the Present English distinction between *exert* (ig·zɔət) and *exercise* (·eksəsaiz), the (s) being preserved unchanged in the latter word because it is followed by a weak vowel. Other examples are *exhibit* compared with *exhibition*, *example*, *anxiety* (æŋ·zaiiti) compared with *anxious* (ænʃəs), where the change of (s) into (ʃ) is a later one (**870**), *dessert*, *disease*, *dissolve*, *transact*.

Exceptions to this rule are the result of analogy. Thus *to absent* (əb·sent) owes its (s) to influence of the adjective *absent* (·æbsənt), *research* to the influence of *search*.

864. Initial (h), which was preserved through First and Second MnE, began to be dropped at the end of the last century, but has now been restored in Standard E. by the combined influence of the spelling and of the speakers cf Scotch and Irish E., where it has always been preserved. It is also preserved in American E., while it has been almost completely lost in the dialects of England—including Cockney E.— as also in vulgar Australian.

865. But (h) is always dropped in weak syllables when not at the beginning of the sentence, as in (-hij sed -ij wɔz redi) *he said he was ready*, whence the distinction between the emphatic (·him) and the unemphatic (-im).

The dropping of *h* in weak syllables is very old. Even in OE we find such spellings as *cora*, *Eadelm — heora* 'their,' *Eadhelm* (a man's name).

866. As we have seen, strong *h* appears in ME in the form of (ç) and (xw). In First MnE the former was weakened to a mere breath-glide, and then dropped, the preceding vowel being lengthened, so that ME *night* (niçt) passed through (niht) into (niit), whence by the regular change (nait). But the older (niht) was still kept up by some speakers, and the co-existence of (nait) and (niht) gave rise to the blending (naiht) or (naiçt), which, although artificial, seems to have been not uncommon in speech. The *gh* in *high*, *nigh*, *weigh*, etc.= ME *high*, *hī* was generally silent. The back-*gh* was kept in such words as *laugh, thought, enough* (lauxw, þouxwt, boxwt, inuxw), and in many words the lip element was exaggerated in Second MnE till it became (f)—(læf, lææf, þoft, þoot, inɐf)—which in *draft* by the side of *draught*—both from ME *draght*—has been adopted in the spelling.

867. **r** was kept unchanged in First MnE, being afterwards gradually weakened till it lost its trill everywhere. Towards the end of the Third period it began to be dropped everywhere except before a vowel, as in the present Standard E.

868. Already in First MnE (r) had developed a glide before it in such words as *fire, flower* (fəiər, flouər) = ME *fir, flur*, and had broadened a preceding *e* into (a), as in *star* (**845**). In Second MnE it began to modify preceding vowels in the direction of (ə), so that *er, ir, ur* came to be levelled under (ər) or (ɐr), as in *her* (hɐr) *fir, bird, fur, turn.* In Third MnE it modified preceding (ee)=*a, ai, ei* to (*ee*), as in *care* (keer). *fair, their* contrasting with *name* (neem), *fail, veil*; and towards the end of this period it broadened a preceding (æ) into (a), as in *star, hard.* ME *ẹr, or* appear in Third MnE sometimes as (iir, uur), as in *fear, moor*, being sometimes broadened into (eer, ɔr), as in *there, bear, floor.* In the present century (r) has been dropped everywhere except before a vowel, *r* final or before a consonant being represented only by a preceding glide-(ə). as in (faiə) = Early MnE (fəiər)=ME *fir*. This (ə)=*r* has broadened preceding (ij, uw) into (i, u), as in *here* (hiə), *poor, cure* (kjuə) contrasting with *he* (hij). *pool* (puwl). The glide-(ə) before (r) was finally absorbed by a preceding mixed or broad vowel, (ɐr) in *her* etc. passing through (ɐə) into (əə), (aə, oə) into (aa, ɔ), as in *star, floor.*

869. **l.** Already in First MnE (l) began to be dropped between (u) and a following consonant, as in *half* (haulf, hauf), *folk* (foulk, fouk); also in *should* (ʃuuld, ʃuld, ʃud), *would, could,* where the (l) was at first dropped only when these words were weak.

870. s, z. In Second and Third MnE the combinations (sj, zj) became (ʃ, ʒ), as in *nation* (neeʃɛn)=Early MnE (nææsjun)=ME *nācioun* (naasi-uun), *sure* (siur, sjuur, ʃuur), *usual* (iuziuæl, juuʒuæl), such words as *nature, verdure* passing through (næætjur, neetjər, verdjur, verdjər) into the present (neitʃə, vəədʒə).

871. w in First MnE was kept before (r), which it rounded, and was then dropped itself, as in *write* (rwəit), the (r) being afterwards unrounded.

We can see the influence of this rounded *r* in the vulgar (rop)=*wrap*, where (rw) had the same rounding effect on the following vowel as in *was* (**844**).

872. In Second MnE *w* was dropped in weak syllables, especially in *-ward, -wards,* as in *Edward* (edərd), *backwards* (bækərdz). We still drop the *w* in *towards* (tɔdz), but it has been restored in the other words through the influence of the spelling, except in vulgar speech. The weak ending *-wich* drops the *w* in all familiar place-names, such as *Greenwich* (grinidʒ).

873. k was kept initially before (n) in First MnE, as in *know* [compare *acknowledge*], the (n) being unvoiced, and the (k) afterwards dropped, so that in Second MnE (knou, knⁿou) became (nℎoo), this (nℎ) being afterwards levelled under the more frequent (n) in *no,* etc.

874. g was dropped before (n) in Second MnE as in *gnaw.*

875. In First MnE medial (ŋg) was shortened to (ŋ) in such words as *singer* (siŋər), *singing*=ME (singer), etc. by the analogy of final (ŋ) in *sing* ; but (ŋg) was kept in the comparison of adjectives, as in *longer, longest.*

876. t, d. In Second MnE (t) preceded by the hisses (s, f) and followed by the vowel-like consonants (l, n, m) was regularly dropped, as in *thistle* (bisl), *fasten* (fææsn), *chestnut*, *Christmas*, *often*.

877. In First MnE (d) preceded by a vowel and followed by (r) was opened into (ð) in many words, such as *father*, *together*, *hither* = OE *fæder*, Late ME *fader*, *fader* (**793**), OE *toˈgædre*, *hider*. Conversely (ð) often became (d) in First MnE in combination with (r) and (l), as in *murther*, *murder*, *rudder*, *fiddle* = OE *morþor*, *roˈþor*, *fiþele*.

878. b. In First MnE final (b) was dropped after (m), as in *lamb*. Hence *b* was added in writing to words which in ME had only *m*, as in *limb*, *numb* = ME *lim*, *inumen* 'taken,' 'seized' = OE *genumen*.

PRESENT ENGLISH.

Stress.

Word-Stress.

879. The characteristic features of Present English stress are some of them of OE origin, while others developed themselves in ME and in the different periods of MnE, some being apparently of very recent origin.

880. In Present English, as in OE, the most general principle of stress is that subordinate words—especially form-words—have weak stress. Thus in *he is a man of the world*, the subordinate words *he*, *is*, *a*, *of*, *the* all have weak stress. Hence the weakened stress in *a ˈpiece of bread*, and the distinction between *ˈsome bread* and *ˈsome ˈpeople* (**61.** 1).

881. The OE principle of putting the stress on the first syllable of a word generally resulted in the principal stress being on the root-syllable of inflected or derived words. This principle is still maintained in MnE in native words, as in *fearful*, *fearfully*, *fearless*, *fearlessness*, *fisher*, *fishery*, *fisherman* (fiʃəmən).

882. We have seen that already in ME many long words of French origin with the stress on the last syllable threw it back on to the first syllable by the analogy of the native stress (**787**). In MnE this tendency has become stronger and stronger, so that the first-syllable stress in such words as *honour*, *pity*, *emperor*, *justify*, which in Late ME was only occasional, has now become fixed. Even in the present century many of these words have thrown back their stress to the first syllable, such as *balcony*, *crystalline*, *recondite*, which in the last century were stressed on their second syllables.

883. Native words which had weak stress on the first syllable in OE and ME, such as *arise*, *become*, *forgive*, *to-day*, still keep this stress in MnE, as also those French words which preserved a similar stress in ME through their resemblance to the above native words, such as *avow*, *defend*.

884. Many other foreign words have also preserved their advanced stress. There are many foreign derivative endings —chiefly Greek and Latin, often modified in their passage through French—which regularly take the stress, such as *-esque*, *-tion*, *-sion* etc., *-bility*, *-graphy*, as in *picturesque*, *grotesque*, *imagination*, *position*, *possibility*, *photography*, in all of which the stress is taken away from the root-syllable, on which it falls in the shorter forms *imagine*, *possible*, *photograph* etc. Many words which were imported from French and other foreign languages in the MnE period keep their advanced stress even when the analogy of other words points to throwing it back on the first syllable, such as *machine*, *caprice*—which show their French origin by the pronunciation of *i* as (ij)—*champagne*, *canoe*, *gazelle*. Words which were imported straight from Latin generally keep the Latin stress, as in *papyrus*, even when the final syllable is dropped, as in *create*, *severe*. Words of Greek origin follow the Latin accentuation as well as the Latin spelling, so that the original Greek stress is preserved in English only when it happens to be preserved in Latin also, as in *genesis, museum* = Greek *genesis, mouseíon.*

885. But foreign words even of recent introduction are always liable to have their stress thrown back on to the first syllable, or, at any rate, towards the beginning of the word, as soon as they become popular, which in Latin words is generally shown by their shortening or dropping their endings, as in ·*audítor* — Latin *au·dítor*, ·*discipline* = Latin *disci·plína*, *phi·losophy* = Latin *philo·sophia* from Greek *philosophía.*

886. When a foreign word is used in different senses, it often happens that in its more familiar meaning it throws the stress back, keeping the original stress in the less familiar meaning. Thus we keep the original Latin stress in the adjective *au·gust* and the name *Augustus* = Latin *au·gustus*, but throw it back in the month-name ·*August*. So also the adjective *mi·nute* keeps its Latin stress, which is thrown back in the more familiar noun ·*minute*.

887. In many cases where the same foreign word is used both as a noun and a verb in English, it keeps its end-stress when used as a verb by the analogy of the native verbs which have the same stress, while the corresponding noun- or adjective-form takes the stress on the first syllable, so that the distinction between such words as the noun ·*accent* and the verb *to ac·cent* is really ultimately due to the analogy of the OE pairs ·*forwyrd, for·weorþan* etc., which analogy was greatly aided by the fact that many verbs of French and Latin origin also threw forward their stress; thus the contrast between the foreign verbs *in·duce, in·vade* etc. and the native nouns ·*income, ·insight* etc. led to the distinction between the noun ·*insult* and the verb *in·sult* from Latin *insul·tāre*. The following are additional examples of such pairs:

·absent	to ab·sent	·compound	to com·pound
·abstract	to ab·stract	·extract	to ex·tract
·affix	to a·ffix	·frequent	to fre·quent

| *object* | *to ob·ject* | ·*produce* | *to pro·duce* |
| ·*present* | *to pre·sent* | ·*rebel* | *to re·bel* |

In some cases, however, the noun- and adjective-forms keep the verb-stress, as in *ad·vice (to ad·vise)*, *ce·ment*.

888. The normal stress of a word is always liable to be changed by considerations of emphasis, even a weak word or syllable being capable of taking strong stress if emphasized, as in *that is ·the thing to do*, especially in cases of contrast, as in *to give and ·forgive, not ·subjective but ·objective*, against the normal stress *for·give, sub·jective, ob·jective*.

In some cases this contrasting stress has permanently altered the normal stress. Thus, while in most words the ending *-or* is pronounced weak (-ər), as in *actor, author*, it is regularly pronounced with strong (ɔr) in those words where it is cor.-trasted with the corresponding passive ending *-ee*, as in *lessor* (le·sɔə) 'one who lets a house' contrasted with *lessee* (le·sij) 'one to whom the house is let,' as the normal pronunciation (lesə) would lead to confusion with the adjective *lesser*.

STRESS IN WORD-GROUPS AND COMPOUNDS.

889. The most characteristic feature of Present English stress is its great development of **even** stress, many combinations which had the strong stress on one syllable only in OE now having it equally distributed over two syllables.

890. Thus in the free groups, adjective or genitive + noun, the regular stress is even, as in *a ·good ·man, a ·virtuous ·woman, a ·great im·provement, the ·king's ·son*. So also to the OE ·*wide :cup* corresponds the Present English ·*widely ·known, ·widely di·ffused*.

891. In OE the combination adjective + noun might be either a free group or a compound, which were distinguished from one another by the adjective being declinable in the group, indeclinable in the compound, both combinations having the stress on the first element. Thus the group ·*god dǣd* 'good deed' and the compound *goddǣd* 'benefit' appear in the dative plural as *godum dǣdum* and *goddǣdum* respectively. So also the compound *cwicseolfor* 'quicksilver,' literally 'living silver' has genitive *cwicseolfres*, the first element remaining undeclined.

892. In MnE, adjectives have become indeclinable, so that it would hardly be possible to distinguish compounds begining with adjectives from free groups, were it not for the difference of stress, the combination adjective + noun with the stress on the first element being a compound in Present English, as in ·*quicksilver*, while the even-stressed ·*good ·deed* can only be regarded as a group, so that the OE compound *goddǣd* must be regarded as having been either lost or separated into a free group in Present English. On the other hand, many OE free combinations of adjective + noun have developed into compounds in MnE, as in *blackberries* = OE *blace berigan*, *Englishman* = OE *Englisc mann*, in the latter example with obscuration of the second element, showing the intimateness of the composition.

893. But the tendency to give adjectives full stress is so strong that even stress is found in many combinations whose meaning is quite as much isolated as in the above instances of uneven stress, such as —

·*high ·road, public house, easy chair, shooting star.*

Prussic acid, Prussian blue, Indian ink.

old age, common sense, safe conduct, high treason, leading article.

Even stress is the rule when the adjective follows the noun, as in *Prince Consort, Princess Royal, poet laureate.*

894. In the OE combination genitive + noun there is nothing to tell us whether it is to be regarded as a group or a compound, for this combination always has the stress on the first element, which, being already inflected, is incapable of any further grammatical modification. But in Present English we can distinguish clearly between even-stress genitive groups such as ·*king's ·son*, and uneven-stress genitive

compounds such as the plant-name *crow's-foot*, whose stress is perfectly parallel to that of other compound names of natural objects (**896**).

Many genitive compounds have been obscured by sound-change and contraction, such as *England* = OE *Engla-land* 'land of the Anglians' (OE plural nominative *Engle*).

895. Even stress has further made its way into some of the old compounds, where the logical relation between the elements of the compound resembles that between the elements of a free group, especially when the first element is felt to be equivalent to an adjective, as in ·*gold* ·*ring* compared with the OE compound *goldfæt* ' gold vessel.' When OE ·*gylden* :*hring*, where *gylden* is a declinable adjective, had been made into the even-stressed ·*golden* ·*ring*, it was natural to transfer this stress to the compound *gold-ring*.

896. But uneven—first-syllable—stress is also preserved in Present English compounds. In some compounds the uneven stress seems to be the result of the second element being less logically prominent than the first, through being a word of general meaning and frequent occurrence in compounds. Thus in such a compound as *appletree* we should expect even stress, as in *apple pudding*, *silk thread*, etc., an *appletree* being simply 'a tree that bears apples,' just as a *silk thread* is a 'thread made of silk'; and the uneven stress is simply the result of the frequency of the second element in *appletree* and the other compounds in -*tree*, there being so many different kinds of fruit-trees that when we hear the words *apple-*, *pear-* etc. as the first elements of compounds, we add the word *tree* almost as a matter of course. In such compounds the second element is, in fact, on the way to become a mere derivative ending, especially when it undergoes phonetic weakening through this very want of prominence, as is often the case with the ending -*man* in such compounds as *shopman* (ʃopmən), *clergyman*, *Englishman*, which are logically on a level with such even-stress compounds as

English boy. The result of these tendencies is that many compound names of natural objects and of classes of human beings, together with some ending in time-words of general meaning, take first-element stress :—

·goldfish, canarybird, turtledove, dragonfly ; appletree, fruit-tree, rosebush, beetroot; sandstone—greyhound, blackbird ; blue-bell, blackberry ; quicksilver—crow's-foot, cat's-mint ; birdseye (a kind of tobacco).

Englishman, Englishwoman, freemason, blacksmith—ladies'-man, lady's-maid, bridesmaid.

summertime, dinnertime ; birthday, dogdays — midnight, midsummer.

897. But in most compounds uneven stress does not imply any logical subordination, but is only a means of joining the two elements more closely together or isolating the meaning of the whole, as we see very clearly by comparing *blackbird* with *black bird.*

898. We may therefore define the logical distinction between even and uneven stress by saying that even stress balances as it were the two elements against one another and puts them on a footing of equality, and to some extent separates them, while uneven stress either subordinates one element to the other, as in *appletree,* or indicates a close logical union, as in *blackbird.*

899. One result of this is that even stress is often preserved in newly-formed compounds or groups merely because the meaning of the two elements is still fresh in the minds of those who use the compound, so that they are balanced against one another, while a similar compound which was formed long ago, and has become traditional, so that the original meaning of its elements is no longer prominent, keeps its original uneven stress, or substitutes uneven for even stress. Thus we have even stress in modern place-names such as *·New ·York, New Zealand, the West End, Redhill,* contrasted with uneven stress in older names such as *New-*

castle, Newport, Longwood, Redlynch—where *lynch*=‘slope of hill.’

Uneven stress in place-names is often the result of the want of prominence of the second element, which is often obscured, as in *the Highlands, the Midlands, Kingston* [-*ton*=*town*], *Bradford* [=*broad ford*].

We will now consider the stress of compounds more in detail, according to the part of speech to which the compound belongs.

Compound Nouns.

900. Compounds of **noun** or **adjective** + **noun** regularly take uneven stress when a causal relation is implied. A very numerous class of causal compounds are those in which the first element expresses the purpose or object of the second; thus *toyshop* is a shop for selling and buying toys, a *watchdog* is a dog for watching. The following are further examples of these purpose-compounds :—

ˈ*greenhouse, diningroom, fireplace, flowerpot, flowerpot-stand, pocketbook; schoolroom, guidebook, footpath, dancing-master, stable-boy, post-office, weathercock; coal-mine, gravel-pit; summer-house.*

901. In other causal compounds the second element expresses the result of the first, or dependence on it; thus *coal-tar* is tar obtained from coal, a *steam-engine* is a machine whose working depends on steam. Other examples are—

ˈ*windfall, rainbow, chillblain; lampblack, water-colours; oil-lamp, sundial; sunflower; thundercloud, thunderstorm, tobacco-smoke, rain-water.*

902. Another well-defined class of uneven-stress noun-compounds are those which express phenomena or actions. In the following the first element may be said to stand in the direct object relation to the second :—

ˈ*painstaking, screwdriver, bookseller, stockbroker; man-*

slaughter, bloodshed ; goldsmith, shoeblack ; flower-show, cart-load.

903. In the following phenomenon-compounds the first element stands to the second in a variety of other relations :—

·earthquake, shipwreck ; grasshopper ; cricket-match, walking-tour, dinner-party ; sunrise, moonlight ; eyesight ; headache ; garrison-life, priestcraft.

904. We now have to consider the use of even stress in noun-compounds. In even stress, as already remarked (**895**), the first element is generally felt to be equivalent to an adjective. This is especially clear in those even-stress compounds in which the first element (*a*) expresses something that resembles the second element, as in *sponge-cake* = ·'sponge-like cake,' 'spongy cake,' (*b*) defines the sex or age of the second element, as in *man cook* = 'male cook,' and (*c*) denotes the material of which the second element is made, as in *silk thread* :—

(*a*) *·bow ·window, rocksalt, loaf sugar ; copper beech, moss rose, silver sand.*

The last three go against the analogy of *goldfish* etc. (**898**) ; but *beech* is evidently too special a word to be subordinated in the same way as *tree* etc.

(*b*) *·man ·cook, lady doctor. boy messenger, infant phenomenon ; tomcat, buck rabbit. poll parrot.* So also in *he-goat. she-goat.*

(*c*) *·brick ·house, stone wall, gravel walk, straw hat, silver spoon ; olive oil ; meat pie, jam tart. ginger ale.*

905. Even stress is also used when a general place-word, such as *road, square,* is defined by another noun—often a proper name—or adjective put before it, as in *Oxford Road.* So also when the name of a place is prefixed to a noun to show where the latter comes from. Examples are—

·Oxford ·Road, Mincing Lane. Hanover Square, London

*Bridge, Wimbledon Common—North Road, South Park—St.
·James's ·Square.*

·*Turkey* ·*carpet, Indiarubber, Cey·lon* ·*tea.*

But when the noun *street* takes the place of *road* etc. in such
compounds, it is subordinated in stress because of its greater
frequency (896) :—

·*Oxford Street, Fenchurch Street—Highstreet—Prince's
Street.*

906. Compounds of **verb + noun** are necessarily phenomenon-compounds, and therefore take uneven stress
(**902**). In them the noun stands sometimes in the object-,
sometimes in the subject-relation to the verb, the relation
being doubtful in some compounds. Examples are—

·*breakwater, scarecrow, telltale, breakfast* (brekfəst) ; *rattle-
snake, leapfrog, drawbridge ; whirlwind, leapyear, washtub.*

Compound Adjectives.

907. Compound adjectives consisting of **noun + adjective-word** generally have uneven stress, especially when the
second element is a participle :—

·*godlike, jelly-like, foolhardy, colourblind, weatherwise,
bloodthirsty, waterproof ; heartrending, spirit-stirring ; sunburnt, careworn, bloodshot.*

Compounds ending in *-ed* tacked on to a noun where there is
no corresponding verb, such as *harebrained, humpbacked,* have
the same stress as *sunburnt,* etc., but they were not originally
participles, having the adjective-ending *-ede* in OE.

908. Combinations of **adjective + adjective** have even
stress ; many of them are used also as nouns :—

·*deaf-·mute, north-west, whitey-brown, greenish yellow ;
half-mad, dead-ripe, redhot, broiling hot.*

909. The analogous combinations of numerals, which are
used both as nouns and adjectives, have the same even
stress :—

·*twenty-one*, a ·*hundred and ·ten*, *two hundred*, *three thousand*.

Compound Verbs.

910. The great majority of compound verbs are made up of adverbs and verbs (**912**), compounds of verbs with other parts of speech being rare, and of modern origin. These compounds of **noun** or **adjective + verb** generally have uneven stress :—

·*browbeat*, originally 'to threaten or censure by contraction of the eyebrows,' *kiln-dry ; whitewash. blindfold.*

Adverbs and Pronouns in Composition.

911. **Noun**-compounds consisting of **adverb + noun.** and **adjective**-compounds consisting of **adverb + preterite participle** generally have uneven stress :—

·*forefinger, foreground, afterthought, bystander, underlip, up train, downfall, outcry, through journey.*

inborn, downcast, thoroughbred.

912. The numerous compound **verbs** formed of **adverb + verb** and of **verb + adverb** have even stress :—

·*forewarn, overcome, undergo, outbid.*

·*pass ·by, draw back, break down, take in, look out, run away.*

913. Nouns and adjectives formed from these verbs by derivation or inflection keep the same even stress :—

·*forerunner, forewarning ; passer by, looking on.*

·*forewarned ; grown up. broken down, worn out.*

914. So also if they are converted into nouns without change of meaning, as in *an ·over·load, a look-out, a break-·wn.*

915. But if they are made into nouns or adjectives with a distinct change of meaning, the stress becomes uneven :—

a ·drawback, a runaway, a go-between, tumble-down (adj.)

916. There are many compounds of **pronoun + pronoun** and of **pronoun + adverb** in which the principle of putting the stress on the modifying element is very clearly carried out ; in the following the modifying element comes first, so that first-syllable stress is the result :—

ʻsomeone	somebody	something	somewhere	somehow
anyone	*anybody*	*anything*	*anywhere*	*anyhow*
everyone	*everybody*	*everything*	*everywhere*	—
no one	*nobody*	*nothing*	*nowhere*	—

So also in *ʻelsewhere*.

917. In other compounds the modifying element follows, so that the stress is thrown forwards :—

someone ʻelse, somewhere else, whatever else.

whoʻever, whosoever, whatever, whenever, wherever, however.

EXTENSION OF COMPOUND-STRESS.

918. In Present English some words made up of inseparable elements take even stress as if they were compound words.

919. Some **prefixes** which have a very definite meaning and are phonetically capable of being detached from the body of a word have in consequence come to be felt as independent words, the prefix and the body of the word being balanced against one another, as it were, by each receiving equal stress. Foreign, as well as native, inseparable prefixes are treated in this way :—

Nouns : *ʻunbeʻlief, ʻmisʻconduct, misunderstanding, nonconductor, ex-manager, sub-committee, archbishop, juxtaposition,* **antiradical.**

Adjectives : *unseen, uncouth, unkind ; superhuman.*

Verbs : *misjudge, unbend, uncover, gainsay, cross-examine ; re-cover* = ' cover again,' *re-examine.*

misʻtake keeps its traditional ME stress because it is isolated from *take*.

920. Even **simple words** of more than one syllable sometimes have their syllables detached in this way. This is frequent with **exclamations**, which naturally tend to take even stress through the endeavour to make each syllable as loud as possible :—

·*hul·lo !, bravo !, amen !, encore !*

Exclamations are also uttered with advanced stress (**929**).

921. The same striving after distinctness leads to even stress in many foreign words, especially proper names :—

·*Ber·lin, Chinese, ·Water·loo.*

922. The *teen*-numerals take level stress on the analogy of the group-numerals *twenty-one,* etc. :—

·*thir·teen, fourteen, seventeen, nineteen.*

GROUP-COMPOUNDS.

923. Group-compounds formed by joining together two nouns by the conjunction *and* or a preposition—generally *of* —throw the stress on to the second element, as being the modifying one. The following are examples of *and*-groups :—

cup and ·saucer, knife and fork, bread and butter.

When other parts of speech are joined together in this way, they keep even stress : ·*now and ·then, to and fro, more and more, five and twenty, black and tan.* *Or*-groups have even stress when the *or* is a strong alternative, as in ·*sooner or ·later,* the stress being thrown back when the *or* is weak, as in *an* ·*hour or so, a step or two.*

924. The following are examples of group-compounds formed with prepositions :—

man of ·property, man-of-war, woman of the world, people of rank, a cup of tea, a pair of gloves, matter of fact, mother-of-pearl ; commander-in-chief, a box on the ear, head over heels.

925. If an adjective precedes the second noun, the chief stress falls on that adjective :—

cat-o·-nine-tails, Jack-of-all-trades.

The stress is thrown back in *father-in-law,* etc.

Stress Advanced in Compounds.

926. In *man·kind* the stress is thrown forward. This is more frequent in words of three or more syllables, especially in proper names and words lengthened by derivative syllables :—

pocket·handkerchief, Southampton, Newfoundland, arch·bishopric [*·arch·bishop*], *out·rageous* [*·outrage*].

So also in *Fitzgerald, portfolio, portmanteau,* which are felt as compounds, though obscured.

927. Stress is thrown forward when a title is followed by a proper name :—

Mr. ·Smith, Miss Carnaby, Lord John, King Henry, Prince Arthur.

928. In exclamations the stress is sometimes even (**920**), but is often advanced, as in *a·ha !, good ·morning !* Hence even-stress compounds such as *·Black·heath, Oxford Road* become *Black·heath,* etc. when used as exclamations, compounds in which the stress is thrown back, such as *·Oxford Street,* keeping their stress unchanged when used as exclamations.

Assumptive (Attributive) Compounds and Groups.

929. When an even-stress compound or group, or simple word stressed like a compound is put before a noun which it modifies assumptively, the stress is thrown on the first element of the compound or group :—

·Berlin ·wool [but *·wool from ·Berlin*], *Waterloo station, a Chinese mandarin ; non-commissioned officer ; underdone meat.*

secondhand bookseller, North Country surgeon, ten-pound note, twenty-five members ; All Saints' day ; goodlooking man, strongminded woman, hardboiled eggs, well-known voice ; turned-up nose, grown-up daughter.

·black-and-tan ·terrier, five-and-twenty blackbirds.

Compare also *a ·seven o'clock ·dinner,* and *a ·good for*

nothing ·fellow with *we dine at ·seven o'·clock* and *he is ·good for ·nothing.*

930. When a group-compound in which the stress is already thrown forward is used assumptively, it keeps its stress unaltered, the stress of the head-word being subordinated:—

cat and ·dog :life, cock and bull story, rag bone and ·bottle :merchant; bank of England note.

931. This is also done with some even-stress groups in which the connection between the elements is not close:—

a drowned ·rat :look, dead letter office, a Michael Angelo style, the Charles Dickens edition.

932. So also in longer groups:

a good all ·round :man, the employers' liability for ·injury :bill, the commons enclosure consoli·dation :act.

Quantity.

933. In MnE there is a general tendency to shorten long vowels. As we have seen (**851, 853**), long vowels are often shortened before certain consonants in native words, as in *blood* (blɐd) = OE and ME *blōd.*

934. There is also a tendency to shorten long vowels—or keep strong short vowels from being lengthened—when followed by a single consonant and a weak vowel, in words of French origin, whether popular or learned, as in *cavern, cavity* compared with *cave; gratify, gratitude* compared with *grateful; perish, method, benefit, relative, astonish, philosophy, astronomy, pleasure* (pleʒə) compared with *please, courage* (kɐridʒ), *flourish.*

935. But when the consonant is followed by two weak vowels the preceding strong vowel is often lengthened, as in *atheist, radiant, patient, tedious,* especially in the derivative endings *-tion, -sion,* etc., preceded by a strong vowel, as in *nation, admiration, adhesion, notion, corrosion,* although *i* is not lengthened under these circumstances, as in *hideous*, *petition*. Short vowels are also preserved when the two short vowels are preceded by certain consonants, such as *n* and *sh*, as in *companion, fashion*.

936. There are also a variety of other exceptions, especially before certain endings, such as *-al, -ive, -y, -n* and *-r* preceded by weak vowels, as in *fatal, decisive, navy* compared with *navigate, bacon, paper, labour*, those in *-n* and *-r* being probably the result of the influence of native words, such as the preterite participles *taken, shaken*, etc., and the numerous derivatives in *-er*, such as *maker*.

937. But some of these words with long vowels shorten them when another syllable is added, as in *national* compared with *nation, tyrannous* compared with *tyrant*.

938. In words which have been imported direct from Latin and Greek, the vowels are generally long under the circumstances described above, as in *basis, ether, regent, crisis, focus, strophe*. But there are several exceptions, such as *simile* (simili), *chemist*, the quantity varying in some words, such as *pathos* (pcipos, pæpos).

939. In Present English we can distinguish three degrees of vowel quantity. Long vowels and diphthongs preserve their full quantity only when final, as in *say, see, no, why*, or when followed by a final voice consonant, as in *home, raise, succeed, wine*. Before breath consonants they become half-long, as in *race, seat, knife*.

940. In all these cases the consonant is short. If a short strong vowel is followed by a single consonant, that consonant is lengthened, as in *fill, win* (winn), *set*, this lengthening having taken place already in ME (**789**). But if the final consonant is voiced—especially if it is a voice stop—the vowel is often lengthened instead of the consonant, as in *bed* (beed), *dog* compared with *dock, his* (hiiz), length being often distributed about equally over the vowel and the consonant. It will be observed that when these naturally short vowels are lengthened in this way, their quality remains unchanged; thus the lengthened vowel of *dog* remains distinct from the (ɔ) of *daub*.

In English, therefore, in the combination strong vowel + final consonant, either the vowel must be long or the consonant. The combination short strong vowel + short final consonant offers great difficulties to English speakers, as in the German *mann* (man).

941. The combination short strong vowel + short consonant occurs in English only before a weak vowel, as in *filling* (filiŋ) compared with *fill* (fill), *lesser, many, cupboard* (kʌbəd), a vowel-like consonant acting like a weak vowel, as in *cattle* (kætl), *written, trouble.* A weak vowel beginning another word has the same effect, if the two words are run together without any pause, as in *fill it* (fil -it), *let us get it* (let -əs get -it) compared with *get them* (gett ðəm). Long vowels and diphthongs under these conditions are partially shortened, as in *tidy* compared with *tide, chosen* (tʃouzn) compared with *chose,* the vowel-like consonant in the latter example acting like a weak vowel. Half-long vowels and diphthongs are partially shortened in the same way, as in *tighter* compared with *tight,* the diphthong in *tighter* being therefore still shorter than in *tidy*.

942. In weak syllables simple vowels become quite short, and a following consonant remains short also, as in *pity, pitied, better, setting.* A vowellike consonant remains short under the same circumstances, as in *settle* (setl), *bitten* (bitn).

943. Final consonants are long, as we have seen, after strong short vowels. In final consonant-groups the separate consonants are short if the last of them is voiceless, as in *built, since, stopped.* A consonant before a voice-consonant is lengthened, especially when a vowel-like consonant is followed by a voice-stop consonant, as in *build* (billd). *bend* compared with *built* (bilt). *bent*.

Two consonants in a weak syllable are, of course, short, as in *bottled* (botld).

944. When long words are drawled, any naturally long sounds they may contain are, of course, lengthened still more. If the word consists of a strong short vowel followed by a single consonant and a short weak vowel, the strong vowel is not lengthened, but the length is thrown on to the weak vowel, which is lengthened without change of quality, and without taking any additional stress, as in *what a pity!* (ˈpitii), *stop her!*

ACCIDENCE.

NOUNS.

Old English.

GENDER.

945. There are three genders of nouns in OE—**masculine, feminine,** and **neuter.** The genders of nouns are most clearly shown by the accompanying definite article 'the'— masculine *se*, feminine *seo*, and neuter *þæt*. The gender is partly natural, partly grammatical. It is to be noted that by natural gender names of children and young animals are neuter: *þæt cild, þæt bearn* 'child,' *þæt cealf* 'calf.' In the same way diminutives are neuter: *þæt mægd-en* 'maiden,' 'girl.' Names of things and abstractions are often neuter, but as often masculine or feminine: *þæt heafod* 'head,' *þæt hus* 'house'; *se finger* 'finger,' *se here* 'army'; *seo hand* 'hand,' *seo wynn* 'joy.' Names of living beings sometimes have a grammatical gender which contradicts the natural gender: thus *þæt wif* 'woman,' 'wife' is neuter.

946. The gender is sometimes shown by the form of the word. Thus all nouns ending in *-a* are masculine, such as *se mona* 'moon,' *seo sunne* 'sun' being feminine.

947. Compound nouns follow the gender of the last element. Hence *se wīfmann* 'woman' is masculine, because *se mann* 'human being' is masculine.

Strong and Weak.

948. All nouns belong to one of two classes—strong and weak. **Weak** nouns are those which inflect mainly with -*n*, such as *se steorra* 'star,' plural nominative *þa steorran, sunne*, genitive singular *þære sunnan*. All others are strong, such as *se stān* 'stone,' genitive singular *stānes*, plural nominative *stanas*.

Cases.

949. OE nouns have four cases, **nominative, accusative, dative, genitive**, which are not always clearly distinguished. The accusative is the same as the nominative in all plurals, in the singular of all neuter nouns, and in the singular of all masculine strong nouns. Masculine and neuter nouns differ very little in their inflections. The inflections of weak nouns are nearly the same in all three genders. The dative plural ending of nearly all nouns is -*um*.

Declensions.

The following are the regular noun-declensions:—

Strong Masculine.

		Sing.	Plur.	Sing.	Plur.
950.	Nom.[1]	*stān*	*stānas*	*ende* 'end'	*endas*
	Dat.	*stāne*	*stānum*	*ende*	*endum*
	Gen.	*stānes*	*stāna*	*endes*	*enda*

Strong Neuter.

		Sing.	Plur.	Sing.	Plur.
951.	Nom.	*hūs*	*hūs*	*scip* 'ship'	*scipu*
	Dat.	*hūse*	*hūsum*	*scipe*	*scipum*
	Gen.	*hūses*	*hūsa*	*scipes*	*scipa*

952. Some neuters have a plural ending -*ru*, such as *cild*, plural *cildru, cildrum, cildra*. The plural ending -*u* is dropped after a long syllable, that is, one containing a

---

[1] Wherever the accusative is not given separately, it is the same as the nominative.

long vowel, as in *hus*, or containing a vowel followed by more than one consonant, as in *folc* 'nations.'

Strong Feminine.

	Sing.	Plur.	Sing.	Plur.
953. Nom.	*caru* 'care'	*cara*	*synn* 'sin'	*synna*
Acc.	*care*	*cara*	*synne*	*synna*
Dat.	*care*	*carum*	*synne*	*synnum*
Gen.	*care*	*carena*	*synne*	*synna*

954. The -*u* of the nom. sing. is, like the -*u* of the neuter plur. nom., kept only after a short syllable. Some strong feminines ending in a consonant have the acc. sing. the same as the nom., such as *dǣd* 'deed,' acc. sing. *dǣd*; but in Late OE most of these are declined like *synn*, with acc. sing. *dǣde*.

Weak Masculine.

955.		Sing.	Plur.
	Nom.	*nama* 'name'	*naman*
	Acc.	*naman*	*naman*
	Dat.	*naman*	*namum*
	Gen.	*naman*	*namena*

Weak Neuter.   Weak Feminine.

	Sing.	Plur.	Sing.	Plur.
Nom.	*ēage* 'eye'	*ēagan*	*ċiriċe* 'church'	*ċiriċan*
Acc.	*ēage*	*ēagan*	*ċiriċan*	*ċiriċan*
Dat.	*ēagan*	*ēagum*	*ċiriċan*	*ċiriċum*
Gen.	*ēagan*	*ēagena*	*ċiriċan*	*ċiriċena*

956. There are besides a number of **irregular** strong nouns. The most important of these are the **mutation**-nouns, such as the masculine *mann* 'man,' *fot* 'foot,' *tōþ* 'tooth,' plur. *męnn*, *fēt* (*fæt*), *tēþ*, the feminine *boc* · book,' *gos* 'goose,' *mus* 'mouse,' *burg* 'city,' plur. *bec*, *ges*, *mȳs*, *byriġ*.

Masculine Mutation-nouns.

	Sing.	Plur.	Sing.	Plur.
957. Nom.	*mann*	*menn*	*fōt*	*fēt*
Dat.	*menn*	*mannum*	*fēt*	*fōtum*
Gen.	*mannes*	*manna*	*fōtes*	*fōta*

Feminine Mutation-nouns.

	Sing.	Plur.	Sing.	Plur.
958. Nom.	*burg, burh*	*byriġ*	*mūs*	*mȳs*
Dat.	*byriġ*	*burgum*	*mȳs*	*mūsum*
Gen.	*burge*	*burga*	*mūse*	*mūsa*

959. The masc. *sunu* 'son' has dat. and gen. sing. and nom. plur. *suna*, the fem. *duru* ' door ' being declined in the same way. So also the fem. *hand* has dat. and gen. sing. and nom. plur. *handa*, the original *-u* of the nom. sing. having been dropped because of the preceding long syllable.

960. Some masc. names of nations occur only in the plur., ending in *-e*, such as *Engle* 'the English,' dat. *Englum*, gen. *Engla*. Some of these have a weak gen. plur., such as *Seaxe* ' Saxons,' *Mierce* ' Mercians,' gen. *Seaxna*, *Miercna*.

961. The relationship-words in *-er, or*, such as *fæder* ' father,' *modor* ' mother,' *brōþor* ' brother ' are partly regular, partly indeclinable, the dat. sing. generally having mutation :—

	Sing.	Plur.	Sing.	Plur.
Nom.	*fæder*	*fæderas*	*brōþor*	*brōþor, brōþru*
Dat.	*fæder*	*fæderum*	*brēþer*	*brōþrum*
Gen.	*fæder, fæderes*	*fædera*	*brōþor*	*brōþra*

962. Some nouns are indeclinable, such as the abstract fem. nouns in *-u*, such as *ieldu* ' old age,' *strengu* ' strength.' The fem. *nieht* ' night ' is indeclinable in the sing. and in the nom. plur., the masc. *mōnaþ* ' month ' being also indeclinable in the nom. plur ; we still preserve these unchanged plurals in the compounds *fortnight*=OE *feowertiene nieht* ' fourteen nights ' and *twelvemonth*. Some nouns are inde-

clinable in the dat. sing., such as *ham* ' home,' as in *æt ham*
' at home.'

The inflection of nouns is attended by various modifications
which fall under the general head of OE sound-changes.

963. Nouns ending in weak *-el, -ol, -en, -er*, etc. often
drop their vowel before an inflection beginning with a
vowel, thus *se engel* ' angel,' *se fugol* ' bird,' *seo sawol* ' soul,'
þæt wæpen 'weapon,' *þæt wundor* 'wonder,' ' miracle,' have
plurals *englas, fuglas, sāwla, wǣpnu, wundru.* This shortening is most frequent after a preceding long syllable, the
weak vowel being generally kept after a short syllable, as in
æcer ' field ' plur *æceras*.

964. For the change of *æ* into *a* in such nouns as *se dæg*
' day,' *se stæf* ' staff,' gen. sing. *dæges, stæfes*, plur. nom.
dagas, stafas, þæt fæt ' vessel,' ' dish,' *þæt dæl* ' dale,' ' valley,'
gen. sing. *fætes, dæles*, plur. nom. *fatu, dalu*, see § **747.**

965. For the dropping of *h* in such nouns as *se Wealh*
' Welshman,' plur. *Wealas, se seolh* ' seal,' plur. *seolas*, see
§ **761.**

966. In Late OE final *h* and medial *g* alternate in such
words as *se troh* (earlier OE *trog*), plur. *trogas, seo burh*, gen.
sing.*burge, se beorh* ' mountain,' plur. *beorgas* (**763**).

967. Final *-u* in the nom. sing. of some nouns, such as *se*
bearu ' grove,' *þæt meolu* ' meal,' *seo sceadu* ' shadow,' ' shade,'
seo sinu ' sinew ' is a weakening of original *w*, which reappears
before an inflection beginning with a vowel, as in the gen.
sing. *bearwes, meolwes, sceadwe, sinwe.* This *-u* is dropped
after a long syllable, as in *seo mæd* ' meadow,' plur. *mædwa*.

968. The dropping of *h* before vowels (**761**) leads to
contraction, as in *þæt feoh* ' money,' gen. sing. *feos*, Oldest
English *feohes*.

Early Middle English.

969. In Early Southern the old gender-distinctions in
nouns were still partially kept up. By degrees, however, the

inflections of the adjectives and the definite article were dropped; and when the Earliest Southern *þe, þeo, þet* were levelled--as they soon were—under the uninflected *þe,* so that *þeo sunne* = OE *seo synn* and *þet hus* became *þe sünne, þe hus,* the old genders were gradually forgotten, simply because there was nothing to mark them.   From the very beginning of the ME period the natural feminine gender of such words as *wummon, meiden* = OE *wifmann, mægden* began to prevail over the grammatical masculine and neuter, these words being referred to by the feminine pronoun *heo* ' she.'

970. The first great change in the old system of inflections was the levelling of weak vowels under *-e* (**794**).   By this change the distinctions of gender in the OE weak forms *mona, sunne, eage* were levelled in the Early Southern forms *mone, sunne, eie* as far as the endings were concerned.   The distinctions of case were almost entirely effaced by this change in such words as OE *sunu,* dat. and gen. sing. and nom. plur. *suna, caru,* acc., dat., and gen. sg. *care,* nom. plur. *cara.* So also the inflections in OE *stāne* (dat. sing.), *stana* (gen. plur.), *scipu* (nom. plur.) were levelled under the same final *-e.*

971. The only endings which could withstand this levelling were the gen. sing. *-es,* the nom. plur. *-as,* which both became *-es* in ME, as in *stones* = OE *stanes, stānas,* the weak *-an,* which became *-en,* the gen. plur. *-ena,* which became *-ene.* The dat. plur. *-um* became *-em* ; but as this was the only case ending in *m,* the consonant was levelled under the more frequent *n,* so that ME *-en* represented OE *-um* as well as *-an,* as in *weren* = OE *geferan, geferum.*

972. The general result of these changes was not only to obscure the distinctions of the cases, but also in some classes of nouns to obscure the distinction between singular and plural.   The confusion was most marked in the feminine nouns, where the changes we have been considering gave the following as the endings corresponding to those of the OE nouns *caru, synn, sunne* respectively :—

Sing. Nom.	*-e*	*-**	*-e*
Acc.	*-e*	*-e*	*-en**
Dat.	*-e*	*-e*	*-en**
Gen.	*-e*	*-e*	*-en**
Plur. Nom.	*-e**	*-e**	*-en*
Dat.	*-en*	*-en*	*-en*
Gen.	*-ene*	*-e*	*-ene*

973. It is evident that the forms marked * in the above table are in the minority, while at the same time most of them obscure the distinction between singular and plural. They were accordingly got rid of by the analogical extension of those forms which were in the majority and more distinctive. The *-e* of *care* and *sunne* was extended to the OE nom. *synn*, which became ME *sunne*. The plural *-en* of *sunnen* = OE *sunnan* was extended to all feminine nouns—ME *caren*, *sünnen* = OE *cara*, *synna*. As *-en* was now the distinctive mark of the plural, it was given up in the singular of *sunne*, whose oblique cases took the same form as the nominative, as in the other two classes. The final result was that all feminine nouns were uniformly declined as follows :—

	Sing.	Plur.
Nom.	*-e*	*-en*
Acc.	*-e*	*-en*
Dat.	*-e*	*-en*
Gen.	*-e*	*-ene*

974. As might be expected, the gen. plur. *-ene* was often levelled under the other plural cases, becoming *-en*.

975. Weak masculines and neuters were declined in the same way—sing. *name*, *eie*, plur. *namen*, *eien*. The only distinction between masculine and neuter weak nouns— namely in the acc. sing. (OE *naman*, *eage*) was thus lost.

976. The originally strong masculine *sune* = OE *sunu* was naturally regarded as a weak noun. and formed its plural *sunen*.

977. *-e* = the OE neuter plur. ending *-u* was made into

-*en* in the same way for the sake of distinctness, as in *deoflen*, *children* = OE *deoflu, cildru*, sing. *deovel, child*.　In many of these words -*e* = OE -*u* was extended to the singular, as in *dale* ' valley,' *bede* ' prayer,' = OE *dæl, gebed*, plur. *dalu, gebedu*. These OE plurals became *dalen, beden* in ME.

978. The remaining masculine and neuter nouns kept their original strong forms.　The dat. sing. in -*e* was kept at first, but often dropped, because such forms as *weie, worde* = OE *wege, worde* suggested a weak singular, and so the dat. sing. was levelled under the nom. in such words—*wei, word* —in accordance with the general ME tendency.　The dat. plur. -*en* = OE -*um* was disused for a similar reason—because it suggested a weak plural—being kept only in a few adverbial phrases, such as *vour sipen* ' four times ' = OE *feower sīþum*, the nom. plur. being used as a dative.　The gen. plur. -*e* = OE -*a* was sometimes kept, but the more distinct weak ending -*ene* was often used instead—*kingene*, as in *alre kingene king* ' king of all kings,' *wordene* instead of *kinge, worde*—both of these forms being gradually supplanted by the nominative. In the neuter plur. the OE undeclined forms were still kept— *hūs, word*—but the strong masc. ending was often extended to the neuters, so as to distinguish the two numbers—*huses, wōrdes.*

The following are then the regular Early Southern ME noun-inflections, those which are liable to be dropped being in (　):—

Strong Masculine and Neuter.

979.

	Sing.		Plur.	
Nom.	*stọn*	*word*	*stọnes*	*word, wordes*
Dat.	*stọn(e)*	*wọrd(e)*	*stọnes, (sīþen)*	*word, wordes*
Gen.	*stọnes*	*wordes*	*stọne(ne), stọnes*	*wọrde(ne), wōrdes*

980. The neuters *child, ęį* ' egg ' have plur. *children, ęįren*, corresponding to OE *cildru, ægru*.

Strong and Weak Feminine.

981.

	Sing.		Plur.	
Nom.	*sünne, chirche*		*sünnen, chirchen*	
Dat.	*sünne, chirche*		*sünnen, chirchen*	
Gen.	*sünne, chirche*		*sunnen, chirchen(e)*	

982. Some originally strong feminines do not take *-e* in the nom. and acc. sing., such as *hond* 'hand,' *miht* 'might,' *cu* 'cow.'

Weak Masculine and Neuter.

983.

	Sing.			Plur.	
Nom.	*ivēre*	*ēie*		*ivēren*	*ēien*
Dat.	*ivēre*	*ēie*		*ivēren*	*ēien*
Gen.	*ivēre*	*ēie*		*ivēren(e)*	*ēien(e)*

984. Those of the old mutation plurals which are still preserved in MnE were of course kept in Early ME as well: *man* (*mon*), *vot*, *tōþ*, *gos*, *mus*, plur. *men*, *vet*, *tēþ*, *ges*, *müs*. The OE *wifmann* plur. *wifmenn* appears in Early Southern ME as *wümmon*, *wümmen*, in Early Midland as *wimman*, *wimmen*. In all these words the mutation was confined to the plur.. such OE datives as *mẹnn* being made into *monne* or *mon*. In the plur. on the other hand the mutated forms were gradually extended to the dat. and gen., *men* supplanting *manne*, *mannen*. Most of the feminine irregular nouns do not take *e* in the nom. and acc. sing. The OE feminine noun *burg* appears in ME sometimes as *burh*, sometimes as *burwe* plur. *burwen*, later *burwes*, the old mutated dat. sing. being preserved as the second element of place-names in the form of *-büri*—in the other dialects *-beri*, *-biri*—as in *Canterbüri* 'Canterbury' = the OE dat. *Cantwarabyrig*. This arose from the phrase 'at the city,' *at* governing the dative in OE, as in *at þære byrig*, which became *at ter büri* in ME (**767**). whence the MnE *Atterbury*. In the case of *boc*, plur. *boken*, *bokes*, the mutation was completely lost.

985. The relationship-words *vader, moder, süster* generally remained unchanged in the sing., having the regular plurals *vaderes, modren, süstren*. *bröþer* of course lost the OE mutation in the dat. sing., which became *bröþer*. But this mutation was transferred to the plur. on the analogy of *fet, men*, etc., so that *bröþre*=OE *bröþru* became *brēþre*, and then, by the usual change of plural *-e* into *-en, brēþren*.

986. *niht, moneþ* and some others remained uninflected in the plural.

987. The OE vowel-change in *dæg*, plur. *dagas*, was preserved in the ME *dęi, dai* plur. *dawes*, although a new plur. *daies* was soon formed direct from the sing. *dai*.

988. Final *e* was dropped after a weak vowel, as in *lęfdi* ‘lady’=OE *hlǣfdige*. The plural ending *-s* without a vowel occurs only in long French words, as in *parlurs* ‘parlours,’ *vestimenz* ‘vestments,’ where *z*=(ts).

In Old French such a word as *vestiment* is inflected thus—

Sing. Nom.	*vestimenz*	Plur. Nom.	*vestiment*
Acc.	*vestiment*	Acc.	*vestimenz*

As the distinction between nom. and acc. had been lost in ME, the French *-s* was naturally identified with the English plur. inflection *-es*.

989. In Early Midland and Northern the distinctions of grammatical gender were entirely lost during the transition from OE, the distinction between strong and weak forms being also done away with, except in a few isolated forms. The natural consequence was that the *-es* of the genitive was extended to weak nouns and to all feminine nouns, the plur. *-es* being then extended in the same way, first to strong neuters, then to weak nouns and feminine nouns generally. The final result was that the only regular inflections left were gen. sing. *-es*, plur. nom. and gen. *-es*, the distinction between nom. and gen. plur. being kept up only in irregular plurals such as *men*, gen. *mennes*.

Late Middle-English.

990. Standard ME follows the Early Midland dialect in its noun-inflections: it has only one case, the genitive; the original nominative, accusative, and dative being now merged in one 'common case':—

Sing. Common	*word,*	*sinne*	'	*man*
Gen.	*wordes,*	*sinnes*		*mannes*
Plur. Common	*wordes,*	*sinnes*		*men*
Gen.	*wordes,*	*sinnes*		*mennes*

991. The *e* of *-es*—the gen. as well as the plur. ending— is often dropped in English as well as French words after a weak syllable, as in *faders* (also *fadres*), *ladys* (also *ladyes*), and after a strong vowel, in order to avoid hiatus, as in *fọs* 'foes.' Also in *pens* = earlier *penies,* of which *pens* was originally the weak form, the word having lost its stress in such combinations as *two penies* [compare the Mn. E. *two-pence* (tɛpəns)].

992. The whole ending *-es* is often dropped in French words and proper names ending in a hiss-consonant, as in the gen. sing. *Troilus, Vẹnus,* and the plurals *cās* 'cases,' *vers* (also *verses*).

This is the result of French influence, for in Old French such a word as *vers,* whose *s* is part of the body of the word, was necessarily indeclinable:—

Sing. Nom. *vers*		Plur. Nom. *vers*	
Acc. *vers*		Acc. *vers*	

993. Originally feminine nouns sometimes keep their earlier *s*-less gen. sing., as in *þe chirche dọre, his lady grace.* We still preserve this form in *Lady-day* compared with *Lord's day.*

994. Many originally neuter nouns with unchanged plurals still keep these, such as *folk, der, hors, nẹt* 'cattle,' *shẹp, swin, kin* 'kind,' *þing, ȝer.* It must be observed that most of these plurals have a collective meaning; thus the plur. *folk* is oftener used in the sense of 'people in general' than in that of 'nations,' and in MnE *swine* is used exclusively in the collective plural sense, not being used in the singular at all. The invariable plurals *night, moneþ, winter* (OE plur. *wintru, winter*) are also kept. But several of these words begin to take the regular plural ending, especially when not preceded by numerals: *þinges, ȝeres, monþes. fot* when used as a measure was also made invariable in the plural on the analogy of the old neuter *pound*, and the other invariable words which were frequently joined to numerals, such as *winter*.

995. In its general meaning *fot* keeps its mutation-plural *fet.* So also *man, wom(m)an, tōþ,* etc. have plurals *men, wom(m)en, tēþ,* etc.

996. The weak plural-ending *-en* is preserved not only in *oxe* plur. *oxen,* but also in other words which have now lost it in the spoken language, such as *asche, aschen, hose, ie* 'eye,' *ien, fo* 'foe,' *fon, to* 'toe,' *ton, scho* 'shoe,' *schon.* In other words this ending is a ME extension, as in *brēþren, children, dohtren, sustren. cow* has plur. *kȳn* = OE *cu,* plur. *cy,* the northern dialect keeping the older form *kī.*

Modern English.

997. By the beginning of the MnE period the *s* of inflectional *-es* had been voiced (**861**), (s) being kept only in monosyllables such as *geese, pence.* In Early MnE the *e* was kept after a hiss-consonant for the sake of distinctness, as in *horses* (horsez), and was dropped everywhere else, the (z) being necessarily unvoiced after a voiceless consonant, as in *beasts* (beests) from *beastes* (beestez), while it was of course preserved after vowels and voiced consonants, as in *days, heads* (heedz).

998. The ME dropping of *-es* after hiss-consonants is still kept up in a few phrases such as *for old acquaintance sake, for Jesus' sake;* but in the spoken language the *-es* is generally kept. as in *St. James's Square*, where it is also written. Such genitives as *Æneas'*, *Socrates' wife* occur only in the literary language ; in the spoken language the full *-es* is added, or else the construction *of Æneas* etc. is used.

One result of the contraction of inflectional *-es* in MnE is that radical *s* has been sometimes mistaken for the plural inflection. so that an original singular has been made into a plural, as in the case of *alms, eaves, riches, summons* : these 'apparent plurals' correspond to the OE singulars *ælmesse, efese* (plur. *efesan*) and the Old French singulars *richesse, semonse*.

Most of these apparent plurals are not used in the singular : but *summons* is used in the sing. without any change—*a summons*. There are some plurals which form a curtailed singular by throwing off the radical final *s*. Thus the collective plural *pease* = the OE weak plural *piosan* has developed a singular *pea*, whence a new orthographic plural *peas* has been formed. In vulgar English such curtailed singulars are frequently formed from names of nations in *-ese*, such as *Chinee*, *Portuguee* from *Chinese, Portuguese*.

Inflectional plurals often come to be used as singulars by change of meaning, such as *news, sixpence*. They may then form new plurals, such as *sixpences*.

999. The ME (and OE) alternation of breath and voice consonants in the inflection of such native words as *wif*, gen. sing. *wives*, plur. *wives* has been kept up only partially in MnE. It has been entirely abandoned in the gen. sing.. which is now formed afresh from the common case—*wife s*. We still keep the voice consonant in such plurals as *wives*, *paths* (paaoz), but such a plural as the earlier MnE *turves* has been made into *turfs*.

We still keep the gen. sing. *calves* in the compounds *calves-head, calves-foot* expressing articles of food : otherwise *calf* has the regular gen. sing. *calf's*.

The following are the main types of noun-inflection in Present English :—

1000. *Sing. Common* hɔs   dog   kæt   waif   guws   mæn

Gen.   hɔsiz   dogz   kæts   waifs   guwsiz   mænz

Plur. Common hɔsiz   dogz   kæts   waivz   gijs   men

Gen.   hɔsiz   dogz   kæts   waivz   gijsiz   menz

Present English has developed a **vocative** case in a few words (**1004.** 1).

Like *horse* are inflected words ending in the hisses (s, z ; ʃ, ʒ), such as *piece, box, size, adze, fish, church* (tʃəatʃ), *age* (eidʒ).

Like *dog* are inflected nouns ending in a vowel or any voiced consonant except (z, ʒ), such as *day, lady, neighbour* (neibə), *mile, dove, son, lord.*

Dice (for gaming) and *pence*, the plurals of *die* and *penny* have (s) because they were shortened to monosyllables already in ME, *dies* (for coining) and *pennies* being new-formations from the singulars on the analogy of the regular plurals *days, ladies*, etc.

Like *cat* are inflected nouns ending in any breath consonant except (s, ʃ), such as *earth, cliff, clerk, bishop.*

1001. All the nouns inflected like *wife*—'voice-breath nouns'—show a long syllable before the inflection in Late ME, as in *staves* = Late ME *staves* (Early ME *staves*), *wolves* = ME *wulves*. Hence nouns with original short *i* never make this change—*piths* (pips), *cliffs*. The only voice-breath noun ending in (s) is *house*, plural *houses* (hauziz). The chief voice-breath nouns in (p) are *bath* (baap), *baths* (baaðz) = Late ME *baþ, baþes* (bap, baaðes), *path, oath, mouth. clothes* was originally the plural of *cloth*, which now forms a regular plural of its own—*cloths*. The great majority of nouns in (p) keep the breath-sound in the plural ; such nouns are *moth, death, hearth, health, birth*. Some, such as *lath, truth, youth* have both pronunciations, that with voice consonants in the plural being, of course, the older one. Nouns in -*f* show the change more frequently : after long Late ME vowels, as in *life, knife, wife, thief, leaf,*

loaf; after *l*, as in *half, calf, elf, self, shelf, wolf*. Nouns in
-rf, such as *dwarf, scarf, turf, wharf*, made this change
in Early MnE—*dwarves*, etc.—but they now generally keep
the *f* in the plural—*dwarfs*, etc. Nouns in *-oof* also keep the
f, as in *hoofs, roofs*. So also *belief*. But the French noun
beef still keeps its plural *beeves*, which, however, is now isolated from its singular, through the latter having lost its
original meaning 'ox.' *staves* was originally the plural of
staff (Late ME *staf, staves*), but having diverged from it in
meaning, it has now developed a new singular *stave*, while
staff itself has developed a new plural *staffs*, as in *army staffs*.

IRREGULAR PLURALS.

1002. The following **mutation-plurals** are still in
common use : *man, men* ; *woman, women* (wumən, wimin),
this plur. being Southern in spelling, though Midland in
pronuncation ; *foot, feet* ; *goose, geese* ; *tooth, teeth* ; *louse, lice* ;
mouse, mice.

1003. The only **n-plurals** in common use are *ox, oxen* ;
child, children. *brother* now has the regular plural *brothers*,
the old plural *brethren* being used only in a metaphorical
sense. *cow* also has a regular plural *cows*, the older *kine*
occurring only in the higher literary language.

1004. *sheep* and *deer* keep their **unchanged plurals**.
Weak (-mən), as in *tradesman, gentleman, Englishman* is also
invariable.

The full sound (-men) is, however, preserved in addressing
a number of people, so we can distinguish the common plural
(dʒentlmən) from the vocative plur. (dʒentlmen).

1005. These are the only absolutely invariable words. In
all other invariable words the unchanged plural implies either
measure or collectiveness. As in Late ME, so also in MnE
many nouns of measure have an unchanged plural only when
preceded by a numeral, as in *two dozen knives* compared with
dozens of knives ; and many of them keep it only in groups or

compounds such as *ten-pound note* compared with *ten pounds*, the earlier MnE *ten pound* being now obsolete or vulgar. It is only when a noun of measure is used also as an ordinary descriptive noun that it occasionally keeps its unchanged plural under all circumstances, as in *how many stone does he weigh?*

1006. While the use of the unchanged plural of measure has been gradually restricted in MnE, the unchanged collective plural has been extended. *swine* has now lost its singular, the sing. and separative plur. being expressed by *pig*, *pigs.* But in most cases the collective and separative plurals are used side by side, as in *to catch fish* compared with *the story of the three fishes.*

These details belong rather to Syntax than to Accidence, and will be considered more fully under the former head.

FOREIGN PLURALS.

1007. Many foreign words—especially Latin and Greek— keep their original plurals, but some of them have also regular English plurals; some have the two plurals in different meanings. Some are used only in the plural. Some are unchanged in the plural.

1008. The most important **Latin** endings are :—

-a . . . -æ : *formula, formulæ* ; *larva, nebula. minutiæ* is used only in the plural.

-us . . . -i : *fungus, fungi*; *hippopotamus, nucleus, radius, terminus, tumulus. anthropophagi, Magi, literati* occur only in the plural. The regular plurals *funguses, hippopotamuses* etc., also occur, especially in the spoken language. *crocus* always has plural *crocuses. genius* in its ordinary meaning has the regular plural *geniuses* ; in that of 'spirit' it keeps the Latin plural *genii.* Latin nouns in -*us* which form their plurals by other endings than -*i*, either keep them, as in *genus*, plur. *genera*, or else make them regular, as in *census*, plur. *censuses* (Latin *census*, plur. *census*).

-um . . . -a: *desideratum, desiderata: erratum. effluvium.*
Many of these are used only in the plural: *addenda, agenda,
arcana, data, ephemera. memorandum* has plur. *memoranda*
and *memorandums.* Others, such as *encomium, millenium*
have only *s*-plurals.

In the spoken language there is a tendency to make the
a-plural into a singular from which a new plural is formed.
Thus *stratum, strata* is made into *strata, stratas* on the analogy
of the ending *-er, -or,* etc., *animalculum, animalcula* is made
into *animalcula, animalculæ* on the analogy of *formula, formulæ.* The difficulties in connection with the last word are
best avoided by using the shortened form *animalcule,* plur.
animalcules.

-is . . . -es: *analysis, analyses; axis, basis, crisis, hypothesis, metamorphosis, oasis. parenthesis. antipodes, aborigines*
are used only in the plur. In these latter the ending is
pronounced distinctly (-ijz). So also in careful speaking we
distinguish the plur. (pərenbisijz) from the sing. (pərenpisis),
but in ordinary speech the *-es* is shortened to (-is) so that
no distinction is made between sing. and plur. in the more
familiar words.

-es . . . . -es: *series, species, superficies.* These plurals
are unchanged both in spelling and pronunciation—(siəriz,
siəriz).

-ix, -yx, -ex . . . -ices: *appendix, appendices; helix,
calyx, vortex.* These plurals hardly occur in the spoken
language, which substitutes the regular forms in familiar
words: *appendixes, calyxes.* The former of these plurals is
also used in writing, the plur. *appendices* being necessary
only when the word has its special mathematical meaning.

1009. There are other isolated Latin plurals: *genus,
genera; stamen, stamina.* But *stamen* generally has a regular
plur. *stamens,* and *stamina* is now used as a sing. in a special
sense.

1010. -on . . . -a is a Greek plur.: *phenomenon, pheno-*

mena; *anacoluthon, automaton, criterion.* The three last also have regular plurals, as also *phenomenon* in the groups *infant phenomenon* etc.

1011. We have Italian plurals in *bandit, banditti* [also *bandits*]; *dilettante, dilettanti*—where the English pronunciation (dili·tænti) makes no distinction between sing. and plur. —*virtuoso, virtuosi* [also *virtuosos*].

1012. The Hebrew plurals *cherubim, seraphim* are collective, and are occasionally used as singulars in Early MnE— *a cherubim. cherub* and *seraph* also have regular plurals, especially in their metaphorical meanings.

1013. The French plural ending *x* in *beaux* (also *beaus*), *flambeaux* is pronounced (z).

1014. The plural of *Mr.* (mistər) is expressed by the different word *Messrs.* (mesəz), in full *Messieurs. Mr.* is a weak form of ME *meister* from old French *meistre*, the corresponding strong form being *master. Messieurs* is the French *mes Sieurs* 'my Lords,' the sing. of which is *Monsieur.* The plural of the feminine *Madam* = French *ma Dame* 'my Lady' is *Mesdames* = French *mes Dames* 'my Ladies,' which, however, is not much used in English.

1015. The tendency of the language now is to get rid of foreign plurals as much as possible, except where the foreign plur. marks a difference of meaning.

INFLECTION OF WORD-GROUPS.

Genitive.

1016. When adjunct-words are joined to a noun so as to form a word-group, the genitive inflection is added to the last member of the group, whether that last member is the head-noun or not, as in *the old king's son, king Alfred's son, the king of England's son, the man I saw yesterday's son.* So also in group-compounds: *the knight-errant's, the son-in-law's.*

1017. In the first example given above the inflections of the words preceding *king's* have simply been dropped—OE *þæs ealdan cyninges sunu.* In the second example the inflection of *king* has been dropped—OE *Ælfredes cyninges sunu.* The third example shows a further step, which was first made in MnE, the ME construction being *þe kinges sune of England.* A still further step is made in the fourth example, in which the genitive ending is added to an indeclinable adverb, inflecting really the whole group *the-man-I-saw-yesterday.* Hence in the first example also we may regard the *-s* as inflecting not *king*, but the whole group *the-old-king*.

Plural.

1018. The principle of group-inflection is not carried so far with the plural ending. When a noun is modified by a following adverb or preposition-group, the noun itself is inflected, as in *hangers-on, fathers-in-law, commanders-in-chief.* If the first element is not a noun, the inflection is naturally put at the end, as in *the three-per-cents, go-betweens, forgetmenots.*

1019. In the rare combination of a noun with a following adjective the same rule was formerly followed, as in *courts-martial, knights-errant,* but now it is more usual to put the inflection at the end, in accordance with the general tendency of the language—*court-martials, knight-errants*—except in such groups as *states-general,* in which the old plural has become fixed, through the sing. being disused. In groups consisting of two titles both elements are inflected, as in *lords-lieutenants, lords-justices, knights-templars.* So also in *men-servants, women-servants.*

1020. When a noun of title etc. is put before another noun, the older rule was that the adjunct-noun took the inflection. We still follow this rule in the combination *Messrs. Smith*; but such combinations as *the Misses Smith, the brothers*

Smith now sound pedantic, the former being also liable to cause confusion with *Mrs.* (misiz), and in colloquial language it is usual to say *the Miss Smiths, the two Doctor Thomsons,* etc., the construction in the case of *brothers,* etc., being often evaded by saying *the Smith brothers.*

SPELLING.

1021. The *e* of the plural *-es* is always kept in writing when pronounced, as in *fishes,* or when required to show the sound of a preceding letter, as in *clothes* compared with *cloths.* But superfluous *e* is still kept in many instances. Thus it is always written after *v* (**824**), as in *shelves.* Final *y* is written *ie* before plural-*s,* as in *spies, cities.* This is a tradition of Early MnE, in which *ie* was written in the singular as well (**825**), as it still is in some words, such as *lie, die*—both of which are verbs as well as nouns—the old equivalent *ye* being still written in *lye, dye* for the sake of distinction. *y* preceded by another vowel is kept unchanged, as in *days, boys.* Weak *-ey* was till lately changed into *ie* before the plural *-s,* and this spelling is still frequent in some words, such as *ponies,* but in most words there is no change—*chimneys, valleys.* *alkali* has plural *alkalies,* the few other words in *-i*—none of which are in frequent use—generally adding the *-s* without *e,* as in *rabbis.* Most words in frequent use have plural *-oes* whether the singular ends in *-oe* or simple *-o: foe, foes; woe, woes; potato, potatoes; negro, negroes.* Nouns in *-io* take only *-s,* as in *folios, ratios,* as also most of the less familiar words: *dominos, grottos, virtuosos, quartos.* The endings *-ies, -oes* were kept to show that the *s* was voiced, =(z), simple *-is, -os* suggesting the breath sound (s), as in *this, crisis, chaos.* The plurals of proper names and of words belonging to other parts of speech used as nouns are sometimes written in the ordinary way, sometimes by adding *s* preceded by an apostrophe, so as to distinguish the body of the word from the ending, the apostrophe being often omitted when there is no fear of confusion : *ayes and noes, ayes and no's, pros and cons, pros and cons, the two Marys, the two Marys, the Percies, to mind ones P's and Q's.* Proper names ending in a hiss-consonant simply add the apostrophe, as in *the Chambers' and Cassells of the future,* also written *Chamberses* in accordance with the pronunciation.

1022. The written genitive ending is *'s,* which is added to the common singular form without any further change : *man s, lady's, negro's.* The regular gen. plur. of nouns is distinguished in writing from the gen. sing. by the apostrophe being put after the genitive inflection, as in *birds' nests* compared with *a bird's nest, the negroes' quarter* (gen. sing. *negro's), beaux'* (gen. sing. *beau's).* The gen. plur. of such irregular nouns as *man* is written in the same way as the gen. sing.: *man's, men's; goose's, geese's.* The apostrophe by itself is often written in the gen. sing. of nouns ending in a hiss-consonant, especially proper names: *Socrates' wisdom, Chambers' Cyclopedia, Cox' cleverness.* This spelling was originally phonetic (998); but the full (-iz) is now always kept in pronunciation, the corresponding spelling *Chambers's,* etc. being also used.   In Early MnE the apostrophe was at first intended only to show contraction of -*es,* and was accordingly used freely in the plural as well as the genitive inflection, the spelling *bird's* being, of course, used for the gen. plur. as well as the gen. sing.   The gradual restriction of the apostrophe to the genitive apparently arose from the belief that such a genitive as *prince's* in *the prince's book* was a shortening of *prince his,* as shown by such spellings as *the prince his book.* This belief and this spelling arose very naturally from the fact that *prince's* and *prince his* had the same sound, weak *his* having dropped its (h) in such collocations even in the OE period (865). Besides being a mark of contraction the apostrophe was found useful in distinguishing between the body of an unfamiliar word and its inflections, being still used for this purpose even in the plural inflection (**1021**).　Hence it was liable to be omitted in familiar words —whether plurals or genitives.　We still generally write the genitives *its, hers, yours* without it, though we write *one's*.

ADJECTIVES.

Inflections.

OLD ENGLISH.

1023. In OE the adjectives have the three genders of nouns, and the same inflections, though with partially different forms, together with the distinction of strong and weak.　In the strong masc. and neut. sing. they have an instrumental case, which in the feminine, in the plural, and in the weak declension—as also in the noun-inflections—is represented by the dative.

1024. Adjectives agree with their nouns in gender, number, and case : *hie comon mid langum scipum, na manigum* 'they came with long ships, not many.'

1025. The weak form is used after the definite article and other defining words, as in *se goda cyning* 'the good king,' *se halga* 'the holy (man),' whence the weak masc. noun *hālga* 'saint,' *þas halgan cyningas* 'these holy kings,' compared with *sum god cyning* 'a certain good king,' *halge menn* 'holy men.' The weak form is also used as a vocative : *þu leofa freond !* 'thou dear friend !'

1026. The following are the strong inflections of *god*, the forms which differ from those of the nouns being marked * :—

		Masc.	Neut.	Fem.
Sing.	Nom.	*god*	*god*	*god*
	Acc.	*godne**	*god*	*gode*
	Dat.	*gōdum**	*gōdum**	*gōdre**

	Instr.	*gōde*	*gōde*	*gōdre**
	Gen.	*godes*	*godes*	*godre**
Plur.	Nom.	*gode**	*god*	*gode**

	Dat.	*gōdum*
	Gen.	*godra**

1027. The weak forms are identical with those of the weak nouns, except in the gen. plur., which, however, sometimes appears as *-ena* with the same ending as in the nouns, instead of taking the ending of the strong adjectives :—

		Masc.	Neut.	Fem.
Sing.	Nom.	*goda*	*gode*	*gōde*
	Acc.	*godan*	*gode*	*godan*
	Dat.	*gōd·n*	*g· 1·n*	*g· dan*
	Gen.	*godan*	*godan*	*godan*

Plur.	Nom.	*gō1·n*
	Dat.	*g· dum*
	Gen.	*godra**

1028. The *-u* of the strong fem. nom. sing. and the strong neut. nom. plur. is kept under the same circumstances as in the noun-inflections; thus *sum* ' some' has *sumu* in the above cases, as opposed to the long-syllable *god*. Adjectives in *-el, -en*, etc. drop the *e* as in noun-inflection ; thus *halig, micel, agen* ' own,' have plurals *halge, micle, āgne*. Where final *-u* is a weakening of *-w*, the *w* is restored before an inflection beginning with a vowel, as in *nearu* ' narrow,' *salu* ' sallow,' *geolu* ' yellow,' plurals *nearwe, salwe, geolwe*. In late OE final *-h* alternates with medial *g* in such forms as *genoh* ' enough ' [earlier *genog*], plur. *genoge*. The dropping of weak *h* between vowels leads to contraction ; thus *heah* ' high.' Mercian *heh*, has plural *hea* (from *heahe*) in Mercian as well as Early West-Saxon, which in the later language is made into *heage* on the analogy of *genoh, genoge*.

1029. Some adjectives are indeclinable, such as *fela* ' many.'

MIDDLE ENGLISH.

1030. The levelling of noun-inflections in ME and the loss of gender distinctions naturally led to the disregard of concord. Hence the case-endings in the singular of strong adjectives began to fall off at the beginning of the ME period. The distinction between singular and plural and between strong and weak inflection was preserved in the adjectives as well as in the nouns. *god* represented the strong singular, *gode* the strong plural and the weak singular. As the weak form of the adjective was generally followed by a noun, it was superfluous to mark the distinction of number in the adjective, and consequently the weak singular ending *-e* was used also in the plural. The result was that in Late ME the adjective had only two inflections, one positive, in *-e*, the other negative, consisting in the absence of the inflectional *-e* :—

| Strong Sing. *god* | Weak Sing. *gōde* |
| Plur. *gōde* | Plur. *gōde* |

1031. The weak form is used much as in OE : *þe yonge sonne* 'the young sun,' *þis ilke monk* 'this same monk,' *my sworne broþer* 'my sworn brother,' *leve brōþer !* 'dear brother !'

1032. Adjectives in *-e*, such as *newe* 'new,' are, of course, invariable. Other adjectives become invariable by dropping the inflectional *-e* after a weak syllable, especially *-i*, as in *þe holi man*, but also in such adjectives as *open, cursed, honest.* ✗

1033. In the Northern dialect all adjectives became indeclinable already in the Early period through loss of final weak *-e*.

1034. The old cases were partially preserved in the Earliest ME. The gen. plur. ending *-re*=OE *-ra*, as in *alre kingene king*=OE *eallra cyninga cyning*, lingered longest, because of its distinctiveness. In Late ME *alder*, from earlier *alre* through *aldre*, became a sort of prefix to superlatives, as in *alderbest* 'best of all'; in Early MnE Shakespere still has *alderliefest* 'dearest of all.'

MODERN ENGLISH.

1035. In MnE the loss of final -*e* made the adjectives in-declinable as far as case and number are concerned. Adjectives thus became formally indistinguishable from adverbs. except by their syntactical relations, the only change of form that was left to them—namely comparison—being shared by adverbs. But Early MnE still preserved a trace of the ME inflections in the distinction between *enough* sing., *enow* plur. =ME *in⁻h, in⁻w⁻.*

Comparison.

OLD-ENGLISH.

1036. In OE the comparative is formed by adding -*ra* and is declined like a weak adjective, as in *leof-ra* 'dearer' masc., *leofre* fem. and neut., the corresponding adverbs ending in -*or* : *leofor, heardor.* The superlative is formed by adding -*ost,* and may be either strong or weak : *leofost* 'dearest.' *se leofosta mann,* The uninflected form of the superlative is used also as an ad-verb : *leofost, heardost.* Some adjectives form their comparison with mutation, the superlative ending in -*est,* as in *lang* 'long,' *lengre, lengest, neah* 'near,' superlative *nīehst, niext* (Anglian *neh, nest, next*). In some comparisons the comparative and superlative are formed from a word distinct from that which constitutes the positive : *god* [adverb *wel*], *betera* [adverb *bet*]. *betst.* The positive of some comparatives and superlatives is represented only by an adverb; thus to *ærra* 'former' (in time) *ærest* 'first' corresponds the adverb *ær* 'formerly.' Many of these form the superlative with -*m,* which is an older form than -*st.* The original form of this superlative is seen in *for-ma* 'first,' the positive of which is represented by the adverb *fore* 'before.' But in most cases the meaning of this old superlative ending was forgotten, and the ending *-st* was added—generally with mutation—giving the double superlative *-mest.* Thus from *forma* the new superlative *fyrmest* 'most foremost,' 'first' was formed. Other examples are *innemest, norþmest* from *inne* 'inside,' *norþ* 'north.'

Middle-English.

1037. In Early ME the endings are *-re, -ere* [adverbial *-er*], *-est : leof, leofre* [*leover*], *leovest.* The insertion of *e* in the comparative ending *-ere* is probably due to the influence of the superlative. In Late ME the final *-e* of *-ere* was dropped, because preceded by a weak syllable, so that the distinction between adjective and adverb was levelled.

Modern English.

1038. In MnE the endings are the same as in Late ME— *-er. -est.* We have also a **periphrastic comparison**, which consists in prefixing the adverbs *more, most,* as in *beautiful, more beautiful, most beautiful* by the side of *hard, harder, hardest.* Periphrastic comparison appears already in Early ME. At first the two methods of comparison were used indiscriminately ; but by degrees the periphrastic comparison has come in MnE to be applied chiefly to longer and more unfamiliar adjectives, the inflectional comparison being restricted more and more to the shorter adjectives, namely—

(*a*) monosyllables, such as *big, high, young, sad.*

(*b*) dissyllabic adjectives with the stress on the last syllable, such as *polite, severe, complete, minute.* But many of these have the periphrastic comparison, which is the more usual of the two when the adjective ends in a heavy consonant-group, as in *abrupt, correct, distinct, ancient, fre- . a nt.*

(*c*) many dissyllabic adjectives with the stress on the

first syllable, such as *tender, bitter, narrow, happy, easy, early, lovely,* and others in *-ly, able, simple, wholesome, cruel.* Those in *-ish, -s,* and *-st* have the periphrastic comparison, so as to avoid the repetition of the hiss-consonant in the superlative : *selfish, childish; adverse; honest, earnest, modest.* So also those in *-ive,* such as *active,* apparently because most of them are long words, the shorter ones being mostly words whose meaning does not lend itself to comparison. Such an adjective as *pleasant,* on the contrary, is compared by inflection in spite of its heavy ending, because its meaning makes it liable to frequent comparison.

1039. The periphrastic comparison is followed—

(*a*) by all adjectives of more than two syllables, such as *difficult, ignorant, important, comfortable, respectable*—all of which have besides heavy endings—*curious, generous, necessary, general, satisfactory.*

(*b*) by those in *-ful,* such as *useful, awful, cheerful, respectful.*

(*c*) by those in *-ed* and *-ing*: *learned, wretched, wicked; cunning, tempting, charming, improving.* These adjectives are not inflected because they have the form of verbals, although some of them, such as *wretched* and *cunning,* are of a different origin. *wicked* sometimes has superlative *wickedest.*

1040. In Early ME such comparisons as *more sad, most sad, beautifuller, beautifullest* were frequent; and they are still used in poetry and the higher prose.

1041. Double comparison was frequent in Early MnE, as in *more braver, most unkindest.* This now survives only as a vulgarism.

Irregular Comparison.

1042. In ME and MnE the old mutation in such comparisons as OE *lang* (*long, lǫng*), *lengre, lengest* was gradually got rid of by the introduction of the vowel of the positive, whence the MnE *longer, longest.* Mutation is preserved only in a few irregular and isolated forms. Other irregularities are the result of ME sound-changes—*late, latter*—of various confusions and mixtures of originally distinct words and forms—*far, further*—and of the retention of different-word comparatives and superlatives—*good, better.*

1043. The double superlative ending *-mest* was naturally associated with *mǣst* 'most,' and already in Late OE we find such forms as *ȳtmǣst* by the side of *ȳtemest* from *ūte* 'outside'; in ME we find the endings *-mest* and *-mǫst* side by side, the latter ultimately getting the upper hand. In the few cases of mutation the vowel of the positive was gradually extended to the other two degrees; already in OE we find *ūtemest* instead of *ȳtemest.* So also OE *fyrmest* was made into *formest* in ME by the influence of *forma* and *fore*, whence the MnE *foremost.* In OE the positives of *æftemest* 'last' and *niþemest* 'lowest' were represented by the adverbs *æfter* 'after' and *niþer, neoþor* 'downwards,' 'down,' these being themselves old comparatives. In ME the full forms of the positives *after, neþer* were introduced into the superlatives, whence the MnE *aftermost, nethermost,* a new superlative *undermost* being formed on the analogy of *nethermost.* A superlative ending *-ermost* having thus established itself, other superlatives of place were formed directly from comparatives by adding *-most,* as in *lowermost, uppermost* in imitation of *nethermost* and *undermost, uttermost* by the side of *utmost, innermost.* So also from *further* was formed a superlative *furthermost,* from which again was formed a double comparative *furthermore,* perhaps partly by the influence of *evermore.* The OE *midmest* was made into *middlemost,* and on the analogy of this form superlatives such as *highmost* were formed direct from adjectives, *highmost* being perhaps regarded as a transposition of *most high.* To the OE superlatives *norþmest, sūþmest* correspond as positives the adverbs *norþ, sūþ,* which were also used as nouns. Hence

in MnE we have superlatives in -*most* formed directly from
nouns, such as *topmost*, *endmost*.

The following are the irregular comparisons of MnE :—

1044.   *old*   { *elder*   *e*
                     { *older*   *oldest* }

OE *eald* (*āld*), *ieldra* (*eldra*), *ieldest* (*eldest*).   The comparisons *elder*, *eldest* are used to express differences of age
from a more abstract point of view than *older*, *oldest*, as in
elder brother compared with *he is older than he looks*.

1045.   *late*   { *latter*   *last* }
                      { *later*   *latest* }

OE *læt* 'slow' [adv. *late* 'slowly,' 'late'], *lætra* [adv.
lator], *latost*.   *latter* — ME *later* with back-shortening.   *last*
is a shortening of ME *latest*, not by phonetic change, but
apparently by the analogy of *best*, *least*, etc.   When *latter* and
last developed special meanings, the new comparisons *later*,
latest were formed directly from *late*.

1046.   *out*   { *utter*   *utmost, uttermost* }
                     { *outer*   *outmost, outermost* }

OE *ute* adv. 'outside,' *ȝterra* [adv. *utor*], *ytmest*, *ytemest*.
Even in OE the vowel of the positive is extended to the
other degrees : *uterra, utemest*, whence by back-shortening
the MnE *utter*, etc., *outer*, etc. being new-formations from *out*.

1047.   *far*   { *farther*   *farthest* }
                     { *further*   *furthest* }

OE *feorr* adv.(and occasionally adj.) far,' *fierra* [adv. *fierr*],
fierrest.   *feorr* became by regular change ME *fer*, MnE *far*.
To the OE adverb *fore* 'before,' 'in front' corresponds the
comparative *furþra* [adv. *furþor*], superl. *fyrest*, *fyrst*, *forma*,
fyrmest.   The comparative adverb *fierr* was soon confused
with the positive *feorr* in ME through the tendency to give
up mutation in comparison, and the more distinct *furþor* took
its place, *fierr* and *furþor* having nearly the same meaning.
When ME *first*=OE *fyrst* became the ordinal numeral

corresponding to *ǫn* 'one'—taking the place of OE *forma* 'first'—a new superlative *furþest* was formed from *furþer* — OE *furþor*. Lastly, the vowel of the positive was extended to the other degrees, giving *farther, farthest*. The old superlative *forma* being no longer recognizable as such, was regarded as a positive, whence a new comparative *former* was made in imitation of *latter*.

1048.   *nigh* $\left\{ \begin{array}{ll} near & next \\ nearer & nearest \end{array} \right\}$

OE *neah* (*neh*) adverb (rarely adjective), *nearra* [adv. *near*], *niehst, nīext* (*next*). The MnE positive adjective and adverb *near* is the old comparative adverb, made into a positive on the analogy of *here, there* as well as *far*. It is compared regularly *nearer, nearest*, the old superlative *next* being isolated from it. The old positive is represented by the adjective and adverb *nigh*, which is obsolete in the spoken language.

1049.   *good* (*well*)   *better*   *best*

OE *god* [adv. *wel*], *bętera* [adv. *bęt*], *bętst*. The dropping of the *t* in *best* is not phonetic, but is the result of the influence of *mǣst*, etc.

1050.   *bad*   *worse*   *worst*

OE *yfel, wiersa* [adv. *wiers*], superl. *wierrest, wierst*, Anglian *wyrsa*, etc. In ME *ill* from Scandinavian *illr* came into use concurrently with *iivel, ivel, evel*, our present *evil* being the Kentish form. In ME a new adjective with the same meaning—*badde*—was developed by change of meaning and shortening from the OE noun *bǣddel* ' effeminate person.' In MnE *bad* has gained the upper hand, though *worse* and *worst* are still comparisons of *evil* and *ill* as well as of *bad*. In the Southern ME *wurse, wurst, u* was developed out of *ü* = Late West-Saxon or Anglian *y* by the influence of the *w*. In Early MnE a new double comparative *worser* was formed. Both *worser* and the double superlative *worsest* occur in Vulgar MnE.

1051. *little* $\left\{ \begin{array}{l} \textit{less} \\ \textit{lesser} \end{array} \right\}$ *least*

OE *lytel, læssa* [adv. *læs*], *last.* The new formation *lesser* is, of course, a double comparative like *worser* (**1051**).

1052. *much* *more* *most.*

OE *micel, māra* [adv. *ma*], *mæst.* In Late West-Saxon *micel* became *mycel* by the influence of the *m*, whence Southern ME *müchel, muche(l).* The Early Midland form is still preserved in the name *Mitchell*, which also shows the original meaning 'big,' 'tall.' In OE *ma*, originally an adverb, is used as a neuter noun governing the genitive in the sense of 'more in number,' as in *ma þara witena* 'more of the councillors.' In ME *mọ̄ =* OE *ma* came to be used as an adjective, and in Early ME *moe* was regarded as the comparative of *many =* OE *manig. moe* has now been levelled under *more =* OE *māra* neut. *mare*, so that *more, most* are the comparisons both of *much* and of *many*. In ME—and already in Late OE—the *a* of *māra, ma* was extended to the superlative, which became *mast, mọst,* MnE *most.*

PRONOUNS.

1053. In OE the inflections of the personal pronouns of the first and second persons—*ic* ' I,' *þu* 'thou '—are altogether peculiar and anomalous. The personal pronouns of the third person—*he* ' he,' *hit* ' it,' *heo* 'she '—have inflections similar to those of the adjectives : compare acc. sing. masc. *hine*, dat. sing. masc. *him* with *godne, godum.* So also the interrogative pronoun *hwā, hwæt* ' who,' ' what,' and the demonstrative pronouns *se* 'that,' 'the' and *þes* 'this' have inflections similar to those of strong adjectives. The main peculiarities of the pronoun inflections as distinguished from those of the adjectives are (*a*) that they are sometimes made up of different

words, thus *ić* acc. *me, se* acc. *þone*, and (*b*) that the neuter
sometimes has a special ending -*t*, as in *hit* 'it' compared
with *he, hwæt, þæt*, which in OE is the neuter of *se*. Some
of the pronouns have, like the adjectives, an instrumental
case. The personal pronouns of the first and second persons have a dual number : *wit* 'we two,' *git* 'ye two.' These
dual forms were kept in the earliest ME, but were soon lost,
together with other characteristic features of the OE pronoun
inflections. But their two main characteristics are still preserved even in MnE in such forms as *I, me* and *who, what*.

1054. The remaining OE pronouns have the inflections of
ordinary strong adjectives, whether they are used as adjectives or nouns. Thus the adjective-pronoun *sum* in *sum mann*
'a certain man' and the noun-pronoun *sum* 'a certain one'
both have plural *sume*, as in *sume menn cwædon, sume cwædon*
'some (people) said'; and there was a singular neuter noun-
pronoun *eall*, as in *sęle eall þæt þu hæfst* 'sell all that thou
hast,' as well as a plural *ealle*, as in *ealle wundrodon* 'all
wondered.' So also *hwęlc* 'which,' *swęlc* 'such,' *ōþer* 'other,'
ænig 'any,' *nan* 'none,' 'no' had the plurals *hwęlce, swęlce,
ōþre, ænige, nāne*, which were used both as adjectives and
nouns. OE pronouns only occasionally take weak inflection, as in *ić selfa* 'I myself' compared with *ić self*, acc. *me
selfne*.

1055. In ME the old plurals in -*e* were kept, as in *alle
men* 'all men,' *alle þat liveþ* 'all that live.' But in MnE the
-*e* was dropped in accordance with the general rule, so that
these pronouns became invariable in the plural, as in *some
think differently, beloved by all, of such is the kingdom of
heaven.*

1056. The regularly inflected pronouns had a gen. sing.
masc. and neut. in -*es* in OE. The OE noun-genitive *ōþres*
'another man's' survives in the MnE *other's, another's*. So
also *either's* — OE *ægþres* from *ægþer = æghwæþer*. The MnE
genitive *one's* is a new-formation.

1057. It is probably the old genitive *other's*—together with the desire of distinctness—which led to the formation of a new plural *others* instead of the invariable *other*, which was still preserved at the beginning of the Early MnE period, as in *when other are glad, then is he sad.*   The plural *ones* of the prop-word *one*, as in *the young ones*, is, of course, a still later formation.

Personal Pronouns.

Old-English.

1058. The following are the inflections of the personal pronouns—including, for convenience, the interrogative *hwā* —later forms being in ( ) :—

Sing. Nom.	*ic*	*þu*	*he*	*hit*	*heo*
Acc.	*mec (me)*	*þeč (þe)*	*hine*	*hit*	*hīe (hy)*
Dat.	*me*	*þe*	*him*	*him*	*hire*
Gen.	*mīn*	*þīn*	*his*	*his*	*hire*

Plur. Nom.	*we*	*ġe*	*hīe (hy, heo)*
Acc.	*usic (us)*	*eowic (eow)*	*hīe (hy, heo)*
Dat.	*ūs*	*eow*	*him (heom)*
Gen.	*ure*	*eower*	*hira, heora*

Sing. Nom.	*hwā*	*hwæt*
Acc.	*hwone*	*hwæt*

Dat.	*hwām (hwām*
Gen.	*hwæs*
Instr.	*hwȳ*

1059. The change of the plur. *him* into *heom* is the result of the influence of the gen. plur. *heora* together with the desire to distinguish between singular and plural.   The late nom. plur. *heo* is the result of levelling under *heom* and *heora*.

1060. Many of the above inflections had weak forms, in which long vowels were shortened, such as weak *þu, heo=* strong *þu, heo.*

1061. The genitives *mīn*, etc. are used not only as possessives, but as pure genitives; thus *ic gemunde þīn* ' I remembered

thee,' *ic gemunde his* ' I remembered him (or it) ' are parallel
to *ic gemunde þæs mannes* ' I remembered the man.'

MIDDLE-ENGLISH.

1062. In ME the genitive of the personal pronouns was
gradually restricted to the function of a possessive pronoun,
though it still retained something of its independence in such
phrases as *oure aller hęle* ' the salvation of us all ' = OE *ure
eallra hǣlu.*

1063. The distinction between accusative and dative was
done away with, these two cases being levelled under one
which we call the ' objective ' case, this objective case being
really the old dative used also as an accusative. This extension of the dative began already in OE, *me, þe, us, eow* being
the regular accusatives even in Early West-Saxon. The explanation is that as the personal pronouns generally refer
to living beings, we naturally think of ' I,' ' you,' etc. not as
mere passive objects of striking, calling, sending, etc., but as
being to some extent actively interested in these processes ;
and hence we are inclined to use the interest-case or dative
to express the personal complement even of purely transitive
verbs. Hence even in OE they began to say *he slog me* ' he
struck me ' instead of *he slog mec* in the same sense as *he slog
þone stān* ' he struck the stone,' but from a different point of
view. In ME the change was carried out consistently, *him*
supplanting *hine* and so on. But with the specifically
neuter pronouns the process was reversed : *it* and *what* being
mainly thought of as passive complements of verbs, not
only kept their old accusatives—which was made still more
easy by these accusatives having the same form as the
nominatives—but used them to express the much rarer relation of interest, and so the old accusative *it* has come to
represent the dative as well as the accusative in MnE, while
the old dative *him* serves as accusative as well as dative.

1064. In ME—as also in OE—all the third person pronouns had weak forms without *h-* : unemphatic or weak *im* by the side of emphatic or strong *him*, although in writing only the emphatic form was used, just as in MnE we write *I saw him*, whether the *him* is emphatic (him) or weak (im). But even in the earliest Midland we find *it* written everywhere by the side of *he*, etc., showing that this originally weak form had supplanted the strong one. The reason is that it was so rarely necessary to emphasize the impersonal pronoun that the strong *hit* was forgotten and disused. But *hit* was preserved in South-Thames English up to the end of the Late ME period.

1065. OE *ic* split up into the two forms *ich* (North-Thames *ic*) and *ī*. The latter—which was, of course, originally the weak form—gradually supplanted the fuller form, which became extinct in Standard ME, although it still survives in the dialects of the West of England.

1066. So also the weak *us* (with short vowel) gradually supplanted the strong *ūs, ous*.

1067. In OE the *o* of *eo, ēo* was often weakened to *a* when these diphthongs were uttered with weak stress, so that such a pronoun as *heora* 'their' developed a weak form *heara*. In Late OE weak diphthongs began to shift their stress on to the second element, the length of *ea, eo* being shifted with the stress. The first elements of the diphthongs were then shortened and weakened till they became a weak (j), which was then liable to be dropped altogether. Hence we get the following changes, which in some cases were fully carried out in Late Old-Northumbrian, while in others they were not carried out till the ME period :—

˙eo	˙ea	eˑa	ja	a
˙ēo		ēˑo	jo	o

Already in Early Old-Anglian we find weak *heara* by the side of the older strong *heora*. In Early ME *heara* passed through (hjare) into *hare*, and in the same way Late OE *heom* 'them' became *ham*. The weak OE *hēo* 'she,' which in Late OE also expressed 'they,' passed through the same change, becoming *ha*. This weak *ha* was then extended to the masc. sing. So in Early Southern we find the following strong and weak pairs with *a* in the latter : *he* (*ha*) 'he,' *heo* (*ha*) 'she,' 'they,' *heom* (*ham*) 'them,' *heore* (*hare*) 'their.' *ha* was liable to drop its *h* by still further weakening, whence the Early MnE *a* = *he* in *quoth'a, quotha, 'a must needs*. It must be noted that such forms as *heo* and *a* represent the two extremes of emphatic strength on the one hand and enclitic weakness on the other, and that there were other intermediate weakenings ; also that when a weak form was developed, that weak form might afterwards take strong stress, and that the original strong form might itself lose its stress and develop a new weakening. Thus we find the strong *heore* weakened into *hore* in the same way as the weak *heare* was further weakened into *hare*.

1068. Strong *heo* 'she' passed through *heo* into (hjoo, jhoo), which last is the Early Midland form, written *gho* parallel to *wha* 'who' = (whaa). But the feminine demonstrative *seo* 'that one,' 'she' gradually took the place of *heo*, at first in the Midland dialect, and then in the Standard ME. *seo* passed through *seo* (sjoo) into *sho* in some dialects with the change of (sj) into (ʃ). This *sho*, being a weak form, existed side by side with the strong *seo*, and in some Midland dialects the two were blended together into a new form *sheo*, which became *she* by the regular change of *eo* into *e*. Strong *heo* was soon discarded, because this vowel change levelled it under the masculine *he*.

1069. *eow* in its weak form passed through (joow) into (juuw), written *ȝuw*, which then became *yow* = (juu), the (w) first changing the *o* into *u*, and then being itself absorbed by the *u*. Early Southern has *ou* with dropping of the *e*, just as in *hore* = *heore*.

1070. The Late OE tendency to confuse *heo* 'she' and *hīe* 'they' under the common form *heo* led to a more extended use of the demonstrative plural *þa* 'they.' In the ME period this usage was especially developed in North-Thames English. But as *þa* also had the strong demonstrative meaning 'those ones,' 'those,' and as Scandinavian influence was strong in North-Thames English, *þa* in the sense of 'they' was made into *þei* by the influence of Scandinavian *þeir* 'they,' where the -*r* is only the inflection of the nom. masc. plur., as in *Danir* 'Danes'= OE *Dęne*. The influence of the Scandinavian dat. and gen. plur. *þeim* 'to them,' *þeira* 'their' also changed the old *þǣm, þara* into *þeim, þeire, þeir* in North-Thames E. In Late ME *þei* found its way into the Standard dialect, which, however, still generally kept the Southern dative *hem* and the possessive *here* from the earlier Southern emphatic *heom, heore*.

1071. The following are, then, the chief forms of the personal pronouns in Early ME, the North-Thames forms being in ( ) :—

Sing. Nom.	*ich, ī (ic, i)*	*þū*	*whǭ (whā), whęt (what)*
Obj.	*mē*	*þē*	*wham*
Plur. Nom.	*wē*	*ȝē*	
Obj.	*ūs, us*	*ōu (ȝūw, ȝū)*	
Sing. Nom.	*hē, ha*	*hit (it)*	*hēo, ha (ȝhō, shō)*
Obl.	*hine, him*	*hit (it)*	*hire*
Plur. Nom.		*heo, ha (þei)*	
Obl.		*heom, ham (þeim)*	

1072. The later forms of Standard ME are—

Sing. Nom.	*ī, ich*	*þow=(þuu)*	*whō*	*what*
Obl.	*mē*	*þē*	*whōm*	*what*
Plur. Nom.	*wē*	*yē*		
Obl.	*us*	*yow=(juu)*		
Sing. Nom.	*hē*	*hit, it*	*shē*	
Obl.	*him*	*hit, it*	*hire, hir, her*	
Plur. Nom.		*þei*		
Obl.		*hem, þeim*		

1073. In Late ME the Early ME *wham* took the vowel of the nom. *who,* in which Early ME *ǫ* was made into close *ō* by the influence of the *w.*

1074. In ME the plural *ȝe, ȝow* was used in respectful and ceremonious address instead of the singular *þow, þe* by imitation of Old French.

1075. In OE weak *mann, man* 'man' was used as an indefinite pronoun = French *on,* with the verb in the third person sing. In ME it was shortened and weakened into *men, me,* as in *me seiþ* 'they say' = OE *man sęgeþ.* In Late ME it was confused with the plur. *men* and gradually disused, *me seiþ* being made into *men seien.*

Modern English.

1076. In Early MnE the use of the ceremonious plural *ȝe, ȝou* was so much extended that it became the usual polite form of address, the singular *thou* being used mainly to express familiarity and contempt, which latter use brought about its complete disuse in the spoken language of the present century, which therefore makes no distinction of number in the personal pronoun of the second person. But we still preserve the old *thou* in the poetical and liturgical language.

1077. In Early MnE the objective form *ȝou* came to be used as a nominative, and in Present English *ȝou* has completely supplanted *ȝe* in the spoken language. The change is partly the result of a general confusion between nominative and objective in MnE, partly of the influence of the singular pronoun *thou.* In Early MnE the ME *þe, ȝe* became (ðii, jii), which were shortened into (ði, ji) when weak. So also ME *þow, ȝow* became Early MnE (ðou, jou) by the regular change of (uu) into (ou), the short (u) of the ME weak forms being necessarily preserved unchanged in the Early MnE (ðu, ju). In Early MnE *thou* and *ȝe* were liable to lose their vowels before another word beginning with a vowel or h + vowel, so that *thou art*, *ye are* were shortened into *th'art*, *y are*, just as *the earth* was shortened into *th'earth*. This gave the following Early MnE forms of the second person pronoun : —

Nom. (ðou, ðu, ð)	(jii, ji, j)
Obj. (ðii, ði)	(jou, ju)

1078. It will be observed that each of these pronouns has two groups of endings which have exactly opposite functions, (-öu), etc. being the nominative ending in the singular *thou*, but the objective ending in the plural *you*, while (-ii) is the objective ending in the singular, the nominative ending in the plural. The natural result of this was that the associations between form and grammatical function became unsettled, and when *ye, you* came to be frequently used in a singular meaning, *thou* (ðou) and *you* (jou) were associated together, till at last *you* came to be regarded as a nominative. This confusion was increased by the shortened forms *y'are*, etc., in which it was impossible to know whether the *y* was a contraction of *ye* or of *you*.

1079. The phonetic similarity between *thee* and *ye* led to the frequent use of *ye* as an objective, especially in the weak form (ji), which was used indifferently as an objective or a nominative, being often further weakened by dropping the consonant, as in *hark'ee, harkee, lookee, thankee*. Such forms as *I tell ye* (ji) were still frequent a few generations ago, and (i) may still be heard in *how do you do?* (hau d i duw), but such forms as (luki, þæŋki) survive only as vulgarisms.

1080. As (ðöu) and (ðu), (jou) and (ju) diverged considerably in sound, one member of each pair was got rid of in the course of the Early MnE period, namely the weak (ðu) and the strong (jou), whose place was taken by (juu),— a lengthening of weak (ju). As this (uu) did not develop till after the change of ME (uu) into (öu) had been completed, it was, of course, preserved from that change.

1081. We have seen that the ending -*e*(*e*) in the second person pronouns is the mark both of the nominative (*ye*) and the objective (*thee*). The same cross-association runs through some of the other pronouns:—

> Nom. : *he, she, we, ye*
> Obj.   : *me, thee*

1082. The fact that in four cases out of six -*ee* is the nom. ending explains how *ye* was able to maintain itself as a nom. in spite of the support given to *you* by the sing. *thou*.

1083. Confusions between nominative and objective may occur in any language through misunderstanding grammatical categories. Thus in the Bible we find *whom do men say that I am ?*, where what ought to be the nominative is put in the objective through attraction (**117**)—through being regarded as the object of the verb *say*; and although OE is strict in its distinction between nom. and accusative, yet the OE version shows the same attraction : *hwæne secgaþ menn þæt sy mannes sunu ?* But as long as a language marks the distinctions of case with clearness, such confusions are confined to isolated constructions. In MnE, however, the distinction between nominative and objective was marked only in a few words, and even there was marked in a way which inevitably led to confusion ; and even apart from this cross-association there was no uniformity : thus in the pairs *I, me ; he, him ; we, us* the objective cases have no formal characteristic in common. Hence in MnE the linguistic sense for the distinction between nominative and objective has been almost as much weakened as that for the distinction between indicative and subjunctive.

1084. In Early MnE the usage was more unsettled than it is now, the nominative being as freely substituted for the objective as vice-versa, as in such constructions as *'tween you and I. you and I* were so frequently joined together as nominatives—*you and I will go together*, etc.—that the three words formed a sort of group-compound, whose last element became invariable.

1085. The tendency of Later MnE is to merge the distinction of nominative and objective in that of **conjoint** and **absolute**, that is, to keep the old nominative forms only when in immediate connection with a verb—*I am ; said he*—so that, as the pronouns in the nominative generally precede the verb, *I, he,* etc. are felt almost to be inseparable verb-forming prefixes, as in *I call*, compared with *to call.* When a pronoun follows a verb, it generally stands in the objective relation ; hence, on the analogy of *he saw me, tell me*, etc., the literary *it is I* is made into *it is me* in the spoken language, so that *me* is felt to be the absolute form of the conjoint *I,* being also used as the answer to the question *who is there?*, etc. In the vulgar language this is carried out consistently, the slightest separation from the verb being enough to elicit the objective form, as in *me and John came home yesterday*=the polite *John and I came home yesterday, them that is here—they that . .* In Standard spoken English the absolute use of the objective forms is most marked in the case of *me*, which is put on a level with the old nominatives *he*, etc.: *it is me, it is he, it is she.* But the usage varies, and in more careless speech such constructions as *it is him, it is us* are frequent.

In the written language the absolute use of the objective forms is not recognized ; and as such expressions as *it is me* are still denounced as incorrect by the grammars, many people try to avoid them in speech as well as writing. The result of this reaction is that the *me* in such constructions as *between John and me, he saw John and me* sounds vulgar and ungrammatical, and is consequently corrected into *I* occasionally in speech, but oftenest in writing, the Early MnE construction being thus revived.

1086. The tendency to use the nominative forms before the verb has had the contrary effect on the pronoun *who.*

Already in Early MnE *whom do you mean?* was made into *who do you mean?* on the analogy of *I mean* . . , *you mean* . . , etc. In Present spoken English *whom* may be said to be extinct, except in the rare construction with a preposition immediately before it, as in *of whom are you speaking?* = the more purely colloquial *who are you speaking of?*

The use of *you* before the verb in *you mean, you see,* etc. seems to be in opposition to the general tendency which made *who* prevail over *whom*. But, as we have seen, the extension of the objective form *you* is not really a case of deliberate substitution of the objective for the nominative, but is the result of the phonetic similarity of the nominative *thou*.

1087. The pronouns *thou, thee* and *ye* are now confined to the liturgical and the higher literary language. In the singular the distinction between nom. *thou* and obj. *thee* is strictly maintained. In the Bible *ye* is the nom. and *you* is the corresponding obj., but in the present language of poetry there is a tendency to use *ye* in the obj. as well as the nom., in order to avoid the prosaic *you* : *ye see, I see ye*.

The old singular second person pronoun is still kept up by the sect known as Society of Friends or Quakers, but in the form of *thee* for the nom. as well as obj. evidently by the influence of *he,* etc., which is confirmed by the fact that in Quaker English *thee* takes the verb in the third person sing. instead of the old second person sing. : *thee has, thee had* = the literary *thou hast, thou hadst*.

1088. In Early MnE *them*—which seems to be a weak form of ME *þeim*—finally got the upper hand of ME *hem,* which has survived only as a weak form, being written *'em* from the mistaken idea that it was a shortening of *them*. We still use (əm) as a weak form of *them* by the side of (ðəm), but only in very familiar speech.

1089. The MnE *it, her* are also equivalent to ME weak forms.

1090. The ME weak *ha* occurs occasionally in Early MnE in the form of *'a, a*, but only in very familiar, careless speech. Such forms as *quotha* are still used in the literary language when quaintness is aimed at.

1091. The following are the present forms of the personal pronouns in literary and spoken English respectively, weak forms being in ( ) :—

Sing.	Nom.	*I*	*thou, you*	*who*	*what*
	Obj.	*me*	*thee, you*	*whom*	*what*
Plur.	Nom.	*we*	*ye, you*		
	Obj.	*us*	*ye, you*		
Sing.	Nom.	*he*	*it*	*she*	
	Obj.	*him*	*it*	*her*	
Plur.	Nom.		*they*		
	Obj.		*them ('em)*		
Sing.	Nom.	ai	juw (ju, jə)	huw (uw)	whot, wot
	Obj.	mij (mi)	juw (ju, jə)	huw (uw)	whot, wot
Plur.	Nom.	wij (wi)	juw (ju, jə)		
	Obj.	ʊs (əs, s)	juw (ju, jə)		
Sing.	Nom.	hij (ij)	it	ʃij (ʃi)	
	Obj.	him (im)	it	həə (əə, ə)	
Plur.	Nom.		ðei		
	Obj.		ðem (ðəm, əm)		

1092. The shortening (-s) = *us* occurs only in *let's*. In Early MnE it was more general.

Possessive Pronouns.

Old English.

1093. The OE possessive pronouns are the genitives of the corresponding personal pronouns : *mīn* 'my,' *ure* 'our,' *þīn* 'thy,' *eower* 'your,' *his* 'his, its,' *hire* 'her,' *hira, heora* 'their.' The possessives of the third person—*his, hire, hira*—together with *hwæs* 'whose,' are indeclinable, those of the first and second person—*mīn, þīn, ure, eower*—being declined like strong adjectives : *mid his freondum* ' with his friends,' *mid mīnum freondum.*

MIDDLE ENGLISH.

1094. In ME *his* was made declinable on the analogy of *mīn*, etc., that is, it took a plural ending *-e*, as in *alle hise men* compared with OE *ealle his męnn.* This being the only inflection of the possessives in ME, those ending in *-e* necessarily remained or became indeclinable. The Early ME *ower, ʒur* = OE *eower* took final *-e* in Late ME by the analogy of *ure*, becoming *youre.*

1095. *mīn* and *þīn* dropped their final *n* before a consonant in Early ME—*mī fader*—keeping it before a vowel or *h* + vowel : *mīn arm, þīn herte.* In Late ME the *n* was often dropped before a vowel as well. The *n* was, of course, always kept when the possessives were used absolutely, or when they followed their noun : *hit is mīn, brōþer mīn!*

1096. In Late ME the possessives ending in *-e* generally take the genitive ending *-s* when used absolutely: *to mīn hous or to youres ; al þis gold is oures* = OE *to mīnum huse oþþe to eowrum ; eall þis gold is ure.* This *-s* is an extension of the *-s* of *his* : *his gold, þat gold is his.*

1097. In the weak forms long vowels were sometimes shortened—*mīn, mi*—and final *e* was dropped : *hir, our,* etc.

1098. In North-Thames English *þei* brought with it the possessive *þeire* = Icelandic *þeira*, which gradually made its way into the London dialect, where it also appears in the weak form *þere* parallel to *þem* = *þeim.*

1099. The following are the possessive pronouns in Standard ME, weak forms being in ( ) :—

Conjoint : *mīn, mi (min, mi) ; þīn, þī (þin, þi) ; his (hes) ; hire, hir (her) ; oure, our ; youre, your ; here, her, þeire, þeir (þere, þer).*

Absolute: *mīn*; *pīn*; *his*; *hires, hirs, heres, hers*; *oures, ours*; *youres, yours*; *heres, hers.*

All those beginning with *h* were, of course, liable to lose it in their weak forms.

1100. The Early ME possessive *whas* became *whos* in Late ME through the influence of *who*.

MODERN ENGLISH.

1101. In Early MnE *his* was still the possessive of *it* as well as *he*: *it* (the serpent) *shall bruise thy head, and thou shalt bruise his heel* (Bible). But already in the Midland dialect of ME the want of a special possessive for *it* was supplied by using the uninflected *it* as a possessive instead of *his*; and this usage appears also in Early MnE: *the hedge-sparrow fed the cuckoo so long that it's had its head bitten off by it young* (Shakespere). Towards the end of the Early MnE period the present genitive *its* came into general use— a form which does not occur at all in the Bible, and very rarely in Shakespere.

1102. The ME distinction between conjoint *mine, thine* and *my, thy* was still kept up in Early MnE, but the shorter forms were frequently used before vowels: *mine eyes, my eyes*. In the higher literary language the distinction is still kept up: *mine eyes, mine host*. But many modern poets drop the *n* before sounded (h), as in *my heart* = Early MnE *mine heart*, keeping it only before vowels and silent *h* + vowel, as in *mine honour*.

1103. The following are the present forms of the possessive pronouns in the literary and spoken languages :—

Conjoint: *my, mine*; *thy, thine*; *his*; *its*; *her*; *our*; *your*; *their*; *whose.*

Absolute: *mine*; *thine*; *his*; *its*; *hers*; *ours*; *yours*; *theirs*; *whose.*

Conjoint: mai (mai, mi); juər, jɔər (jor, jər); hiz (iz); its; həər (ər); ðeər (ðər); huwz (uwz).

Absolute: main; juəz, jɔəz; hiz; its; həəz; ðeəz; huwz.

One's in *one loses one's time* may be regarded as an indefinite possessive pronoun.

Self.

OLD-ENGLISH.

1104. In OE the emphatic *self*—Late West-Saxon *sylf*—is added to nouns and personal pronouns, being generally inflected like a strong adjective in agreement with its head-word: *God self hit geworhte* 'God himself made it,' *swā-swa hīe cwǣdon him selfum* 'as they said to themselves,' *he forgeat his selfes* 'he forgot himself.' In the nominative the weak-inflected *selfa* is used in the same way: *God selfa, ic selfa.*

Weak *self* is also used in the sense of 'same,' being treated like a pure adjective: *þy* (instr.) *sylfan dæge* 'on the same day.'

1105. In OE the personal pronouns are used also as reflexive pronouns, as they still are in such phrases as *he looked about him* compared with *he must take care of himself.* OE *self* does not make a pronoun reflexive, but simply emphasizes one that is already so, as in *wyscton him selfum*, the shorter *wyscton him* being enough to express the meaning 'wished for themselves.' Hence such a phrase as *he ofsticode hine* might mean either 'he stabbed him' (some-one else), or 'he stabbed himself.' By degrees *he ofsticode hine selfne*, which at first meant both 'he stabbed that very man' and 'he stabbed himself,' was restricted to the latter meaning, the simple *hine, him*, etc., being restricted more and more to the non-reflexive meaning, so that already in Early ME we find *self, sulf* used very much as in MnE.

1106. In OE a personal pronoun in the dative is often added reflexively to a pronoun in the nominative, but without materially affecting its meaning, as in *he ondred him þone mann* 'he was afraid of the man,' literally 'feared for himself,' *hie gewiton him* 'they departed.' This pleonastic dative is often added to *self, selfa* in this way : *he biþ him self gehwæþer, sunu and fæder* 'he (the phœnix) is himself to-himself both (pronoun), son and father,' *ic me self gewāt* 'I myself departed,' *hē him selfa sceaf reaf of līce* 'he to-himself himself pushed the robe from the body'='he took off his robe.'

1107. *self* in OE was occasionally used as a noun without any accompanying head-word : *sleaþ synnigne ofer selfes mūþ!* 'strike ye the sinful one on his mouth!'

MIDDLE ENGLISH.

1108. In ME the meaning and function of the datives *me* and *þe* in the combinations *ich me self, þu þe self,* etc., were soon forgotten, so that these constructions became unmeaning, which led to the change of *me* and *þe* into the possessives *mī, þī, self* being regarded as a noun, as shown in such constructions as *mī self haveþ* 'myself has' compared with *þī self havest* 'thyself hast.' On the analogy of *miself, þiself* the plurals *ureself, ȝūreself* were formed. The dative was preserved in *himself* 'himself, itself,' plur. *himself* (Late ME also *þemself*). *hireself* 'herself' could of course be regarded either as dative or possessive. The forms *-selve, -selven* also occur : *miselve, miselven, himselve, himselven. selven* is probably the OE dat. sing. or plur. *selfum, selve* being either a shortening of *selven* or else = OE weak *selfa.*

MODERN ENGLISH.

1109. In Early MnE *self* came to be regarded more and more as a noun, which led to such constructions as the Shakesperian *thy fair self, Tarquin's self.* A new plural *selves* was now formed on the analogy of *shelf, shelves,* etc. : *myself, ourselves, to your gross selves* (Shakespere).

1110. But the older dative was still preserved in *himself,* *themselves.* *itself* must also be regarded as containing the objective (= dative) case of *it* rather than as a contraction of *it's self.* In Present English we have the forms *his self, their selves* in vulgar speech; and even in the Standard dialect these forms are necessary when *own* is added: *his own self.*

1111. The following are the forms of the spoken language :—

Sing. *myself*; *yourself*; *himself, itself, herself.*
Plur. *ourselves*; *yourselves*; *themselves.*

To these may be added the indefinite *oneself.*

1112. It will be observed that *yourself, yourselves* make a distinction between sing. and plur. which is lost in the simple *you,* the sing. *thyself* being, of course, preserved only in the higher literary language. So also a form *ourself* occurs occasionally in older writers in the sense of 'myself'; but in the present literary language an author speaks of himself as *ourselves,* if he uses the plural.

1113. In the literary language *self* is used as an independent noun : *till Glory's self is twilight* (Byron); *then, all forgetful of self, she wandered into the village.*

1114. In the spoken language the emphatic and reflexive meanings of *myself,* etc., are distinguished by the stress, these forms having strong stress when emphatic, weak when reflexive, as in *I did it myself* compared with *he roused himself.*

The OE *self* as an adjective is represented by the compound *self-same* in MnE : *the selfsame thing.*

Demonstrative.

Old English.

1115. The OE demonstrative *se* 'that, this, the, he,' etc., and *þes* 'this, this one' are inflected as follows :—

	Masc.	Neut.	Fem.	Masc.	Neut.	Fem.
Sing. Nom.	sē (se)	þæt	sēo	þēs (þes)	þis	þēos
Acc.	þone	þæt	þā	þisne	þis	þās
Dat.	þǣm, þām		þǣre	þissum		þisse(re)
Gen.	þæs		þǣre	þisses		þisse(re)
Instr.	þȳ		þǣre	þȳs		þisse(re)
Plur. Nom.	þā			þās		
Dat.	þǣm, þām			þissum		
Gen.	þāra, þǣra			þissa, þissera		

The forms *sē*, *þēs* are used only as noun-pronouns in the sense of 'this one,' 'he.'

Middle English.

1116. In ME the *s* of the OE *se, se, seo* was made into *þ* by the influence of the more numerous forms beginning with *þ*, and of *þes, þis, þeos*.

1117. The resulting *þe, þat, þeo* was at first used, as in OE, both as a demonstrative and as a definite article. But by degrees the neuter sing. *þat* and the plur. *þa* were restricted to the demonstrative meaning. In Early Southern *þẹt hus* = OE *þæt hus* is still used in the sense of 'the house' as well as of 'that house'; but in Late ME *þat* is restricted to the more emphatic meaning, as in MnE. This restriction was still more marked in the plur.; already in the Earliest ME *þọ men, þọ hus* were used only in the demonstrative meanings 'those men,' 'those houses.'

1118. *þọ* was now regarded as the plur. of *þat*, and was completely disassociated from the definite article. Hence it became necessary to eliminate the old *þa*-forms—acc. sing. fem. and nom. plur.—from the inflection of the definite article. This was done by extending the nom. sing. fem. first to the acc. sing. fem.—*þeo sünne* = OE *þa synne* as well as *seo synn*—and then to the plur. nom.: *þeo sunnen* = OE *þa synna*.

1119. The old *þas*—the acc. sing. fem. and nom. plur. of þes—was now associated with the old þa, till at last ME þę and þǫs were completely confused, þęs being regarded as þę with the plural -s added, so that þę men, þęs men both came to mean 'those men.'

1120. The form þęs was now eliminated from the inflection of þes in the same way as þę was eliminated from the inflection of þe, the fem. sing. nom. þeos being extended first to the acc. fem. sing. and then to the nom. plur. : þeos sünne = OE þeos synn and þās synne, þeos sünnen = OE þas synna.

1121. The following are the full inflections of the Early Southern demonstratives corresponding to OE se and þes :

		Masc.	Neut.	Fem.	Masc.	Neut.	Fem.
Sing.	Nom.	þe	þęt	þeo	þes	þis	þeos
	Acc.	þene	þęt	þeo	þesne	þis	þeos
	Dat.	þen	þen	þer	þisse	þisse	þisse
	Gen.	þes	þes	þer	þisses	þisses	þisse
Plur.	Nom.		þeo			þeos	
	Dat.		þen			þissen	
	Gen.		þer			þisse	

1122. But already in Early Southern there was a tendency to make the definite article indeclinable—þe. The main causes of this were (*a*) the want of stress of the article, which made its endings indistinct, (*b*) the general loss of the sense of gender- and case-distinctions, and (*c*) the confusion which arose from using þęt both as an article and a demonstrative.

1123. The new demonstrative þat was in like manner extended to the masc. and fem. sing. and then to the oblique cases of the sing., so that þat hus, þat man were sharply distinguished from þe man, þe hus.

1124. The neuter þis was extended in the same way : þis man, þis hus, þis cu = OE þes mann, þis hus, þeos cu.

1125. At first the indeclinable þat was not always restricted to its demonstrative meaning, but was used also as an article in all three genders. This usage survived in Late ME in a few combinations : þat on 'the one,' þat oþer 'the other,' þat *ilke* ' the same ' = OE *se ilca, þæt ilce*, etc.   The final *t* of the *þat* was often regarded as the beginning of the next word, and the *a* was weakened to *e* so as to make the curtailed *þat* into the definite article *þe*, the first two of the above combinations being written *þe tọn, þe tọþer*.   *The tother* has been preserved to the present day in vulgar English.   In Early MnE *the tother* and *the other* were blended into *t'other*, which was still used in the literary language of the last century.

That ilk is still used in Scotland in the phrase *A. of that ilk*, meaning that Mr. A.'s surname is the same word as the title of his estate.   In newspaper English the combination is ignorantly made into the pleonastic *the same ilk*, as in *consumption, and endless other ills of the same ilk* (Pall Mall Gazette).

1126. In the plural, where there was no distinction of gender, *þọ, þọs* and *þeos* became indeclinable even sooner than the singulars *þat, þis*.

1127. The plural *þeos* ' these ' was discarded in Late ME, and a new plural was formed direct from *þis* by adding the regular adjective plural ending *e*, giving *þise*, which also appears in the weak form *þese*, like *hese = hise*. *þese* may, however, be the result of the influence of the older *þeos, þeos*, which in Late ME would become *þes, þes*.

Modern English.

1128. Standard MnE finally settled down to the demonstrative forms—

Sing.	*that*	*this*
Plur.	*those*	*these*

1129. In Early MnE the article *the* is often shortened to *th'* before vowels and *h* + vowels, as in *th'enemy, th'hill*, and even before other consonants, as in *th world*, where the *w* was probably dropped.

1130. In the present spoken English *the* has two forms, (ði) before a vowel, as in (ði enimi), (ðə) before a consonant, as in (ðə mæn, ðə hɔs).

one, a ; none, no.

1131. In OE the numeral *an* 'one,' which was inflected like a strong adjective (but with acc. sing. masc. *ǣnne*), was occasionally used also in an indefinite sense, which sometimes approached very near to that of the indefinite article : *an mann* = 'a certain man,' 'a man '; although in most cases the indefinite article was not expressed at all : *on ǽlcre byrig biþ cyning* 'in each city there is a king.'

Weak *ana* is used in the special sense of 'alone' : *ic ana siod* 'I stood alone.' MnE *alone* = OE *eall ana* 'entirely alone.'

1132. From *an* was formed the negative *nan* 'none' = *⁎ne an* 'not one,' which was used both as a noun—*nǽnne ne gehǽlþ* 'he heals no one'—and, more frequently, as an adjective : *nan mann* 'no man,' *nan þing* 'no thing,' 'nothing.'

1133. In ME *an* developed into a regular indefinite article. When used in this way it lost its stress and shortened its vowel, becoming *an.* As this shortening took place before the change of *a* into *ǫ*, the article *an* was isolated from the numeral *ǫn* 'one.'

1134. In ME *ǫn, nǭn, an* dropped their final *n* in the same way as *min* and *þin* before a consonant, keeping it before a vowel or *h* + vowel : *ǫ man* 'one man,' *ǫn arm, she dǫþ nǫn harm to nǫ man, a man, an old man. ǫn* and *nǫn* kept their *n* of course when used absolutely.

1135. In MnE the strong words *ǫn* and *nǫn* levelled these distinctions, but in different ways. In the case of *one* the shortened form was given up, *one* being used before vowels as well as consonants : *one man, one arm.* It is to be noted that in Early MnE *one* kept the sound (*ōn*). But already in the Western dialects of ME it had been diphthongized into (wun), whence the present (wʊn), the other pronunciation being still preserved in *alone, only.*

1136. *none* went the opposite way, the fuller form being preserved only absolutely—*I have none*—the shorter *no* being used as the conjoint form before vowels and consonants alike : *no man, no other*.

1137. The article *an* has kept the ME variation : *a man, an enemy*. In Early MnE the full form was also kept before *h* : *an house*. We now say *a house, a history*, etc. But we generally use *an* before *h* in weak syllables, where it is then dropped in pronunciation, as in *an historical event*. As *one* itself is now pronounced (wɛn), it takes *a* before it : *such a one*. So also *u* = (juw, iuə) now takes *a* before it, as in *a unit*, like *a youth*. But *an unit, an useless waste of life* are still found in the literary language, being traditions of the earlier pronunciation of *u* as (·iu).

In ME the distinction in meaning between *ǫn* and *an* was not always strictly carried out at first, the strong *ǫn* being sometimes used as an indefinite article, and *an* being sometimes used in the sense of 'one.' This latter usage has survived to the present day in a few phrases, such as *a day or two, they are both of an age*.

Interrogative and Relative.

1138. The interrogative pronouns in OE are *hwa, hwæt*, whose inflections have been already given (**1058**), *hwelc, hwilc*, Late West-Saxon *hwylc* 'which' (implying 'more than one'), and *hwæþer* 'which of two.' *hwelc* is a shortening of **hwalic*, *hwilc* of **hwilic* (with the *a* assimilated to the following *i*), where *hwa-* is the original short form of *hwa* (**745**), and *-lic* is a shortening of *līc*, the original meaning of the compound being 'who-like' or 'what-like.' *hwæþer* was originally formed from **hwa* with the same comparative derivative ending as in *furþor* (**1048**). *hwelc* is used both as a noun and an adjective, generally in a more definite sense than *hwa*, *hwæt*, though it must sometimes be translated by *who* or *what*, especially when an adjective, *hwelc* being the only adjective form of *hwa* and *hwæt*, as in *hwelce mede hæbbe ge?* 'what reward have ye?'

1139. In ME *hwęlc* dropped the *l*, probably at first only when unstressed: Early Southern *hwüch* from Late West-Saxon *hwylc*, Late ME *which* being a Midland form.

1140. In OE *hwā* and *hwæt* were used only as nouns, but in ME *what* was used as an indeclinable adjective of all three genders : *what þing*, *what man*. This early use of *what* as an adjective was helped by its resemblance to *þat*. The OE use of *hwæt* with a noun in the gen. plur., as in *hwæt manna ?* 'what kind of men,' 'what men' also paved the way for the later use of the word as an adjective, just as *ma* + gen. plur. developed into an adjective (**1052**). When the language was able to distinguish between *what thing* and *which thing*, the latter pronoun was gradually restricted to its more definite meaning.

1141. *hwæþer*, Anglian *hwæþer* from **hwaþir*, was used both as a pronoun = 'which of two,' and as an adverb and a conjunction = 'whether.' It now survives only as an adverb, *which* having taken the place of the pronoun. The pronoun *whether* still survived in Early MnE, as in *whether of them twain did the will of his father ?* corresponding to the OE *hwæþer þara twegra dyde hæs fæder willan ?*

1142. There were no simple relative pronouns in OE, there being only an indeclinable relative particle *þe*, which was generally joined to the noun-pronoun *se* : *se mann se-þe* . . 'the man who . . ,' *þa męnn þæm-þe* . . 'the men to whom . .' *se* by itself was also used as a relative : *se mann sē* . . , *he þæt beacen geseah þæt him geiewed wearþ* 'he saw the beacon that was shown to him.' In ME *that* became an indeclinable relative as in MnE : *he that will* . .

1143. Although the OE interrogative pronouns were not used relatively. they were freely used conjunctively, a usage which naturally grew out of their interrogative meaning, *hwæt wilt þu ?* 'what do you wish?' for instance, suggesting such constructions as *he ascode þone cyning hwæþer he wolde* 'he asked the king which of the two he wished,' *he hordap and nāt hwām* 'he hoards and knows not for whom.' In ME *whọ* soon came to be used as a relative, as also in MnE: *the man who* . . , *the woman who* . . , *what* being still restricted to the conjunctive use.

Definite.

1144. Besides *se* and *þes* there was in OE a third demonstrative pronoun *geon*, which however became obsolete already in Early West-Saxon. It was preserved in North-Thames English, being still in common use in the north of England and Scotland in the form of *yon*. In MnE *yon* has been confused with the adverb *yond, yonder*—*yond cloud, yonder hill*—of which it was supposed to be a shortened form, and was consequently written *yon*. *yond* is now completely obsolete, and *yonder* is more frequent than *yon* in the literary language, both being obsolete in the spoken language.

1145. The OE demonstrative of quality *swelc, swilc*, Late West-Saxon *swylc=*swalic*, *swilic* 'so-like,' *swa* being the older form of *swā* ' so,' dropped its *l* in ME in the same way as *hwelc* did, Southern *swüch* becoming *swuch* by the influence of the *w*, which was then absorbed by the *u*, giving *such*. The tradition of the Midland form *swich* is still preserved in the vulgar *sich*.

Indefinite.

1146. The particle *a* ' always ' was in OE prefixed to pronouns and adverbs—especially interrogative ones—to give them an indefinite sense, as in *āhwǽr* 'anywhere,' *ahwæþer* 'either of two.' Interrogative pronouns and adverbs were also used in an indefinite sense without any prefix, as in *gif hwā þas bōc āwrītan wile* 'if anyone wants to make a copy of this book.' The indefinite meaning grows naturally out of the interrogative, such a question as ' who? ' being necessarily indefinite, for if we knew who the person was, we should not ask the question. The indefinite meaning was made more prominent by putting the interrogative word between *swā* . . *swā* 'as . . as': *swā-hwā-swā* 'whoever,' *swā-hwæt-swā* 'whatever,' *swā-hwelc-swā* 'whichever.' In ME the first *swā* was dropped in these groups : *whǫ-sǫ, what-sǫ.* In Late OE. *ǣfre* 'ever,' 'always' is sometimes added like the older *ā*—though more loosely—to express indefiniteness, as in *eall þæt ǣfre betst wæs* (Chronicle 1048) 'whatever was best'; and in ME this usage was much extended, whence the MnE *whosoever, whatsoever,* and, with dropping of the now superfluous *so, whoever, whatever, whichever,* etc.

1147. In OE the noun *wiht* 'creature,' 'thing,' came to be regarded almost as a pronoun, and when the indefinite *a-* was prefixed to it, the origin of the resulting noun-pronoun *āwiht* was forgotten, and it was contracted to *āuht, āht, aht.* The prefix *a-* also appears in the form of *ō-*, whence the parallel forms *ōwiht, oht.* Hence ME has both *auht, aht,* and *ouht, oht.* In OE negative forms were obtained by prefixing *n-* : *nāwiht, nauht, naht, nōwiht, noht,* whence ME *nauht, naht,* and *nouht, noht.* The fluctuation between *au* and *ou* in these words still continued in MnE, even when the two spellings had come to represent the same sound (ɔ). We now write only *aught,* making an arbitrary distinction between *naught* and *nought.* In OE *nauht,* etc. were used as adverbs='not at all,' 'by no means,' and in ME they became less and less emphatic, especially in the weak forms, which dropped the *h,* becoming *nat, not,* which at last became equivalent to the older *ne* 'not.' In the Present spoken English the strong forms *aught* and *naught, nought* have been superseded by *anything* and *nothing* from OE *ǣnig þing, nān þing.* But we still keep the derivative *naughty,* which in Early MnE had the older meaning 'good for nothing,' 'worthless'; and we use *nought* to express the zero in arithmetic, writing *naught* in the sense of 'nothing'—a sense which is now obsolete in the spoken language. But (ɔt) is in common colloquial use as a shortened form of *nought*, as in (desiməl ɔt wɛn)＝·oı. This form probably arose from the frequent use of *nought* after numbers ending in *n—one, seven, nine, ten*—(wɛn nɔt) being naturally shortened to (wɛn ɔt), the shortened form being then used after all the other numerals as well.

1148. some＝OE *sum* has two forms, strong (sɛm) and weak (səm) [61]. It is still used as a plural noun-pronoun. the singular being represented by the compounds *someone, somebody, something*. In ME the two indefinite pronouns *sum* and *what* were combined in *sumwhat* to express the same meaning as *something*: *somewhat* is now used only as an adverb.

1149. any＝the OE noun and adjective *ǣnig*, formed from *an* 'one' by the derivative ending -*ig*, which causes mutation of the preceding vowel. In Late ME *ēni* was back-shortened (**793**) to *eni*, which was often made into *anı* by the influence of *an*. Early MnE has both *eny* and *any*; and MnE keeps the former in speech, the latter in writing. The OE negative *nānig* was supplanted by *nǫn* in ME. *any* is now used only as an adjective, the corresponding noun being represented by the compound *anyone, anybody. anything*. In Early MnE *any* was still used as a noun: *who is here so vile? . . . if any, speak!* (Shakespere).

1150. other＝the OE strong noun and adjective *ōþer*: *þæs ōþres nama* 'the other man's name,' *þa ōþre menn* 'the other men.' For the later inflections of *other* see §§ **1056. 1057.**

1151. The reciprocal noun-pronouns *one another*, *each other* are now inseparable compounds, but their elements were originally separate words with independent inflections; *they love each other* meant originally 'they love, each-one (nom.) the-other (acc.).' In OE we find such constructions as *ǣghwæþer ōþerne oftrǣdlīce utdrǣfde* 'each the-other repeatedly drove out' (said of the five sons of a king); and even in Early MnE we still find reminiscences of the original

construction : *with greedy force each other doth assail*
(Spenser).

Quantitative.

For *much, more, most · a little, less, least,* see §§ **1051, 1052.**
For *enough* see § **1035.**

1152. both = ME *bŏþe* from OE *ba-þā 'both those,' 'both
the,' *bā* being the fem. and neut. form corresponding to the
masc. *begen* ' both,' just as the fem. and neut. *twā* ' two ' correspond to the masc. *twegen.*

1153. each = OE *ǣlc* from *āgilīc, literally 'ever each,'
where the *ge-* has the same collective meaning as in *gefera*
'companion,' etc. *ǣlc* in ME became *ęlch,* and—with the
same dropping of the *l* as in *which—ęch,* the Northern form
being *ilk,* which was thus confounded with *ilk* 'same '= OE
ilca. each is still a noun as well as an adjective, though there
is also a compound noun-form *each one.*

1154. every is a ME compound of *ǣfre* (**1146**) and *ǣlc,*
the earliest ME form being *ęvręlch,* then *ęvrich,* which in
Late ME was shortened to *ęveri. every* is now used only as
an adjective, the noun being represented by the compounds
everyone, everybody, everything.

1155. either = OE *ǣgþer, ǣghwæþer* from **āgihwæþer.*
OE *ǣgþer* has the meaning of Latin *uterque* 'each of two,'
' both of two,' the meaning ' one of two,' Latin *alteruter,*
being expressed by *āhwæþer* without the collective *ge-,* which
often shortened to *āuþer, āþer.* The difference of meaning is
is seen in such sentences as *on ǣgþere healfe eas* ' on both sides
of the river ' and *gif he āuþer þissa forlǣtt* ' if he gives up
either of these two things.' In ME the pronoun *ouþer* = OE
āuþer was gradually disused, and *ęiþer* = OE *ǣgþer* was used
to express both meanings. In MnE *either* is now restricted
to the alternative meaning *alteruter.*

In ME both *ęiþer* and *ouþer* continued to be used as conjunctions, weak *ouþer* being contracted to *ęþer, ęr, or. ōþer .. or*

'either .. or'—in which the first member kept its fuller form because it kept the strong stress—was in Late ME made into *eiþer .. or*, as in MnE.

1156. In OE there was a negative form corresponding to *auþer*: *nahwæþer*, *nāuþer*, *nāþer*, *nohwæþer*, *nōþer*. In ME it was preserved as a conjunction, the weak form being shortened to *nor*. The strong form *nouþer* was, on the other hand, made into a new-formation *neiþer* on the analogy of *eiþer*, being used both as a pronoun and as the first member of the correlative conjunction-group *neiþer . . . nor*, as in MnE.

1157. In MnE *either* and *neither* are used both as adjectives and as nouns.

1158. There are a few quantitative pronouns remaining, whose etymology and history deserves notice :—

several has the same form in ME and old French; it comes from the Late Latin *sēparālis*, corresponding to Old Latin *sēparabilis* 'separable.'

few = OE *fēa*, *fēawe* plur.

many = OE *manig*, Late West-Saxon *mænig* by the analogy of *ænig*. ME *mani*, *meni* with back-shortening. Early MnE (mani, meni).

NUMERALS.

Cardinal.

1159. The cardinal numerals 1–12 are expressed by the following isolated words :—

one. OE *an*.

two. OE masc. *twēgen*, neut. and fem. *twā*. Already in the Earliest ME *twā* was extended to the masc.: *twā men* = OE *twēgen menn*. But *twēien*, *twēie* = OE *twēgen* was preserved, and, indeed, survives in the present literary English in the form of *twain*, but was used indiscriminately in all three genders. In Late ME *two*=OE *twā* became *two* by the same influence of the *w* as in *who* (1073). In Early MnE the (w) of (twuu) was soon absorbed, giving (tuu).

three. OE *þrīe*, neut. and fem. *þreo*. In ME the latter form was extended to the masc., becoming *þre* in Late ME.

four. OE *feower*, which in ME became *fōwer*, *four*, the *e* being absorbed by the two lip-consonants between which it stood.

five. OE *fīf*, absolute *fīfe*. *fīf*, like the other isolated numerals above three, though uninflected when joined to a noun, is generally inflected when used absolutely : *fīf mẹnn*, *heora wǣron fīfe* 'there were five of them.' In ME both forms were kept, the conjoint *fīf* and the absolute *fīve*, the latter being by degrees extended to the conjoint use, whence the MnE *five*.

six. OE *siex*, *six*, Anglian *sex*.

seven. OE *seofon*.

eight. OE *eahta*, Anglian *æhta*, whence ME *eighte*.

nine. OE *nigon*. ME *niȝen*, *nīn*, absolute *nīne*.

ten. OE *tien*, Anglian *ten*. ME *ten* with shortening.

eleven. OE *ẹndleofan*. ME *enleven*, *elleven*, absolute *e·levene*.

twelve. OE *twẹlf*, absolute *twẹlfe*. ME *twelf*, *twelve*.

1160. The teen-numerals 13–19 are compounds of the units with -*tīene*, Anglian -*tene* :—

thirteen. OE *þrītiene*, *þrittiene*, *þreotiene*. ME *þrittene*. The MnE form shows the same consonant-transposition as in *third* (1170).

fourteen. OE *feowertiene*.

fifteen. OE *fīftiene*. In ME *fiftene* the *ī* was shortened before the consonant-group.

sixteen. OE *sixtiene*.

seventeen. OE *seofontiene*.

eighteen. OE *eahtatiene*, Anglian *æhtatene*. ME *eightetene*, contracted *eightene*.

nineteen. OE *nigonfiene.*   ME *nigenlene, nīnlēne.*

1161. The ty-numerals 20—90 are formed in OE by combining the units with *-tig*, which was originally a noun meaning 'a lot of ten,' 'half a score,' so that *twenty* originally meant 'two tens.' The numerals 70—90 also prefix *hund-* : —

twenty. OE *twentig* from **twegen-tig, twentig.*

thirty. OE *þritig, þrittig.*   ME. *þritti.* Late East-Midland *þirti*, with the same transposition as in *third*.

forty. OE *feowertig.*

fifty. OE *fiftig.*   ME *fifti.*

sixty. OE *sixtig.*

seventy. OE *hundseofontig.*   ME *seofenlig. sefenti.*

eighty. OE *hundeahtatig*, Anglian *hundæhtatig.*

ninety. OE *hundnigontig.*

1162. In OE the ty-numerals are sometimes declined as adjectives. as in *æfter þritigra daga fæce* 'after the space of thirty days.' When undeclined they are used in their original function of nouns governing the genitive : *sixtig mila brad* 'sixty miles broad.'

1163. The high numerals hundred and thousand are in OE neuter nouns. *hund. hundred* and *þusend.* governing the genitive : *twā hund wintra* 'two hundred winters (years),' *þusend manna* 'a thousand men.'

1164. In OE there was no numeral higher than thousand. million, ME *millioun.* is the French form of Late Latin *milliō,* acc. *millionem* formed from Latin *mille* 'thousand.' *billion, trillion*, etc. are much later formations, in which the Latin prefixes *bi-* and *tri-* (as in *biennial, triennial*) were substituted for the initial syllable of *million*, so that *billion* was regarded as a sort of contraction of **bimillion.   milliard* is a Modern French formation from Latin *mille,* or rather from *million.* by substituting the augmentative ending *-ard* for *-on*, so that the word means 'big million,' *million* itself originally meaning 'group of thousands.'

1165. Numeral-groups are either cumulative, as in

twenty-five = 20 + 5, or **multiple**, as in *two hundred* = 2 × 100. In such cumulative groups as *twenty-five* the units always came first in OE—*fif and twentig manna*—and we still say *five-and-twenty* as well as *twenty-five*, but only with the lower ty-numerals; thus we hardly ever say *he is five and fifty*.

1166. In speaking we generally count by hundreds up to 1900, especially in dates. Thus 1066, 1891 are called *ten hundred and sixty-six, eighteen hundred and ninety-one*, or, more briefly *ten sixty-six, eighteen ninety-one*.

1167. The high numerals are not used alone, but require *a* or *one* before them, the latter when emphatic, as in *one hundred, not two hundred*. *a* in *a hundred, a thousand*, etc. may be the indefinite article, but is more probably the weak *one*, as in *a day or two* (**1137. 1**).

1168. In MnE all the numerals are treated as adjectives followed by nouns in the plural, *a-hundred*, etc. being a kind of group-adjective: *ten men, twenty men, a hundred men, two thousand men*.

1169. But all the numerals can also be used as nouns with plurals in -*s*. They necessarily become nouns when their head-word is suppressed, as in *units, tens, and hundreds, to go on all fours, there were ten of us*; but even when the head-word is expressed, the numeral may be made into a noun whenever it has any independence of meaning, as in *thousands of people*.

Ordinal.

1170. Most of the ordinal numerals are derivatives of the cardinal ones, but the first two ordinals are expressed by distinct words :—

first is the OE *fyrest*, which originally meant 'foremost' (**1047**); but this meaning was sometimes so much weakened that *fyrest* became practically equivalent to *forma*, which is the regular OE ordinal corresponding to *an*.

second was introduced in ME, being the French form of Latin *secundus*.   The OE word was *ōþer*, which was discarded because of the ambiguity resulting from it having also the meaning ' other.

third = OE *þridda*, Late Northumbrian *þirda*, ME *þirde*.

The other OE ordinals below 20 are formed from the cardinals by adding *-þa*, the *þ* becoming *t* after *s* or *f*, and final *n* of the cardinals being dropped :—

fourth = OE *feowerþa*, *feorþa*, ME *fourþe* [Cp. *fourteen*, *forty*.]

fifth = OE *fīfta*, ME *fifte*, Early MnE *fift*.   In later MnE the *th* was restored by the influence of the other ordinals, as also in Early MnE *sixt*.

sixth = OE *sixta*.

seventh = OE *seofoþa* is a Late ME new-formation direct from the cardinal.   So also *ninth*, *tenth*, *eleventh*.

eighth = OE *eahtoþa*, Anglian *æhtoþa*, where the *o* is the older form of the *a* in the cardinal *eahta*, *æhta*.

ninth = OE *nigoþa*.

tenth = OE *teoþa* with the unmutated vowel of the cardinal *tien*.

eleventh = OE *endleofta*.

twelfth = OE *twelfta*.

1171. The OE teen-ordinals end in *-teoþa*, which in ME was made in *-tenþe*, a new-formation from the cardinal ending *-tēne*, as in *fiftenþe* = OE *fifteoþa*.

1172. The OE ty-ordinals end in *-tigoþa*, *-tiogoþa*, which in ME became *-teoþe*, and then *-tiþe* by the influence of the cardinals : OE *twentigoþa*, Late ME *twentiþe*.   In Early MnE *e* was introduced by the analogy of the verb-inflection *-eth*, but these ordinals were still pronounced (twentiþ, þirtiþ), etc., although the spelling has now altered the pronunciation into (twenti-iþ), etc.

1173. In Early MnE the ordinal ending *-th* was extended to the high numerals, which before had no ordinal forms :

hundredth, which was pronounced (hundreb), *thousandth*, *millionth*.

1174. The OE ordinals were inflected as weak adjectives.

1175. In ordinal groups only the last member of the group takes the ordinal form, the others being left in the shorter cardinal form : *twenty-fifth* or *five-and-twentieth*, *hundred and second*. This usage prevailed already in OE, as in *on þam twa-and-twentigoþan dæge*, where *twā* is kept in the neuter, although *dæg* is masculine, because it forms a sort of group compound with the ordinal.

1176. The ordinals are used as nouns in MnE in the combination of two ordinals to express fractional numbers, as in *two thirds of an inch*.

VERBS.

Old-English.

INFLECTIONS.

1177. There are two main conjugations of verbs in OE, **strong** and **weak**, distinguished mainly by the formation of their preterites and preterite participles. If we compare these parts of the verb with its infinitive, we find that strong verbs, such as *bindan* 'to bind,' form their preterite by vowel-change — *band* 'he bound' — and add -*en* in the preterite participle with or without vowel-change, *ge*- being often prefixed, in weak as well as strong verbs — *gebunden* 'bound'; while weak verbs, such as *hīeran* 'hear,' form their preterite and preterite participle with the help of *d* or *t* : *hīerde, gehīered*.

1178. The following are the chief verb endings of the active voice, including the preterite participle passive. Where two endings are given, the second is that of the weak verbs. Observe that all three persons have the same ending in the plural, and that the imperative exists only in the second person.

		Indicative.	Subjunctive.
Present Singular	1	-e	-e
	2	-st	-e
	3	-þ	-e
Plural		-aþ	-en
Preterite Singular	1	-, -de	-e, -de
	2	-e, -dest	-e, -de
	3	-, -de	-e, -de
Plural		-on, -don	-en, -den
Imperative Singular		-, -, (e-, -a)	Infinitive -an
Plural		-aþ	Gerund -enne
Participle Present		-ende	
Preterite		-en, -ed.	

1179. Verbs whose root ends in a vowel generally contract; thus *seon* 'to see,' *gān* 'to go,' conjugate *ic seo, ic gā, we seoþ, we gāþ* compared with *ic binde, we bindaþ.*

1180. For the plural ending -*aþ*, both indic. and imper., -*e* is substituted when the pronoun comes immediately after the verb: *ge bindaþ*, but *binde ge*. So also *gā ge !* compared with *ge gāþ*. These forms were originally subjunctives, *binde ge* being a shortening of *binden ge*. So also in *gā we* 'let us go.' This change was often extended by analogy to the ending -*on*, as in *mote we* 'may we,' *sohte ge* 'ye sought' compared with *we moton, ge sohton.*

1181. The passive voice, and many forms of the active voice as well, are expressed by the combination of auxiliary verbs with the pret. partic. and, more rarely, the pres. partic. The chief auxiliary verbs are *wesan* 'be,' *weorþan* 'become,' and *habban* 'have,' as in *he wæs gefunden, he wearþ gefunden* 'he was found,' *he is gecumen* 'he has come,' *he hæfþ gefunden* 'he has found.'

1182. But besides the pret. partic., there is a trace of the old Germanic passive in the form *hātte* from *hātan*, which is both pres. 'is named, called,' and pret. 'was called.'

1183. The infinitive was originally an indeclinable abstract noun formed from the corresponding verb, so that *bindan* originally meant 'binding,' 'act of binding.' The gerund is a similarly formed noun in the dative case governed by the preposition *tō*, which always precedes it, as in *he is to cumenne* 'he is to come' = Latin *venturus est*. It often takes the *a* of the infin.—*to cumanne*.

1184. The pret. partic., as already stated, generally takes *ge-* before it; but not if the verb already has *ge-* or a similar inseparable prefix, as in *forgiefen* 'forgiven,' *alīesed* 'redeemed.' In West-Saxon *hīeran* generally takes *ge-* throughout: *gehīeran, gehīered*.

1185. Both participles are declined like adjectives: *wē sindon gecumene, he hæfþ hine gefundenne* 'he has found him,' literally 'he possesses him found.' But in the later language the pret. partic. in combination with auxiliary *habban* became indeclinable through the original meaning having been forgotten: *he hæfþ hine gefunden*.

1186. In the older language the second person sing. ends in -*s*: *þu lufas* 'thou lovest,' *þu lufades*. But already in Early West-Saxon the regular forms are *lufast, lufadest*.

1187. In Late Northumbrian inflectional *þ* became *s*: *he bindes, wē bindas*.

1188. In Late OE the subj. plur. ending -*en* was made into -*on* by the influence of the indic., as in *gyf hȳ wǣron* 'if they were,' compared with Early West-Saxon *gif hīe wǣren*.

1189. In Late OE the -*st* of the 2nd pers. sing. pret. indic. of weak verbs is extended to the subj.: *gyf þu lufodest* 'if you loved' = Early West-Saxon *gif þu lufode*.

Strong Verbs.

1190. In the strong verbs the plur. of the pret. indic. often has a vowel different from that of the sing.: *ic band, wē bundon*. The 2nd sing. pret. indic. and the whole pret. subj. always have the vowel of the pret. plur. indic.: *þu bunde, gif ic bunde, gif wē bunden*. The following are the Early West-Saxon inflections of the strong verb *bindan*:—

		Indic.	Subj.
Pres. Sing.	1	*binde*	*binde*
	2	*bindest, bintst*	*binde*
	3	*bindeþ, bint*	*binde*
Plur.		*bindaþ*	*binden*
Pret. Sing.	1	*band*	*bunde*
	2	*bunde*	*bunde*
	3	*band*	*bunde*
Plur.		*bundon*	*bunden*
Imper. Sing.		*bind*	Infin. *bindan*
Plur.		*bindaþ*	Gerund *tō bindenne*

Partic. Pres. *bindende*

Pret. *gebunden.*

1191. Some strong verbs are inflected like weak verbs every-where except in the preterite forms. Thus *swęrian* ' swear,' pret. *swor*, is inflected like *fęrian* (**1208**) : pres. indic. *swęrige*, *swęrest, swęreþ, swęriaþ ;* subj. pres. *swęrige, swęrigen ;* imper. *swęre, swęriaþ ;* pres. partic. *swęrigende.* Many strong verbs with double consonants, such as *biddan* ' pray,' ' ask' pret. *bæd*, are inflected like *sęttan* (**1207**) : pres. indic. *biddc. bitst* (*bidcst*), *bitt* (*bideþ*), *biddaþ ;* subj. pres. *bidde, bidden ;* imper. *bide, biddaþ ;* pres. partic. *biddende.*

All of these verbs, both strong and weak, had a *j* before their endings in Germanic (**768**)—**swarjan, *farjan, *bidjan, *satjan ;* and hence all of them mutate their root-vowels. The strong verb *wépan* ' weep' is also a ' j-verb,' as shown by its mutation, the Anglian form being *wāpan*, and is declined like the weak verb *hieran*, which however has the same endings as a strong verb in the infinitive and present tenses, and so there is nothing to distinguish the inflections of *wépan* from those of the ordinary j-less strong verbs : pres. *wépe, wepst* (*wépest*), *wepþ* (*wépeþ*), *wépaþ ;* imper. *wép*, etc.

1192. The Germanic forms of the endings -*st*, -*þ* were -*is*, -*iþ*, which are still preserved in the oldest English : *bindis*, *bindiþ.* In West-Saxon these endings mutated a preceding vowel and then dropped their own vowels, as in *þu lycst, hit greuþ* from *lucan* ' close,' ' lock,' *grōwan* ' grow.' The re-

sulting consonant-combinations were modified in various;
ways (**767**): *þ, dþ, ddþ* were made into *tt, t*, as in *lǽtt* 'lets,'
bītt 'waits,' *bitt* 'asks,' *stęnt* 'stands' from *lǽtan* 'let,' *bīdan,
biddan, standan*; and *sþ* became *st*, as in *cīest* 'chooses' from
cēosan. Similar changes took place in the 2nd pers. sing.:
þu bitst 'you ask,' *þū cīest*. In Anglian the full endings
-es (*-est*), *-eþ* were restored, the unmutated vowels being at
the same time restored: *leteþ, bīdeþ, bīdeþ, biddeþ, stǫndeþ;
biddes, cēoses.*

1193. The vowel-changes in the strong verbs are generally due to gradation (**770**), which is often accompanied by
consonant-change, as in *weorþan, geworden* (**766**). But in
some verbs the vowel of the pret. is the result of contraction
of Germanic and Arian reduplication; thus *hēold* 'held'
(infin. *healdan*) is a contraction of **hehold,* **hehald.* Traces
of this reduplication are preserved in a few OE preterites,
such as *he-ht*, later *hēt* (infin. *hātan* 'call,' 'command')=
Germanic *hehait (Gothic *haihait*).

1194. The following are the classes under which the
strong verbs fall according to their vowel-changes, each
class being named after a characteristic verb. A few examples only are given of each class. The special Anglian
forms are given in ( ). The forms are given in the order
infin., pret. sing., pret. plur., pret. partic.

I. **Reduplicative** or **fall**-class.

1195. The pret. sing. and plur. has *eo* or *e*, the pret.
partic. keeping the vowel of the infin.:—

feallan (*fallan*) 'fall'	*fēoll*	*fēollon*	*feallen* (*fallen*)
healdan (*hāldan*) 'hold'	*hēold*	*hēoldon*	*healden* (*hālden*)
cnāwan 'know'	*cnēow*	*cnēowon*	*cnāwen*
grōwan 'grow'	*grēow*	*grēowon*	*grōwen*
bēatan 'beat'	*bēot*	*bēoton*	*bēaten*
hātan 'command'	*hē(h)t*	*hē(h)ton*	*hāten*
lǣtan 'let'	*lēt*	*lēton*	*lǣten*

. II. **Shake**-class.

1196. These verbs have in the infin. *a, ea,* or, in j-verbs the mutations *g, ie,* in the pret. sing. and plur. *o,* in the pret. partic. *a, æ :*—

faran 'go'	*fōr*	*fōron*	*faren*
scacan 'shake'	*scōc*	*scōcon*	*sċacen*
hebban (768) 'raise'	*hōf*	*hōfon*	*hafen, hæfen*

III. **Bind**-class.

1197. In the infin. *i, ie, e, eo* followed by two consonants one at least of which is nearly always a vowellike consonant—*r, l, n, m ;* in the pret. sing. *a, æ, ea ;* in the pret. plur. *u ;* in the pret. partic. *u, o.*

bindan 'bind'	*band, bond*	*bundon*	*bunden*
gieldan (geldan) 'pay'	*geald (gald)*	*guldon*	*golden*
helpan 'help'	*healp (hālp)*	*hulpon*	*holpen*
berstan (764) 'burst'	*bærst*	*burston*	*borsten*
weorþan 'become'	*wearþ*	*wurdon*	*worden*
feohtan (fehtan) 'fight'	*feaht (fæht)*	*fuhton*	*fohten*

IV. **Bear**-class.

1198. In the infin. *e, ie, i* followed by a single consonant which is generally vowellike ; in *brecan* the vowellike consonant precedes the vowel ; in the pret. sing. *a, æ, ea ;* in the pret. plur. *æ, ea, o, a ;* in the pret. partic. *o, u* :—

beran 'carry'	*bær*	*bāron*	*boren*
brecan 'break'	*bræc*	*brācon*	*brocen*
sċieran (sċeran) 'cut'	*scear (scær)*	*sċēaron (sċēron)*	*scoren*
niman 'take'	*nam, nom*	*nomon, namon*	*numen*

V. **Give**-class.

1199. In the infin. *e, ie,* and, in the j-verbs *i,* followed by a single, non-vowellike consonant, this class differing from the last only in the pret. partic., which keeps the vowel of the infin., the mutated *i* of the j-verbs returning to *e* :—

sprecan 'speak'	*spræc*	*sprǣcon*	*sprecen*
giefan (gefan) 'give'	*geaf (gæf)*	*geafon (gēfon)*	*giefen (gefen)*
sittan 'sit'	*sæt*	*sǣton*	*seten*
licgan 'lie'	*læg*	*lagon, lǣgon*	*legen*

VI. Shine-class.

1200. In the innn. *ī*; pret. sing. *a*; pret. plur. and pret. partic. *i* :—

drīfan 'drive'	*drāf*	*drifon*	*drifen*
scīnan 'shine'	*scān*	*scinon*	*scinen*
wrītan 'write'	*wrāt*	*writon*	*writen*

VII. Choose-class.

1201. In the innn. *eo, ū*; pret. sing. *ēa*; pret. plur. *u*; pret. partic. *o* :—

bēodan 'command'	*bēad*	*budon*	*boden*
cēosan 'choose'	*cēas*	*curon*	*coren*
frēosan 'freeze'	*frēas*	*fruron*	*froren*
būgan 'bend'	*bēag, bēah*	*bugon*	*bogen*

Weak Verbs.

1202. The weak verbs fall under two main groups, according as the vowel of the infin. is mutated or not. The mutation-group comprises two classes, the **near**-class (*hīeran*) and the **wean**-class (*węnian*), the unmutated verbs constituting the third or **love**-class (*lufian*).

I. Hear-class.

1203. The following are the Early West-Saxon forms :—

		Indic.	Subj.
Pres. Sing.	1	*hīere*	*hīere*
	2	*hīerst*	*hīere*
	3	*hīerþ*	*hīere*
Plur.		*hīeraþ*	*hīeren*
Pret. Sing.	1	*hīerde*	*hīerde*
	2	*hīerdest*	*hīerde*
	3	*hīerde*	*hīerde*
Plur.		*hīerdon*	*hīerden*

Imper. Sing.	*hīer*	Infin.	*hīeran*
Plur.	*hīeraþ*	Gerund	*to hīerenne*
Partic. Pres.	*hīerende*		
Pret.	*hīered.*		

1204. This class adds *-de* in the pret. and *-ed* in the pret. partic., where the *e* is liable to be dropped when an inflectional vowel is added, as in the nom. plur. *gehīerde*. Verbs ending in *t, d, c* drop the *e* in the uninflected form also, as in *asęnd* 'sent' (infin. *asęndan*), where *d* is a shortening of *dd*. After the breath-consonants *t, c* the inflectional *d* is unvoiced, and *c* becomes *h*: *mētan* 'find,' 'meet' *gemētt*, *tǣcan* 'show' *getǣht*. But the full forms *āsęnded, gemēted* also occur, especially in Anglian. Similar changes take place in the pret. *-tde, -þ(þ)de* become *-tte, -þte*, as in *gemętte* 'found,' *dypte* 'dipped' (infin. *dyppan*). The inflectional *d* is also unvoiced after *ss* and the other breath-consonants, as in *missan* 'miss' *miste*, compared with *rǣsde* 'rushed' from *rǣsan*, where the *s* = (z). In *dypte* the *p* is, of course, a shortening of *pp*. There are similar shortenings in *sęndan, sęnde, fyllan, fylde*, etc.

1205. I b. Seek-class. In this subdivision of the hear-class the vowel of the infin. is unmutated in the pret. and pret. partic., the inflections being the same as in the other verbs of the hear-class:—

sęllan 'give'	*sealde (sālde)*	*geseald (gesāld)*
sēcan (sǣcan) 'seek'	*sohte, sohte*	*gesoht, gesoht*

1206. Those with *n* followed by *c* or *g*—*þęncan* 'think,' *bringan* 'bring'—drop the nasal and lengthen the preceding vowel and modify it in other ways: *þęncan, þohte, geþoht* = Germanic **þankjan, *þanhta*, *an* before *h* having been regularly changed to nasal *a*, which in OE as regularly became *ō*. Long vowels were shortened in OE before *ht*, so that *þōhte*, etc. became *þohte*. Seek-verbs in *-ęcc* carry the mutated vowel *ę* into the pret. and pret. partic. in Late West-Saxon: *streccan,* ' stretch,' *streahte, streaht (stræhte, stræht)* later *strehte, streht.*

1207. It will be observed that all verbs of the hear-class have long syllables in the infin.—either a long vowel, as in *hieran,* or a vowel followed by two consonants, as in *sęndan, fyllan.* In the latter verb the *ll* is Germanic [cp. the adjective *full*], and is therefore kept through all the inflections of the verb, except where *l* is written for *ll* befcre a consonant in contracted forms : pres. indic. *fylle, fyllest (fylst), fyllęþ (fylþ), fyllaþ*; imper. sing. *fyll,* etc.   But most of the verbs of this class with double consonants in the infin., such as *sęttan* ' set,' are inflected like strong j-verbs such as *biddan* (**1191**). the double consonant being also shortened in the pret. and pret. partic. : pres. indic. *sętte, sętst (sętes), sętt (sęteþ), settaþ*; subj. *sętte(n)*; imper. *sęte, sęttaþ*; pres. part. *sęttende*; pret. *sętte* = **sętede,* pret. partic. *gesęted, gesętt.* Some of these verbs belong to the seek-division, such as *sęcgan* ' say ' : pres. indic. *sęcge, sęgst (sęges), sęgþ (sęgeþ), sęcgaþ*; imper. *sęge, sęcgaþ*; pres. partic. *sęcgende*; pret. *sægde,* pret. partic. *gesægd.* So also *sęllan* has pres. indic. *sęlle, sęlþ (sęleþ), sęllaþ,* imper. *sęle, sęllaþ,* etc.

II. **Wean**-class.

1208. All of these verbs have infin. *-ian* and a short rootsyllable with a mutated vowel. They form their pret. in *-ede,* and their pret. partic. in *-ed,* which is never contracted. The following are the Early West-Saxon forms of *węnian* ' accustom ' :—

		Indic.	Subj.
Pres. Sing.	1	*węnige*	*węnige*
	2	*węnest*	*węnige*
	3	*węneþ*	*węnige*
Plur.		*węniaþ*	*węnigen*

		Indic.	Subj.
Pret. Sing.	1	*węnede*	*węnede*
	2	*węnedest*	*węnede*
	3	*węnede*	*węnede*
Plur.		*węnedon*	*węneden*

Imper. Sing.	*węne*	Infin.	*węnian*
Plur.	*węniaþ*	Gerund	*tō węniġenne*

Partic. Pres. *węniġende*
Pret. *ġewęned.*

So also *fęrian* ' carry ' [*faran* ' go '] *styrian* ' stir.'

III. Love-class.

1209. In Germanic these verbs had infinitives *-an, -ōn*, of which *-ian* is a later development and therefore does not cause mutation like the *-ian* of the wean-class, which is of Germanic origin. The following are the Early West-Saxon forms :—

		Indic.	Subj.
Pres. Sing.	1	*lufiġe*	*lufiġe*
	2	*lufast*	*lufiġe*
	3	*lufaþ*	*lufiġe*
Plur.		*lufiaþ*	*lufiġen*
Pret. Sing.	1	*lufode*	*lufode*
	2	*lufodest*	*lufode*
	3	*lufode*	*lufode*
Plur.		*lufodon*	*lufoden*

Imper. Sing.	*lufa*	Infin.	*lufian*
Plur.	*lufiaþ*	Gerund	*tō lufiġenne*

Partic. Pres. *lufiġende*
Pret. *ġelufod.*

So also *āscian* ' ask,' *macian* ' make,' and many others.

Irregular Weak Verbs.

1210. Some weak verbs, such as *libban* ' live,' show a mixture of the inflections of the hear- and the love-class : pres. indic. *libbe, leofast, leofaþ, libbaþ* ; subj. *libbe(n)* ; imper.

leofa, *libbaþ*; pres. partic. *libbende*; pret. *lifde*, pret. partic. *ġelifd*.

Preterite-present Verbs.

1211. These verbs have for their presents old strong pre-terites; thus the preterite-present verb *wat* 'I know' was originally a strong preterite of the shine-class. The present of these verbs differs however from the strong preterites in the 2nd sing. indic., which ends in *t* or *st*, a *t* before the inflectional *t* also becoming *s*: *iċ sċeal* 'I shall,' *þu sċealt*; *iċ cann* 'I know,' *þu canst*; *iċ wat* 'I know,' *þu wast*.

1212. From these presents new weak preterites are formed with various irregular changes: *sċeolde*, *cuþe*, *wiste*.

1213. Many of these verbs are defective, the infin., imper., and participles being often wanting. The subj. is often substituted for the imper. sing. The following are the inflec-tions of *witan* 'know':—

		Indic.		Subj.
Pres. Sing.	1	*wāt*		*wite*
	2	*wāst*		*wite*
	3	*wāt*		*wite*
Plur.		*witon*		*witen*
Pret. Sing.	1	*wiste*		*wiste*
	2	*wistest*		*wiste*
	3	*wiste*		*wiste*
Plur.		*wiston*		*wisten*
Imper. Sing.		*wite*	Infin.	*witan*
Plur.		*witaþ*	Gerund	*tō witenne*
		Partic. Pres.	*witende*	
		Pret.	*witen.*	

Middle-English.

Early Middle English.

1214. The ME levelling of weak vowels under *e* had a comparatively slight effect on the verb inflections, especially

in Early Southern, where the OE verb-inflections were preserved very faithfully. But the inevitable change of *-a, -ast,
-aþ, -ode* into *-e, -est, -eþ, -ede,* as in *luve, luvest, luveþ, luvede*
= OE *lufa, lufast, lufaþ, lufode,* necessarily led to a complete
levelling of the old wean- and love-classes of weak verbs, the
ME love-class including all the OE ian-verbs whether accompanied by mutation or not.

1215. The Southern tendency to drop final *n* first affected
the infin. and pret. partic.: Early Southern *binden, binde;
ibūnd n, ihūndc.*

1216. The tendency to shorten double consonants in weak
syllables made the OE gerund *to bindenne* into ME *to
bindrnc.*

1217. The tendency to drop final weak *e* after another
weak syllable (**794**) led to the shortening of *to bindene* into
to binden, which made it liable to be confused with the infin.
So also *luvie* = OE *lufige, lufian* was often shortened to *luvi.*

In the South-Thames dialects this *-i* afterwards came to be
regarded as the special mark of the infin., being sometimes
extended to strong verbs as well as weak verbs with OE infin.
-an.

1218. In Early Southern the pres. partic. ending is *-inde,*
as in *bindinde, herinde,* which probably owes its *i* to the influence of the verbal nouns in *-inge, -ing* = OE *-ing, -ung,* such
as *lerninge* = OE *leornung.*

1219. Early Southern keeps the prefix *i-* = OE *ge-: ibunden.
ihēred* = OE *gcʰundcn, gchēred.*

1220. The most important change in the strong verbs is
that many of them became weak. Already in OE such verbs
as *slǣpan* 'sleep,' *ondrǣdan* 'fear,' had the weak preterites
slǣpte, ondrǣdde by the side of the strong *slēp, ondred;* in
Late West-Saxon *hebban* 'raise' has the weak pret. *hefde*
by the side of strong *hōf,* and so on. In ME this is carried
much further. Thus even in the earliest ME we find the
OE strong preterites *lēt* 'let,' *weop* 'wept' represented not

only by *let, weop*, but also by the weak *lette, wepte*, although such forms as *wep* still survive in Standard Late ME. Many other weak and strong forms existed side by side for a long time; and although in MnE the weak forms have nearly always prevailed, this was not always the case in ME, where, for instance, such a weak pret. as *hefde* 'raised' was in the Late ME period discarded in favour of the new-formed strong pret. *haf*, the old *hōf* being also preserved.

1221. The inflections of the strong verbs that remained were modified by various levelling influences. The mutation in the contracted forms of the OE presents was got rid of by bringing in the unmutated vowel of the infin., etc., as in *berþ* 'carries,' *tret* 'treads,' *stont* 'stands,' infin. *beren, treden, stonden* = Early West-Saxon *bierþ (bireþ), tritt, stent.*

1222. The gradation of consonants in the OE *ceosan, gecoren*, etc. was got rid of by carrying the *s* through: *cheosen, chēsen, chēs, ichosen.*

1223. In this last verb we can also observe the extension of *ch* = OE *c* to the original *c* of the pret. partic., so as to make initial *ch* uniform through the whole verb. We can observe the opposite levelling of *ch* under *c* in such verb-forms as *kerven, karf* = OE *ceorfan, cearf*, which have taken their back-consonant from the OE pret. plur. *curfon* and pret. partic. *corfen.*

1224. But in some verbs the old consonant-gradations were preserved, as in *forlesen* 'lose,' *forlēs, forloren.*

1225. Some of the ME changes had the contrary effect of creating new distinctions. Thus OE *ǣ, ǽ* was regularly shortened before consonant-groups, and the resulting *æ* was afterwards broadened to *a* (**797**), as in the OE pret. *tǣhte* 'showed,' which in ME passed through *tæhte* into *tahte*, whence MnE *taught*. In many preterites and pret. participles these changes gave rise only to divergence of quantity, as in *meten, mette, imet* = OE *gemetan*, etc., and in Northern *ledde* = Southern *ladde* from *lēden* 'lead' = OE *lǣdan, lǣdde.*

1226. The following are the inflections of the strong verb *bīnden*, and of the weak verbs *heren* 'hear' and *luvien*, as representatives of the two classes of weak verbs in Early Southern :—

Pres. Indic. Sing.	1	*bīnde*	*hēre*	*luvie*
	2	*bīndest, bintst*	*hēr(e)st*	*luvest*
	3	*bīndeþ, bint*	*hēr(e)þ*	*luveþ*
	Plur.	*bīndeþ*	*hēreþ*	*luvieþ*
Pres. Subj. Sing.		*bīnde*	*hēre*	*luvie*
	Plur.	*bīnden*	*hēren*	*luvien*
Pret. Indic. Sing.	1	*bǭnd*	*herde*	*luvede*
	2	*būnde*	*herdest*	*luvedest*
	3	*bǭnd*	*herde*	*luvede*
	Plur.	*būnden*	*herden*	*luveden*
Pret. Subj. Sing.	1	*būnde*	*herde*	*luvede*
	2	*būnde*	· *herdest*	*luvedest*
	3	*būnde*	*herde*	*luvede*
	Plur.	*būnden*	*herden*	*luveden*
Imper. Sing.		*bīnd*	· *hēre*	*luvie*
	Plur.	*bīndeþ*	*hēreþ*	*luvieþ*
Infin.		*bīnden*	*hēren*	*luvien*
	Gerund	*bīndene*	*hērene*	*luviene*
Partic. Pres.		*bīndinde*	*hērinde*	*luviinde*
	Pret.	*ibūnden*	*ihēr(e)d*	*iluved.*

1227. In the forms *bīnde gē, būnde gē,* -*e* is substituted for -*eþ* (1180).

1228. It will be observed that the distinction between the two classes of weak verbs is very slight, the *i* of the love-class being often dropped—*ī luve, we luveþ,* etc.—while the imper. sing. *here* has taken the *e* of *luvie, luve*.

Midland.

1229. In Early Midland many levellings which are only just beginning in Early Southern are fully carried out. The love-class lost their *i* entirely, and as the hear-class generally had the full Anglian endings -*est,* -*eþ,* there is only one set of inflections for the two classes: *heren, lufen* = Southern *heren, luvien*. On the other hand, the contracted forms of the hear-class are extended to the love-class, as in *birþ* 'befits,' 'becomes' pret. *birde* = OE *gebyreþ, gebyrede,* infin. *gebyrian* (wean-class).

1230. The characteristic feature of the Midland verb is its extension of the plur. ending *-en* of the subj. pres. and of the pret. indic. and subj.—*gif þei lufen, þei comen* 'came,' *gif þei comen, þei brohten*—to the present indic. plur.: *we lufen, þei cumen* = Southern *we luvieþ, heo cumeþ.* But the older *-(e)þ* is kept in the imper. plur.: *cumeþ!, beþ!* 'be ye' = Southern *cumeþ, beoþ.*

1231. In Early Midland the gerund was completely levelled under the infin.: *to binden, to heren.*

1232. In Midland the pres. partic. keeps the old ending: *bindende, herende, lufende.* The *n* of the infin. and strong pret. partic. is never dropped as in Southern. The pret. partic. loses its prefix *ge-*.

1233. The distinction between single and double consonant forms in the old j-verbs, such as *hebban, hefeþ, hof, hafen* and *libban, leofaþ, lifde,* which was still kept up in Early Southern—*hebben, heveþ; libben, leveþ, liveþ*—began to break down in Early Midland through the extension of the single consonant forms; thus in Early Midland we find pres. plur. indic. *lifen* = Early Southern *libbeþ,* although the older infin. *libben* is still kept in Early Midland; but *hefen* is used not only as a pres. plur., but also as an infin.

Northern.

1234. In the Northern dialect inflectional *þ* had been changed to *s*, and final *n* had begun to drop off already in the OE period: Old Northumbrian *bindes, bindas, binda* = Mercian *bindeþ, bindaþ, bindan.* In the Early Middle period weak final *e* was dropped, so that the infin. *binde* = Old Northumbrian *binda* became monosyllabic *bind,* under which the gerund *to bind* was levelled.   The subj. *bīnde* = Old North. sing. and plur. *bīnde* was reduced to the same monosyllable. Hence also the pret. plur. *herden* was reduced to the same form as the sing.—*herd*.   The effect of these changes on a strong pret. such as that of *bīnd* was to leave only two forms —*band* 1st and 3rd pers. sing. indic., and *būnd* 2nd pers. sing. and plur. and subj. generally—and the vowel change was soon got rid of by extension of the vowel of the 1st and 3rd person sing. indic. : *ī band, þu band, we band.*

1235. In Late Old Northumbrian the old ending of the 2nd person pres. *-es, -as*, etc. was preserved by the influence of the new 3rd person *-es, -as = -eþ, -aþ*.   Hence in Early Northern *-es* became the common ending of the 2nd and 3rd persons indic. pres. sing.   In the pres. indic. plur. *-es* = older *-as, -ias* was dropped when the verb was immediately preceded or followed by its pronoun : *we þat bīndes, men bīndes; we bīnd, þaı bīnd.*   The 'absolute' form was afterwards extended to the 1st pers. sing. as well ; *ī þat bīndes.*

1236. The *n* of the strong pret. partic. was not lost in Old Northumbrian because of the inflected forms *gebundene*, etc., by whose influence the *n* was restored in the uninflected form ; hence it was always kept in the ME Northern dialect as well.

1237. The Northern form of the pres. partic. is *-and*: *bīndand, herand* = Midland and OE *bīndende, herende*, Southern *bīndinde, herinde.*   This *a* is the result of Scandinavian influence : Icel. *bindandi, heyrandi.*

1238. The following are then the most distinctive verb-inflections of the three dialects in their Early Middle periods :—

	Southern.	Midland.	Northern.
Indic. Pres. Sing. 1	*bīnde*	*bīnde*	*bīnd*
2	*bīndest, bintst*	*bīndest*	*bīndes*
3	*bīndeþ, bint*	*bīndeþ*	*bīndes*
Plur.	*bīndeþ*	*bīnden*	*bīnd(es)*

	Southern.	Midland.	Northern.
Imper. Sing.	*bīnd*	*bīnd*	*bīnd*
Plur.	*bīndeþ*	*bīndeþ*	*bīnd(es)*
Pres. Partic.	*bīndinde*	*bīndende*	*bīndand*

LATE MIDDLE-ENGLISH.

1239. The most important change in Standard ME and in Late South-Thames English generally is the further assimilation of the pres. partic. to the verbal nouns in *-inge* by which the earlier *bīndinde* became *bīndinge*, a change of which we see traces already in Early Southern, as in *heo riden singinge* 'they rode singing' = OE *hīe ridon singende*. But as the verbal nouns also occur without final *-e*, the distinction between *lerninge* partic. and *lerning* noun was not entirely lost.

1240. Early ME *d* was changed to *t* in the weak pret. and pret. partic. of verbs in *rd, ld, nd*: *girte, girt*, infin. *girden*; *bilte, bilt* infin. *bilden*; *wente, went* infin. *wenden* = Early Southern *gürde, gürd*; *bülde, büld*; *wende, wend*. This change served to distinguish such forms as *he sende* pres. subj. and *he sente* pret., which in Early ME were both expressed by the first form. But it is also carried out in some words with *l, ll, n, nn*: *felen* 'feel' *felte*; *dwellen, dwelte*; *menen, mente*; *brennen* 'burn,' *brente*; and after *s* = (z) and *v*, where it unvoices these consonants: *losien* = OE *losian, loste*; *lēven* — OE *lǣfan, lefte, lafte*.

1241. In Standard ME we see the same levelling and simplifying tendencies at work as in Early Midland and Northern. The old vowel-change in such preterites as *bǫnd* is still kept up, but the short form *bǫnd* is often extended throughout the pret.: *þu bǫnd, we bǫnd* as well as *þū bounde, we bounde(n)*.

1242. In some verbs of the bear- and give-class the *e* of the plural is sometimes extended to the sing. as in *ber, set* by the side of *bar, sat* = OE *bær, sæt* plur. *bǣron, sǣton*, Anglian *bēron, sēton*.

1243. Influence of the strong plur. pret. on the sing. is also seen in such sing. preterites as *slow, saw* = Early Southern *sloh* plur. *slōwen*, Late OE *sloh, slogon*, OE *seah, sawon*.

1244. In Late ME the pret. partic. begins to influence the pret. plur.   As a general rule the old pret. plurals were preserved in Late ME only when they had the same vowel as the pret. partic., as in *þei bounden, þei dronken, þei wonnen* (class 3), *riden, writen* (class 6) ; otherwise the plur. pret. took the vowel of the pret. partic.: *þei holpen, foghten, chosen*.

1245. The sing. of the imper. began to be extended to the plur : *bind* ' bind ye ' by the side of *bīndeþ*.

1246. In the love-class of weak verbs the *i* was dropped entirely, and the pret. ending *-ede* was often shortened to *-ed* in accordance with the general principle of dropping weak *e* after a weak syllable : *he loveþ, he loved*.

1247. Some of the above changes may be the result of Midland influence, of which we have an undoubted example in the substitution of *-en* (*-e*) for *-eþ* in the plur. indic. pres. *-eþ* was, of course, kept in the plur. imper., although here also the Midland ending seems to occur in its shortened form *-e* : *bīnde*.

1248. The following are the Standard ME inflections of the three verbs whose Early ME inflections have been given already :—

Pres. Indic. Sing.	1	*bīnde*	*hēre*	*lŏve*	
	2	*bīndest*	*hēr(e)st*	*lŏvest*	
	3	*bīndeþ, bint*	*hēr(e)þ*	*lŏveþ*	
	Plur.	*bīnde(n)*	*hēre(n)*	*lŏve(n)*	
Pres. Subj. Sing.		*bīnde*	*hēre*	*lŏve*	
	Plur.	*bīnde(n*	*hēre(n)*	*lŏve(n)*	
Pret. Indic. Sing.	1	*bŏnd*	*herde*	*lŏved(e)*	
	2	*bounde, bŏnd*	*herdest*	*lŏvedest*	
	3	*bŏnd*	*herde*	*lŏved(e)*	
	Plur.	*bounde(n), bŏnd*	*herde(n)*	*lŏvede(n), līved*	
Pret. Subj. Sing.	1	*bounde*	*herde*	*lŏved(e)*	
	2	*bounde*	*herde(st)*	*lŏvede(st), līved*	
	3	*bounde*	*herde*	*lŏved(e)*	
	Plur.	*bounde(n)*	*herde(n)*	*lŏvede(n), līved*	

Imper. Sing.	*bind*	*her(e)*	*lŏve*
Plur.	*binde(þ), bind*	*here(þ), her*	*lŏve(þ)*
Infin.	*binde(n)*	*here(n)*	*lŏve(n)*
Gerund	*binden(e), bīnde*	*heren(e), here*	*lŏven(e), lŏve*
Partic. Pres.	*bindinge*	*heringe*	*lŏvinge*
Pret.	*(i)bounde(n)*	*(i)herd*	*(i)lŏv(e)d.*

The following examples will show the regular development
of the different classes of strong verbs : —

I. Fall-class.

1249.	*fallen*	*fell*	*fellen*	*fallen*
	hǫlden	*hēld*	*hēlden*	*hǫlden*
	grōwen	*grēw*	*grēwen*	*grōwen*
	knǫwen	*knēw*	*knēwen*	*knǫwen*

II. Shake-class.

1250.	*shāken*	*shōk*	*shōken*	*shāken*
	wāken	*wōk*	*wōken*	*wāken*
	laughen	*laugh, low*	*lowen*	*laughen*
	drawen	*drough, drow*	*drowen*	*drawen*

Observe that the preterites of this class have split up into
two groups, one with *ō*, the other with (uu) [806].

III. Bind-class.

1251.	*bīnden*	*bǫnd*	*bounden*	*bounden*
	singen	*sǫng*	*sŏngen*	*sŏngen*
	drinken	*drank*	*drŏnken*	*dronken*
	winnen	*wan*	*wŏnnen*	*wŏnnen*
	kerven	*karf*	*korven*	*korven*
	helpen	*halp*	*holpen*	*holpen*
	fighten	*faught*	*foghten*	*foghten*

IV. Bear-class.

1252.	*stēlen*	*stal*	*stēlen, stal*	*stǫlen*
	bēren	*bār, bēr*	*bēren, bār*	*bǭren*

V. Give-class.

1253.	*gēten*	*gat*	*gēten, gat*	*gēten*
	sitten	*sat, sēt*	*sēten, sat*	*sēten*

VI. Shine-class.

1254.	*rīden*	*rǫd*	*riden*	*riden*
	wrīten	*wrǫt*	*writen*	*writen*

VII. Choose-class.

1255.	*crēpen*	*crēp*	*crǫpen*	*crǫpen*
	chēsen	*chēs*	*chǫsen*	*chǫsen*

Modern English.

1256. The main innovation in the MnE verb-inflections was the introduction of the Northern -*s* in the 3rd pers. sing. pres. indic.—*he calls*—which was introduced into Standard English through the medium of the Midland dialect. It did not entirely supplant the older -*th*—*he calleth*—which still survives in the higher literary language.

1257. The MnE verb is further characterized by the development of a **gerund**. When the pres. partic. ending -*inge* lost its final vowel, the last vestige of a formal distinction between such a pres. partic. as *lerning* and the verb-noun *lerning* disappeared. In OE the number of verb-nouns in -*ung*, -*ing* was limited, especially in the earlier stages of the language. In ME their number increased, and when the pres. partic. in -*inge* was fully established, and became indistinguishable in form from the ing-nouns, these could be formed at pleasure from any verb; or, in other words, every pres. partic. could be used as a verb-noun. At first—in Early MnE as well as ME—these words were used entirely as nouns—taking the article *the* before them and the preposition *of* after them, etc.—as in *he thanked him for the saving of his life,* where *saving* is used exactly like the abstract noun *preservation*; but by degrees they were treated like infinitives, the article being dropped and the following noun joined on to them as to the corresponding finite verb; so that the above sentence was shortened to *he thanked him for saving his life.*

In such constructions, which began in Early MnE, *saving* etc. are true noun-verbals or gerunds.

1258. In MnE the dropping of weak final *e*, together with the ME tendency to drop final weak *n*, had a great effect in simplifying the verb-inflections. The monosyllabic *bind* became the representative of the following ME forms: pres. indic. 1st pers. sing. *ī binde*, plur. *we binde(n)*, etc., pres. subj. *binde*, *binde(n)*. The levelling of the distinction between the pret. and pret. partic. which had begun in ME was completed in the MnE forms *herd* (*heard*), *loved* representing ME. *herde*, *loved(e)* and *(i)herd*, *(i)loved*. Such weak verbs as *set* and *cast* became invariable in the pret. and pret. partic.: infin. *set*, pret. *set*, pret. partic. *set*=ME *sette(n)*, *sette*, *(i)set*. Moreover in such verbs the distinction between strong and weak conjugation is effaced: compare *set* pret. *set* with *let* pret. *let*=OE *sęttan*, *sętte*; *lætan*, *let*.

1259. The weak vowel of the endings *-est*, *-eth*, *-es*, *-ed* was dropped in Early MnE in the spoken language, except that full *-est*, *-es* was always kept after the hiss-consonants (s, z; ʃ, ʒ), being subject to exactly the same rules as the noun-inflectional *-es* (**997**), as in *missest, misses, risest, rises, wishes, singes*. Full *-ed* was preserved after the point-stops *t*, *d*, as in *hated, wanted, wedded, wounded*=ME *hatede*, etc. Otherwise all these endings were shortened in speech without regard to the ME forms—in *loves* (luvz), *lovest, loveth* (luvþ), as well as *heares, hears, hearest, heareth*. In this way the distinction between the two classes of weak verbs was finally done away with as far as the endings were concerned, the distinction being only partially recognizable in the sound-changes in such verbs as *hear, heard* (hiir, hard); *feel, felt*; *teach, taught*.

1260. But in the higher language the full endings *-est*, *-eth*, *-ed* were freely used after all consonants indifferently, especially in poetry, for the sake of the metre. *-es* was not used in this way because the less familiar *-eth* could always be

substituted for it.   Some very common verbs were, however,
used only in the short forms, such as *dost, doth, mayst, wouldst,*
especially the contracted *hast, hath, had* = ME *havest, hast*
etc.   *-est* was generally shortened in weak preterites, as in
lovedst, criedst.   *-est* and *-eth* are obsolete in Present English
except in the higher language, in which they naturally keep
their full forms, except in *dost, hath* etc.   The higher language also keeps full *-ed* in many forms where the spoken
language contracts, as in *beloved* (bı·levid) compared with
loved (lɛvd), *blessed are the peacemakers.*

1261. The vowel of the full endings is now weak (i), as in
(raizist. raiziz, raiziþ, heitid), and in Early MnE as well as
Late ME it was often written *i, y* instead of *e*, as in Early
MnE *thou spekyst, he dwellith, puttyth, passid, armyd.*

1262. In writing, the silent *e* of *-es* was generally omitted
in Early MnE, as in *sits, binds*; but not after *v*, as in *loves*,
nor, of course, where required to show the pronunciation of a
preceding letter, as in *shines.*   The other endings were sometimes written in full, sometimes without the *e*, whose absence
was often marked by an apostrophe : *seemed, seem d, seemd.*
The first two spellings continued in common use up to the
second half of the last century, the full spelling being now
preferred.   But *-aid* is written without the *e* in monosyllables
such as *said, paid* (Early MnE also *paied, payed, payd*).   The
omission of the *e* in *heard* compared with *feared* is necessary
to show the pronunciation.

1263. The consonant of shortened *-es* was assimilated as
regards breath and voice to the preceding consonant in the
same way as in the noun-inflections : *lets, leads* (leedz), *loves*
(luvz).   The same assimilations took place with shortened
-ed: loved (luvd), *breathed* (breeðd), *thanked* (þaŋkt), *blessed.*
-ed being thus used to express (t), this spelling was often
extended to such preterites as *burnt, smelt,* which were written
burned, smelled, although they come from ME *brente, smelte.*
But the phonetic spellings *thank t, thankt (thank'd), dropt,*

crost (*cross'd*), *accurst* also came into partial use, and some of them have become fixed, such as *past* in *half past one* compared with *the time has passed quickly*.

The above are organic changes. We have now to consider the internal changes in the verb-inflections, beginning with those of a levelling character.

1264. The change of strong to weak verbs which we observe in ME went on in the transition from ME to MnE, and, in some cases, in MnE itself. Thus the Early MnE preterite *clomb* and the pret. partic. *molten* have now become *climbed*, *melted*. But some of the weak forms that arose in Early MnE have now been discarded, such as the Shakesperian pret. participles *comed*, *becomed*.

1265. On the other hand, several weak verbs have been made strong by the analogy of strong verbs, such as *stick*, *stuck* (OE *stician*, *sticode*) by the analogy of *sting*, *stung*; *wear*, *wore*, *worn* (OE *werian*, *werede*) by the analogy of *swear*, *swore*, *sworn*. So also several weak verbs in *-ow* have taken pret. participles in *-own* by the analogy of *know*, *known*, etc., keeping the original weak pret.: *show*, pret. *showed*, pret. partic. *shown* (OE *sceawian*, *sceawode*).

1266. The levelling of the short quantity of the vowels in the sing. of strong preterites under the long quantity of the pret. partic. and infin. seen in Late ME *bar* = Early ME *bẹr*, *bar* is carried much further in MnE, as in *brake*, *spake* = Late ME *brak*, *spak*, pret. partic. *brọken*, infin. *brẹken* etc. When a certain number of preterites in *a* had been thus lengthened, others were lengthened without regard to the length of the other parts of the verb, such as *came*, *bade* = ME *cam*, *bad*, infin. *comen*, *bidden*, although the latter had a long vowel in the pret. partic. *bẹden*.

1267. There is also a regular process of voice-levelling in the MnE strong verb, by which final (s, f) in the pret. sing. becomes voiced as in the infin. and pret. partic., as in *rose*, *chose, gave, drove*=ME *rǫs, chęs, gaf, drǫf,* infin. *risen, driven* etc., pret. partic. *driven* etc.

1268. The distinction between pret. sing. and plur. was levelled, as we have seen, in the MnE weak verbs by phonetic changes. In the strong verbs it was levelled by external, analogical changes. Already in ME strong verbs the vowel of the sing. was often carried into the plur., especially when the plur. had a vowel different from that of the pret. partic., as in *þei stal* instead of *þei stelen* (pret. partic. *stolen*). Hence such Early MnE preterites as *bare, brake, gave, sat* correspond to ME singulars.

1269. In many cases, however, MnE strong preterites have the vowel of the ME pret. plur. We have seen that in Late ME there was an intimate connection between the vowel of the pret. plur. and of the pret. partic. in strong verbs, so that at last the pret. plur., when it differed from the pret. sing., almost always had the vowel of the pret. partic. Hence in MnE the vowel of the pret. plur. when thus supported by the pret. partic. was often able to supplant the original singular-vowel. This was carried out consistently in those verbs of the bind-class which had ME (uu) in the pret. plur. and pret. partic.: *bound, found*=ME *bǫnd, fǫnd.* plur. *bounden* etc. The same change took place in other verbs of the bind-class, and in some of the shine- and choose-class, many verbs having two preterites in Early MnE, one representing the ME pret. sing., the other with the vowel of the plur.: *began, begun; sang, sung; stang, stung; faught, fought*=ME *bigan, sǫng, stǫng, faught—bit; rode, rid; wrote, writ*=ME *bǫt, rǫd, wrǫt.* The present forms of these preterites are *began, sang, stung, fought, bit, rode, wrote.* the tendency evidently being to favour the original sing. forms.

1270. But there has been in MnE a further assimilation of the pret. to the pret. partic., which has affected nearly all verbs of the bear-class with ME *ǫ* in the pret. partic.: already in Early MnE we find the preterites *bore, broke, spoke* by the side of *bare, brake, spake* = ME *bar, brak, spak,* ME *stal* being represented by *stole* only in Early MnE. In Present English *bare* etc. survive only in the higher language.

1271. When a direct association had thus been established between the pret. and pret. partic. the two parts of the verb began to be confused—a confusion which was helped by the pret. partic. in *I have seen* etc. having nearly the same meaning as the pret. *I saw* etc.—so that the pret. began to be substituted for the pret. partic. in some verbs, especially when the older form of the pret. partic. was liable to be forgotten through not being in very frequent use—as in the case of ME *shinen* from *shīnen*—or ambiguous—as in the case of ME *stǫnden,* which was both pret. partic. and infin.—or anomalous and irregular in any way, as in *sę̄ten* compared with the infin. *sitten.* Hence in MnE the original preterites *shone, stood, sat* have supplanted the older pret. participles. In Early MnE this was carried still further than in Standard Present English, as in *took, shook, arose* = *taken, shaken, arisen.*

1272. In the above examples the pret. participles *shone* etc. lost their final *n* through the substitution of a form with a different vowel. Such pret. participles as *bound, begun* = ME *bounden, bigǫnnen* may be considered either as the result of extension of the MnE pret. forms *bound* etc., or of dropping the *e* of the curtailed ME forms (*1*)*bounde,* etc.

It sometimes happens that the pret. partic. ending *-en* is dropped in a verb, but preserved in an adjective formed from the pret. partic. before it had lost the *-en,* as in the adjectives *drunken, bounden* (in *bounden duty*) compared with the pret. participles *drunk, bound.*

1273. In Early MnE the ending *-est* was extended to the pret. indic. of strong verbs : *thou boundest. thou spakest* = ME *bounde, bond, spak.* The rare Early MnE dropping of *-st* in weak as well as strong preterites, as in *thou saw, thou maked, thou had* is probably the result of Northern influence. But in

Present English, poets often instinctively drop this harsh and heavy inflection, especially when the verb is separated from its pronoun: *where thou once formed thy paradise* (Byron). Verbs whose pret. is the same as the pres.—especially those in *-st*—frequently drop the inflectional *st*, or else add it with an intervening *-ed* for the sake of distinctness: *thou castedst* or *thou cast.*

1274. The following is the Early MnE conjugation of the strong verb *see* and the weak verb *call*:—

Indic. Pres. Sing.	1	*see*	*call*
	2	*seest*	*call(e)st*
	3	*seeth, sees*	*call(e)th, calls*
Plur.		*see*	*call*
Subj. Pres.		*see*	*call*
Pret. Indic. Sing.	1	*saw*	*call(e)d*
	2	*saw(e)st*	*calledst*
	3	*saw*	*call(e)d*
Plur.		*saw*	*call(e)d*
Pret. Subj.		*saw*	*call(e)d*
Imper.		*see*	*call*
Infin.		*see*	*call*
Pres. Partic. and Gerund		*seeing*	*calling*
Pret. Partic.		*seen*	*call(e)d*

Besides the above inflections there are others which occur only as isolated archaisms. The contracted *-t=-eth* has left a trace in the form *list* 'wishes,' 'likes,' as in *let him do it when he list* = OE *lyst* (*lysteþ*) from the weak verb *lystan*. All three ME indic. plurals are found in the Early MnE literary language, the most frequent of which—the Midland *-en*—survives in the Shakesperian *they waxen in their mirth.* The Southern *-eth* and the Northern *-es* are much less frequent. The infin. or gerund in *-en* survives in Shakespere: *to killen.*

1275. The following examples will show the regular development of the different classes of strong verbs in literary MnE. It will be observed that the best-preserved classes are the 3rd and the 6th, the others being so reduced in the number of their verbs, and there being so much divergence of form, that they retain hardly a trace of their OE characteristics : —

I. **Fall**-class.

1276. *fall*	*fell*	*fallen*
hold	*held*	*held, beholden*
grow	*grew*	*grown*
know	*knew*	*known*

II. **Shake**-class.

1277. *shake*	*shook*	*shaken*
take	*took*	*taken*

The Late ME preterites in (-uu)＝OE -*oh*, such as *drow*, *slow*, were in Early MnE levelled under the more numerous *ew*-verbs of the fall-class : *draw, drew* ; *slay, slew*.

III. **Bind**-class.

1278. *sing*	*sang*	*sung*
drink	*drank*	*drunk*
sting	*stung*	*stung*
swing	*swung*	*swung*
bind	*bound*	*bound(en)*
find	*found*	*found*
fight	*fought*	*fought*

IV. **Bear**-class.

1279. *bear*	*bare, bore*	*born(e)*
steal	*stole*	*stolen*

V. **Give**-class.

1280. *give*	*gave*	*given*
weave	*wove*	*woven*
sit	*sat*	*sat*

VI. **Shine**-class.

1281. *drive*	*drove*	*driven*

write	*wrote*	*written*
bite	*bit*	*bitten*
shine	*shone*	*shone*

The occasional Early MnE preterites *drave*, *strave*, etc., are probably Northern forms.

VII. Choose-class.

| 1282. *freeze* | *froze* | *frozen* |
| *choose* | *chose* | *chosen* |

PRESENT ENGLISH.

1283. In the present Spoken English the earlier substitution of *you see, you saw* for *thou seest, thou sawest*, and of *he sees* for *he seeth* has been completely carried out, so that the older -*st* and -*th* survive only in proverbs and in phrases taken from the higher literary language. where the older forms still survive.

Having traced the English verb down to its most reduced MnE form, it will now be more instructive to regard it from a purely descriptive, unhistorical point of view.

1284. If we examine the Present English verb from this point of view, the first thing that strikes us is that the traditional distinction between strong and weak verbs can no longer be maintained : without going back to ME we cannot tell whether such preterites as *sat, lit, led, held*, infinitives *sit, light, lead, hold*, are strong or weak.

1285. We are therefore compelled to make a new division into **consonantal** and **vocalic**. Consonantal verbs are those which form their preterites and pret. participles by adding *d* or *t*, such as *called, looked, heard, burnt*, infinitives *call, look, hear. burn.* Vocalic verbs are those which form their preterites or pret. participles by vowel-change without the addition of any consonant, except that the pret. partic. of some of these verbs adds -*en* : *sing, sang, sung* ; *bind, bound, bound* ; *run. ran, run—drive. drove, driven* ; *speak, spoke, spoken* ; *see, saw, seen.* Under the vocalic verbs we must also

include the **invariable** verbs : *let, let, let* ; *cast, cast, cast.*
Mixed verbs show a mixture of consonantal and vocalic
inflection : *crow, crew, crowed* ; *show, showed, shown.*

1286. The great majority of verbs belong to the regular consonantal conjugation, their pret. and pret. partic. ending being—

    a. (-id) after (t) and (d) : *delighted, nodded.*

    b. (-d) after the other voice sounds : *played, raised, saved,
turned, dragged.*

    c. (-t) after the other breath consonants : *hissed, pushed,
looked.*

1287. Compared with these verbs those of the vocalic class
must be regarded as irregular, although many of them fall
under more or less uniform classes. There are also irregular
consonantal verbs, such as *burn, burnt,* compared with the
regular *turn, turned.* There is also a small class of specially
irregular or **anomalous** verbs, such as *be, was, been,* some of
which—mostly comprising the old preterite-present verbs—
are defective, such as (*I*) *can, could,* which has no infin.
or participles. The irregular verbs therefore comprise all
the vocalic and anomalous verbs together with some of the
consonantal, all regular verbs being consonantal. All newly
formed verbs are conjugated consonantally, the consonantal
inflections being the only living or productive ones.

1288. As regards the relation of consonantal and vocalic
to weak and strong, the following general rules may be laid
down :—

    a. Vocalic verbs with pret. partic. in *-en* are strong.

    b. Vocalic verbs not ending in *t* or *d* in the pret. are
strong.

    c. Vocalic verbs ending in *t* or *d* in the pret. may be
either strong or weak.

    d. Invariable verbs—which always end in *t* or *d*—are
almost always weak.

1289. The following are the inflections of the consonantal
verb *call* and the vocalic verb *see* in Spoken English :—

Pres. Indic. Sing. 1	kɔl	sij
2	kɔl	sij
3	kɔlz	sijz
Plur.	kɔl	sij
Pres. Subj.	kɔl	sij
Pret. (Indic. and Subj.)	kɔld	sɔ
Imper.	kɔl	sij
Infin.	kɔl	sij
Pres. Partic. and Gerund	kɔliŋ	sijiŋ
Pret. Partic.	kɔld	sijn

1290. Observe that in the regular conjugation the only ıstinctive ' positive ' inflections are -*s*, -*d*, -*ing*, the common ɔrm *call* being only a negative inflection; also that the ommon form represents the whole of the pres. indic. and ubj. except the 3rd pers. sing. pres. indic., the imper., and he infin. (and supine); while -*ed* represents the pret. indic. ınd subj. together with the pret. partic.; and even -*ing* has two distinct functions, the only unambiguous inflection being the *s*, which has, however, the same form as the two noun-inflections, the gen. and the plur.

In Vulgar English the inflectional -*s* is extended to all the other persons of the pres. indic. : *I says, you says, we says, they says*. This cannot be the result of Northern influence, for in Northern the *s* was not added when the pronoun was prefixed, the Northern forms being *I say* etc. It is more probable that the *s*, being the mark of the pres., was extended for distinctness.

1291. The subj. is very little used even in the educated form of Spoken English, and in vulgar speech it disappears entirely.

Irregular Verbs in Modern English.

1292. In the following sections the vowel-changes are arranged in the alphabetic order of the vowels of the pre-terites in their phonetic spelling, to which the alphabetic order of the vowels of the infinitive is subordinated, thus (ei ... e) as in *say*, *said*, and then (ij . . e), as in *flee, fled,* precede (iə . . əə), and this is followed by (uw . . o), etc. Forms that occur only in the higher literary language are marked *.   Obsolete forms are marked †.

CONSONANTAL VERBS.

With Vowel-change.

Verbs which take the regular consonantal inflection (d, t), but with vowel-change :—

Vowel-change (ei . . e).

1293. say, said (sei, sed).   In this verb the vowel-change in the pret. is exceptionally carried out in the 3rd sing. pres. indic. as well—(sez) *says*.   OE weak I b *seġan*, *sæġde*, *sæġd*. In ME the *ġ*-forms of this verb were preserved in South-Thames English; but in the North-Thames dialects the *g*-forms *seġest*, *seġeþ*, imper. *seġe* were extended to the original *ġ*-forms: *i seie*, infin. *sein*, *seien*, pres. partic. *seiende*.   These became the Standard ME forms also.   The OE pret. *sæġde* — Late West-Saxon *sǣde*—developed regularly in *saide* in ME, which was also made into *seide* by the influence of the other parts of the verb.   In Early MnE we find the shortened (sed)— which was probably at first a weak form—as well as the full (said); (sed) is probably an Early MnE shortening of (ee)= ME (ai)—a shortening which also took place in *says*.   All the other OE *ġ*-verbs show a similar extension of the *g*-forms in ME, so that the OE infinitives *liċgan*, *leċgan*, *byċgan* appear in MnE as *lie* (ME *lien*), *lay* (ME *leien*), *buy* (ME *bien*), which correspond phonetically to the OE imperatives *liġe*, *leġe*, *byġe*.

Vowel-change (ij . . e).

1294. flee, fled (flij, fled).   OE strong VII *fleon* (Oldest English *fleohan*), *fleah*, plur. *flugon*, pret. partic. *flogen*.   There was another OE verb of the same class, some of whose forms were identical with forms of *fleon*, namely *fleogan* 'fly,' *fleag* (*fleah*), pret. plur. *flugon*, pret. partic. *flogen*.   As the two

verbs were similar in meaning also, they were frequently confounded in Late West-Saxon, the distinctive forms of *fleogan*
being used in the sense of 'flee' as well as in that of 'fly,'
and *fleon* being used in the sense of 'fly.' This confusion
has lasted to the present day, in as far as many modern
writers use *fly* consistently in the sense of 'run away.' *Flee*
is now obsolete in the spoken language. In ME the confusion between the two verbs was often avoided by using the
weak verb *fleden* = OE *fledan* (*flædan*) 'flow,' 'be at high tide'
(said of the sea) from OE *flod* ' flood' in the sense of 'flee,' its
pret. *fledde* coming gradually to be regarded as the pret. of the
old strong *fleon, flen.* This development was probably helped
by the Scandinavian weak verb *flyja* ' flee,' pret. *flyþi.*

1295. creep, crept (krijp, krept). OE strong VII *creopan,*
creap, cropen. In ME *crepen* developed a weak pret. *crepte* by
the side of the strong *crep.*

1296. leap, lept (lijp, lept). OE strong I *hleapan, hleop,*
hleapen. ME *lēpen, lep* and *lepte.*

1297. sleep, slept (slijp, slept). OE strong I *slǣpan,*
slep, slǣpen, there being also a weak pret. *slǣpte.* ME
slēpen, slēp and *slepte.*

1298. sweep, swept (swijp, swept). OE strong I *swapan,*
sweop, swapen, which in ME became by regular change
swopen, swep, swopen. There was a weak OE verb *swipian.*
sweopian, 'beat,' which in ME became *swepien, swēp(i)en,*
and was then confused in meaning with *swopen.* The MnE
sweep seems to point to a blending of ME *swēpen* and the
pret. *swep.*

1299. weep, wept (wijp, wept). OE strong I j-verb
wepan (*wæpan*), *weop, wopen.* ME has pret. *wēp* and *wepte.*

Vowel-change (iə . . əə).

1300. hear, heard (hiər, həəd). OE weak I *hieran,*
hierde. Anglian *heran, herde,* whence ME *heren, herde* with
the usual shortening. In Early MnE the (e) of the pret. was

regularly broadened to (a) before the (r), giving (hiiər, hard'
The spelling *heard* shows the not unfrequent lengthening c
ME *e* before (r)-combinations, which, of course, preserved i
from the change into (a); (heerd) was then shortened tc
(herd), whence the Present English (həəd).

Vowel-change (uw . . o).

1301. shoe, shod (ʃuw, ʃod). OE *scoian, scode, gescod*
ME *shoɪn*, pret. partic. *ished*. The MnE shortening is
parallel to that in *rod* compared with *rood*, both=OE *rod*
shod is now used chiefly as an adjective, *shoe* being conjugated
regularly *shoed*.

Vowel-change (e . . ou).

1302. sell, sold (sel, sould). OE weak I b *sęllan, sealde,*
Anglian *salde* 'give.' ME *sellen, sęlde, isęld.* In OE the
meaning 'sell' was only occasionally implied in the mɔrε
general one of 'give,' as in *sęllan wiþ weorþe* 'give for a
value (price)' ='sell.'

1303. tell, told (tel, tould). OE weak I b *tęllan, tealdε*
Anglian *talde.* ME *tellen, tǫlde.*

With t instead of d.

1304. burn, burnt. In OE the intransitive 'burn' was
expressed by the strong verb III *biernan*, Late West-Saxon
byrnan, Anglian *beornan*, pret. *born, barn*, pret. plur. *burnon,*
pret. partic. *geburnen*; the transitive by the weak *bærnan.*
bærnde. In these two verbs the *r* had been transposed, the
Germanic forms being **brinnan, *brannjan*, with which compare the Scandinavian strong *brinna*, pret. *brann*, pret. partic.
brunninn, and the weak *brenna, brendi*. In ME the originally transitive and intransitive forms came to be used indiscriminately in both senses, the weak forms gradually getting
the upper hand. In Standard ME the Northern—originally

Scandinavian—form *brennen, brente* was used both transitively
and intransitively, the strong Northern form—also originally
Scandinavian—*brinnen* occurring less frequently, generally in
its original intransitive sense.   The other dialects show a
great variety of forms : Early Southern *beornen, bęrnen, bernen*, Early Midland *bęrnen, bernen, brennen*, Early Northern
brin (transitive as well as intrans.), *bren*.   The infin. *burnen*
seems to occur first in Late Midland ; the *u* is either taken
from the old pret. partic. or is more probably the result of
the influence of the lip-consonant *b* on the following *eo* of
Anglian *beornan*.   The pret. *brent* survived for some time in
Early MnE.

1305. dwell, dwelt.   ME *dwellen, dwelte* from Scandinavian *dvęlja* ' remain,' not from OE *dwęlian*, which had the
meaning ' lead astray.'

1306. learn, learnt.   OE *leornian, leornode*; ME *lern(i)en,
lernde*, later *lernte*.   The adjective *learned* preserves the fuller
form of the pret. partic.

1307. pen, pent.   OE *pęnnan, pęnde* ' impound '; ME
pennen, pende, pente.

1308. smell, smelt.   OE *smęllan* ' strike.'

1309. spell, spelt.   OE *spellian, spellode* ' relate ' [*spell*
neut. ' tidings '].   ME *spellien* ' spell.'

1310. spill, spilt.   OE *spildan, spillan*, pret. *spilde*
' destroy.'

1311. spoil, spoilt.   ME *spoilen, despoilen* from Old
French *spolier, despoiller* [from Latin *spoliare* 'strip,' 'plunder']
was associated with *spillen* from OE *spillan*, so that when
spillen took the special sense ' waste liquids,' ' spill,' *spoilen*
took the old meaning of *spillen*, namely ' destroy,' and formed
a pret. *spoilte* on the analogy of *spilte*.   *spoil* in the sense of
' plunder ' is regular.

With t instead of d and Vowel-change.

Vowel-change (ij . . e).

1312. (be)reave, *bereft, bereaved. OE *(be)reafian,* *reafode.* ME *birẹven, birẹvde, birefte, birafte,* the last being the Standard ME form.

1313. cleave, cleft 'divide,' 'adhere.' OE strong VII *cleofan, cleaf, clofen* 'divide'; ME *cleven, clọ̄f, clọven.* OE weak III *cleofian, clifian* 'adhere'; ME *clẹvien, clẹvede.* There was also a strong verb VI in OE *clifan* 'adhere,' ME *cliven* pret. partic. *cliven* 'adhere,' 'climb.' In ME *clọ̄f,* Northern *clāf,* originally pret. of *cliven,* was used also as pret. of *cleven,* whose pret. partic. *clọven* had in Late ME the same vowel as *clọ̄f.* A new weak pret. *clefte* was then formed from *cleven.* In the Earliest MnE *cleeve* 'divide' kept (ii) = ME close *e,* but was soon confused with *cleave* (kleev) 'adhere' = Early ME *clẹvien,* Late ME *clẹvien,* so that it was written with *ea.* The MnE pret. *clove* may be regarded either as the descendant of the OE pret. *clāf* or as the ME pret. *clẹ̄f* (from OE *cleaf*) levelled under the pret. partic. *clọven.* The other MnE pret. *clave* is of course the Northern form of OE *clāf.* The following are the forms of the two verbs in MnE:—

　　cleave 'divide'; *clove,* †*clave, cleft*; *cloven, cleft,* †*cleaved.*
　　cleave 'adhere'; †*clave, cleaved*; *cleaved.*

The latter is now obsolete in the spoken language; and the other *cleave* is not much used except in some special technical expressions. *cloven* survives only as an adjective, as in *cloven foot.*

1314. deal, dealt (dijl, delt). OE *dǣlan, dǣlde.*

1315. dream, dreamt, dreamed (drijm, dremt, drijmd). OE *drieman,* Anglian *dreman* 'modulate' [*dream* 'melody,' 'joy']. The ME *dremen, dremde, drem(p)te* got the meaning 'dream' from the Scandinavian *drøyma* 'dream' [Scandina-

ian noun *drọumr* 'dream']. In Early MnE the verb was
evelled under the noun *dream*, the ME pret. being however
:ept in spelling—*dremt*—as well as pronunciation by the side
)f the new pret. *dreamed*. The spelling *dreamt* is, of course,
ι blending of *dremt* and *dreamed*.

1316. feel, felt. OE *felan* (*fælan*) *felde*.

1317. lean, leant, leaned (lijn, lent, lijnd). OE *hleonian*
hlinian), *hleonode*; ME *lēnien* (*linien*), *lēnede*. The pret.
'eant comes from another OE verb meaning 'to lean,' namely
hlēnan, hlænde; ME *lēnen. lende, lente*.

1318. kneel, knelt. ME *knelen, knelde, knelte* of Scandinavian origin.

1319. leave, left. OE *lǣfan, lǣfde*. ME *lēven, lefte,
lafte*.

1320. mean, meant (mijn, ment). OE *mǣnan, mǣnde*
'mean,' 'complain.' ME *mēnen, mende, mente*.

Vowel-change (ai . . ɔ).

1321. buy. bought (bai, bɔt). OE *bycgan, bohte*. ME
büggen, biggen, būen, bīen (1293), pret. *bohte, bouhte*.

Vowel-change (uw . . ɔ).

1322. lose, lost. OE strong VII *forleosan, forlēas,
forloren* 'destroy,' 'lose,' weak III *losian* 'go to waste,' 'get
lost.' ME *lesen, forlesen* 'lose,' *lēs, forlēs, loren, forloren*.
The dropping of the *for-* is due to the influence of *losien* =
OE *losian*, whose transitive use, as in *he losede al his folc* 'he
lost all his people (army)' is due to the influence of *forlesen*.
Hence the pret. partic. *ilosed*, later *lost*, came to be used as
the pret. partic. of *lesen*, when the old pret. participles *loren,
forloren* had come to be isolated from their verbs in meaning
—MnE **lorn* in *love-lorn*, etc., *forlorn*, which are now used
only as adjectives. In Early MnE *lese* took (uu) from the
adjective *loose* and verb *loosen* [ME *los, losnen* from Scandinavian

lǫuss 'free,' 'loose,' *lǫusna* 'get loose'], being at first written
loose, then *lose,* to distinguish it from the adjective *loose.*

With t instead of -ded.

1323. gird, girt. girded. OE *gyrdan, gyrde.*

1324. build, built, †builded. OE *bylden, bylde.*

1325. gild, gilt, gilded. OE *gyldan, gylde.*

1326. bend, bent, †bended. OE *bęndan* 'bind,' 'bend'
[*bindan,* pret. *band* 'bind']. The pret. *bended* is now used
only as an adjective in *bended knee.*

1327. blend, †blent, blended. OE strong I *blandan*
'mix.' Weak ME *blęndan* has only the meaning 'blind.'

1328. lend, lent. OE *lænan, lænde.* ME *lęnden, lenden*
is a new-formation from the OE preterite-forms, possibly
with influence of *senden* 'send'; from *lenden* a new pret.
lende, lente was formed on the analogy of *senden, sente,* etc.

1329. rend, rent. OE *ręndan (hręndan), ręnde.*

1330. send, sent. OE *sęndan, sęnde.*

1331. †shend, †shent. OE *scęndan, scęnde* 'put to
shame' [*scand* disgrace].

1332. spend, spent. OE *spęndan, spęnde* from Latin
expendere.

1333. *wend, went. OE *węndan* 'turn' trans. [*windan*
strong III 'turn' intrans.] The pret. *went* is now used only
as the pret. of *go* (**1458**).

With Consonant-loss.

1334. make, made. OE *macian, macode.* ME *makien,
makede, imaked,* Late ME *makien,* contracted *made, (i)mād.*

With Consonant-loss and Vowel-change.
Vowel-change (ou . . æ).

1335. clothe, clad, clothed. OE *clāþian, claþode* [*clāþ*
'cloth']. Scandinavian *klæþa, klæþdi,* whence ME *clęþen,
cladde* northern *cledde* as well as *clōþ(i)en, clōþede.*

Vowel-change (æ . . ɔ).

1336. catch; **caught**. ME *cacchen, caughte* from Old French *cachier* [Low Latin *captiare* = Latin *captare*, a frequentative of *capere* 'seize']. *cachier* is probably a North-East French (Picard) form; the Parisian form being *chacier* (Modern French *chasser*), whence the MnE *chace, chase*. ME *cacchen* having the same meaning and the same termination as *lacchen, laughte* from OE *læccan, gelæhte* 'seize,' 'catch' [compare MnE *latch*], naturally formed its preterite in the same way.

1337. distract; †**distraught, distracted**. OE *streccan* 'stretch,' pret. *streahte, strehte*, appears in ME in the form of *strecchen, straughte, straghte*, the pret. partic. *streight* being still kept in MnE as an adjective—*straight* literally 'stretched out.' In Late ME the Latin *distractus* was imported as an adj. *distract* (French *distrait*). which was made into *distraught* by the influence of *straught*. When *distract* was made into a verb in Early MnE, *distraught* was naturally regarded as its participle. Through further confusion *straught* itself was used in the sense of 'distracted.' and a new partic. †*bestraught* was formed on the analogy of *beset*.

Vowel-change (əə . . ɔ).

1338. work; *****wrought, worked** (wəək, rɔt). OE *wyrcan*, Anglian *wircan*, the corresponding noun being *weorc*, Late West-Saxon *worc*, Anglian *werc*, which in ME influenced the verb. The ME forms are: Southern *würchen, worchen* with the usual change of *wü-* to *wu-*, Midland *werken*, Northern *wirk*. The OE pret. *worhte* underwent the usual r-transposition in ME, becoming *wrohte*, MnE *wrought*, which in ordinary speech survives only as an adjective, as in *wrought iron*.

Vowel-change (i . . ɔ).

1339. bring; **brought** (briŋ. brɔt). OE *bringan, brohte*.

1340. think ; thought. In OE there were two weak Ia verbs of allied form and meaning: *þęncan, þohte* 'think'; *þyncan, þuhte* 'seem,' which was impersonal, *me þynčþ* 'it seems to me' having much the same meaning as *ic þęnce.* In ME *þęncan* became regularly *þenchen* in South-Thames English, *þenken* in North-Thames English; and *þyncan* became *þunchen, þinchen* in South-Thames English, *þinken* in North-Thames English. The pret. *þuhte* was soon disused, *þo(u)hte* taking its place : *he þohte* 'he thought,' *him þohte* 'it seemed to him.' In Standard ME the two verbs were still kept apart in the infin. and present tenses, which had the Midland forms *þenken, ī þenke ; þinken, me þinkeþ,* etc.; but in the compound *biþinken* 'consider'=OE *beþęncan,* the latter had already begun to encroach. In Northern *þink* completely supplanted *þenk,* as in MnE. Hence MnE *think* is historically = OE *þyncan,* and its pret. *thought* = OE *þohte,* the pret. of the lost *þęncan.*

Vowel-change (ij . . ɔ).

1341. seek ; sought ; beseech ; besought. OE *sēčan (sǣcan), sohte.* ME South-Thames *sechen, bisechen,* North-Thames *seken, biseken.* The MnE *seek* and *beseech* are therefore from different dialects of ME. Shakespere has the Midland form not only in *seek,* but also in *beseek.*

1342. reach ; †raught, reached. OE *rǣcan, rǣhte.* ME *rēchen, ra(u)ghte,* Northern *reghte.*

1343. teach ; taught. OE *tǣcan, tǣhte* 'show.' ME *tęchen, ta(u)ghte,* which gradually supplanted *lęren* 'teach' = OE *lǣran.*

INVARIABLE VERBS.

(aa).

1344. cast. ME *casten* from Scandinavian weak *kasta, kastaþi.* In Early MnE there is also a regular pret. *casted.*

(ai).

1345. *dight 'adorn' as in *storied window richly dight* (Milton). OE *dihtan* 'arrange,' 'appoint' from the Latin *dictāre*.

(ʙ).

1346. cut. ME *kutten*.

1347. shut. OE *scyttan* 'lock,' 'bolt' [*gescot* 'shot,' 'dart'; *sceotan* strong VII 'shoot']. ME *schütten, schutten*.

1348. thrust. ME *þrüsten, þrusten* from Scandinavian *þrȳsta*.

(e).

1349. let. OE strong I *lǣtan, let, lǣten*. ME *leten*, pret. strong *let*, and weak *lette* from **lette*. In MnE the short vowel of this weak pret. was extended to the infin., etc. The obsolete verb *let* 'hinder,' still preserved in the phrase *let or hindrance*, is the OE weak *lettan, lette*, connected with *læt* 'slow,' *late* adv. 'late.'

1350. set. OE *settan, sette*. connected with the strong verb V *sittan*. pret. *sæt*.

1351. shed. OE strong I *scādan, sceadan, sced* 'separate,' a meaning still preserved in the noun *watershed*. ME *schēden* formed a weak pret. *schadde, schedde*, and developed the new meaning 'separate into drops,' 'shed.' In MnE the short vowel of the pret. was extended to the pres., etc., as in *let*.

1352. shred. OE *screadian, screadode*. ME *schreden, schredde*, the short vowel being afterwards extended to the pres., etc.

1353. spread. OE *sprædan, sprædde*. ME *sprēden, spradde, spredde*, the short vowel of the pret. being afterwards extended to the other parts of the verb.

(əə).

1354. burst. OE strong III *berstan, bærst, burston, geborsten.* In this verb the *r* is transposed, having its original position in the Scandinavian forms *bresta, brast, brustum, brostinn.* The Scandinavian verb influenced the ME forms: *beorsten, bursten, bresten, brusten*; pret. *barst, brast*; pret. partic. *borsten, bursten, brosten, brusten.* The Standard ME forms are *bresten, brast, brosten.* The *u* of the infin. *bursten* is the result of the influence of the lip-consonant *b* on the earlier *eo*, as in *burn* (**1304**), the *u* being afterwards extended to the pret. partic. The strong pret. partic. *bursten* survived in Early MnE.

1355. hurt. ME *hurten, hurten.*

(i).

1356. hit. ME *hitten* from Scandinavian *hitta* 'find.'

1357. knit. OE *cnyttan* 'tie' [*cnotta* 'knot']. The invariable pret.-form is now preserved only as an adjective in *well-knit*, etc. Otherwise the pret.-form is regular—*knitted.*

1358. quit. ME *quiten* pret. *quitte* from Old French *quiter* from Latin *qvietus.* In MnE the shortened vowel of the pret. was extended to the rest of the verb. The derivative *requite* keeps its original length, having a pret. partic. *requit* in Early MnE. *acquit* is invariable in Early MnE. All these verbs are now regular.

1359. rid. ME *redden, rüdden, ridden* 'rescue,' 'separate fighters' is apparently a blending of OE *hreddan* 'rescue' and Scandinavian *ryþja* pret. *rudda* 'clear away.'

1360. slit. OE strong VI *slītan, slat, sliten.* ME has both strong *sliten*, pret. partic. *sliten*, and a weak verb *slitten*, which may have existed in OE.

1361. split. ME *splatten*, of which Early MnE *splette* is probably a Northern form. *splet* seems to have been made into *split* by the influence of *slit.*

ɔ**ı**.

1362. cost.   ME *costen* from Old French *coster* (Modern French *couter*) from Latin *constāre*.

u

1363. put.   ME *pullen*.

Vocalic Verbs.

Vowel-change (ai . . au).

1364. bind ; bound.   OE strong III *bindan, band, bunden*. The older pret. partic. is still preserved in *bounden duty*.

1365. find : found.   OE strong III *findan, fand*— more generally weak *funde—funden*.   ME pret. *fond, founde*.

1366. grind ; ground.   OE strong III *grindan, grand, runden*.

1367. wind : wound.   OE strong III *windan, wand, wunden*. The verb *wind* in *to wind a horn* was formed direct from the noun *wind*, and was conjugated weak—pret. *winded*—in Early MnE. The noun *wind* had the same sound as the verb *wind* in Early MnE—(waind) ; so that when the noun came to be pronounced (wind), as it is in Present English, the verb *wind* 'blow,' which kept the older pronunciation, was isolated from the noun *wind* and associated with the old strong verb *wind*, and took a strong preterite-form *wound—he wound the horn.*

Vowel-change (ai . . ʊ).

1368. strike : struck.   OE strong VI *strican, strac, stricen* 'move about,' 'touch lightly.'   ME *striken, strok* (Northern *strak*), *striken*.   Early MnE *strike*, pret. *stroke, strake, struck*, pret. partic. *stricken, strucken, struck*.

Vowel-change (æ . . ʙ).

1369. hang; hung, hanged. OE strong I *hon* (from earlier **hohan*), *heng, hangen*, the *g* being a weakening of the *h* of the infin., where *o* = Germanic *an* (1206), so that *hon* = Germanic **hanhan*. There was also a weak intransitive *hangian, hangode, hon* itself being used transitively. In Early ME the consonantal variation in the strong verb was soon levelled : sometimes the infinitive form was extended to the pret. partic. which was made into (*a*)*hon* ; but afterwards the ng-forms got the upper hand, being supported by the weak verb *hangien*, and a new strong infin. *hangen* was formed, pret. *heng*, pret. partic. *hangen*. In some dialects the pret. was shortened to *heng* with short close (e), which being an unfamiliar sound in ME was made into *i*. This new pret. *hing*, which is frequent in some Midland dialects, was made into an infin. in Northern by the analogy of the bind-class, with pret. *hang*, which afterwards made its way into the Standard dialect in the form of *heng* parallel to *seng* 'sang.' A pret. partic. *hung* was further developed on the analogy of *sing, sang, sung*, and *hung* was then extended to the pret. sing. in the same way as *clung*, etc. (1269), the older infin. *hang* being preserved in the Standard dialect. In MnE the strong form *hung* is both transitive and intransitive, *hanged* being used only transitively, contrary to the OE usage.

Vowel-change (i . . ʙ).

1370. dig; dug, †digged. ME *diggen, diggede*, equivalent to OE *dician* [*dīc* 'ditch'], of which it seems to be a modification by some analogical influence. The vocalic pret. *dug* developed itself towards the end of the Early MnE period ; it is not found in the Bible.

1371. cling; clung. OE strong III *clingan, clang, clungen* 'wither.' ME *clingen, clong, clungen* 'shrivel,' 'adhere,' 'hang.'

1372. fling; flung. ME strong III *flingen* from weak Scandinavian *flengja* [compare ME *wing* from Scandinavian *vengr*]. *flingen* was, of course, made strong on the analogy of *sling* and the other strong verbs in -*ing*.

1373. sling; slung. ME strong III *slingen* from Scandinavian *slongva*, which passed through *slengen* into *slingen*, and then became strong in the same way as *fling*. The pret. *slang* occurs in the Bible.

1374. slink; slunk. OE strong III *slincan*.

1375. spin; spun. OE strong III *spinnan*. The pret. *span* is now obsolete.

1376. stick; stuck, †sticked 'pierce,' 'adhere.' OE *stician* (*stiocian*), *sticode* 'pierce,' 'adhere.' ME strong V *steken, stak, steken* and *stoken* [like *spoken* = OE *specen*] 'pierce,' 'imprison,' which may represent an OE strong verb. *stuck* may owe its *u* to the influence of *stung*.

1377. sting; stung. OE strong III *stingan*.

1378. string; strung. stringed. This verb is a MnE formation from the ME noun *string* from Scandinavian *strengr*, with the usual change of Scandinavian -*eng* into -*ing*. We keep the older consonantal inflexion in *stringed instruments*.

1379. swing; swung. OE strong III *swingan*.

1380. win; won. OE strong III *winnan* 'make war,' *gewinnan* 'conquer,' 'gain.'

1381. wring; wrung. OE strong III *wringan*.

Vowel-change (e . . æ . . e).

1382. run; ran; run. OE strong III *irnan, iernan* (*eornan*), Late West-Saxon *yrnan*, pret. *orn, arn*, pret. partic. *urnen*, with the same transposition of the *r* as in *burn*, the older forms being preserved in *gerinnan* 'coagulate,' literally 'run together,' *gerann, gerunnen*. The ME verb was influenced by the two Scandinavian verbs, the strong *rinna, rann, runninn* and the weak *renna, rendi*, the Standard ME forms being indeed entirely Scandinavian : *rennen, ran, irunnen*. The Early Southern forms of the infin. are *irnen, eornen, urnen* probably — *ürnen* from Late West-Saxon *yrnan*. The infin. *run* appears in Northern by the side of the Scandinavian *rin*. As there is no reason why the regular *rin, ran, run* should have been disturbed by the extension of the pret. partic. form to the infin., etc. against the analogy of *win*, etc., it seems most probable that the *u* of the infin. was originally a Southern development out of *ürnen*, perhaps by the influence of *burn*.

Vowel-change (i . . æ).

1383. sit ; sæt. OE strong V j-verb *sittan, sæt, seten*. ME *sitten, sat, seten* and also *siten* with the vowel of the infin. From the ME partic. *siten* is derived the obsolete MnE pret. and pret. partic. *sit*, which made the verb invariable. The obsolete MnE pret. *sate* is due to the analogy of *came, spake*, etc., the short *sat* being kept up at the same time by the short vowel of the infin. *sit*.

1384. spit ; spat. There were in OE two weak verbs of the same meaning *spittan, spitte* and *spātan, spætte*, both of which were kept in ME, where the pret. *spætte* became regularly *spatte*. The MnE *spit, spat* is, therefore, a mixture of two distinct verbs.

Vowel-change (i . . æ . . v).

1385. begin ; began ; begun. OE strong III *beginnan, onginnan*, later *aginnan*. The MnE shortened 'gin appears early in ME ; the coexistence of *risen* and *arisen* no doubt led to the shortening of *aginnen* into *ginnen*.

1386. drink ; drank ; drunk. OE strong III *drincan*. The OE pret. partic. *drunken*, ME *dronken* survives in the adjective *drunken*, the shortened form *drunk* being also used as an adjective. In MnE the use of *drank* as a partic.—as also of *began*, etc.—was formerly more frequent ; but the partic.

drank is still frequently used, apparently in order to avoid the form *drunk*, which suggests *drunken*.

1387. **ring; rang: rung.** OE (*h*)*ringan* is apparently weak.

1388. **shrink; shrank; shrunk.** OE strong III *scrincan*.

1389. **sing; sang: sung.** OE strong III *singan*.

1390. **sink; sank: sunk.** OE strong III *sincan*. The full pret. partic. is still preserved as an adjective, as in *sunken rock*.

1391. **spring; sprang; sprung.** OE strong III *springan*.

1392. **stink; stank; stunk.** OE strong III *stincan* 'rise' (said of dust, vapour, etc.), 'have a good or bad odour,' as in *wel-stincende* 'fragrant.'

1393. **swim; swam; swum.** OE strong III *swimman*.

Vowel-change (i .. æ .. i-n).

1394. **(for)bid; -bad; -bidden.** OE strong V j-verb *biddan, bæd, beden* 'pray,' 'ask'; strong VII *beodan, bead, boden* 'offer,' 'command.' The corresponding ME forms are *bidden, bad, bēden* and—by the analogy of the infin.— *bidden; beden, bēd, bōden*. But already in Early ME the two verbs began to be confused. *bidden* in the special sense of 'ask to one's house,' 'invite' soon got confused with *bēden*, which developed the meaning 'offer an invitation,' the confusion being aided by the weak verb *bōd(i)en* = OE *bodian* 'announce'—itself connected with *beodan*. Hence even in Early ME we find *iboden* used in the sense of 'invited.' It was still more natural to soften down the command expressed by *beden* by the substitution of the milder *bidden*. The pret. *bad* soon supplanted *bēd* by taking to itself the meaning 'commanded,' except in the emphatic *forbeden*, which in Standard ME only rarely has the pret. *forbad* instead of *forbēd*. The following are the Standard ME forms—

bidden, beden ; bad ; będen, bǫden.

forbeden ; forbęd (forbad) ; forbǫden.

In the transition to MnE the *bid*-forms were gradually extended till they entirely supplanted the others. The relation between the two forms *bad* and *bade* is the same as that between *sat* and *sate* (1266). In Early MnE the pret. partic. was often shortened to *bid*, which was used also as a pret., so that the verb became invariable. The simple *bid* is now obsolete in the spoken language, its place being taken by *tell*.

Vowel-change (ij . . e).

1395. bleed ; **bled.** OE weak *bledan (blædan), bledde.* [*blod* ' blood '].

1396. breed ; **bred.** OE weak *bredan (brædan), bredde.* [*brod* ' brood '].

1397. feed ; **fed.** OE weak *fedan (fadan), fedde.* [*foda* ' food '].

1398. lead ; **led.** OE weak *lædan, lædde.*

1399. meet ; **met.** OE weak *metan (mætan) mette.* [*gemot* ' meeting '].

1400. read : **read** (rijd ; red). OE weak *rædan, rædde.*

1401. speed ; **sped.** OE weak *spedan (spædan), spedde.*

Many verbs analogous to the above now follow the regular conjugation, such as *greet, seem* = OE *gretan, grette,* etc.

Vowel-change (ij . . e . . ij-n).

1402. eat ; **ate** ; **eaten.** OE strong V, with exceptional (Germanic) lengthening in the pret. sing., *etan, æt,* pret. plur. *æton,* pret. partic. *eten.* ME *ēten, et, at, ēten,* the pret. *at* being of course due to the influence of the other verbs of the same class.

Vowel-change (ou . . e).

1403. hold ; **held.** OE strong I *healdan, haldan ; heold ;*

gehealden, gehalden ME *holden* ; *held, held, hild* ; *iholden.* We still preserve the fuller form of the pret. partic. in *beholden.*

Vowel-change (ɔ . . e . . ɔ-n).

1404. fall; fell; fallen. OE strong I *feallan, fallan* : *feoll* ; *feallen, fallen.* ME *fallen* ; *fel, fel, fil* ; *fallen.*

Vowel-change (ai . . ei . . ei-n).

1405. lie ; lay ; lain. OE strong V j-verb *licgan, læg, gelegen,* imper. sing. *lige,* etc. The ME development of this verb is analogous to that of the other cg-verbs (1293). In Early Southern the infin. *liggen* was preserved by the side of the imper. *lie;* but in the North-Thames dialects it was levelled under the g-forms, becoming *lin, lien.* The Standard ME forms are *lien, lai,* pret. partic. *leien, lein.* In vulgar MnE the preterite-forms have led to the complete levelling of this verb under the transitive *lay* ; and this change is making its way into educated speech.

Vowel-change (ɐ . . ei . . ɐ).

1406. come ; came ; come. OE strong IV, with anomalous weak vowel in the pres. and infin. and exceptional extension of the vowel of the pret. plur. to the pret. sing. : *cuman* ; *cwom. com* ; *c(w)omon* ; *cumen.* The pret. *com* was preserved in Standard ME, but was partially supplanted by the new formation *cam* on the analogy of the strong verb IV *nimen* 'take,' *nam, nomen.* *cam* underwent the usual lengthening into *came* in MnE.

Vowel-change (i . . ei . . i-n).

1407. give : gave ; given. OE *giefan, gyfan, gefan, geyfan* ; *græf, gæf* ; *giefen, gyfen, ᵹefen.*

Vowel-change (ai . . i).

1408. light ; lit, lighted. OE weak *lihtan, lihte* 'illuminate' and 'make light,' 'alleviate' [*leoht* adj. 'light of

colour' and 'light of weight']. There was a third OE weak
verb *lihtan, alihtan* 'alight from a horse.' The MnE verb
light in *light on* must be referred to this last. The consonantal preterite-form *lit* does not, of course, appear till *light*
had become (ləit), that is, in the MnE period, when it arose
from imitation of *bite, bit,* etc. The verb *alight* still keeps
the older consonantal inflexion, which is also used in the
other verbs.

Vowel-change (ai . . i . . i-n).

1409. bite ; bit ; bitten. OE strong VI *bītan.* The
shortened pret. partic. is still kept in the phrase *the biter bit.*

1410. chide ; chid ; chidden. OE weak *cīdan, cīdde.*
ME *chīden, chidde.* In Early MnE the verb was made strong
chide, chode, chidden—on the analogy of *ride, rode, ridden.*
The pret. partic. was then shortened to *chid,* and extended to
the pret. The verb is nearly obsolete in the present spoken
English.

1411. hide, hid, hidden is a strong verb of similar recent
formation, except that it does not seem to have developed
any pret. analogous to Early MnE *chode* : OE *hȳdan, hȳdde,*
ME *hīden, hidde.*

Vowel-change (ij . . ij . . ij-n).

1412. beat ; beat ; beaten. OE strong I *beatan, beot,
beaten.*

Vowel-change (ai . . o).

1413. shine ; shone. OE strong VI *scīnan, scan, scinen.*

Vowel-change (e . . o . . o-n).

1414. forget ; forgot ; forgotten, got. In OE the
strong V verb *gietan, gytan, getan* : *geat, gæt; gieten, gyten,
geten* occurs only in the compounds *begietan* 'get,' *ongietan*
'understand,' *forgietan* 'forget' and a few others. In ME

begiten, begeten was shortened to *giten, geten* through the influence of the Scandinavian *geta, gat, getinn* ' get,' or rather the Scandinavian word was substituted for it.

1415. tread; trod; trodden. OE strong V. *tredan, trǣd, treden.* ME *tręden, trad, tręden* and—by the analogy of *broken,* etc.—*troden, troden.*

Vowel-change (ij . . o . . o-n).

1416. seethe; †sod, seethed; sodden, †sod, seethed. OE strong VII *seoþan, seaþ, soden. sodden* is now used as an adjective, which has been made into a verb with a pret. partic. *soddened,* which is extensively used instead of *sodden.*

Vowel-change (uw . . o).

1417. shoot; shot. OE strong VII *sceotan, sceat, scoten.* Standard ME *scheten, schęt, schoten.* There is also an infin. *schuten* in ME, whose *u* probably = *ü* from OE *eo*, as in *choose* (**1437**), which afterwards became (uu) and was written *oo* in Early MnE.

Vowel-change (ai . . ou).

1418. climb; †clomb, climbed. OE strong III *climman, clamm, clummen* and also *climban, clamb, clumben,* although the latter is found only in late texts. ME *climmen, clam, clommen* and *climben, clǫmb (clamb), clomben.*

Vowel-change (ai . . ou . . i-n).

1419. (a)bide; †bode, †bid, bided; †biden, †bid, bided. OE strong VI *bidan* ' wait,' *abidan* ' endure.' ME *(a)biden, bǫd, biden,* there being also a weak pret. *abidde.*

1420. drive; drove, †drave; driven. OE strong VI *drifan.* Like the other verbs of this series *drive* had in MnE a curtailed pret. partic. (driv), which was extended to the pret. It was not much used in writing because, being necessarily written *drive,* it was liable to be confounded with the pres.

1421. ride ; rode, †rid ; ridden, †rid.   OE strong VI *rīdan*.

1422. (a)rise ; rose ; risen.   OE strong VI (*a*)*rīsan*. The MnE preterite-form (riz) was not much used in writing because there was no convenient way of expressing its sound.

1423. shrive ; †shrove, shrived ; shriven.   OE strong VI *scrīfan* ' decree.'

1424. smite ; smote ; smitten.   OE strong VI *smītan* ' smear.'

1425. stride ; strode ; †stridden, strode.   OE *strīdan*.

1426. strive ; strove ; striven.   ME strong VI *striven, strōf, striven*, which is the Old French *estriver* [from Old Low-German *strīp* ' strife '] made into a strong verb on the analogy of *driven*.

1427. thrive ; throve ; thriven.   ME *þriven* from the Scandinavian strong reflexive verb *þrīfask*.

1428. write ; wrote, †writ ; written, †writ.   OE strong VI *wrītan*.

Vowel-change (ei . . ou).

1429. wake ; woke, waked.   OE strong II *wacan, wōc, wacen*, generally compounded with *on-* —*onwacan, awacan*. (*on*)*wacan* and the weak *a*(*wæcnian*), *wacian* ' keep awake ' are intransitive.   The corresponding transitive verb is *weccan, weahte, wehte*.   ME has (*a*)*waken, wōk, waken* and *wakien, wakede* ; *wakenen, wak*(*e*)*nede*.   The (ou) instead of (uw) in the MnE *woke* is probably due to the influence of the numerous preterites of the shine-class—*rose*, etc.

1430. stave ; stove, staved.   This verb was first formed in MnE from the noun *stave* ' piece of a cask,' itself a late formation from *staves*, plur. of *staff*.   Its vocalic inflexion is of course the result of analogy.

Vowel-change (ei . . ou . . ou-n).

1431. break ; broke, †brake ; broken, †broke.   OE strong IV *brecan, bræc, brocen*.

Vowel-change (ij . . ou . . ou-n).

1432. freeze; froze; frozen. †frore OE strong VII *frēᵕsan, frᵕᵛᵛᵗ, fᵢ ᵛᵛn.*

1433. heave : hove. heaved; †hoven, hove, heaved. OE strong j-verb II *hebban, hōf, hafᵢn.* ME *hebben, hₑven ; hōf, haf; hₑᵛen, hₑᵛen,* the last form being due to the influence of the infin., while *haf, hₒᵛen* are due to the influence of *wₑᵛen, waf, wₒᵛen* (1436). There was also a weak ME pret. *hefde, hₑᵛede.* The MnE *hoᵛe* probably points to a ME pret. *hₒf* with the vowel of the pret. partic.

1434. speak; spoke, †spake : spoken. †spoke. OE strong V *sprecan, sprœc, sprecen.* In Late OE this verb began to drop its *r*—especially in the Kentish dialect. In ME the *r* disappeared entirely, and the pret. partic. took *o* on the analogy of *broken,* etc. : *spₑkₑn, spak. spₑkₑn, spₒken.*

1435. steal; stole; stolen. OE strong IV *stelan, stₐl, stolen.*

1436. weave; wove, weaved : woven. weaved. OE strong V *wefan, waf, wefₑn.* ME *wₑᵛen, waf, wₑᵛen, wₒᵛen.*

Vowel-change (uw . . ou . . ou-n).

1437. choose : chose; chosen. OE strong VII *ceosan, ceas, coren.* ME *chₑsen, chₑs, chosen.* There was also a West-Midland infin. *chüsen* with the regular West-Midland change of OE *eo* into *ü.* In Early MnE (tʃiuz) became (tʃuuz), which was written phonetically *choose,* although the older spelling *chuse* survived till the end of the last century. *chese* also occurs in Early MnE.

Vowel-change (ai . . ɔ).

1438. fight; fought. OE strong III *feohtan (fehtan); feaht (faht): fohten.* ME *fighten, faught, foughten.* In the pret. Early MnE fluctuates between *au* and *ou.*

Vowel-change (eə . . ɔ . . ɔ-n).

1439. bear : bore. †bare; born(e). OE strong IV

beran, bær, boren. MnE makes a distinction between *born* in the sense of French *né* and *borne*='carried' which did not exist in OE or ME.

1440. swear; swore, †sware; sworn. OE strong j-verb II *swęrian, swōr, swaren, sworen,* the *o* of the last form being due to the influence of the preceding *w.* ME *swerien, swǭren; swor, swār; sworen. swār* is, of course, due to the analogy of *bęren, bar.*

1441. tear; tore, †tare; torn. OE strong IV *teran.*

1442. wear; wore, †ware; worn. OE weak *węrian, węrede* 'wear clothes.' The vocalic forms were first developed in Early MnE by the analogy of *bear.*

Vowel-change (ei . . ɔ).

1443. freight; *fraught, freighted. The Late ME weak verb *fraughten* [imported from Dutch?] was made into *freight* in Early MnE by the influence of the synonymous *fret,* and *fraught* itself came to be regarded as the pret. of this new verb *freight* by a vague association with *work, wrought,* etc. But *fraught* was still used as a pres. in Early MnE: *the good ship . . . and the fraughting souls within her* (Shakespere).

Vowel-change (iə . . ɔ . . ɔ-n).

1444. shear; †shore, †share, sheared; shorn, †sheared. OE strong IV *scieran (sceran); scear (scær); scoren.*

Vowel-change (ij . . ɔ . . ij-n).

1445. see; saw; seen. OE strong V *seon; seah (sæh); sāwon (segon); sewen (segen).* In Late Northumbrian the adjective *gesene*=West-Saxon *gesīene* 'visible' was used as the pret. partic. Early ME *seon, sen; seih* (Southern), *sah, sauh* pret. plur. *sęwen, sęien;* pret. partic. *seien, sein.* In Late ME the pret. sing. forms dropped the *h* by the influence of the pret. plur. and pret. partic., giving *sei, sai* and *saw,* the last being the usual North-Thames form, especially in

Northumbrian, which also kept the Old-Northumbrian pret. partic. in the form of *sen*. The Standard ME inflections are *se(n)*; *seigh, sai*; *(i)sein*. In MnE the Northern pret. *saw* and pret. partic. *seen* were introduced into the Standard dialect.

Vowel-change (æ . . . u).

1446. stand; stood. OE strong II with *n* inserted in the pres. etc.: *standan, stod, standen*.

Vowel-change (ei . . . u . . . ei-n).

1447. forsake; forsook; forsaken. OE strong II *forsacan* 'renounce,' 'deny.'

1448. shake; shook; shaken. OE strong II *scacan*.

1449. take; took; taken, *ta'en. ME strong II *taken, tok, taken* from Scandinavian *taka, tok, tękinn*. In Northern this verb was contracted like *make*, and the pret. partic. *ta en* passed into Standard MnE.

Vowel-change (ai . . . uw . . . ou-n).

1450. fly; flew; flown. OE strong VII *fleogan* (*flegan, fligan*); *fleag, fleah* (*fleh*); *flugon*; *flogen*. ME *flen, flien*; *fleigh, fley*—with the same dropping of final *h* as in *sei* = OE *gesæh—fly*; pret. plur. *flowen, flǫwen* (influence of pret. partic.); pret. partic. *flǫwen*. The Early MnE pret. *flew* (fliu) probably arose in the same way as *drew*, etc. (**1277**).

Vowel-change (ei . . . uw . . . ei-n).

1451. slay; slew; slain. OE strong II *slean* (from *sleahan*); *slog, sloh*; *slagen, slægen, slęgen*. ME Southern *slęn*, Midland *slǫn*, Northern *slā*; *sloh*, Late ME *slough, slow* = (sluu); pret. partic. *slawen, sleien, slain*. In MnE, the *ai* of the pret. partic. was extended to the infin., and the *ow* of the pret. underwent the usual analogical change into *ew*. The archaic forms *slee = slea*, pret. *slue* still lingered in Early MnE.

Vowel-change (ou . . . **uw** . . . ou-n).

1452. **blow ; blew ; blown, blowed.** OE strong I *blāwan* 'blow' (of wind), *bleow, blāwen* and *blowan* 'bloom,' *bleow, blōwen.* ME *blǫwen, blew, blǫwen* and *blōwen, blew, blōwen.*

1453. **crow ; crew. crowed ; +crown, crowed.** OE strong I *crāwan, creow, crāwen.*

1454. **grow ; grew ; grown.** OE strong I *grōwan, greow, growen.*

1455. **know ; knew ; known.** OE strong I *cnāwan, cnēow, cnāwen.*

Vowel-change (ɔ . . . **uw** . . . ɔ-n).

1456. **draw ; drew ; drawn.** OE strong II *dragan ; drōg, droh ; dragen.*

MIXED VERBS.

1457. There are several verbs which have a strong pret. partic. in *-en* with a regular consonantal pret. Some of these are old strong verbs which have become partially consonantal ; but others are weak verbs which have taken the partic. ending *-en* by the influence of old strong verbs which they happen to resemble. In the following list the latter class are marked ‡.

1458. **go ; went ; gone.** OE strong I *gan, gangan ; geong, code* (weak) ; *gegān, gegangen.* ME *gǫ(n), gange(n) ; yōde, wente ; gǫ(n), gangen.* In ME the longer form *gang* was gradually restricted to the Northern dialect. The curtailed Southern pret. partic. *gǫ* is still preserved in the adverb *ago* = OE *agan* 'passed' (of time).

1459. **grave, graved ; graven, graved.** OE strong II *grafan, grōf, grafen.*

1460. **hew ; hewed ; hewn, hewed.** OE strong I *heawan, hēow, hēawen.*

1461. †lade, load; †laded, loaded; laden, †laded, †loaden, loaded. OE strong II *hladan, hlod, hlæden, hladen.* The MnE change of *lade* into *load*—the older form being still preserved in *bill of lading* as well as in the pret. partic. *laden*—is through the influence of the noun *load*, ME *lode* = OE *lad* (fem.) 'leading,' 'way'—a meaning still preserved in *loadstar*—connected with *lædan* 'lead,' which had also the meaning 'carry,' as it still has in the dialectal expression *lead hay*, etc. Thus in ME *lode* came to mean 'load,' and was at last confused with the verb *laden.*

1462. melt; melted; molten. melted. OE strong III *mellan. mollen* is now used only as an adjective.

1463. mow; mowed; mown, mowed. OE strong I *māwan, meow, māwen.*

1464. rive; rived; riven, rived. ME strong VI *riven, rōf, riven* from the Scandinavian *rīfa.*

1465. ‡saw; sawed; sawn, sawed. ME weak *saw(i)en.* MnE *sawn* by the analogy of *drawn.*

1466. shape; shaped; shapen, shaped. OE strong II j-verb *scieppan, scyppan (sceppan)*; *scop*; *scapen, scæpen.* In ME this verb was influenced—or rather supplanted—by the Scandinavian verb *skapa, skop.*

1467. shave; shaved; shaven, shaved. OE strong II *scafan, scōf, scafen.*

1468. ₊show; showed; shown, showed. OE weak *sceawian, sceawode* 'survey,' 'look at.' ME *schew(i)en, schowien,* Northern *schaw.* Early MnE *shew* and *show. shown* by the analogy of *known*, etc.

1469. sow; sowed; sown, sowed. OE strong I *sāwan, sēw, sāwen.*

1470. ‡strew; strewed; strewn. strewed. OE weak *strewian, streowian.* ME *strewen, strowen, strawen. strewn* by the analogy of *hewn.*

1471. swell; swelled; swollen, swelled. OE strong III *swellan.*

Isolated Forms.

1472. Some obsolete verbs occur only in isolated forms, namely *quoth, hight, iclept, wont.*

1473. quoth. OE strong V *cweþan, cwaþ, cwǽdon, gecweden* 'say.' In ME the strong consonant of the infin. was kept throughout: *cweþen, cwaþ, icweþen*; so also *bicweþen* 'bequeath,' which in MnE is consonantal—*bequeathed*. In Late ME the simple *cweþen* was gradually disused except in the pret. sing. As *cwaþ* was often unstressed in such combinations as *cwaþ ·he*, it developed a weak form *cwod, quod* through the regular rounding of unstressed *a* into *o* after a lip-consonant, as in OE *Oswold*=earlier *Oswald*. The explanation of the *d* is that *cwaþ he* etc. were made into (kwaþ·ee) which became (kwað·ee, kwoð·ee); and when (kwoð) was detached and received strong stress—as it naturally would—the final (ð), being an unfamiliar sound in strong syllables, was changed into (d). The form *quoth* is a blending of strong *quath* and weak *quod*. *quoth* being obsolete is now generally pronounced artificially (kwoup) on the analogy of *both*; but the older colloquial pronunciation was (kwʊp) or (keþ).

1474. hight 'is named, called,' 'was called,' ME *highte* is a blending of the OE passive form *hātte* (**1182**) and *heht*, the active pret. of the same verb *hātan*.

1475. iclept= ME *iclēped*, OE *gecleopod* 'called' the pret. partic. of the weak verb *cleopian, clipian.*

1476. wont 'accustomed'= OE *gewunod*, pret. partic. of the weak verb *gewunian* [*gewuna* 'custom,' 'habit.'] Being unfamiliar, this word is now artificially pronounced (wount) instead of the earlier and correct (wʊnt).

Anomalous Verbs.

1477. Most of the MnE verbs that we class as anomalous are old preterite-present verbs. Two of these preterite-present verbs—*dare* and *owe* = OE *dearr, ag*—have been made regular in certain meanings. The original inflections of these verbs have been much curtailed in MnE, most of them having only the inflections of the finite present and preterite. The only one which has an infin. is *dare*, which seems to have taken it from the regularly inflected verb *dare*. Two of the old preterite-present verbs—*must* and *ought*—occur now only in the OE preterite forms, which have taken the place of the OE present *mot* and *ag*, so that these verbs are incapable of marking the distinction between pres. and pret.

1478. In the present Spoken English the preterite-present verbs, together with *need* and the other anomalous verbs *be, have, do*, are the only ones which have the particle *not* joined to them directly instead of with the help of an auxiliary verb, as in *I cannot* (kaant) compared with *I do not see*. the *not* being shortened to (nt), often with modification of the verb itself. Most of the anomalous verbs have also very distinct weak forms, which we will put in (   ).

1479. can, canst : could, couldst. OE *cann, canst*. plur. *cunnon* ; pret. *cupe*; infin. *cunnan* ' know.' There is a weak OE verb *cunnian, cunnode* 'try,' which must not be confounded with *cunnan* ' know ' ; from this *cunnian* comes the MnE *con* ' peruse,' ' study,' which, being unfamiliar, is now pronounced artificially (kon) instead of the correct (kɐn). ME *can, canst*, plur. *connen, can* ; *coupe, coude* ; infin. *connen. coude* is a weakening of *coupe* ,which probably began like that of *quap* into *quod* (**1473**), in such combinations as (kuup·ee, kuuð·ee)=*coupe he*, the detached (kuuð) being made into (kuud), which became *coude* by blending with *coupe*. The Late ME participle-adjective *conninge* seems to have been introduced from the Northern dialect, where it appears in the form of *cunnand*, which is no doubt the Scandinavian adjective and pres. partic. *kunnandi* 'knowing,' ' sagacious,' from *kann* ' knows,' infin. *kunna*. The Scandinavian noun formed from this adj.—*kunnandi* (fem.) ' knowledge '—was also in-

troduced into MnE, being made into *conninge* in the Standard
dialect. In the transition to MnE the weak *coude* entirely
supplanted the strong *couthe*, and in Early MnE it was made
into *could* on the analogy of *should* and *would* = OE. *scolde*,
wolde. The (uu) of *coud*, *could*, was shortened when unstressed, which prevented it from being diphthongized like the
(uu) in *house*; and the (l) of all three verbs was dropped in
their weak forms, so that *could* had two forms, the strong
(kuld) and the weak (kud). At the same time the meaning
'knowing' gradually developed into 'being able.' The
Spoken English forms of this verb, including the weak and
negative forms, are :—

kæn (kən), kaant; kud (kəd), kudnt.

The defective forms of this verb are supplied by *be able* : *can
you do it ? ; I shall not be able to do it.*

1480. **dare, darest, (he) dare, †dares ; durst; infin.
dare.** OE *dearr, dearst, durron*; *dorste*; ME *dar, dār* (as
in the pret. *bar*), *darst*; *dorste, durste* with the *u* of OE
durron; infin. *durren, ādren*, of which the former represents
the probable OE infin. *durran*, the latter being a new-formation from *dār*. In MnE *dare* in the transitive sense of
'challenge' has become quite regular: *he dared him to do it*.
The intransitive pres. partic. *daring* is used only as an adjective. The pret. *durst* is little used in the spoken language,
where the literary *I durst not interrupt him* is represented by
I did not dare to interrupt him. The pres. *dare* is most frequent in the phrase *I dare say* = ' I think,' ' it is probable.'

1481. **may, mayst; might, mightst.** OE *mæg, þu
meaht (mæht), miht*, plur. *magon*; pret. *meahte (mæhte) mihte*
' be able.' [Compare *mægen, meaht, miht* 'power,' 'force.']
The ME forms seem to have been influenced by another OE
preterite-present verb of similar meaning, namely *deag, deah*
' avail ' plur. *dugon*; pret. *dohte*; infin. *dugan*. The ME
forms are : *mai, miht*, and, very late, *mayst*, plur. *mawen*,

muwen, moun ; pret. *mahte, mihte, mohte*. This last survived as a vulgarism (mɔɔt) to the end of the 17th century. The meaning of the verb developed in MnE into that of 'have permission.' The Spoken English forms are :—

mei, meint ; mait, maitnt.

1482. †mote (muut) ; must. OE *mot, most, moton* ; *moste* ' may.' ME *mot, most, moten* ; *moste*. The pres. survived only as an archaism in Early MnE : *as fair as fair mote be* (Spenser). Already in ME the pret. was used in the sense of the pres., and in Early MnE this usage became fixed. It began with the use of the pret. subj.—which was practically indistinguishable from the pret. indic.—to express mild command, so that *þou moste*='you would be able,' 'you might' was understood to mean 'you will have to,' 'you must.' The vowel of *moste* passed through (uu) into (u) in Early MnE, the shortening having probably begun in the weak form. The Spoken English forms of this verb are :—

mɐst (mɔst, mɔs), mɐsnt.

1483. (owe) ; ought. OE *ag, ah, þū aht, aht*, plur. *agon* ; pret. *ahte, ahte* ; infin. *agan* · possess.' The adjective *āgen* 'own' is an old pret. partic. of this verb. From *āgen* is formed the weak verb *āgnian*, 'appropriate,' 'possess.' In Early ME *ahte* developed regularly into *a(u)hte*, but afterwards *ǫ* was introduced from the infin. etc., giving *ǫ(u)hte*. In ME *ǫwen* in the sense of 'possess' soon took regular weak inflection—*ī ǫwe, we ǫweþ*, etc.—still keeping the older *ǫuhte* as its pret. The meaning 'possess' gradually developed into that of 'have a debt,' 'owe,' which, again, developed the abstract meaning 'ought,' especially in the pret., which by degrees took the function of a pres. in the same way as *must* (1482). The Spoken English forms are :—

ɔt, ɔtnt.

1484. shall, shalt, should. shouldst. OE *sceal (scæl). sceall (scæll), sculon* ; *scolde*, Northumbrian *scalde* by the analogy of *walde* (1485)=*wolde*. ME *schal, schall, schulen, schullen* (by the analogy of *willen*); *scholde, schulde* (by the influence of *schulen*). In Northern, weak *sh* became *s*, as in *Inglis*=*English* [compare Scotch *Scots* from *Scottish*], whence the Northern (originally only weak) forms *sal, sald*. Of the two Early MnE forms of the pret., strong (ʃuld) and weak (ʃud), only the latter has survived. The spoken forms are :—

ʃæl (ʃl), ʃaant ; ʃud (ʃəd), ʃudnt.

1485. will, wilt ; would, wouldst ; imper. **will**. This verb was in OE originally a strong subjunctive preterite, with which pres. indic. forms were afterwards mixed : *wile, wille, will, willaþ*; *wolde, walde* (originally weak?) ; infin. *willan*. In OE this verb has, together with several other verbs in very frequent use, special **negative** forms, the result of contraction with a preceding *ne* 'not' : *ic nyle, þu nylt, he nyle, we nyllaþ* ; *nolde*, etc. One of these negative forms is still preserved in the phrase *willy nilly*, Early MnE *will he, nill he*=OE *wile he, nyle he*. The ME forms are : *wile, wole, will, woll, willeþ, willen, wollen* ; *wolde, walde, wolde*, whose (u) is the result of the influence of the pres. forms *wole*, etc., which were probably at first weak forms, in which the *w* rounded the following vowel and gradually assimilated it to itself. In Early MnE (wud) was the weak form of (wuld). The spoken forms are :—

wil (l), wount ; wud (wəd, əd), wudnt.

1486. †wot ; †twist. OE *wāt, wāst, witon* ; *wiste* ; *witan* ; *witende*. The adjective *gewiss* 'certain' is an old pret. partic. of this verb. ME *wot, wost, witen* ; infin. *witen* ; pres. partic. *witinge*. In Early MnE *wot* was sometimes made the base of a regular verb : *he wotteth, wots*, pret. *wotted*, pres. partic. *wotting*. The old pres. partic. still survives in the adverb *unwittingly*, and the infin. in the adverb phrase *to wit*=viz.

The ME adjective *iwis*—OE *gewiss* has in MnE been often wrongly divided *i wis*, as if it were the pronoun *I* with a verb equivalent to *wot*, a view which has been further supported in recent times by the chance resemblance of the Modern German equivalent of *wot*, namely *weiss*, plur. *wissen*.

1487. need. This verb agrees with the preterite-present verbs in having no *s*-inflection and in taking *not* without any auxiliary—*he need not* (nijdnt). The loss of the *s*—which seems to have begun in the transition from ME to MnE—is apparently partly the result of similarity of meaning to that of the preterite-present verbs; but the absence of the inflectional *s* is partly due to the verb *need* 'require' being formed directly from the noun *need* through the ambiguity of such sentences as Early MnE *what need all this waste?* There were two weak verbs formed from the noun in OE—*nīedan, nydan* (*nedan*) and *neadian*. Both had the meaning 'compel,' which they kept in Early ME. The later meaning 'require' was probably the result of making the noun *need* in such sentences as that quoted above into a verb.

We now come to the anomalous auxiliary verbs *be, have, do*.

1488. The verb *be* in OE is made up of three distinct roots; that seen in (*a*) *is, are*, (*b*) *was*, and (*c*) *be* :—

		Indic.	Subj.
Pres. Sing.	1	*eom* (*eam*); *bēo*	*sīe, sy; bēo*
	2	*eart* (*earþ*); *bist*	*sīe, sy; bēo*
	3	*is; biþ*	*sīe, sy; bēo*
Plur.		*sind, sindon, ǝ ǝ ǝ ǝ ǝ ǝ ǝ ǝ ǝ*	*sīen, sȳn; bēon*
Pret. Sing.	1	*wæs*	*wǣre*
	2	*wǣre*	*wǣre*
	3	*wæs*	*wǣre*
Plur.		*wǣ ron*	*wǣ ren*
Imper. Sing.		*wes; bēo*	Infin. *wesan; bēon*
Plur.		*wesaþ; bēoþ*	Gerund *to wesenne; to bēonne*

Partic. Pres. *bēonde*

1489. The *ea* in *eart* and the Anglian *eam*, *earon* is a weakening of *eo* (**1068**), preserved in the West-Saxon *eom* and the occasional *eort, eorun*. In Late Northumbrian this *ea* undergoes the usual further weakening into *a*: *am, arþ, aron.*

1490. The Standard ME forms are: *am, art, is, be(n)*; subj. *be, be(n)*; pret. *was, wẹr(e), was, wẹre(n)*; pret. subj., *wẹr(e), wẹre(n)*; imper. *be, béþ*; infin. *be(n)*; participles *beinge, be(n)*. The ME pret. partic. is, of course, an analogical new-formation. The North-Thames plur. *ar(n)* is still rare in Standard ME, but is firmly established in Early MnE, which inflects: *am, art, is, are*; subj. *be*; pret. *was, wast, wert*, plur. *were*; subj. pret. *were, wert, were*; infin. *be*; partic. *being, been*. The use of *be* in the pres. indic. is still kept up in Early MnE: *I be, thou beest, they be,* etc.; the form *he bes* is, however, very rare. There is in MnE a tendency to get rid of the distinctively subjunctive inflections of this verb not only by using *thou beest* as if it were a subjunctive—*if thou beest = if thou be*—but also by substituting *if I was* for *if I were,* etc. *was = were* was frequent in the last century not only as a subjunctive, but also in the indic. *you was.* In the present Spoken English the distinction between *was* and *were* is strictly maintained, the substitution of *was* for *were* being a vulgarism. The subj. pres. is, on the other hand, extinct in the spoken language, except in a few phrases. The following are the inflections of *be* in spoken English:

Pres. Indic. and Subj. Sing.	1	æm (m)
	2	aar (ər)
	3	iz (z, s); iznt
Plur.		aar (ər)
Pret. Indic. Sing.	1	woz (wɔz); woznt
	2	wəər (wər); wəənt
	3	woz (wɔz); woznt
Plur.		wəər (wər); wəənt
Pret. Subj.		wəər (wər); wəənt

Imper. and Infin.　　bij
Pres. Partic. and Gerund　　bijin
Pret. Partic.　　bijn, bin

1491. The negative forms left blank in the pres. are generally supplied by (eint) in familiar speech, which is, however, felt to be a vulgarism, and is avoided by many educated speakers, who say (aim not) instead of (ai eint), (aa ju not) instead of (eint ju).

1492. have. The OE inflections resemble those of *libban* (1210): *hæbbe, hafast, hæfst, hafaþ, hæfþ*, plur. *habbaþ*; su'j. *hc¹¹·, hc·¹' n*; pret. *h fá·*; imper. *hæfa, ha''ıþ*; infin. *habban*; partic. *hæbbende, gehæfd*. In ME the old *bb* was gradually supplanted by the *v* = OE *f* of the other forms, the *v* itself being often dropped by contraction. The Standard ME forms are : *have*, weak *hav, hast, haþ*, plur. *hāve(n), han, han*; pret. *hadde*; pret. partic. *had*. In ME the weak short-vowel forms gradually supplanted the long-vowel ones ; but we keep the long-vowel forms in the derivative *behave*, pret. *behaved* = ME *behaven*. The MnE literary forms are : *have, hast, hath, has* plur. *have*; subj. pres. *have*; pret. indic. *had, hadst*; pret. subj. *had*; imper. and infin. *have*; partic. *having, had*. Early MnE still kept the shortened infin. *ha, a* = ME *han* : *she might a been* (Shakespere). In Present English the infinitive (ə) occurs only in vulgar or very indistinct speech. The distinctive spoken forms of *have* in Present English are :—

hæv (əv, v), hævnt; hæz (əz, z, s), hæznt; hæd (əd, d), nædnt; hʌviŋ.

The distinction between subj. and indic. is entirely lost.

1493. do. OE *do, dest (dæst), dēþ (daþ)*, plur. *dōþ*; pret. weak *dyde*; imper. *do, dōþ*; infin. *don*; partic. *donde, gedon*. The mutation in *dest, dēþ* is common to all the dialects. In Standard ME the *o* of the other parts of the verb supplanted the older *e* : *do, dost, dōþ*, plur. *don*; *dide*; imper. *do, dōþ*; partic. *doinge do(n)*. In MnE (uu) = ME *o*

was shortened in the weak forms of *dost, doth, does, done,*
whence the present forms (dʊst, dʊp, dʊz, dʊn), which have
supplanted the Early MnE strong forms (duust), etc.   The
spoken forms in Present English are :

   duw (də, d), dount ; dʊz (dəz), dʊznt ; did, didnt ; dʊn.

PARTICLES.

1494. All the OE particles are either **primary** or
secondary (337). The secondary particles are formed
from other (declinable) parts of speech ; thus *ham* in *he*
eode ham 'he went home' is formed from the masc. noun
ham 'home,' 'homestead.' Primary particles, such as *be*
'by,' *swā* 'so' are not formed from other parts of speech.
There is no strict division between the three classes of
particles, most of the prepositions being used also as adverbs,
some adverbs being used also as conjunctions. Thus *ær* is a
preposition in *ær dæge* 'before day(break),' an adverb in *he*
eft wæs papa swā he ær wæs 'he was pope again as he was
before,' and a conjunction in *ær þæt flōd com* 'before the
flood came.'

   1495. Some of the particles are **simple**, some **derivative**,
such as *uf-an* 'above,' some **compound** (group-compounds),
such as *be-neoþan* 'beneath,' which is compounded with the
preposition *be*. The above are primary adverbs. Secondary
particles also admit of the same divisions, such as *ham, sōþlice*
'truly,' *ealne-weg* 'always,' literally 'all (the) way.'

Adverb-endings.

   1496. In OE, adverbs are regularly formed from adjectives
by adding *-e*, a preceding *æ* being generally changed to *a* :
deope 'deeply,' *hearde* 'strongly,' 'severely,' *nearwe* 'narrowly,'
late 'slowly,' 'with delay' from *deop, heard* 'hard,' 'strong,'
'severe,' *nearu, læt* 'slow,' *swiþe* 'very' from the obsolete
adjective *swiþ* 'strong,' preserved in proper names such as

Swiphun 'Swithin,' literally 'strong cub.' Adjectives with a mutated vowel often have an unmutated vowel in the adverb, as in *sōfte* 'gently,' 'luxuriously,' *swote* 'sweetly' corresponding to the adjectives *sēfte* (*sǣfte*), *swete* (*swǣte*). The numerous adjectives in *-lic* form their adverbs in *-līce*, the original length of the vowel being kept, as in *egeslīce* 'terribly,' *gesǣliglīce* 'blessedly,' 'happily' from *egeslic*, *gesǣliglic* [*egesa* 'terror,' *sǣl* 'favourable time,' 'luck']. But *gesǣliglic* occurs also in the shorter form *gesǣlig*; and hence in this and similar cases the adverb could be regarded as formed directly from the shorter adjective—*gesǣlig-līce* from *gesǣlig*. In this way *-līce* came to be regarded as an independent adverb-ending equivalent to *-e*, which, through being more distinct, it gradually supplanted in many words. Hence *-līce* was sometimes added directly, without there being any adjective in *-lic*.

1497. In ME the two endings *-e* and *-līche* were both kept, the latter appearing as *-līke* in Early Midland, as in *deplīke* compared with Early Southern *deoplīche*.

1498. When final *-e* was dropped in North-Thames English the distinction between the adj. *hard* and the adverb *hard(e)*, etc. was lost. By degrees also the adverb-ending *-līke* was levelled under the adjective-ending *-li=* Southern *-lich*, and *-li* then became a regular adverb-ending. In Late ME it was introduced into the Standard dialect, where it supplanted the Early Southern *-līche*, as in *deply*, *hardly*, *openly*. But *-ly* was also retained as an adjective-ending, as it still is in such a word as *goodly=* OE *godlic*, ME *godlich*, *godli*. Some of the MnE adverbs which have the same form as adverbs, as in *pull hard*, *speak loud*, *talk like a foreigner* compared with *a hard pull*, etc. are, of course, the descendants of the OE adverbs in *-e*, such as *hearde*, *hlude*, *gelīce*; but others are new-formations on the analogy of these traditional ones, especially those in *-y=* OE *-ig*, as in *pretty well*, *mighty fine*, for the OE adjectives in *-ig* formed their adverbs in *-iglīce* (*mihtiglīce*) to avoid the ambiguity of *-ige*, which might be mistaken for the plur., etc. inflection.

1499. In Old French the uninflected forms of adjectives —originally the neut. sing.—were used as adverbs, which were introduced into ME, whence such MnE adverbs as in *just ready, shut close* [Old French *clos* from Latin *clausum*], *quiet* [Latin *qvietum*], *very*=ME *verrai* 'true,' 'truly,' Old French *verai* [Modern French *vrai*] from Latin *verax, vērācem.*

1500. In Present English, adverbs in *-ly* are formed freely from all kinds of adjectives, as in *deeply, foolishly, willingly, affectedly.* Through the shortening of double consonants the (l) is dropped after adjectives ending in (l), as in *fully* (fuli), *nobly.* The addition of *-ly* is attended by various changes of spelling, as in *merrily, gaily* [old-fashioned English and American *gayly*], *fully, nobly* from *merry, gay, full, noble.* Adverbs in *-ly* are not often formed from adjectives that already end in *-ly*, these adjectives generally forming their adverbs by periphrases, such as *in a lively manner, in a friendly way.* Some MnE adverbs in *-ly* are formed direct from nouns, such as *namely*; but such adverbs as *daily, yearly, quarterly* in *he is paid quarterly* are old adjectives used as adverbs.

A less frequent adverb-ending in OE was *-unga, -inga*, by which adverbs were formed from adjectives: *eallunga* 'entirely,' *ierringa* 'angrily,' from *eall, ierre.* There was also in OE a class of adverbs formed from nouns—mostly names of parts of the body—by adding *-ling* and prefixing the preposition *on*, such as *on bæcling* 'backwards.' By blending these two endings a new ending *-lunga, -linga* was formed, as in *grund-lunga* 'from the foundations,' 'completely.' In ME the ending *-linge* is frequent, the adverbial *-es* **(1504)** being often added, as in *hēdlinge(s)* 'headlong,' *nęselinge(s)* 'on the nose,' 'at full length,' *sidelinge(s)* 'sideways.' In MnE this ending has been confused with the adjective *long.* Hence in Early MnE we find *sideling, sidelong* 'sideways,' *flatling* and *flatlong*, as in *the blow fell flatlong*, that is, 'was given with the flat of the sword instead of the point.' In Present English *headlong* is still an adverb, *sidelong* being an adjective—*a sidelong glance.* The older *sidelinge* was regarded as a pres. partic., and from it was formed a verb *to sidle (up to).* So also the ME adverb *grovelinge* ' grovellingly' was made into the verb *grovel.*

1501. In ME and MnE some new adverb-endings arose out of OE adverbial phrases. Thus the OE *on ōþre wisan* ' in another way' [*wise* weak fem. ' manner,' ' way'] was shortened and hardened into the group *ōþrewīse, ōþerwīse;* and in MnE *-wise* was used to form new adverbs, such as *likewise, nowise.* The noun *way* was used in like manner to form adverb-groups such as *midway, noway,* whence *noways* with the usual addition of *-s.* *-wise,* and *-ways* were often confused, as in *lengthwise—lengthways, endwise, coastwise.* The nouns *time* and *while* = OE weak masc. *tīma* and strong fem. *hwīl* ' time,' have also come to be used as adverb-endings in such words as *meantime, sometime(s), ofttimes, oftentimes, meanwhile, somewhile, otherwhile(s),* the last two being now obsolete.

Adverbs formed direct from Nouns and Adjectives.

1502. Many OE adverbs are formed direct from nouns or adjectives, either inflected or uninflected. The following are uninflected, being formed from nouns in the acc. sing. and adjectives in the neut. sing.: *ham, norþ, sup. east, west; eall* ' entirely,' *neah* ' nearly,' *genog* ' sufficiently.'

The most important inflectional endings are *-um* and *-es :—*

1503. **-um** : *hwīlum* 'sometimes,' *stundum* 'at intervals' [*stund* strong fem. ' period ']. *-mǣlum* from the neut. noun *mǣl* ' mark,' ' point of time ' is a frequent adverb-ending, as in *styccemǣlum* ' piecemeal,' *floccmǣlum* ' in troops.' From adjectives are formed *miclum* ' greatly,' *lȳtlum and lȳtlum* ' by little and little,' ' by degrees.' The isolated ME *whilom* is still preserved in the higher language. *-mǣlum* in ME passed through -*melen* into -*mēle*, as in *dropmele, pecemele,* where *stycce* was replaced by its French equivalent.

1504. -es in OE was extended to fem. nouns as an adverb-ending : *dæges and nihtes* ' by day and by night,' *sumeres and wintra* [*wintra* masc. gen. like *suna*], *nīedes* ' of necessity ' [*nīed* fem.] ; *ealles* ' entirely,' *elles* ' otherwise ' from a lost adjective. The adverb-ending -*weardes* interchanges with the uninflected -*weard,* as in *hamweard(es)* ' homewards.'　　In ME and MnE this ending was dropped in some words, as in Late ME *day and night*; but it was more often extended, especially to adverbs which in OE ended in a vowel or *n,* in order to make them more distinct, as in *always* = Early MnE *alwai,* OE *ealneweg, ones* ' once ' = OE *æne,* the mutated *æ* being supplanted by *ā* = the OE *a* in *an, twīes* ' twice,' *þrīes* ' thrice ' = OE *twiwa, þriwa.* OE *heonone* ' hence ' **(1509)** became *he(o)nne* in Early MnE, and by the addition of -*s, hennes,* OE *þanon* ' thence,' *hwanon* ' whence ' becoming Late ME *þennes, whennes* by the influence of *hennes.* So also OE *siþþan* **(1511)** ' since ' passed through *siþþen, sin* into *siþens, sins.* This extension of -*s* went on in MnE also, as in *sometimes* = earlier MnE *sometime,* which is still preserved in the higher language.

Some adverbs in -*es* took final *t* in Early MnE or Late ME, as in *amidst, betwixt, whilst, amongst* = ME *amiddes* — a blending of OE *onmiddan* and *tomiddes* · *betwix(t), whiles, among.*

1505. The following are examples of OE **group-adverbs** : *ealneweg, ealneg* ' always,' *georstandæg* ' yesterday,' *on weg* ' away,' *on bæc* ' backwards,' ' back,' *ofdune* ' down,' literally ' off the hill,' *todæg* ' today,' where *to* governs an exceptional form of the dative. All the above show isolation either of form or meaning, and therefore approximate to compounds. Such collocations, on the other hand, as *on līfe* ' alive ' literally ' in life,' *on slǣpe* ' in sleep, asleep,' *on eornost* ' in earnest ' show no isolation either of meaning or form.　　But in ME there was a tendency to shorten weak *of* and *on* to *a* whenever they were closely associated with the following word. Hence the ME forms *adune, adun* 'down' adv., *awai, abak, alīve, aslēpe*, the *a* having been dropped in the MnE adverbs *down, back*. The same weakening took place in ME and Early MnE combinations, as in *aclock*, now written *o'clock = of (the) clock*, and also in freer combinations, as in *go a fishing =* OE *gan on fiscnoþ, twice a day =* OE *twiwa on dæge*.

In MnE this *a* was taken for the indef. article, so that in *jackanapes = jack-of-apes* it was made into *an* before a vowel.

Some French group-adverbs formed with the preposition *a* were introduced into ME, where they were of course put on a level with the similar native combinations: *apart, apas —* MnE *apace*.

1506. In ME the OE preposition *be* became *bi* (1535), but the old *be* was kept in compounds such as *beforen =* OE *be-foran*, and also in some traditional collocations such as OE *be sīdan* 'by the side,' ME *beside*, which was now completely isolated from *bi þe(re) side*, just as *alīve* was isolated from *in al his līf* etc. But the new preposition *bī* was sometimes introduced into these groups, being however shortened to *bi*: *bifore, biside*. On the analogy of the older compounds the new-formation *bī cause* 'by the cause' was made into *bicause*, *because*.

1507. In ME and MnE the place of a lost or obscured ending was sometimes supplied by a preposition, giving rise to new group-adverbs, such as *of a truth =* OE *sōþes, of right =* OE *ryhtes, bī pecemele =* OE *styccemǣlum, by little and little —* OE *lytlum and lytlum*.

Sometimes a preposition was added even when the ending was clear, as in *at unawares*.

Pronominal Adverbs.

1508. Among the OE primary adverbs there is a symmetrical group of adverbs of place, connected with the pronouns *he*, *þæt*, *hwæt*, their endings expressing respectively rest, motion to, and motion from :—

Rest	Motion to	Motion from
her 'here'	*hider* 'hither'	*heonon* 'hence'
þær 'there'	*þider* 'thither'	*þanon* 'thence'
hwær 'where'	*hwider* 'whither'	*hwanon* 'whence'

The ME *th* in *hither* etc. is due to the influence of the *r* (877).

1509. The ending *-er*, *-an*, *-on* of the other primary adverbs has no very definite meaning : *of-er* 'over,' expressing both motion and rest, *und-er*, *æft-er* ; *inn-an* 'within,' *uf-an* 'above' [connected with *ofer*], *hindan* 'behind,' *foran* 'in front.' The ending *-an* was, however, extended to the noun-derived adverbs *norþ* etc., where it kept its definite meaning : *norþan* 'from the north,' *suþan* 'from the south.' *-on*, *-an* often takes final *-e*: *heonone*, *utan(e)* 'outside.' The adverbs *þonne* 'then,' 'than,' *hwonne* 'when' are also pronominal.

1510. Many OE adverbs are formed directly from pronouns. The neuter *þæt* is used as a conjunction exactly as in MnE: *he sægde þæt*; *he sægde þæt he wære gearu*, literally 'he said that: (namely) he was ready.' So also the pronoun *hwaþer* is used in the same way as *whether*. The indeclinable *þe* is used as a relative pronoun, both alone and in combination with *se* (1142), and is used also as a particle in a variety of meanings—'when,' 'because' etc. It is also added to particles to make them into conjunctions, or mark them more distinctly as such, as in *þeah-þe* 'although' conjunction, *þeah* 'though' being an adverb, *þætte* 'that' conj.=*þæt þe* (767). Inflected pronouns are also used as particles. *þy*, the instrumental of *þæt*, is used in the sense of 'therefore,' 'because,' and to express measure and proportion, as in *þy ma* 'the more,' correlative *þy . . . þȳ*=MnE *the . . . the* in *the more the merrier*. The change of *þy* into *the* is the result of loss of stress and confusion with the indeclinable *þe*. *hwy*, the instrumental of *hwœt*, is used in the sense of its MnE descendant *why*.

1511. There are many group-particles in OE consisting of a preposition governing a pronoun in the dat. or instr. The combination with the preposition alone generally forms an adverb—*for þœm, for þon, for þy* 'therefore'—the corresponding conjunctions being formed by the addition of *þe*— *for þœm þe, for þon þe, for þy þe* 'because,' *œr þœm þe* 'before,' *after þœm þe* 'after'—or *þœt*: *to þœm þœt, to þon þœt* 'in order that.'

siþþan, seoþþan 'since' contains an obsolete preposition *$*sīþ* 'since'—*siþþan = sīþ-þon* with shortening of the *ī*.

1512. There are similar group-particles formed by combinations of pronouns with nouns and adverbs formed from adjectives, such as *þa hwīle þe* 'while,' literally 'the time when' [*þa hwīle* acc. fem. sing.], *nā þy lœs* 'nevertheless,' 'notwithstanding,' literally 'not by-that less,' *þy lœs þe* 'lest,' literally 'by-that less that.'

1513. The group-adverbs *for-þī, for-þan, for-hwī* continued in use throughout the ME period, but became obsolete in MnE. The groups in *-þe* were modified in various ways. In the Early MnE the ambiguous *þe* was generally made into *þat*, as in *for-þī-þat, þe-while-þat*, or dropped entirely, as in *þeih, þouh* conj.= OE *þeah þe*. *þat* often took the place of the inflected pronoun, as in *for-þat, er-þat, after-þat*, and the new-formations *til-þat, before-þat*. But even in the Earliest ME the pronouns were dropped, so that the bare prepositions *for, er, before* etc. were used as conjunctions, as in MnE, this shortening being helped by the fact that even in OE the prepositions *œr* 'before' and *būtan* 'without' were used also as conjunctions, the latter in the sense of 'except,' 'unless.' *þe-hwīle-þe* was shortened to *þe-hwīle* and then to *hwīle*, whence the later *whiles, whilst*, the older *the while, while* still surviving in the higher language. OE *þy lœs þe* dropped the *þy* in Early MnE, and *sþ* was made into *st* (767), giving *læste*, shortened *leste, lest*.

Correlative Particles.

1514. OE correlative particles are : *þy* . . . *þȳ* (**1510**); *swa* . . . *swa*, as in *swa hwīt swa snāw* 'as white as snow'; *þa* . . . *þā, þonne* . . . *þonne* 'then . . . when' as in *þa he com, þa eode ic* 'when he came, I went,' the second (demonstrative) *þa, þonne* being omitted in MnE. Indefinite adverbs are formed like indefinite pronouns (**1146**) with correlative *swa—swa hwǣr swa* 'wherever.'

1515. In ME the first two groups were preserved in the form of *þe* . . . *þe* and *alswǫ* . . . *ase, as* . . . *as, alswǫ* being a strong, *as(e)* a weak form of the OE group *eall-swa* 'entirely so.' In the other correlative groups one of the members was generally omitted in ME, as in the ME and MnE equivalents of the OE *þa* . . . *þa, þonne* . . . *þonne*, where the relative *when* was substituted for *þenne* = OE *þonne*, the second member being omitted.

So also *swa hwǣr swa* appears as *whēr so* in ME.

Pronominal Conjunctions.

1516. In OE the neuter pronouns *āuþer, nāuþer, ǣgþer* (**1146, 1155**) are often used adverbially in connection with the correlative conjunction-pairs *ge* . . . *ge* 'both . . . and,' *oþþe* . . . *oþþe* 'either . . . or,' *ne* . . . *ne* 'neither . . . nor,' standing in a kind of opposition to them : *hīe cuþon ǣgþer, ge gōd ge yfel* 'they knew each-of-the-two, both good and evil'; *se geswęnced biþ āuþer, oþþe on mōde oþþe on līchaman* 'he who is afflicted either-way, either in mind or in body'; *hīe ne cuþon nan-þing yfeles, nāþer ne on sprǣce ne on weorce* 'they knew nothing of evil, no-way, neither in speech nor in action.'

1517. In Early ME the first correlative conjunction was dropped in such combinations, so that the adverbial pronoun was brought into direct correlation with the second conjunction, OE *nāþer ne . . . ne* being made into *nọþer . . . ne, neiþer . . . ne* (1156) etc.: *nọþer on speche ne on werke.* The original pronoun afterwards supplanted the second conjunction as well, where, being unstressed, it was liable to shortening, whence the pairs *ọþer (eiþer) . . . or, nọþer (neiþer) . . . nor: ẹveri man schal have ọþer god ọþer üvel—eiþer god or üvel.* The weak *or, nor* were only rarely introduced into the first clause as well; but in the higher language we still use *or . . . or* instead of *either . . . or.* The new conjunctions soon came to be used without any correlative, as in the Early MnE *he mihte riden ọþer gọn.* The correlative *both . . . and* arose in the same way as *either . . . or* etc., the beginning of it being seen in such an OE construction as *hie bu geseoþ, þæt he hie gengrede, and him eac forgeaf ece līf,* 'they see both (neut. sing.) that he has saved them, and has also given them eternal life.'

Negation and Affirmation.

1518. The negative particle in OE is *ne*, which drops its vowel in some combinations before a vowel, or *h* or *w* followed by a vowel, these consonants being also dropped, *nwi-* being made into *ny-*; thus *eom* 'am,' *hafþ* 'has,' *hæfde* 'had,' *wat* 'knows,' *wiste* 'knew,' *wile* 'will,' *wolde* 'would' have the negative forms *neom* 'am not,' *nafþ, nafde, nāt, nyste, nyle, nolde.* Some pronouns and adverbs have similar negative forms, such as *nan* 'none,' *nāhwæþer, nauþer* 'neither,' *nāwiht, naht, nọwiht, noht* 'nothing,' *nā* 'not' from *an, ahwæþer, āwiht (ọwiht), a* 'ever.' In sentences the *ne* is prefixed to the verb, being contracted with it if possible, and to all the other words in the sentence that admit of contracted negative forms: *nan ne dorste nan þing āscian* 'no-one durst ask anything.' If the sentence does not contain any such contracted negatives in addition to the negatived verb, the stronger *na* or *naht* is added to support the *ne* before the verb: *þæt hus nā ne feoll* ' the house did not fall.'

1519. In ME the usage is often the same as in OE: *he nǣver nadde nǫþing.* But the weak form of *nāwiht*, namely *nat, not* (**1147**) from being a mere strengthening of the *ne*, began to supplant it, as in *to me sche wol nat do þat grace*, although *ne* is often kept, as in *Dẹþ ne wol nat hān mī līf.*

1520. In MnE *ne* disappeared entirely. At the same time the influence of Latin grammar led to the adoption of the logical principle that ' two negatives contradict each other and make an affirmative,' which is now strictly carried out in the Standard language, spoken as well as written, though the old pleonastic negatives are still kept up in vulgar speech, as in *I don't know nothing about it*=the educated *I do not know anything about it* or *I know nothing about it.*

1521. Although OE *naht* was preferred to *nā* as the auxiliary negative in ME, the latter held its ground in certain collocations, especially before comparative adjectives and adverbs, and is still kept in such phrases as *he is no better ; no more of this !* And *no* is always used as the absolute negation—in answer to questions etc.—together with *nay*, which is the Scandinavian *nei* ' no,' literally ' not-ever.' *nay* is now obsolete in speech.

1522. The OE particles of affirmation are *gea*, Anglian *gǣ, ge*, ME *yẹ̄*, Early MnE (jee) Second MnE (jii, jee), which is now obsolete ; and *yes*=OE *gise*, Anglian *gese*, ME and Early MnE *yis, yes. gise* is an old group-compound of *gea* and the subjunctive *sīe* ' be it ' ; it was therefore originally an emphatic affirmative.

Comparison of Adverbs.

1523. The comparison of adverbs has already been treated of under Adjectives (**1036**). In OE the regular forms of adverb-comparison were *-e, -or, -ost* and *-līce, -licor, -liocor,*

-*licost*, -*liocost*: *deope*, *deoplīce*; *deopor*, Late OE *deoppor* (769), *deoplicor*; *deopost*, *deoplicost*. There was also a smaller class with mutation in the higher degrees, the endings being -*e*, -, -*est*, as in *lange* 'for a long time,' *leng*, *lengest*. Most of the adverbs which admit of comparison are formed from adjectives; but primary adverbs also admit of direct comparison, with and without mutation : *oft* 'often,' *oftor*, *oftost*; *ær* 'before.' *āror*, *ærest*.

1524. In MnE the comparison -*er*, -*est* is, as a general rule, applied only to those adverbs which have no special adverbial ending in the positive, especially those which have the same form as the corresponding adjectives, such as *hard* —as in *pull harder*, *pull hardest*—*loud*, *quick*, *fast*, *long*. The comparison of primary adverbs, as in *often*=OE *oft*, *oftener*, *oftenest*, has in some cases been carried further than in OE, as in *soon*, *sooner*, *soonest*, *seldomer*. the OE *sona*, *seldon* not admitting of comparison. Adverbs in -*ly* are compared periphrastically : *fully*, *more fully*, *most fully*. But in the spoken language these adverbs often form their comparisons by inflection from the corresponding adjective : *easy*, *easier*—as in *easier said than done*—*easiest*; *cheaply*, *cheaper*, *cheapest*— as in *where it can be done cheapest*.

1525. The following adverbs are compared irregularly in MnE :—

well; *better*; *best*.   OE *wel*; *bet*; *betst*. which dropped its *t* in ME *best* on the analogy of *must*, etc.

badly (*evilly*, *ill*); *worse*, *worst*.   OE *yfle*; *wiers* (*wyrs*) ; 'rr ... u ·. ū rr... wyrs. .

much, *more*, *most*.   OE *micle*; *mā(re)* ; *mǣst*.

little, *less*, *least*.   OE *lȳtle*, *lȳt*; *lǣs* : *lǣst*.

far ; *farther*, *further* ; *farthest*, *furthest*.   OE *feorr* ; *fierr* ; *ı rr··ı.*

1526. There are besides various isolated forms which have been treated of under the comparison of adjectives. From the comparative adverb *rather*=OE *hraþor* 'quicker,' 'sooner' a positive adjective *rathe* was formed in MnE—*the rathe prim-rose* (Milton)—which is now obsolete.

1527. From some of the isolated comparatives and super-latives, whose meaning has been forgotten and which have come to be regarded as positives, adverbs have been formed by adding -*ly*: *formerly, latterly, lastly.*

PREPOSITIONS.

OLD-ENGLISH.

1528. Of the OE prepositions some are **simple**, some **compound.** Most of the latter are made up of prepositions—especially *be*—and place-adverbs ending in -*an*, -*on*, *be*- becoming *b*- before a vowel, such contracted forms as *bufan* 'above' = *be-ufan, being made into new compounds, such as *onbufan* 'above.' The following are the most important of these compound prepositions :—

æt: *ætforan* 'before.'

be 'by': *baftan* 'behind,' *beforan* 'before,' *begeondan* 'beyond,' *behindan* 'behind,' *binnan* 'within,' *beneoþan* 'beneath,' *bufan* 'above,' *butan* 'outside.'

on: *onforan* 'before,' *oninnan* 'within,' *onbufan* 'above,' *onuppan* 'upon,' *onbutan* 'around.'

to: *tōforan* 'before.'

under: *underneoþan* 'beneath.'

wiþ 'towards': *wiþinnan* 'within,' *wiþutan* 'without.'

ymb 'around': *ymbutan* 'around.'

1529. Other compound prepositions are formed of prepo-sitions + nouns or adjectives in the four cases governed by OE prepositions—the acc., dat., instr., gen. : *ongemang* 'among,' literally 'into the crowd'; *ongean*, Anglian *onggegn*, *ongen*, 'against,' and *togeanes*, Anglian *togegnes*, *togenes* 'towards,' 'against' contain an obsolete noun of uncertain meaning; *tomiddes* 'amidst' is formed from the adj. *midd* 'middle'; *betweonum, betwix* are formed from an obsolete adjective connected with *twiwa* 'twice.'

1530. Those OE prepositions which govern both acc. and dat., generally take the acc. to express motion, the dat. (or instr.) to express rest : *he eode on þæt hus* 'he went into the house'; *he wunode on þæm huse* 'he remained in the house.'

1531. As we see in the last examples the preposition *on* does duty for *in*, which became extinct in Later OE.

1532. The OE prepositions are closely allied to the adverbs. Most of them can be used as adverbs without any change of form. Thus *on* is an adverb in *he dyde on his byrnan* 'he put on his corslet,' the MnE *don* and *doff* being contractions of OE *dō(n) on, do of.* So also in *he him to cwæþ* 'he said to him' compared with *he cwæþ to him.* Some prepositions however, such as *for*, are not used as adverbs, while others undergo change of form. Thus the adverbs corresponding to *be* and *in (on)* are *bī* and *inn : he stōd bī, he stōd him bī, he eode inn* compared with *he stōd be him* 'he stood by him,' *he eode in (on) þæt hus.* The preposition *be* is, of course, the weak form due to want of stress, *bī* being the original strong form.

1533. In such combinations as *þæron, þærto,* which in OE are regularly used to express *on it, to it*, etc. (379), *on* and *to* must, of course, be regarded as adverbs. *therein, herein* are, indeed, often expressed by *þærinne, herinne* with the pure adverb *inne = innan.*

1534. It is to be observed that the prepositions were originally all adverbs, which could modify either verbs (*he stood by*) or nouns. Adverbs were originally added to inflected nouns to express more definitely the meanings already indicated by the inflection. Thus 'motion to' was originally expressed by the acc. alone, as we see in the Latin *domum venit* 'he came home' and also in the adverb *home* itself, and the prepositions *on, in, through,* etc. were put before the acc. of motion to define it more exactly. So also in *on þæm huse* the idea of 'rest in a place' was primarily expressed by the dative, which here represents the Arian locative.

MIDDLE AND MODERN ENGLISH.

1535. In ME the adverb *bī* was extended to the function of a preposition—a change which had already begun in OE —so that *be* was preserved only in compounds and traditional groups such as *beforen, beside*.　　By the change of *-an, -on* into *-e* the OE adverb *foran* and the preposition *fore* 'before' were levelled under the latter, and by the analogy of the adverbs *inne, ūte = innan, utan*, the preposition *mid* 'with' when used as an adverb was made into *mide*, as in *permide =* OE *þarmid*. So also *for*, which had no corresponding adverb-form in OE, developed a ME adverb *fore*, as in *perfore, wherfore*. The confusion that thus arose between OE *for* and *fore* was avoided by an extended use of the compound *before(n)*.

1536. In ME *innan* 'inside' came into general use as a preposition so as to avoid the ambiguity of OE *on* = 'on,' 'in.' Being generally unstressed, it was shortened first to *ine* and then to *in*, the original distinction being thus restored.

1537. In ME *fro* from Scandinavian *frā* and *from* = OE *fram* were used both as adverbs and prepositions. We now use *fro* only as an adverb in the phrase *to and fro*.

1538. In ME the preposition *mid* ' with ' got confused with *wiþ* 'against'—a confusion which would easily arise in such phrases as *fight with* (OE *feohtan wiþ*), *deal with*, where the relation between the parties might be considered either from its original point of view as 'towards,' 'against,' or from that of 'participation,' 'having in common.' By degrees the more marked meaning of OE *wiþ* was expressed by *against*, and ME *wiþ* took the meanings of *mid*, which then became extinct.

For the differentiation of OE *of, wiþ* into MnE *of, off*, (wið, wiþ) see § 861.

1539. In ME the rare construction of prepositions with the genitive was soon given up—except of course in isolated groups such as *tomiddes*—and when the distinction between the other oblique cases and the nom. was lost in the nouns, and nothing was left but the distinction of nom. and objective in some of the personal pronouns, the only trace left of case-government by prepositions was that they were sometimes followed by a personal pronoun in the objective case.

1540. In OE the adverbial ending -*weard* is sometimes used detached in connection with the preposition *to* in such constructions as *wiþ hire* (dat.) *weard* 'towards her.' In ME this is often carried further, as in *to wode ward, to Troie wardes = toward þe wode, towardes Troie, fro Bordeux ward* compared with *framward Teukesbüri*, where *framward* is a new formation on the analogy of *toward*. In Early MnE the Bible still has *to God ward*.

1541. In ME the *a* of *amiddes* was restored to its full form *on*, for which *in* was afterwards substituted. The body of the word was then regarded as an independent noun, so that at last *inmidst* developed into *in the midst* (*of*).

INTERJECTIONS.

1542. Interjections are **primary** and **secondary**. Primary interjections are mostly imitations of sounds that accompany emotions : *ah, o, oh, pah, pooh, hush*. From them other parts of speech may be formed ; thus *hush* is used as a verb—*to hush*. Such interjections as *what! dear me!* are secondary. There are also **mixed** interjections, made up of primary interjections combined with other parts of speech, such as *alas* from Old French *halas, alas* [Modern French *hélas*], made up of the interjection *a* and *las* = Latin *lassum* 'weary.'

1543. The OE *la! ealā!* 'oh!' seem to be primary.

wā! 'woe!' is the same word as the noun *wāwa, wā* 'misfortune.' *wālā! wālāwā!* 'alas!' are therefore mixed interjections.

1544. Interjections may stand in various grammatical relations to other words. Hence in OE, *wā* sometimes governs a dat., as in *wā þæm menn!* 'woe to the man!' *wālā* governs a gen. in such phrases as *wālā þære iermþe!* 'alas for the misery,' on the analogy of the gen. after verbs of repenting, etc. As we see from the above examples, interjections are frequently connected with prepositions in MnE.

COMPOSITION.

Old-English.

1545. The normal way of forming compounds in OE is by joining together two words—which may be themselves compound or derivative words—the former word being uninflected, the latter, if declinable, keeping its power of inflection, and, if a noun, determining the gender of the whole compound. Thus the neuter noun *gold* and the masculine noun *smiþ* can be combined to form the compound masculine noun *goldsmiþ* 'goldsmith.' So also *ǣfen-tīd* 'evening time' is feminine because its last element is a feminine noun. These compounds of **noun + noun** are the most frequent. There are also compounds of **adjective + noun**, such as *hālig-dæg* 'church festival' literally 'holy-day,' *cwic-seolfor* 'quick-silver,' 'mercury,' literally 'living silver'; of **noun + adjective**, such as *wīn-sæd* 'satiated with wine,' and of **adjective + adjective**, such as *wīd-cūþ* 'widely known.'

1546. In the above examples the part of speech of the whole compound is determined by that of the last element. But there is a class of adjective + noun compounds having the function of adjectives, such as *glæd-mōd* 'having a glad mood,' *blīþ-heort* 'blithe of heart,' 'cheerful,' formed from the adjectives *glæd*, *blīpe* and the nouns *mod, heorte*. As we see from the last example, the noun is sometimes shortened in such compounds. We call these compounds **conversion-compounds**, because they involve the conversion of a noun into an adjective. They are very old formations, such conversion-compounds as the Greek *dus-menes* 'having an evil mind,' having apparently been formed in Parent Arian.

Parent Arian had also **double conversion-compounds**, consisting of two nouns. An example of such compounds is afforded by the Greek *rhodo-dáktulos* 'having rose-fingers,' 'rosy-fingered' (an epithet of the Dawn).

The OE ending *-lic* is really the obscured second element of old conversion-compounds (1614).

1547. The form-isolation of compounds in OE consists in the indeclinability of the first element. It is only by this criterion that we can distinguish such compounds as *gōddǣd* 'benefit' from the word-group *god dǽd* 'good action,' as in the dative plural *goddǽdum* compared with *godum dǽdum*.

1548. It is only occasionally that the first element of a compound in OE shows any variation from the form it has when detached. But final vowels are often dropped, as in *gum-cynn* 'mankind,' from *guma* 'man,' *sunn-beam* 'sunbeam,' from *sunne* 'sun,' compared with *sige-lean* 'reward of victory.'

1549. Normal OE compounds take the stress on the first element ; but as word-groups beginning with the genitive of a noun or an inflected adjective do the same, stress is in OE no criterion of composition as opposed to mere grouping. Hence there is in OE no formal distinction between such a word-group as *cyninges sunu* 'king's son,' in which the meaning of the whole follows from that of its elements, and one in which there is isolation of meaning, such as the plant-name *geaces-sure* 'sorrel,' literally 'cuckoo's-sour.' But as most of the latter class developed into true compounds in MnE through keeping their uneven stress (894), it is convenient to regard them as 'genitive-compounds' in OE as well. The following are examples of such OE genitive compounds, many of which, it will be observed, have been obscured in MnE :—

Tiwes-dæg 'Tuesday,' literally 'day of the war-god (*Tiw*), the name being a translation of the Latin *dies Martis* (French *Mardi*), *Sunnan-dæg* 'Sunday' [*sunne* 'sun'], *Monan-dæg* 'Monday' [*mona* 'moon'], *Engla-land* 'England,' literally 'land of the Anglians' [*Engle* plur. 'Anglians,' 'English'], *witena-gemōt* 'parliament.' literally 'meeting of the wise men or councillors,' often erroneously written *witangemot, dæges-eage* 'daisy,' literally 'eye of day.' These combinations are especially frequent as place-names, such as *Seoles-ieg* 'Selsey,' literally 'seal's island,' *Oxena-ford* 'Oxford,' literally 'ford of oxen,' *Buccinga-ham.* 'Buckingham,' literally 'home of (the tribe or family of) the Buccings,' *Defena-scīr* 'Devonshire,' literally 'province of Devonia ' (OE *Defen*).

1550. Verbs are very rarely compounded directly with nouns or adjectives in OE, although there is nothing to prevent verbs being formed from compound nouns or adjectives. Thus from the compound noun *wuldor-beag* 'glory-crown,' 'aureole' is formed the verb *wuldorbeagian* 'to crown,' there being no separate verb *beagian. But the frequent combinations of verbs with prefixes, such as *mis-don* 'act amiss.' 'do wrong,' led to combinations with certain adjectives in similar adverbial meanings, such as *full* in *full-fyllan* 'fully fill,' 'fulfil,' *full-wyrcan* 'fully work,' 'complete.' and *efen* 'even,' 'equal,' which in composition expresses the idea of community or association, as in *efen·prowian* 'sympathize,' literally 'suffer in common with.' The want of stress in the first elements of these compounds shows that they are felt as mere prefixes.

Modern English.

1551. In MnE some compounds are formed by adding

to the first element the Latin and Greek connecting-vowel *o*, but only when the first element is in a Latin or Latinized form, as in *Anglosaxon, Anglo-Indian, Franco-German,* a *concavo-convex lens.*

The connecting vowel *o* is very frequent in Greek compounds, such as *hippo-damos* 'horse-taming,' *philo-sophia* 'philosophy,' literally 'loving wisdom.' In such forms as *hippo-, philo-* are preserved one of the most frequent forms of uninflected nouns and adjectives in a primitive stage of Parent Arian. When inflections were fully developed. these old uninflected forms survived only as the first elements of compounds. It is possible that such OE compounds as *dæge-weorc* 'day's work.' *nihte-gale* 'nightingale.' literally 'night-singer,' from *dæg* and *niht*, still preserve remains of the old connecting vowel.

The *ng* in the MnE *nightingale* may be due to the influence of *evening*. In MnE *handiwork* the *i* is the OE prefix *ge-*, preserved in *enough* = OE *genog*. the OE form of the compound being *hand-geweorc*. The *i-* was preserved in MnE probably through association with the adjective *handy*. *handicraft* = OE *handcræft* probably owes its *i* to the influence of *handiwork* and *handy*.

1552. One of the formal tests of composition in MnE as well as in OE is the inseparability and indeclinability of the first element. But owing to the scantiness of the inflections in MnE and its more rigid word-order, these tests are not so decisive in it as in OE, especially when an adjective is the first element. The great extension of even stress in MnE, on the other hand. makes stress the main criterion for distinguishing between compounds and word-groups (889).

1553. One result of this further development of stress-distinctions in MnE is that we are able to recognize a special class of MnE genitive-compounds. distinguished from mere genitive-groups in the same way as compounds beginning with an adjective are distinguished from the corresponding word-groups, namely by having uneven instead of even stress (894).

1554. Hence also the OE compounds *goldfæt, goddád*

have in MnE been separated into the groups *gold vessel, good deed*, such OE compounds as *goldsmiþ, cwicseolfor* being preserved as compounds in the form of *goldsmith, quicksilver* by their uneven stress; while the OE groups *domes dæg, blæc berige* have been made into the compounds *doomsday, blackberry*.

1555. Some compounds of MnE formation have a noun in the plural as their first element, but only when this noun in the plural has developed a meaning of its own different from that of the singular, so that it is isolated from its singular, the connection between them being sometimes forgotten. Such compounds are *clothesbrush, clothes-basket,* etc., *newsboy, newspaper* (njuwspeipə), where the compound is obscured by the change of the (z) of *news* (njuwz) into (s).

1556. As regards the use of the different parts of speech in composition, the most noticeable difference between OE and MnE is the greater freedom with which in MnE verbs enter into composition with nouns and adjectives, the result of the combination being sometimes a noun, as in *breakwater, clasp-knife*, sometimes a verb, as in *browbeat, whitewash*, according as the last element is a noun or a verb. But such compounds are still comparatively rare, the main combinations of verbs being with particles, as in OE.

Meaning of Compounds.

1557. The general rule of English—as also of Parent Arian—composition is to put the adjunct-word before the head-word, on the same principle of putting the modifier before the modified word as we follow in the group adjective + noun. Hence the order in the compound *blackbird* is the same as in the group *black bird*.

In such groups as *man-of-war, bread-and-butter*, on the contrary, the modifying element follows, instead of preceding, and accordingly the stress is thrown on to the second element.

The end-stress in *mankind* seems to show that even in a

normal compound the second element may sometimes be regarded as the modifying one.

1558. In many cases the logical relation between the
elements of a compound may be defined with certainty and
accuracy, as may be seen from the lists given under the head
of stress in compounds (**896** foll.).   Thus it is perfectly
clear that in *goldfish* the first element defines the second one
by stating something that the second element resembles, the
compound being equivalent to 'gold-resembling fish,' or
more definitely 'gold-coloured fish.'   So also it is evident
that *sight* in *sightseer* stands in the same relation to *seer* as
it does to the verb *see* in *he saw the sights*, and that the
elements of *churchgoer* stands to one another in the same
relation as *church* and *go* do in *he goes to church*.

1559. But in many cases these logical relations are less
definite.   Thus a *water-plant* might mean a plant growing
in the water, or a plant growing near the water, or, on the
analogy of *water-melon*, we might suppose it to mean a plant
containing a great deal of moisture, and perhaps growing
in a comparatively dry place.   The logical relations between
the elements of causal and phenomenon-compounds are
often difficult to define accurately, even when the meaning of
the compound itself is definite, as in *sundial*, which might be
explained either as a 'dial *for* showing the position of the
sun,' or as a 'dial worked—as it were—*by* the sun instead
of by clockwork, etc.'

1560. It must, indeed, be borne in mind that this very
vagueness is the chief reason why composition is resorted
to : it is only by leaving open the logical relations between
the elements of compounds that we are able to form them
as we want them without stopping to analyze exactly the
logical or grammatical relations between the words we join
together, as we might have to do if we connected them
together by more definite means, such as prepositions or
inflections.

1561. An important general distinction between compounds as regards their meaning is the **closeness** of the logical connection between them. We may from this point of view distinguish between **co-compounds** and **sub-compounds** in the same way as we distinguish between co-complexes and sub-complexes (**456**). Thus in a causal compound the relation between the two elements is an intimate one, like that between the clauses of a causal complex sentence. There are hardly any pure co-compounds in English, such a combination as *deaf-mute* = 'a person who is deaf and dumb' being an even-stress group-compound and not a pure compound. Pure co-compounds are found in Greek, and are very frequent in Sanskrit, where we find long 'copulative' compounds such as *god-angel-man-serpent-demons* meaning simply 'gods, angels, men, serpents, and demons,' that is, 'all living creatures.' As we have seen, the less close the logical relation between the elements of a compound, that is, the more co-ordinative the compound is, the greater the tendency in Present English to resolve it into an even-stress word-group.

DERIVATION.

Native Elements.

PREFIXES.

1562. Some of the OE prefixes are **strong** (strong-stressed), some **weak** (weak-stressed). Noun- and adjective-prefixes— that is, prefixes added to nouns and adjectives respectively— are generally strong, as in *mis-dǽd* 'misdeed,' *un-cúþ* 'unknown'; while verb-prefixes are generally weak, as in *forgiefan* 'forgive.' When the same prefix is used both with nouns (and adjectives) and with verbs, it generally takes a shortened and weakened form in the latter combination, which is the natural result of its weak stress. The following are examples of such pairs of originally identical prefixes :—

·and-giet 'intelligence'	*on·gietan* 'understand'
·æf-þunca 'grudge'	*ofþyncan* 'to grudge'
·or-þanc 'device'	*a·þencan* 'devise'
·bī-gang 'circuit'	*be·gan* 'practise'

1563. When a verb is formed direct from a noun or adjective, the strong form of the prefix is preserved unchanged, as in *·andswarian* 'to answer' from the noun *·and-swaru* 'answer.'

Originally there was a verb **on·swerian* corresponding to *andswaru* in the same way as *ongietan* corresponds to *andgiet*; and the frequent OE form *andswerian* is a blending of the original verb and *andswarian* or *andswaru*.

1564. Conversely, in a noun formed from a verb the verb-prefix is preserved unchanged, as in *ā·līesednes* 'redemption,' literally 'loosenedness,' from *a·līesan* 'release,' 'redeem.'

It sometimes happens that a noun which originally had a strong prefix takes the corresponding weak one by the influence of a verb of similar meaning. Thus *bīgang* is often made into *be·gang* by the influence of *be·gan*.

1565. In some cases older distinctions between the strong and weak forms of prefixes have been levelled. Thus the weak *for-* in *for·dōn* 'destroy,' *forweorþan* 'perish' appears in the earliest OE as *fer-* (*fer·dōn*), *for-* being then used only as the corresponding strong form in such nouns as *·forwyrd* 'destruction,' from which it was gradually extended to verb-forms. So also the weak *tō-* in *tō·brecan* 'break to pieces' is represented by *te-* in earlier OE (*te·brecan*). Its strong form was originally **tor-*, parallel to the strong *for-*; *tor-* was made into *tō-* by contraction, and then extended to the weak forms.

1566. In the case of these two prefixes the weak stress was kept in the originally weak forms in spite of the adoption of the strong forms. But in some cases the prefix not only kept its strong form when transferred to a verb, but also its strong stress : thus the prefix *mis*- has strong stress in *·misdon* as well as in *misdǣd*.

1567. The prefix *ge-*, on the other hand, always has weak stress. not only before verbs, as in *ge·seon* 'to see,' but also in nouns, such as *ge·sihþ* 'sight,' where it originally had a strong form **gǣ-*, **gea-* with strong stress.

1568. Prefixes to pronouns and particles are sometimes weak, sometimes strong.

The following are the most important of the OE prefixes, the strong being marked (·).

1569. a-. This prefix, whose strong form is *or*- (**1562**), is cognate with the German *er*-, as in *er·lauben* ' allow,' strong *ur*-, as in *·urlaub*, the noun corresponding to *erlauben*. Its original meaning was ' out,' ' from,' ' forth,' which may still be traced in such verbs as *ārīsan* 'arise,' *awacan* 'awake' (German *erwachen*), while in many cases it is practically unmeaning—or, at most, emphatic—as in *āberan* ' carry,' ' endure,' *ābysgian* ' occupy' [*bysig* ' busy '].

1570. ·a- is a shorter form of *āwa* ' always.' It is a strong prefix which is used only with pronouns and particles to give them an indefinite meaning, as in *·āhwæþer* ' either of two,' *āhwǣr* ' anywhere,' from *hwæþer* 'which of the two?' and *hwǣr* ' where ? '

1571. ·æg- was originally *ā* ' always ' followed by the prefix *ge*- in its older form *gi*- (**1574**), whose *i* mutated the preceding *ā* into *æ*, and was then dropped, giving *æg*-. The *a* in this prefix served merely to emphasize and generalize the collective meaning of the *ge*-, so that *æg*- is equivalent to ' all ' or ' every,' as in *·æghwæþer* ' each of two,' *æghwǣr* ' everywhere.'

1572. be- has *bī*- for its strong form. It is the same word as the preposition *be* ' by,' whose strong form is the adverb *bī* ' by.' As *be* and *bī* are therefore still independent words, *began*, *bīgang*, etc., may be regarded as compounds rather than derivatives. But the prefixes *be-*, *bī-* have diverged so much in meaning from the independent words *be, bī*, that from an unhistorical point of view the two pairs have no connection with one another. Thus as prefixes *be-* and *bī-* preserve the meaning 'around,' kept also in Greek *amphi-*, which represents the fuller Arian form of which *bī* is a shortening. This primitive meaning is seen in *bigang, began*, in which 'going round' developed into the meanings 'worship,' 'cultivate.' The most general function of *be-* is to specialize the meaning of transitive verbs, as in *behon* 'hang with,' *besęllan* 'beset,' and to make an intransitive verb transitive, as in *bewepan* 'bewail,' *bepęncan* 'consider' from *wepan* 'weep,' *pęncan* 'think.' In some cases it is privative, as in *beniman* 'deprive' [*niman* 'take']. *beheafdian* 'behead.'

1573. for, earlier *fer-*, strong *for-* (1565) is quite distinct from the preposition *for* : it expresses destruction, loss, etc., as in *fordon* 'destroy,' *forweorþan* 'perish' from *don* 'do,' *weorþan* 'become,' originally 'turn' [compare Latin *vertere*], being sometimes only intensitive, as in *forbærnan* 'burn up.'

1574. ge-, which is prefixed equally to verbs, nouns, adjectives, pronouns, and particles, has primarily a collective meaning, as in *gefera* 'companion,' originally 'fellow traveller,' from *for* 'journey' [*faran*, 'go,' 'travel'], *gebrōþru* 'brothers' [*brōþor*, 'brother'], *gehwā* 'each one' from *hwa* 'who?', being cognate with the Latin *cum* 'with.' It is often only intensitive, and often practically unmeaning, as in *gemunan* 'remember,' *gemynd* 'memory,' 'mind.' As a prefix to the preterite participle of verbs, as in *gebunden* 'bound.' it is really a grammatical inflection (74).

1575. mis- is a prefix both to verbs and nouns, as in *mislician* 'displease,' *misdǣd* 'misdeed.'

1576. of- is cognate with the preposition and adverb *of* 'off, of.' The strong form *æf-* (1562) is of rare occurrence; in such words as *ofsṗring* 'progeny,' it has been supplanted by the weak form. In this word the original meaning of the

prefix has been preserved, but in most cases it is only intensitive, as in *ofslean* 'kill' [*slean* 'strike'], or unmeaning, as
in the preterite participle *ofþyrsted* 'thirsty.'

1577. **on-**, strong *and-* (**1562**), is represented in German
by *ent-*, *em(p)-*, strong *ant-*, as in *empfangen* 'receive'= OE
onfōn, *ant-wort* 'answer,' with which compare OE. *and-wyrde*
'answer,' literally 'against-wording,' where it still preserves
its original meaning of 'against,' being cognate with the
Greek *antí* 'against.' In some words it expresses 'separation,' 'change,' as in *onbindan* 'unbind,' *onlucan* 'unlock,'
'open,' *onwęndan* 'overturn,' 'change to the worse.' In
many words it is unmeaning, as in *ondrǣdan* 'dread,' *onginnan* 'begin.'

1578. *on*-derivatives such as the above must be carefully
distinguished from compounds with the preposition or adverb
on 'on,' such as *on-winnan* 'make war on,' 'assail,' *ongean*
'against' [Modern German *entgegen*= older German *engegen*,
ingegin owes its *ent-* to confusion with the prefix *ent-*].

1579. **to-**, earlier *te-*, strong *to-* (**1565**), is represented in
German by *zer-*, as in *zerbrechen*=OE. *tobrecan* 'break to
pieces,' *zertheilen*=OE *todǣlan* 'distribute' [*dǣl* 'portion,'
'share']. This prefix always keeps its original meaning of
'separation,' 'destruction,' and is thus easily distinguished
from compounds with the preposition *to* 'to,' such as *tocyme*
'arrival' [*cyme* 'coming'], *togǣdre* 'together.'

1580. **un-** 'un-' is a prefix to nouns, adjectives, and
secondary adverbs, and is generally purely negative, though
sometimes intensitive in the sense of 'bad': *undǣd* 'wicked
deed,' 'crime,' *uncuþ* 'unknown,' *unsōfte* 'ungently,' 'severely.'

1581. **wan-** 'un-' [*wana* adjective 'wanting,' *wanian*
'curtail,' 'wane'] is prefixed to adjectives, as in *wanhāl* 'un-
healthy' [*hal* 'whole,' 'sound'].

1582. In ME *ge-* was weakened to *i-*, as in *īvere*, *ibūnde(n)*.
It soon began to be dropped in the North-Thames dialects,
as in *līc* 'like'= South-Thames *ilich*, OE *ʒelīc*. In Standard

ME the grammatical *i-* is sometimes kept, sometimes not —being generally dropped, as in *fere, kinde*=OE *gefera* 'companion,' *gecynd* fem. 'kind,' 'nature,' *gecynde* 'natural.' The prefix seems to have been preserved in poetry for the sake of the metre after it had become extinct in the spoken language. But it has been kept to the present day in *enough*=ME *inoh*, OE *genog, handiwork* (1551. 2), and in the obsolete *ywis*=OE *gewiss* 'certain'—sometimes made into a verb (1486. 1), and in the preterite participles *yclept* =OE *gecleopod* 'called,' *yclad*. Also through confusion with *every* in *everywhere* from OE **æfre gehwær*.

alike must be referred to the OE *onlic*, which had the same meaning as *gelīc*.

1583. In ME the prepositions *of* and *on* were liable to be weakened into *a* (1505). The same change took place with the prefixes *of-* and *on-*, and as OE *a-* was shortened to *a-*, all three prefixes were often levelled under one form. This levelling was helped by the fact that already in OE there was a certain confusion between these endings through the vagueness of their meanings in many words. Thus we find in OE *abīdan, onbīdan* 'await,' *onwacan* and *awacan* 'awake,' *ondrǣ-dan* 'fear,' *ofdrǣdd* pret. partic. 'afraid,' the difference of meaning being often very slight in other cases, as in *asendan* 'send,' *onsendan* 'send forth,' *agiefan* 'render,' *ofgiefan* 're-linquish.' *of-* was preserved in *ofspring* through its strong stress. So also *and-* in *andsware, answare*. Towards the end of the ME period the prefix *a-* was dropped in many words, partly through its vagueness of meaning, partly through its indistinctness of sound. It is now preserved only in a few words, such as *arise, awake, awaken*=OE *arīsan, awacan, awæcnian, acknowledge*=ME *aknōulēchen*, to which corresponds OE *oncnawan. ashamed*=OE *ofsceamod, abide*=OE *onbīdan* 'wait,' and the obsolete *athirst*=OE *ofþyrst-t*.

1584. But those verbs in *on-* which expressed a definite reversal of the meaning of the verbs they were formed from, such as *onbindan*, saved their prefixes from being weakened into the ambiguous *a-* by identifying it with the almost synonymous noun- and adjective-prefix *un-*, whence the MnE. *unbind. unlock*, and many new-formations—from French as well as English verbs—such as *unsettle, unhook, unarm, unchain*.

1585. *to-* was preserved in ME, as in *tobreken, torenden*, but has become obsolete in MnE, though the Bible still has *all tobrake his scull*, where *all* is adverbial.

1586. *for-* is still preserved in MnE, as in *forbid, forswear, forlorn* = OE *forloren*, preterite participle of *forleosan* 'lose'; but many of the ME derivatives have become obsolete, and *for-* is no longer a living prefix. In *forego* = OE *forgan* 'go without,' 'forego' the prefix has been confused with the separable prefix or adverb *fore* = OE *fore* 'before.'

1587. The mainly noun- and adjective prefixes *mis-* and *un-* are still living prefixes, being freely used to form new derivatives, such as *misadventure, misrepresent, unrest, unlimited, unchain*.

1588. The only old verb-prefix that can be regarded as still living is *be-*, with which an immense number of new verbs have been formed in MnE as well as ME. Many of these have been formed directly from nouns—French as well as English—such as *befriend, benighted, besiege*. The noun *byword* still keeps the strong form, being formed on the analogy of ME *bispel* = OE *bispell* 'parable'; but such nouns as *bystreet, bystander*, may be regarded rather as compounds with the adverb *bi*. Some nouns have taken *be-* from the corresponding verbs, such as *belief* = OE *geleafa*, the corresponding verb being *believe* = OE *geliefan*, Late OE *belefan*.

SUFFIXES.

1589. Of the OE endings some, which contained *i* or *j* in Germanic, cause mutation of the preceding vowel, as in *gylden* 'golden.' When the same ending sometimes mutates, sometimes not, the mutated forms are generally the original ones, the unmutated forms being the result of later influence of the unmutated word from which the derivative was formed. Thus *beren* 'belonging to a bear' = earlier *biren* owes its *e* to the influence of the noun *bera* 'bear.'

Noun-forming.

(*a*) *Concrete.*

1590. -cen is a diminutive neuter ending, which, although preserved only in a very few words, such as *tyncen* from *tunne* 'tun,' 'cask,' was no doubt in common use in the spoken language. It is an extension of the originally diminutive ending *-en* in *mægden*. In ME and MnE it appears in the form of *-kin*, *-ikin*, whose full vowel and *k* instead of *ch* is probably the result of the influence of the French *-quin*, itself of Low German origin. Thus *manikin* 'dwarf' is the French *mannequin*, which is itself a Low German diminutive of *man*. Other examples are *lambkin*, *napkin* [French *nappe* 'tablecloth'], *canakin*, *kilderkin*. In *bumpkin* the meaning smallness passes over into that of contempt. In ME this ending was freely used to form nicknames from proper names, many of which afterwards became surnames: *Wilekin*, *Wilkin* from *William*, whence the MnE *Wilkinson*, which was again shortened to *Wilkins*, *Perkin*, shortened from *Peterkin*, *Halkin*, whence by phonetic spelling *Hawkin(s)*, from *Hal*, a child's mispronunciation of *Harry* = *Henry*.

1591. -end '-er' is the noun-form of the present participle ending *-ende*, and forms nouns denoting agents from verbs, such as *hælend* 'healer,' 'Saviour,' *sceotend* 'shooter,' 'warrior.' It became extinct in ME, its place being supplied by the ending *-ere*. But it still survives disguised in *friend* = OE *freond* literally 'lover,' and *fiend* — OE *feond* 'enemy,' literally 'hater.'

1592. -ere, -ære, masc. '-er' forms agent-denoting nouns from verbs: *bindere* 'binder,' *fiscere* 'fisher,' *leornere* 'learner,' *godspellere* ' evangelist ' from the verbs *bindan, fiscian, leornian, godspellian.* It will be observed that of these verbs two are formed directly from nouns—*fiscian* from *fisc, godspellian* from *godspell*—originally *godspell* ' good tidings '—while *leornere* is associated in meaning with the noun *leornung. bocere* ' scribe ' seems, indeed, to be formed directly from *boc* on the model of the Latin *librarius.* In ME the *ǽ* in the form -*ǽre* was shortened, and underwent the regular change into *a,* so that in Early ME we find such forms as *fischare* by the side of *fischere.* In Late ME there was a good deal of confusion between these endings and the French and Latin endings -*er, -ier, -eer, -our, -or,* which often had the same meanings as the native ending (**1685**). This confusion was increased in Early MnE by the levelling of -*er, -ar, -or,* etc. under (ər) [**859**]. Hence such forms as *liar* = OE *leogere, sailor* compared with *a fast sailer* [OE *seglan* ' sail '].

1593. **-estre** fem. ' -ess ': *bæcestre* ' female baker ' [*bæcere* ' baker '], *tæppestre* ' female tapster,' *witegestre* ' prophetess ' [*witega* ' prophet ']. In ME this ending, being unstrest, soon lost its final *e,* and the resulting -*ster* came to be regarded as an emphatic form of -*er,* and consequently was applied to men as well as women, so that the Early ME feminines *bakstere, tappistere* developed into the Late ME masculines *baxter, tapster.* Many of these trade-names in -*ster* survive only as proper names, such as *Baxter, Brewster, Webster.* In MnE this ending is also used to express ' one who does a thing habitually,' generally with an implication of contempt, as in *punster, trickster.* The only noun in -*ster* which is still distinctly feminine is *spinster,* which has, however, lost its meaning of ' female spinner,' being now used only in that of ' unmarried woman.'

1594. **-ing** masc.: *earming* ' poor wretch ' [*earm* ' poor '] *lytling* ' little one ' [*lytel* ' little ']. The late OE *niþing* ' coward,' ' object of contempt,' is probably of Scandinavian origin (Icelandic *níþungr*). This ending is specially used to

form patronymics, such as *æþeling* 'son of a noble,' 'prince'
from *æþele* 'noble,' 'aristocratic,' *cyning* 'king,' literally 'son
of a king,' the underived *cyne* being preserved only in
compounds such as *cynehelm* 'crown,' literally 'king-helm.'
These patronymics are formed freely from personal names :
Scielding, Æþelwulfing, Elising 'son of Elisha.' Many of
them are preserved as proper names, such as *Manning,
Harding*, especially in place-names, such as *Billingsgate,
Islington, Reading*, so called from the clans of the *Billingas*
'sons of Bill' etc.

This ending is also found in names of animals, as in *hæring*
'herring,' and in names of things, especially coins, such as
scilling, pening, feorþing (feorþung, feorþling) 'farthing,' literally
'fourth part (of a *pening*)' from *feorþa* 'fourth.'

1595. -ling masc. in OE generally expresses affection,
familiarity, or contempt : *deorling* 'favourite,' from *deore*
'dear,' 'precious,' ME *derling*, MnE *darling*. *fosterling*
'foster-child,' *hyrling* 'hireling,' *underling*. There are many
others in MnE, some of which may be of OE origin, such as
foundling, others being new-formations, such as *starveling,
worldling, nurseling, changeling*. This suffix is frequent in
names of animals, generally expressing youth or smallness,
as in *youngling* 'young animal,' also used in the sense of
'young human being,' *yearling, nestling, duckling, gosling*.
Some of these may be of OE origin.

1596. -en fem. with mutation : *gyden* 'goddess,' *fyxen*
'vixen' from *god. fox*.

This ending has, besides, a variety of meanings. It is diminutive in *mægden*, and in the compound ending *-cen* (1590) ; and
occurs, interchanging with *-on. -n*, in a number of words without
showing any definite meaning, as in *heofen* 'heaven,' *mægen*
'power,' *þegen, þegn* 'retainer,' 'nobleman.'

(*b*) *Abstract.*

1597. -nis(s). -nes(s) fem. is the regular ending for forming abstract nouns from adjectives : *godnis* 'goodness,'

gelīcnis 'likeness,' *beorhtnis* 'brightness.' This ending is still in living use in MnE, being added to foreign as well as native adjectives, as in *closeness, graciousness*, although many of these do not take it because they are already provided with corresponding abstract nouns of foreign formation ; thus to *possible* corresponds *possibility*, to *charitable, charity*, to *mediocre, mediocrity*, although such derivatives as *inevitableness* are freely formed whenever it is found convenient.

Words in *-ness* only rarely take concrete meanings, as in *witness, wilderness*.

1598. **-u** fem. with mutation forms abstract nouns from adjectives : *lengu* 'length,' *strengu* 'strength,' *brǣdu* 'breadth,' *hǣlu* 'salvation,' *hǣtu* 'heat,' *ieldu* 'old age,' archaic MnE *eld, wrǣþ(þ)u* 'anger,' ME *wraþþe*, MnE *wrath*, from the adjectives *lang, strang, brad, hal* · sound,' *hat, eald, wráþ*.

1599. **-uþ, -þ** fem. with and without mutation : *treowþ* 'fidelity,' *þiefþ* 'theft,' ME *þiefþe, þefte*, from *treowe* 'faithful,' *þeof* 'thief,' *slǣwþ* 'sloth,' which in ME became *slouþe* by the influence of the adjective from which it was formed, namely OE *slaw*, ME *slow* · indolent.' To *geoguþ* 'youth' corresponds the adjective *geong* 'young.' In ME the ending *-þe* = OE *-þ* was substituted for the equivalent *-e* = OE *-u*, as being more distinct, whence the MnE *length, strength, breadth, health* = ME *lengþe*, OE *lengu*, etc. Similarly OE *diepe* from *deop* 'deep' has become *depth*. So also ME *wele*, MnE *weal* = OE *wela* 'prosperity,' · wealth,' has developed a secondary form *wealth* on the analogy of *health*. In ME and MnE some new derivatives in *-th* have been formed, not only from adjectives, as in *warmth, dearth*, but also directly from verbs, as in *growth, stealth*, the latter on the analogy of ME *þiefþe* 'theft.'

1600. **-ung, -ing**, fem. forms abstract nouns from verbs : *blētsung* 'blessing,' *geendung* 'ending,' · end,' *leornung, leorning* 'learning,' *rǣding* 'reading,' from the verbs *blētsian*, *gegndian, leornian, rǣdan* (weak verb). In OE this ending is restricted in its use, and is very rarely used to form derivatives from strong verbs because these are generally provided with other derivatives, such as *cyme* 'coming,' *gang* 'going' corresponding to the strong verbs *cuman, gan*. In ME the use of *-inge, -ing* was so much extended that at last abstract nouns could be formed with it from any verb, till it finally developed into a purely grammatical form—the gerund **(1257).** In MnE many words in *-ing* have assumed concrete meanings, such as *being* = ' creature.' In most cases these concrete words in *-ing* express either the result of the action expressed by the verb, as in *building* 'what is built,' 'edifice,' *dripping, leavings*, or the instrument of the action of the verb, as in *clothing, covering, wrapping, footing* 'ground to put the foot on.' In some words *-ing* has a collective meaning, as in *paling, shipping*. Some of these words, such as *shipping, shirting*, seem to be formed directly from nouns. This probably arose from the ambiguity of such words as *flooring*, which might be referred either to the noun *floor* or the verb *to floor*.

The following endings were originally independent words in OE itself :—

1601. -dom masc. is from the noun *dom* 'judgment,' 'authority,' and expresses first 'rank,' and then—especially in combination with adjectives—condition generally : *cynedom* 'royal authority,' 'kingdom,' *king* having been substituted for the less familiar *cyne* **(1594)** in ME, *biscopdom* 'bishopric' [*-ric* — OE *rice* 'government,' 'kingdom '], *martyrdom, cristendom, freodom* 'freedom,' *wisdom*. In MnE there are a few new-formations, such as *dukedom. christendom* and *heathendom* have now become concrete. In OE itself *lǣcedom* 'medicine' from *lǣce* 'leech,' 'physician' had a concrete meaning.

1602. -had masc. from the noun *had* ' rank,' ' condition, 'character,' 'nature': *biscophād* 'rank of bishop,' 'episcopacy,' *preosthad* 'priesthood,' *cildhad*, *mægphad* 'virginity,' the more familiar *mægden* being substituted for *mægþ* 'virgin,' 'maid' in the ME. *maidenhod*. *widwan-had* 'widowhood' is really a group-compound of *had* and the genitive of the weak noun *widwe*. In ME this ending became -*hod* with close *o* instead of *ǭ*, whence the MnE -*hood*; this change cannot well be organic, and may be due to the combined influence of -*dōm* and the noun *hod* 'hood.' The frequent ME form -*hę̄de*, -*hę̄d* is the result of the influence of another ending of similar meaning, namely -*rę̄de* from OE -*rǣden* (1604), the form -*hode* being another result of these blendings. In OE -*had* is used only with nouns, but its ME and MnE representatives form derivatives from adjectives also, such as *hardihood*, *likelihood*, *falsehood*. Many of the derivatives from nouns have taken concrete—mostly collective—meanings, as in *priesthood* and the new-formations *brotherhood*, *neighbourhood*. The ME form -*hę̄de* is now almost extinct, surviving only in *maidenhead* and *Godhead*, such Early MnE forms as *lustihead* being now obsolete.

1603. -**lac** neut. from the noun *lac*, whose ordinary meaning is 'gift,' but which shows traces of the older meanings 'game,' 'fight,' 'action in general,' agreeing with those of the verb *lacan* 'play' etc. : *reaflac* 'robbery' [*reafian* 'plunder'], *scinlāc* 'phantasm,' 'delirium,' 'fury' [*scin* 'phantasm,' 'ghost' from *scinan* 'shine,' 'appear'], *wędlāc* 'marriage' [*wędd* 'pledge,' 'contract']. This ending survives only in *wedlock*, whose *o* is the ME *ǫ* shortened.

1604. -**ræden** fem., gen. -*rǣdenne*, from the noun *rǣden* 'regulation,' 'agreement' [connected with *gerǣdan* 'put in order,' 'arrange' and the MnE *ready*]: *geferrǣden* 'fellowship,' 'agreement,' *freondrǣden* 'relationship,' 'friendship,' *mannrǣden* 'allegiance,' *teonrǣden* 'injury' [*teona* 'insult,' 'injury']. In OE this ending was applied only to nouns. ME keeps many of the OE derivatives, *frendrę̄de*, *sibrę̄de* 'relationship' = OE *sibbrǣden*, and on the analogy of these forms the new derivative *haterǝde, hatrǝde* 'hatred' [ME *hate* is a blending of the OE noun *hęte* 'violence,' 'hostility' and the corresponding verb *hatian*]. The analogy of *sibrǝde*, etc. also led to the ME change of OE *cynren* 'line of descendants,' 'family'—which is a shortening of **cynn-ryne* 'kin-course' [*ryne*, 'running,' 'course,' connected with *iernan* 'run']— into *kinrǝde*, whence, by the usual insertion of *d* (821), the MnE *kindred*.

1605. -scipe masc. '-ship,' from a lost noun connected with the verb *scieppan* 'shape,' 'create': *hlāfordscipe* 'lordship' 'authority,' *frēondscipe, weorþscipe* 'honour' [*weorþ* noun and adjective ' worth,' 'worthy']. Concrete in *gebēorscipe* 'convivial meeting,' 'banquet' from *gebēora* 'boon-companion,' literally 'fellow-beerdrinker' [*ge*-collective + *bēor* 'beer'] and some others. This ending is frequently used in MnE to form new derivatives, especially from personal words, as in *ownership, consulship, relationship.* In OE it is used to form derivatives almost exclusively from nouns, but in MnE we have such derivatives as *hardship, courtship* from the adjective *hard* and the verb *to court. Landscape*—of which the older spelling was *landskip*—was introduced into English in the 17th century from Dutch, where *landschap* (lantsxap) 'province,' 'country' came to be used by painters as a technical term to express the background in a painting, in which sense it came into English, the ending being at first blended with *-ship* into *-skip*.

Adjective-forming.

1606. -ede forms compound adjectives from names of parts of the body preceded by a modifying word: *sūrēagede* 'blear-eyed,' literally 'sour-eyed,' *micelhēafdede* 'big-headed,' *prihēafdede* 'three-headed.' In MnE this ending has been necessarily shortened to *-ed*, and so has become indistinguishable from the preterite participle inflection.

1607. -en with mutation generally denotes material, being

also used in the more general sense of 'belonging to': *æcen*
'of oak' [*āc* 'oak'], *gylden* 'golden,' *wyllen* 'woollen' [*wulle*
'wool'], *stænen* 'of stone,' *hæþen* 'heathen' [*hæþ* 'heath'],
In *beren* from *bera* 'bear,' as in *beren fell* 'a bear's skin,'
earlier *biren*, the *e* has been brought in from the noun; so
also in *leaden* 'leaden' [*lead* 'lead']. In MnE these adjectives restore the unmutated vowel everywhere, as in *golden*,
woollen, on the analogy of which new derivatives had been
formed, such as *wooden*, *hempen*. In MnE the simple nouns
are generally used instead of the material adjectives in *-en*, as
in *gold watch, stone wall*, the full forms being used only in
special meanings, as in *golden hair*, although we still use
wooden, woollen etc. as material adjectives. The similarity of
meaning between material nouns and adjectives (155) has
in some cases led to the conversion of adjectives in *-en* into
nouns, as in *linen* = OE *linen* 'flaxen' from *līn* 'flax,' and the
tree names *aspen* = OE *æspe*, *linden* = OE *lind* fem. [*linde(n)tre*
passed through *lindetre* into *līntre* in ME, whence the Early
MnE *linetree*, now *lime-tree*].

Some adjectives in *-en* with mutation were originally preterite participles of strong verbs: *druncen* 'intoxicated,' *agen*
'own,' *fægen* 'glad,' whence MnE *fain*, from *drincan, agan*
'possess,' *gefēon* 'rejoice,' the strong verb corresponding to
open 'open' being lost.

1608. -ig ' y- ' corresponds sometimes to Germanic *-ig, -īg*,
sometimes to Germanic *-ag*, etc., causing mutation in the
former case, but not in the latter: *halig* 'holy' [*hāl* 'entire,'
'sound'], *modig* 'proud,' *mistig* 'misty,' *īsig* 'icy'; *hefig*
'heavy' [connected with *hebban*, preterite participle *hafen*,
'lift'], *bysig* 'busy,' *dysig* 'foolish,' whence MnE *dizzy*.   In
MnE this ending has been widely extended, and in many
words it has taken the place of the material *-en*, as in *fiery* =
OE *fyren* [*fyr* 'fire'], *clayey*, *gluey*, where the Early MnE
spelling -*ey* is preserved, as it regularly is after vowels.

-ig is also a noun-ending, as in *bodig* 'body,' *īfig* 'ivy,' *hunig*

‘honey.' The final *-y* with which nouns are made into diminutives or words of contempt in MnE seems to be this ending :
puppy, baby from *pup, babe, dummy,* formed from *dumb* after
the *b* had become silent, *Billy* from *Bill = William, Betty,
Betsy, Lizzie,* all three from *Elizabeth,* and many other familiar
names, the earlier spelling *-ie* being kept in some of the female
names.

1609. -isc ' -ish ' with mutation—which is sometimes got
rid of by the influence of the underived word—is most frequently used to form names of nations, but also in derivatives
from common nouns : *Englisc. Frencisc* ' French ' [*Francland*
' land of the Franks.' ' France ']. *Scyttisc* ' Scotch ' [*Scottland,*
' Ireland.' afterwards ' Scotland ']. *Wēlisc* ' Welsh '; *cierlisce
menn* ' serfs ' [*ceorl* ' serf '], *mēnnisc* ' human,' *folcisc* ' popular,'
' vulgar.' In ME some of the names of nations were con-
tracted by omission of the vowel of the ending, whence the
MnE *French, Scotch* by the side of the fuller *Scottish,* in both
of which the unmutated vowel has been restored by the influence of *Scot, Scotland.* So also *Welsh.* the unmutated
vowel of ME *Walsch*—due to the influence of *Wāles* = OE
Wealas ' Welshmen '—being preserved only in the proper
name *Walsh.* In the other words formed from nouns *-ish*
generally expresses contempt, as in *mannish. womanish*
compared with *manly. womanly, childish* compared with
childlike, brutish. swinish, uppish. Such adjectives as
bookish, roguish, in which there is no depreciation implied,
tend to become obsolete. *-ish* added to an adjective expresses simple diminution, as in *oldish, youngish. sweetish.
longish,* especially with names of colours, such as *reddish,
yellowish.*

1610. -sum ' -some ' forms adjectives from nouns, adjectives, and verbs: *sibbsum* ' peaceful.' *wynsum* ' pleasant '
[*wynn* ' joy ']; *langsum* ' tedious '; *hiersum* ' obedient ' [*hieran*
' hear,' ' obey ']. There are many ME and MnE new-formations : *burdensome. handsome, troublesome ; wholesome. weari-
some ; buxom.* ME *buhsum,* formed from the OE verb *bugan*

'bow,' 'bend,' the original meaning of the adjective being 'pliable,' 'goodnatured.'

The following endings were independent words in Germanic :—

1611. -feald '-fold' [Compare the verb *fealdan* 'fold'] forms adjectives from adjective-words, especially numerals : *manigfeald* 'manifold,' 'various,' *scofonfeald*, *hundfeald*, 'hundredfold.'

1612. -full '-ful,' sometimes weakened to *-fol*, from the adjective *full* 'full,' forms adjectives from abstract nouns : *carfull* ' careful,' *sorgfull* ' sorrowful,' *synnfull* ' sinful.' There are numerous new-formations in ME and MnE—some from concrete nouns : *artful, powerful, fruitful, masterful*. In Present English this ending is shortened to (-fl), by which it is distinguished from the compounds *handfull* (hændful), *spoonfull* etc.

1613. -leas '-less' from the adjective *leas* 'deprived of,' ' without ' [Compare *forleosan* 'lose'] forms adjectives from nouns and verbs : *arleas* ' without honour,' ' wicked,' *geleafleas* ' unbelieving,' *slapleas* ' sleepless '; *giemeleas* ' careless,' *recceleas* ' careless,' from *gieman* ' take care of,' *reccan* ' reck.' From *-leas* abstract nouns in *-least* are formed, where the *t=þ* (**767**), such as *slapleast* ' sleeplessness.' In ME this ending appears both as *-les* and as *-les* with the vowel shortened, which may be due to the influence of *lesse* ' less.' It is frequently used in new-formations, such as *fearless, useless*.

1614. -lic '-ly' : *eorþlic* ' earthly,' *wiflic* ' feminine,' *cynelic* ' royal,' *freondlic* ' friendly,' *gearlic* ' annual.' These derivatives were originally conversion-compounds with *lic* ' body,' the weak vowel being afterwards shortened, so that *wiflic*, for instance, meant originally ' having the body or form of a woman ' (**1546**). Derivatives in *-lic* from adjectives and adverbs are less frequent : *godlic* ' pleasant,' *deadlic* 'mortal,' *lāþlic* 'hateful,' *ǣnlic* 'unique' [from *an* 'one,' with exceptional mutation], *uplic, upplic* 'sublime.'   This ending is freely used in new-formations in ME and MnE, as in *princely, quarterly, sickly.*

1615, -weard, '-ward,' from an obsolete adjective connected with *weorþan* = Latin *vertere*, forms adjectives from nouns, adjectives, and adverbs: *hāmweard, middeweard, inneweard* from *ham* 'home,' *midde* 'middle' adj., *inne* 'within.'

Verb-forming.

1616. -na is a Scandinavian suffix forming weak intransitive verbs, mostly inchoative, from verb roots and adjectives, as in Icelandic *brotna,* 'get broken,' connected with *brjóta* 'break' (pret. partic. *brotinn*) = OE *brēotan* (pret. partic. *broten*), *hvītna* 'become white,' *harþna* 'become hard.' Many of these verbs were imported in ME, such as *harþna*, which became *hardnen* by the influence of the ME adjective *hard*. There have been many new-formations in ME and MnE, some from adjectives, such as *gladden, redden*, some from nouns, such as *frighten* [OE *fyrhtu* 'fear'], *lengthen*. In English these verbs are used transitively as well as intransitively.

The native verbs *awaken, fasten* are not formed direct from *wake* and *fast*, but the OE weak verbs *awæcnian, fæstnian* are formed from the nouns *wæcen* 'watching,' *fæsten* 'fastness,' 'fort,' which are, of course, derivatives of *wacan* 'wake' and *fæst* 'fast,' 'firm.'

1617. -sian with mutation: *clǣnsian* 'cleanse,' *blǣdsian, bletsian* 'bless,' from *blōd* 'blood,' with shortening of the *ǣ*, the original meaning being 'to sprinkle (the altar) with blood.' In Scandinavian this ending appears as -sa, as in *hreinsa* 'purify' [*hreinn* 'pure']. whence our *rinse.*

1618. -læcan from *lac* (1603): *genēalæcan* 'approach' from *neah* 'near,' *geryhtlæcan* 'correct.' In ME a new verb *cnþulęchen* was formed with this ending from OE *cnawan* 'know,' whence in Late ME a noun *cnþulęche* was formed, which, by the change of weak *ch* into (dȝ) gave MnE *knowlędge.*

Foreign Elements.

1619. The foreign derivative elements in English are mainly of French, Latin, and Greek origin. Many which were at first introduced into English in their popular French forms were afterwards Latinized, at first in spelling only, but afterwards, in many cases, in pronunciation also. In some cases they were wholly or partially Latinized in French itself, though sometimes—in Late Old French—in spelling only. In some cases false etymological spellings of derivative elements of Latin origin were introduced either in French or English, some of which have corrupted the pronunciation.

1620. Although foreign derivatives are often so disguised as no longer to be recognizable as derivatives, yet many foreign derivative elements have remained as distinct as the native ones. Many of them are freely used to form new derivatives from words of native as well as foreign origin. Some of them are even detached and used as independent words, such as *extra.*

Prefixes.

1621. In Latin many of the prefixes are liable to various changes according to the nature of the initial consonants of the word they modify, the full form of a prefix ending in consonants being generally preserved before a vowel, while before consonants the final consonants of the prefix are liable to assimilation and loss; and these variations have generally been preserved when the words containing them were imported into French and English.

1622. The foreign prefixes will now be treated of in their alphabetical order. Specially French prefixes are marked *,

Greek prefixes are marked †, Latin prefixes being left unmarked.

1623. ab-, abs-, a-, 'from, away': *ab-erration, ab-hor, ab-rupt; abs-cond, abs-tinent; a-vert.* The above are formed from verb-roots. *abnormis,* which in English was made into *abnormal* on the analogy of the Latin adj. *normalis,* is an example of an *ab*-derivative from a noun—Latin *norma* ' pattern.' All the above words were taken directly from Latin or from learned French. In popular French *ab-* became *av-,* but the Latin form was generally restored, as in *abus* from *abusum,* whence MnE *abuse.* But Latin *ab-b-* was shortened, as in *abregier* from Latin *abbreviāre,* whence MnE *abridge,* of which MnE *abbreviate* is a learned doublet, taken direct from Latin.

1624. ad-, a-, also in the assimilated forms *ag-. af-* etc., according to the consonant that follows, ' to.' In Old French this prefix was shortened to *a-,* not only before consonants, as in *aventure* ' adventure' from Latin *res adventura* ' a thing about to happen,' but also before vowels, as in *aourner* ' adorn' from Latin *adornāre.* The double consonants in such Latin words as *aggravāre, assentāre=adgravāre, adsentāre* were shortened both in pronunciation and writing in Old French—*agrever, asenter*—double *s* being, however, often kept (*assenter*) to show that the *s* was pronounced (s) and not (z). But in Late Old French the *d* was often introduced again by the influence of the Latin orthography, whence the spellings *adventure, adorner* etc., the latter word being at the same time Latinized in its vowel. Hence many of these words appear in ME in a variety of forms, one, of early introduction. pure Old French. the other or others more or less Latinized, while in some cases the Latinized form does not appear till after the ME period. Thus in ME we have *aventure* and a contracted form *aunter,* in Early MnE *adventer,* which in the Present English has been further Latinized into *adventure*; while the Latinized *adornen* appears already in ME by the side of the pure French form *aurnen*, there being also a blending *adurnen*. The double consonants were restored in the same way, sometimes in ME, but generally not till later; thus we have ME *agreven, asenten* (also *assenten*)=MnE *aggrieve, assent.* Sometimes the prefix *a-* was made into *ad-* from a mistaken etymology, as in *advance, advantage*=ME *avancen, avantage,* Old French *avancer* being a verb formed from the particle *avant*—Latin **ab-ante.*

1625. amb-, am-, an-, 'around': *amb-ition*; *am-putate, per-am-bulate*; *an-cipital* 'two-headed,' 'doubtful.'

1626. †amphi- 'around': *amphi-bious, amphi-theatre.*

1627. †an- before vowels and *h* + vowel, **a-** before other consonants, 'un-': *an-archy* [compare *mon-archy*], *an-hydrous* 'without water'; *a-theist, a-tom* literally 'uncut,' 'undivisible.'

1628. †ana- 'up,' 'again,' 'apart,' 'according to,' 're-versal' etc.: *ana-thema,* originally 'thing put up or dedicated.' *ana-baptist,* 're-baptist,' *ana-tomy* literally 'cutting up,' *ana-logy* 'according to proportion,' *ana-gram* 'transposition of letters,' *ana-chronism.*

1629. ante-, anti- 'before': *ante-cedent, ante-diluvian*; *anti-cipate.* Freely used in new-formations, such as *ante-chamber, anteroom, antedate.*

1630. †anti- 'against': *Anti-christ, antidote* literally 'given against,' *anti-pathy, anti-podes, anti-thesis.* Freely used in new-formations, such as *anti-radical, anti-constitutional, anti-Gladstone, anti-spasmodic.*

1631. †apo-, before vowels **ap-,** before *h* **aph-,** the *h* itself being dropped: 'from,' 'away,' 'forth' etc.: *apo-cope* literally 'cutting away,' *apo-logy, apo-strophe* literally 'turning away,' *apo-stasy*; *aph-orism.*

1632. bi- 'half,' 'twice': *bi-ennial* [compare *annual*], *bi-sect, bi-valve. bi-cycle* is a newly formed hybrid from Greek *kuklos* 'circle.'

1633. †cata-, cat-, cath-, 'down,' 'through' etc.: *cata-*

ract, catastrophe, catalogue; *cat-echize*; *cath-edral. cath-*
.

1634. circum-, circu- 'round': *circum-navigate, circum-scribe, circumstance, circumlocution, circumspect, circumvent; 'rcu-it-us.*

1635. cis- 'on this side of': *Cisalpine.*

1636. com-, con-, co- 'with,' 'together,' being another form of the preposition *cum* 'with'; often merely intensive, like the cognate OE *ge-*.   In Old French the vowel of this prefix was made into *o* through the influence of *cum*, which was often lengthened in ME words taken from French, whence the MnE (v, au) in *comfort, council, counsel* etc., the (o) in such words as *conduit*, earlier MnE (kʊndit) being due to the spelling.   In Old French—as also occasionally in Latin itself—the final consonant of this prefix was often dropped before consonants, whence the MnE *covent = convent* in *Covent Garden* [Latin *conventio*], *covenant*. The following are further examples of this prefix: *combine, commit, comprehend, comfort* [Old French *comforter, conforter*]; *confess, convince, conclude, concern, conduct, contain*; *co-agulate, coincide, cohere; col-league, connect, corrupt.* This prefix is used in new-formations, such as *com-mingle, compatriot*, especially in the form of *co-*: *co-exist, co-operation, co-tenant.* The predominance of the latter ending has led to the change of *contemporary* into *cotemporary*; but the former is now preferred, as being nearer the Latin form.

1637. contra-, contro-, *counter- 'against,' originally used only to form verbs.   The Old-French form is *cuntre-, cōntre-* with the *o* made into *o* on the analogy of Old French *com-, con-*, out of which English *counter-* has developed in the same way as in *counsel* etc.   But in Old French *contre-* was often made into *contre-* by the influence of the Latin spelling.   The Latin forms are less frequent than the French: *contradict, contravene, contra-st* [French *contraster* from *contrā-stare*], *contraband* [literally 'contrary to the proclamation ']; *controversy, controvert.* The form *counter-* is used not only in French words, such as *counterfeit, countermand, counterpart, counterpoise,* but also in new-formations, such as *counter-attraction, counterbalance, counter-revolution, counterweigh. counter* is also used as an independent adverb, as in *to run counter to,* being partly the Old French adverb and preposition *contre,* partly the detached prefix.

1638. de- is partly the Latin (and French) *de* 'from,' ' away,' also expressing ' difference,' ' negation,' ' completion,' being often only intensitive, which is both a preposition and a prefix ; partly French *des-, dé-* from Latin *dis-* 'asunder,' ' apart,' which often develops the same negative meaning as *de* = Latin *de-*: *degrade, derive, devious,* literally ' out of the path,' *dethrone, devote, deny. de* = Latin *dis-* (also *dī-,* and assimilated *dif-*) : *defeat* [Latin **disfacere, disfactum*]. *defy* literally ' renounce faith,' *delay* [Latin *dilātum*], *depart, detach.*

1639. ***demi-** ' half' from Latin *dimidium* : *demigod, demi-semibreve. demy* (di·mai) is used as an independent word.

1640. †**di-** ' twice': *digraph, di-phthong, dilemma, diploma.* The double *ss* in *dissyllable* was introduced in French through confusion with the Latin prefix *dis-.*

1641. †**dia-, di-** ' through ': *diadem, diagnosis, diameter* ; *diocese, diorama.*

1642. dis, di-, assimilated **dif-** ' asunder.' ' apart,' ' privation,' ' negation.' The Old French form *des-* [Modern French *des-, dé-*] is still preserved in *descant* ' tune with modulations.' In the other derivatives taken from Old French the Latin *dis-* has been restored, as in *disarm* = Old French *desarmer, disappoint* [compare Modern French *désappointer*], *disdain* [compare Modern French *dédaigner*]. *dishonest, disease, distress* [Latin *districtiare]. The following are of direct Latin origin : *discreet, dispute. dissolve, distant ; different. difficult.* The form *di-* is rare in words of French introduction, such as *diminish,* and not very frequent in

words of Latin form : *divide, dilate, digress, direct, divert.*
dis- is freely used in new-formations, such as *disconnect, dis-
inherit, disingenuous,* being frequently added to English
words, as in *disburden, disheartened, disown.* In *dislike* =
ME *mislíken* it has been substituted for a similar-sounding
native prefix ; so also perhaps in *disbelieve, distrust.*

*en-, *em- ' in ' : see in-, im-.

1643. †en-, em-, assimilated el-, ' in ' : *encyclopedia,
energy, enthusiasm* ; *emblem, embryo, emphasis, emporium* :
ellipse.

1644. †endo- ' within ' : *endogamous* ' marrying within
the tribe,' *endogenous* ' growing from within.'

*enter- ' between ' ; see inter-.

1645. †epi-, ep-, eph- ' upon ' : *epigram, epitaph, epi-
demic* ; *ephemeral.*

1646. ex-, e-, assimilated ef- ' out of.'   The Old French
form is *es-,* Modern French *é-. es-* has been preserved in
English only in a few obscured words, such as *essay, escape.*
Wherever the meaning of the prefix has been kept clear it
has been restored to its Latin form in English : *exchange*
from Old French *eschangier, extend, extinguish.*   The other
Latin forms are seen in *elegant, erect, evade* ; *efface, effect.*   As
x = (ks), an initial *s* is often dropped after *ex-,* as in *ex-pect*
[compare *re-spect*], *exude, extirpate* [from Latin *sudare*
' sweat,' *stirps* ' stem ']. *ex-* is frequently used in new-
formations to express ' one out of office ' etc., as in *ex-king,
ex-president, ex-secretary* ; so also in the adjective *ex-
official.*

1647. †ex-, ec- ' out of ' : *exodus* ; *ec-stasy.*

1648. †exo- ' outside ' : *exogamous* ' marrying outside the
tribe,' *exoteric* ' suitable for outer world, for people in
general.'

1649. extra- ' beyond ' is used in Latin chiefly with adjectives : *extramundane, extraordinary, extravagant* ; so also
in the new-formations *extra-official, extra-parochial.   extra*

by itself is used in English as an adjective and adverb, being either the Latin adverb and preposition *extra* 'beyond,' or else the detached prefix. Hence such combinations as *extra work, extra pay, extra careful, extra-superfine* are not derivatives, but word-groups or compounds.

1650. †**hyper-** 'over,' 'beyond': *hyperbole, hyperborean, hypercritical.*

1651. †**nypo-, hyp-, hyph-** 'under': *hypodermic* 'belonging to the parts under the skin,' *hypocrite, hypothesis; hyphen.*

1652. in-, im-, in-, i-, assimilated **il-** etc. 'un-'—with which it is cognate as well as with Greek *an-*—is joined to adjectives and occasionally to nouns. The following are examples of words which had this prefix in Latin itself: *insane* [Latin *insānus*], *insipid, inestimable, injury, injustice; impious, imbecile; ignoble* [Latin *ignobilis*], *ignorant; illiberal, immortal.* In English this prefix is applied only to foreign words of some length, as in *inequality, injustice* compared with *unequal, unjust.* If new words are formed from foreign words by means of English endings *un-* is prefixed, as in *ungrateful, undecided,* compared with *ingratitude, indecisive.* But *un-* is also prefixed to some words with exceptionally familiar Latin endings such as *-able,* as in *uneatable, unconquerable* compared with *intolerable, invincible.*

1653. in-, im-, il-, etc. 'in,' 'into' is mainly a verb-former. The French form of this prefix is *en-, em-,* preserved in English in such words as *endure, engage, envoy; embellish, employ.* But in many words of French introduction the Latin form has been restored, as in *indite,* ME *enditen, inquire, imprint.* As the spelling makes no difference in the present pronunciation—*en-, em-*=(-in, -im)—it fluctuates in some words between the Latin and French forms, the latter being now preferred in such cases of doubt, as in *encage, enjoin, entitle, embark,* formerly written also *incage* etc., although *impeach* now follows the Latin spelling.

The following are examples of purely Latin words with this prefix : *inaugurate, induce, invade* ; *impel* ; *illuminate, immerse, irruption* ' breaking in.'   There are many new-formations with the French form of the prefix : *enlarge* ; *embody, enkindle, enliven.*   In *impoverish* and *improve* the Latin form of the prefix has taken the place of the less distinct *a-* from Latin *ad-*, the former word being the Old French *apovrir* [Latin **appauperire*], while the latter is a variation of *approve* = *aprove.*   In a few words, such as *inborn, income* the prefix is of English origin.

1654. inter-, *enter- ' between.'   The French form is preserved only in *enterprise, entertain*, the Latin form having been substituted in all other words of French introduction : *intercede, interfere, interpose, interpret, interval.*   In *intellect, intelligent* and their derivatives the Latin assimilation before *l* is kept, which is disregarded in other words, such as *interlace, interlude.*   This prefix is frequently used in new-formations, such as *interchange. international, intertwist.*

1655. intro- ' within,' ' into ' : *introduce, introspection.*

1656. †meta-, met-, meth- ' with,' ' after,' ' change ' : *metaphysics* ' the study that comes after physics,' *metamorphosis* ; *method.*

1657. ne- ' not ' : *nefarious, ne-uter, neutral.*

1658. non- ' not.'   The adverb *non* ' not ' is not used as a derivative in Latin, occurring only as the first element of a few group-compounds such as *non-nulli* ' some,' literally ' not-none,' *nonnunquam* ' sometimes.'   In Modern French and English it is used as a prefix in such words as *nonsense, nondescript* [Latin *non descriptum* ' not described '], *nonentity*, as it already was in Late Latin in *non-entitas.*   It is freely used in new-formations, such as *non-conductor, non-appearance, non-intervention.*

1659. ob-, o(b)s-. o-, assimilated **occ-** etc., ' towards,' ·against ' : *obedient, oblong, ob-stacle, obviate* ; *os-tensible* ; *omit* ; *occasion, occur, offend, opposite.*   In some cases the full *ob-* has taken the place of an assimilated form, as in *obfuscate.*

*par- see **per-**.

1660. †para-, par-, parh- 'beside,' 'against': *paradox, paragraph; parenthesis, parody; parhelion.*

1661. per- 'through,' occurring also as a preposition. The assimilated *pel-* is preserved in English only in *pellucid.* The French form both of the prefix and of the preposition is *par,* preserved in English only in *pardon* [Late Latin *perdonāre*] and *parboil* (**1540**). *par-* in *paramount, paramour* is the preposition, these words being really adverbial groups, meaning originally 'through (by) above,' 'through love.' In all other words the Latin form has been restored, as in *perfidy, perfume, permit, pervade.* ME *parfit* from Latin *perfectus* through French *parfait* was Latinized in ME first into *perfit,* then into *perfect.*

*por-, see **pro-**.

1662. post- 'after': *posthumous, postpone, postscript.*

1663. pre- Latin *prae-* 'before.' French *pre-*: *precept, precede, prefer, prescribe, present, pretend.* It is freely used in new-formations in the sense of 'before in time,' as in *preconceive, preingage, prepossess*—now used only metaphorically— *presuppose.*

1664. preter- Latin *praeter-* 'beyond': *preter-ite, pretermit, preternatural.*

1665. pro-, prod- 'before,' 'forth,' 'away from,' 'deprivation,' as in *profane* literally 'away from the temple' *prohibit,* 'acting as substitute,' as in *proconsul,* 'relation,' as in *proportion. pro* 'before,' 'for' etc. is also an independent preposition. There was in Latin an allied prefix *por-,* as in *portendere* 'portend.' The popular Old French form of *pro-* and the preposition *pro* was *pur, por* [modern French *pour*], which was probably a blending of *pro* and *per.* This form is preserved in such words as *purchase* [Latin *procaptiāre], *purloin, purpose, pursue; portray, portrait; poursuivant, pur-*

suivant 'state messenger or attendant.' The following are examples of the Latin form : *procede, pro-duce, progress, proclaim, protract, provide* ; *prod-igy, prodigal.*

1666. †pro- 'before' : *problem, programme, prologue.*

1667. †pros- 'towards' : *pros-elyte* literally 'coming towards,' *prosody.*

*pur-, see pro-.

1668. re-, red-, 'back,' 'repetition,' as in *repeat,* 'opposition,' as in *resist,* having often only an intensitive force, as in *rejoice.* In French *re-* often became *r-* before a vowel, but the full form was restored in English, as in *reenter* from French *rentrer.* The fuller form *red-* is preserved in *redeem, redound* literally 'flow back' [Latin *redundare*], *redolent, redintegrate.* In Spoken English *re-* has two forms: weak (-ri) in traditional derivatives such as *receive, repeat, reveal* ; strong (·rij) meaning 'repetition,' which is freely used in new-formations, such as *reenter, reconsider, reintroduce, recover an umbrella* distinct from the traditional *recover.*

1669. retro- 'backwards' : *retrograde, retrospection.*

1670. se-, sed- 'apart,' 'away' : *secede, seduce, seclusion, select, separate* ; *sedition.*

1671. semi- 'half' : *semicircle, semivowel* [Latin *semi-vocalis*], *semicolon, semibreve.* Also in new-formations, such as *semi-detached.*

1672. sine- 'without' : *sinecure.*

1673. sub-, assimilated suc- etc. 'under,' whence a great variety of secondary meanings—'near,' 'behind,' 'following,' 'inferiority,' 'diminution,' 'approaching,' 'help,' 'completion,' the primary meaning also developing into that of 'stealth,' 'secrecy' : *subterranean, subscribe, suburb, subsequent, subordinate, subdivide, subvention, suborn* ; *succumb, suggest, support, suffix, suffice, supply, succour, surreptitious.* sub- is freely used in new-formations, such as *subcutaneous, subsoil, subway,* especially to express subordination etc., as in *sub-com-*

mittee, sub-editor, sub-lieutenant, sublet, and diminution, as in the adjectives *subacid, sub-transparent, sub-tropical.*

1674. subter- 'under': *subterfuge.*

1675. super- 'above,' 'beyond' became *sur-* in Old French, which is frequently preserved in English, as in *surmount, survey, surpass, surface* by the side of its Latin original *superficies.* It expresses 'beyond in time' in *survive, superannuated.* Its most frequent metaphorical meanings are 'addition,' 'excess,' 'superiority,' as in *surname* [which is an Anglicised form of French *surnom*]; *surfeit, supernatural, superfluous; surpass, supereminent.* The Latin form of the prefix is freely used in new-formations, generally to express 'excess': *super-sensual* 'beyond the reach of the senses,' *super-phosphate, super-heat* 'to heat steam till it resembles a perfect gas.' *super* is used in stage-language as an independent noun in the sense of *supernumerary,* of which it is a contraction.

1676. supra- 'above,' 'beyond': *supramundane.*

*sur-, see **super-**.

1677. sus- has the same meaning as *sub-,* being a contraction of *subtus: susceptible, suspend, sustain* [Latin *sustinere* through French]. *susst-* etc. are shortened to *sust-* etc.: *su-spect, suspicion.*

1678. †syn-, sy-, assimilated **syl-** etc. 'with,' 'together': *synagogue, synod, synopsis, syntax; sy-stem; syl-lable, symmetry.*

1679. trans-, tra- 'across,' 'through,' 'beyond.' The old French form is *tres-,* preserved in English only in *trespass,* compared with the Latin form of the prefix in *transgress. transs-* is shortened to *trans-* as in *tran-scend.* Various shades of the primary meaning are seen in such words as *transient, transitory, transpire, tra-duce. trans-* often expresses 'change,' both of place as in *transplant, transpose,* and of quality as in *transform, transmutation, translate, travesty.* It is used in new-formations, as in *Transatlantic, tranship.*

*tres-, see **trans-**.

1680. ultra- 'beyond,' both of place and of quantity and superiority: *ultramontane* 'beyond the mountains,' that is, 'belonging to the Italian party in the Church of Rome,' *ultramarine* 'a colour brought from beyond the sea,' *ultramundane*. Freely used in new-formations to express excess : *ultra-radical, ultra-clerical*, whence the detached *ultra* has come to be used as an independent adjective in the sense of 'extreme,' as in *ultra measures*, whence the derivatives **ultraist, ultraism**.

Suffixes.

1681. The foreign suffixes will now be treated of under the general heads of 'noun-forming' etc., and the sub-divisions 'personal,' 'abstract,' the suffixes under each section being arranged so that those which consist entirely of vowels come first, and are followed by those that contain consonants in the alphabetic order of those consonants.

Noun-forming.

Personal.

1682. *-ee is the strong form of French *-é* from Latin *-atus*, and denotes the person who takes a passive share in an action or agreement, the corresponding active agent being denoted by *-or, -er*. Thus *lessee* is the person to whom a house is let on lease, as opposed to the lessor ; so also *grantee, legatee, mortgagee*. Some of these derivatives have no special active word corresponding to them, such as *patentee, referee, trustee*. In these words the passive meaning is less prominent, and *patentee*, for instance, may be taken to mean either 'one to whom a patent is granted,' or 'one who takes out a patent'; and in some cases *-ee* is a purely active suffix as in *absentee, devotee, refugee*.

The weak form of this suffix is *-y, -ey*, as in *attorney* = Old French *atorné* (**1695**).

-iff, see -ive under 'Adjective-forming.'

-an, -ean, -ian, -ine, -nt, see under 'Adjective-forming.'

1683. -ar, -er, -eer, -ier from Latin -*ārius*, -*arīs*, Low Latin -*erius*, whence the Old French -*ier*, which in ME became -*er*. In ME -*er* was shortened to -*er* when weak, whence such MnE derivatives as *barber*, *officer*, *prisoner*, *sorcerer*, *stranger*.   In ME it was often levelled under the English suffix -*ere*, as in *scolere, templere*.   Many words took the ending -*ar* through the influence of the original Latin forms, some already in ME, such as *vicar*, others later, such as *scholar*, *Templar*. The MnE -*eer*, -*ier* comes from the strong form of the French suffix, both forms being freely used in new-formations, especially -*eer*: *cavalier* — of which *chevalier* is the Modern French form introduced into MnE — *cuirassier*, *gondolier ;* *muleteer*, *pioneer* [Early MnE *pioner*], *pamphleteer*, *privateer*, *volunteer*.   *gazetteer*, originally 'newspaper-editor,' now means 'geographical dictionary.'

1684. -or from Latin -*or*, *-our from Latin -*orem*, through Old French -*or*.   In Latin this ending is preceded by derivative *t*, which under certain conditions becomes *s*: *imperātor*, *professor*.   In Old French the *t* was weakened and then dropped, leaving a hiatus, as in *empereor*, *sauveor* (Latin *salvatorem*).   The *t* was of course kept in learned words of later importation into French, and was reintroduced into popular words when they were Latinized, whence the MnE forms *autour*, *author* (**831**) [Latin *auctorem*], *creditor*, *orator*.   In Early MnE the spelling -*our* was still preserved, but we now write the Latin -*or* even in words that have not been otherwise Latinized, such as *emperor*, *governor*, *tailor*, *conqueror* = earlier *emperour*, *taylour* etc., though we still write *saviour*.

1685. -*or* has in many words taken the place of French -*er* (as also in some English words, § **1592**): *bachelor* [Early MnE *bacheler*], *chancellor*, *proprietor*, *warrior* = OE *bacheler*, Modern French *bachelier* etc.   This is partly the result of

-or and *-er* having the same sound (ər) even in Early MnE (859). In some words the opposite change has taken place, as in *miner, robber* = ME *minour, robbour*.

1686. *-or* is generally weak, but in legal words such as *grantor, lessor,* where it is contrasted with the passive *-ee* (1682), it takes strong stress for the sake of emphasis and distinctness — (leˑsɔr).

-**ary**, see under ' Adjective-forming.'

1687. -**ard**, -**art**. Although introduced into English from French, this suffix is of Germanic origin. In the Germanic languages *-hard* 'hard' in the sense of 'strong,' 'brave,' was a frequent termination of proper names of men, many of which were introduced into Old French, whence they passed into English, such as *Richard. Reynard. Renard* was originally a man's name—Old High German *Reginhart*—which was given to the fox in the story of ' Renard the fox,' which was introduced into France in the twelfth century from Flanders. In Flemish the name of the fox is *Reinaert,* which in French became *Renart*; and the story became so popular in France that *renard* is now the only French word for fox, the Old French *goupil* ' fox ' surviving only as a proper name. The name-suffix *-ard, -art* was soon used in Old French and the other Romance languages to form personal nouns, which were at first nicknames, and had a depreciatory sense. Thus from the Romance forms of Latin *cauda* ' tail ' was formed Italian *codardo,* Old French *cŏart* ' coward,' literally '(dog) with his tail between his legs.' Other examples are *bastard, wizard,* which were imported from French, and English formations, such as *braggart, drunkard, dullard, niggard, sluggard.* This suffix is used to express nationality in *Spaniard, Savoyard,* probably at first with an idea of ridicule. It was also used to form names of animals, as in *bustard, mallard* ' wild drake ' [formed in French from the adjective *male*]; rarely to form names of things, as in *petard, poniard* [Old French *poing* ' fist '.]

-ese, see under 'Adjective-forming.'

1688. **-ess*, French *-esse* from Latin *-issa* denotes female persons and—more rarely—female animals : *goddess, prophetess, priestess, prioress, baroness, countess, shepherdess, hostess, patroness, manageress ; lioness, tigress.* Exceptional formations in point of meaning are : *Jewess, negress ; mayoress=* 'wife of mayor.' Final weak and silent vowels are omitted before this suffix, as in *princess, negress, votaress* from *prince, negro, votary.* Nouns in *-er, -or* often throw out the vowel when *-ess* is added, as in *tigress, actress* from *tiger, actor.* Nouns in *-erer, -eror,* and some in *-urer* drop the second of these two weak syllables before *-ess,* as in *murderess, sorceress, conqueress, treasuress* from *murderer, sorcerer, conqueror, treasurer.* Similarly in *governess* from *governor.* Some words show further changes : *abbess, anchoress* from *abbott, anchorite ; duchess (duke), marchioness (marquis), mistress (master),* the last being a weak form corresponding to the masc. *Mr.* (mistər).

1689. *†-ist*, Latin *-ista* from Greek *-istes,* generally expresses 'trade,' 'pursuit,' or adherence to a party, dogma etc.: *artist, florist, pugilist, chemist, scientist,* which is a convenient neologism for 'man of science' ; *communist, nihilist, royalist, deist.* It is used in a more general sense in such derivatives as *bigamist, copyist, provincialist.* In *tobacconist* from *tobacco* an *n* is inserted on the analogy of *botanist, mechanist* etc., in *egotist* by the side of *egoist* a *t* on that of *dramatist,* both insertions being prompted by the desire to avoid hiatus.

The parallel *†-ast* in *phantast, enthusiast.*

1690. *†-ite*, Latin *-ita* from Greek *-ites,* is used to form names of nations, sects etc: *Canaanite, Israelite, the Stagirite* 'he who was born at Stagira,' that is, the philosopher Aristotle, *Carmelite ; jacobite.*

1691. *-trix* is the Latin fem. of *-tor : executrix, testatrix* from *executor, testator.*

Diminutive.

1692. -ule, -cule : *capsule, globule, pastule*; *animalcule* — also in the fuller Latin form *animalculum—corpuscule.* The latter ending was shortened to -*cle* in French in most words where the diminutive meaning was not prominent, whence the English *article, oracle, miracle, spectacle* etc. But several of them retain the diminutive meaning, especially where *i* precedes: *cuticle* ' outer thin skin,' *particle, versicle.*

1693. -et, -let.   -*et* forms diminutive nouns and adjectives: *cabinet, coronet, circlet, islet, cygnet, leveret; dulcet, russet.*   On the analogy of *circlet* from *circle* etc., where the *l* came to be regarded as part of the suffix, a new diminutive -*let* has developed itself, which is freely used in new-formations, such as *leaflet, ringlet, streamlet, troutlet.*   In many words these suffixes have lost their diminutive meaning.

Abstract.

1694. *-y, -ey.   -*y* represents Early MnE, ME and Old French -*ie* from Latin -*ia*, and is chiefly used to form abstract nouns, as in *fury, modesty, perfidy*, and in more popular French words, such as *barony, company, courtesy, fancy.* Some of these words have more special and concrete meanings, such as *comedy, tragedy, family, navy.*

-*y* = Latin -*ia* is frequent in names of countries, as in *Italy, Germany, Sicily, Normandy*, although in most cases the full Latin ending has been restored, as in *Arabia* (*Araby* in poetry), *Asia, India, Austria.*   -*y* also corresponds to the Latin neuter ending -*ium*, as in *augury, monastery, remedy, study*, forming concrete as well as abstract words.

1695. -*y* is also the MnE representative of weak ME -*e*, which when strong becomes -*ee* in MnE (1682**).   -*y* = ME -*e* from French -*é* = Latin -*ātus* (**1716**), is sometimes abstract, but generally concrete in a collective sense or in names of districts: *treaty*—the learned doublet of which is *tractate*—[Latin *tractatus*]; *clergy*; *county, duchy.*

1696. It often answers to Old French *-ee* from Latin (generally Late Latin) *-āta* with the same meaning as *-ātus*: *destiny*, *entry*; *army*, *jury*; *country*.

1697. The spelling *-ey* is a mere variety of *-y*, as in *Turkey* (ME *Turkīe*), *attorney* (French *-é*), *journey* (French *-ee*).

-y and *-ey* represent a variety of other Fench vowels in isolated words.

1698. -ice, *-ess, *-ise from Latin *-itia*, *-ities*, Late Latin *-icia*, which in Latin were used chiefly to form abstract nouns from adjectives: *avarice*, *justice*, *malice*, *notice*. The popular Old French form was *-esse*, kept in ME words such as *largesse* 'largess' [*large* 'liberal'], *richesse* 'riches' (**998.** 1). These suffixes were also used in Old French to form derivatives from nouns, whence the MnE *cowardice*, *merchandise*. which has a concrete meaning. There are some English new-formations in *-ice*, *-ise*: *practice*, *practise*, *treatise*.

1699. -cy, -sy. These suffixes were first developed from the Latin combinations *-t-ia*, *-c-ia* in such words as *constancy*, *fallacy* from Latin *constantia* (Late Latin *constancia*). *fallacia*, themselves formed from the derivative adjectives *constans* (*constantem*), *fallāx* (*fallacem*). In MnE they are still associated with derivative *t* and *c*, often taking the place of other endings of Latin origin, especially *-tion*, as in *conspiracy* [compare *conspirator*], *degeneracy* [*degenerate*], *obstinacy* — Latin *conspiratiō* etc. They have the same abstract meaning in many other new-formations, such as *intricacy*, *intimacy*, *lunacy* from *intricate*, *intimate*, *lunatic*, where the second suffix *-ic* is disregarded. In these words the *c* is still felt to be a modification of the derivative *t*, but in the still more recent formations *idiotcy* [also *idiocy*], *bankruptcy* the *t* is kept before it, so that the *-cy* has developed into an independent, primary suffix. A special use of these suffixes is to denote rank and office: *curacy*, *episcopacy*, *magistracy*, *papacy*, *cornetcy*, *ensigncy*;

minstrelsy. Some of the above have also a collective sense. *legacy* has a concrete meaning.

1700. †-ad, -id were used to form titles of epic poems, as in *Iliad* 'the tale of Ilium or Troy,' *Aeneid* 'the adventures of Aeneas,' whence many new-formations in modern times, such as *Lusiad, Columbiad,* the suffix -*ad* being often used to form titles of satirical poems, such as *The Dunciad* 'epic of dunces.'

1701. The Greek -*ad* occurs also in other functions, being used especially to form abstract nouns from numbers, as in *monad, triad, myriad,* and *decade* with the French form of the suffix.

1702. *-ade is a French adaptation of Italian -*ada* from Latin -*ata,* of which -*ée* is the regular French form, as in *armée,* whence the English *army* [compare the Spanish *armada*]. -*ade* generally forms collective nouns from other nouns : *balustrade, barricade, colonnade*; sometimes from verbs, as in *cavalcade* [Italian *cavalcare* 'ride']. It also forms abstract nouns from nouns and verbs : *blockade, parade, promenade, serenade.*

1703. *-age from Latin -*aticum* forms nouns from various parts of speech with a great variety of meanings, the most marked of which are (*a*) collectiveness, as in *baggage, luggage, bandage, cordage, plumage, cellarage*; (*b*) profit or charge in relation to the root-word, as in *mileage* 'payment or allowance for travelling per mile,' also collectively 'aggregate of miles,' *postage, poundage, leakage*; (*c*) action or state (rank, quality): *carnage, coinage, language, tillage, voyage; bondage, courage, peerage.*

-al, see under 'Adjective-forming.'

1704. -ment, Latin -*mentum,* forms nouns from verbs. It forms abstract nouns expressing action, state, or result, as in *argument, emolument,* which in Latin means both 'labour' and 'gain.' So also in many new-formations : *agreement, enjoyment, government, employment, punishment, treatment,* which are formed from French verbs, and *endearment, bereavement, fulfilment,* which are formed from English verbs. In concrete words *-ment* expresses sometimes the means of an action, as in *instrument, ligament, pavement, ornament,* sometimes its result, as in *apartment, fragment, segment.*

1705. From *-ment* is formed the adjective-suffix -**mental** (**1730**), as in *experimental, fundamental, instrumental,* whence again is formed the abstract noun-suffix -**mentality** (**1718**), as in *instrumentality.*

-**in**, -**ine**, see ' Adjective-forming.'

1706. -**ion** (-sion, -tion) from Latin *-iō* (*-ionem*), which forms abstract nouns from verbs: *opinion, rebellion, religion*; *compulsion, passion, session*; *education, action, fiction, description.* Some have developed concrete meanings, such as *nation, legion, region.* The popular Old French form of this suffix was *-on,* the *i* being absorbed into the preceding sound in various ways, whence MnE *reason* [compare the more learned *ration, rational*], *arson, treason.* In less familiar words the Latin *i* was restored, whence the ME forms *opiniūn, condicioun,* etc. In Early MnE (-iuun) was shortened to (-iun), being often made into (-ion) by the influence of the spelling. The spelling *-ion* was sometimes introduced into purely popular words, as in *fashion* = French *façon* from Latin *factio,* whence the learned *faction.*

1707. -**ana** is used in new-formations from names of persons to signify literary gossip about them, as in *Johnsoniana* ' sayings of, or anecdotes about Dr. Johnson,' *Walpoliana,* also publications bearing on them and their literary works, as in *Shakesperiana.* This suffix is the Latin neut. plur. of adjectives in *-anus* (**1735**), as used in such phrases as *dicta Vergiliana* ' sayings of Virgil ' (*Vergilius*). The detached *ana* has come to be used as a noun either in the plur. or sing.—in which latter case it takes a plur. *anas, ana's*—to signify ' collection of anecdotes of celebrities ' etc., the plur. *ana* being now the most usual.

1708. -ance, -ence from Latin *-antia* (*-ancia*), *-entia* (*-encia*), which form abstract nouns from the present participle endings *-āns, -ens,* acc. *antem, -entem* (**1742**), as in *arrogance, ignorance; experience, innocence, penitence, licence,* which is also written more phonetically *license,* with an arbitrary distinction of meaning. The above words preserve their Latin roots, but most of the derivatives in *-ance* are of French formation : *entrance, grievance, repentance.*

1709. These endings often take on the suffix *-y* (**1694**), giving -ancy, -ency, as in *brilliancy, consistency* by the side of *brilliance, consistence.* In the case of *excellence, excellency* there is a difference of meaning. Some occur only in the longer form, such as *constancy* [*Constance* only as a proper name], *infancy, agency, clemency.*

1710. -or, *-our from Latin *-or, -orem* forms abstract nouns, chiefly from verbs. In MnE the French spelling *-our* is preferred to the Latin *-or,* especially in more popular words, the usage being the contrary of that which prevails with the personal ending *-or* (**1684**); but in America the shorter *-or* is consistently extended to the abstract or-derivatives as well, as in *honor* = British English *honour,* parallel with *author.* The following are examples of this suffix : *colour, clamour, honour, vapour; liquor, splendor, tumor.* There are some new-formations : *demeanour, behaviour.*

1711. The lengthened ending -ory = Latin *-orius, -oria,* forms adjectives and abstract nouns—in which *t,* (*s*) precede the ending—such as *obligatory, compulsory, cursory; history, oratory, victory.*

1712. *-ry, Old French *-rie,* arose from the addition of the abstract suffix *-ie* (**1694**) to the French ending *-(i)er* (**1683**), as in *chevalerie, chivalerie* ' body of knights,' ' chivalry' from *chevalier* ' rider,' ' knight' [Late Latin *caballarius*]. In English also it was associated with the personal suffix *-er* through such derivatives as *fisher-y.* In MnE this suffix is mainly used in derivatives from nouns, and occasionally from adjectives, expressing (*a*) actions or qualities, as in *bigotry*, *devilry*, *drudgery*, *pedantry*, *revelry*, *pleasantry*; (*b*) condition, as in *outlawry*, *slavery*; (*c*) occupation, trade, art etc., as in *casuistry*, *palmistry*, *chemistry*, *heraldry*; (*d*) the place of actions, occupations etc., as in *nunnery*, *nursery*, *vestry* 'place where vestments are kept'; (*e*) the result or product of action etc., as in *poetry*, *tapestry*; (*f*) collectivity, as in *infantry* literally 'band of youths,' *peasantry*, *yeomanry*.

1713. -**ure** from Latin *-ura*, which is generally preceded by derivative *t*, (*s*). In popular Old French forms the *t* disappeared, in the same way as in *-ée* (**1682**); thus Latin *armatura* becomes in Old French *armeure*, which in MnE has become *armour* by the influence of the suffix *-our*. The *t* is of course preserved in learned words, such as *nature*. The chief function of this suffix is to form abstract nouns, generally from verb-roots : *figure* ; *capture*, *departure* ; *censure*, *composure*. It also forms concrete nouns, such as *furniture*, *picture*. In some words it has taken the place of *-ir*, *-or*, as in *leisure*, *pleasure*, *treasure* = Old French *leisir*, *pleisir*, *tresor*.

-**ese**, see under 'Adjective-forming.'

1714. †-**ism**, Latin *-ismus*, from Greek *-ismos* is freely used to form abstract nouns expressing action, habit—especially habits of language or pronunciation—or attachment to some creed, party etc. : *Anglicism*, *archaism*, *provincialism* ; *despotism*, *patriotism*, *mannerism*, *pugilism* ; *Calvinism*, *positivism*, *conservatism*. *egotism* by the side of *egoism* owes its *t* to *egotist* (**1689**).

1715. In Greek this suffix is added to adjectives in *-ikós* forming the compound suffix *-ikismos*, Latin *-icismus*, whence English -**icism**, as in *Atticism*, *empiricism*, *fanaticism*, *Scotticism*, *witticism*. In the last two *-icism* must be regarded as a simple derivative, there being no corresponding adjective in *-ic*.

1716. -**ate** from Latin *-atus*, gen. *-atus* expresses office, function, as in *consulate*, *episcopate* and the new-formations *cardinalate, professorate*, being sometimes used to express the holder of the office, as in *magistrate*, and also in a collective sense, as in *syndicate, electorate* 'body of electors' (also 'dignity of Elector').

1717. -itude from Latin *-itūdo* forms abstract nouns from adjectives : *beatitude, fortitude, lassitude, sollicitude*.   In *multitude* it has developed a concrete meaning.

1718. *-ty Latin *-tas, -tatem*, Old French *-te*, ME *-te* forms abstract nouns from adjectives : *liberty* ; *variety* ; *antiquity, dignity, insipidity, vanity*.   *-ity* is often added in this way to adjective-suffixes, so that, for instance, **-city** corresponds to *-cious*, as in *capacity* (*capacious*), *ferocity*, **-idity** to *-id*, as in *insipidity, timidity*, **-ality** to *-al*, as in *reality, vitality*, **-ility** to *-il* and *-ile*, as in *civility, fertility*, **-arity** to *-ar*, as in *regularity, vulgarity*, the most regular and frequent correspondence being that between *-ble* (**1719**) and **-bility**, as in *nobility, durability, solubility*.   The above are all of direct Latin origin.   Others have passed through French changes, such as *certainty, plenty, poverty, pity, property*, the two last having the learned doublets *piety, propriety*.   In some words this suffix has a concrete meaning, as in *city, deity, gratuity, university*.

Adjective-forming.

1719. *-ble from Latin *-bilis*, as in *nobilis* 'noble,' *flebilis* 'weeping,' 'doleful,' 'to be wept over,' 'lamentable,' whence Old French *fleble, feble*, whence, again, our *feeble*, of which *foible* is a later French doublet, *tolerabilis* 'tolerable,' *terribilis* 'terrible.'   In English *-ble* is generally preceded by *a* or *i*—these being the vowels that most frequently precede it in Latin—only exceptionally by other vowels, as in *soluble*.   In Latin it has no very definite meaning, and is used both in an active and passive sense (as in *flebilis*); but in English the passive meaning prevails, *-ble* being associated with the adjective *able* from Latin *habilis, navigable*, for instance, being regarded as equivalent to 'able to be navigated.' So also in *admirable, malleable, tolerable, flexible, legible, soluble.* In some however the suffix has an active meaning, as in *durable, favorable, peaceable; forcible, sensible.* There are many new formations in *-able,* such as *unbearable, eatable*; *reliable, dependable,* formed from *rely on, depend on.* In the colloquial *getatable* the preposition is kept for the sake of distinctness.

1720. There is another suffix *-ble* of French origin, from Latin *-plex (-plicem)* '-fold,' which we have in the English word *double, treble,* the *p* of the Latin form being restored in *triple* and in formations from the higher numbers, such as *quadruple,* and in *multiple.*

1721. *-bund,* *-bond : *moribund, rubicund*; *vagabond,* which is also a noun.

1722. *-ic,* French *-ic, -ique* from Latin *-icus* and Greek *-ikos,* forms adjectives, generally from nouns, many of these derivations being also used as nouns, some exclusively so. Thus we have the Latin *domestic, generic, public, rustic,* the Greek *catholic, cynic, mythic, tonic.* This suffix also forms part of the Latin compound suffix *-atic,* as in *aquatic, fanatic, lunatic.* There is also a Greek ending *-tic* preceded by different vowels, in which the *t* is part of the body of the word : *emphat-ic, systematic* [compare *systemat-ize*]; *athletic, phonetic*; *despotic.*

1723. *-ic* is also used to form names of races and languages, as in *Celtic (Keltic), Germanic, Italic,* and new-formations such as *Finnic, Indic, Tungusic, Hanseatic,* formed from *Hansa, Hanse-towns* on the analogy of *Asiatic* from *Asia.*

1724. Of the nouns in *-ic* some denote persons, such as *catholic, domestic, rustic* and the collective *public,* all of which are also nouns, and *lunatic,* which is now used chiefly as a noun ; while others denote things, such as *tonic,* others language, such as *Celtic, Gaelic,* which however is generally

expressed by *-ish* (1757).   There are also many which denote
arts and sciences, such as *arithmetic, logic, music,* especially
in the plur. : *phonetics, physics* [the sing. *physic* has now a concrete meaning], *mathematics, optics.*   In Greek *logic* was called
he logike tékhne 'the reason science,' where the adjective *logikós*
is in the fem., agreeing with *tékhne*; afterwards *logike* by itself
was used as a fem. noun, which was adopted into Latin, either
unchanged—*logice*—or with the Latin fem. ending—*logica* ;
and from Latin this and the other words of the same kind
passed through French into English.   In Greek these adjectives were also used as nouns in the neut. plur., as in *ta
mathematiká*, literally ' the mathematical (things).'   The MnE
use of the plur. *mathematics* is an imitation of this usage,
aided by the English habit of making adjectives into nouns
by adding the plur. *-s*, as in *greens, news* and the vulgar
rheumatics = rheumatism.

1725. *-ic* rarely corresponds to Latin *-icus, -iqvus*, as in
pudic.   Latin *antiqvus, anticus* passed through French into
English, where it came to be written and pronounced
antic(k), the meaning ' ancient ' developing into ' quaint,'
' odd,' the more learned spelling *antique* afterwards giving
rise to the pronunciation (æn·tijk) in imitation of French,
the two forms *antic* and *antique* being completely isolated
from one another through the former having become a
noun.

1726. Derivations in *-ic* often take on the adjective suffix
-al, the new *-ical* and the shorter *-ic* being often used
almost indifferently, as in *generic(al), mythic(al), poetic(al),*
while in other cases the addition of *-al* is accompanied by
a marked divergence of meaning, as in *politic(al), comic(al).*
When a word in *ic(s)* is used exclusively as a noun, the
corresponding adjective always take *-al* for the sale of distinction, as in *cynic(al)*—though we still say *cynic philosopher*
in the sense of ' philosopher who is a cynic '—*music(al),*
mathematical.

1727. †-iac forms adjectives—which are sometimes also used as nouns—from nouns, the ending -*al* being often added, as in the case of -*ic* (**1726**): *maniac, demoniac(al), hypochondriac(al), Syriac.*

1728. -id forms adjectives from adjectives, verbs, and nouns : *acid, fluid, intrepid, morbid, languid, splendid, vivid.* Some of these, such as *acid* and *fluid*, are also used as nouns.

1729. †-oid. Greek -*eides* from *eídos* 'form' makes nouns into adjectives, such as *anthropoeides* 'having the form of a man.' In Latin Greek *ei* is written *i*, and as the ending was generally preceded by *o*, -*oid* has come to be regarded as an independent suffix in such words as *anthropoid* 'resembling man,' *cycloid, rhomboid* ; on the analogy of which there are numerous new-formations, such as *alkaloid, aneroid, tabloid*, most of which are nouns.

1730. -al. Latin -*alis* is a very frequent adjective-ending, as in *equal, eternal, natural, real, royal*, which is the French form corresponding the learned *regal*, both from Latin *regalis.* So also -ial : *essential, martial, pestilential.*

1731. -*al* is often added to the adjective-suffix -*ic* (**1722**), the resulting -ical being often regarded as an independent suffix, whence such new-formations as *lackadaisical, whimsical.*

1732. -*al* also forms nouns with a great variety of meanings, such as *individual, general* ; *animal* ; *mineral, journal, capital*, all of which were originally adjectives, many of them being still used as such.

1733. -*al* is especially used in MnE to form abstract nouns, mostly from verbs, such as *arrival, denial, funeral, proposal, refusal, trial.* Some of these—such as *funeral*—had the same ending in ME, while others had the ending -*aille*, which is the old French form of the Latin adjective neut. plur. -*alia* from -*alis.* Thus *victuals* appears in ME in the form of *vitaille*, which is also the Old French form, from Latin *victuālia*, which afterwards influenced the spelling of the word.

1734. -il, -ile, Latin -*ilis*, -*īlis*, the former being mainly from verb-roots, the latter from nouns. From -*ilis*: *ductile*, *fertile*, *fragile*, *missile*. From -*īlis*: *civil*, *hostile*, *juvenile*, *servile*. In *gentle* we have an English shortening of French *gentil*, which was re-introduced into MnE in the form of *genteel*, *gentile* being a third doublet which represents the original Latin form *gentilis* 'belonging to a *gens* or family.' The shortening is French in *humble*, *stable*, *subtle*, also written in the more learned form *subtile*. In Early MnE -*il*, -*ile* were both pronounced (-il), but now many words written -*ile* are pronounced with (-ail) through the influence of the spelling.

1735. -an, -ane from Latin -*anus* forms adjectives denoting persons, such as *human*, *pagan*, *republican*, *veteran*, many of which are also used as nouns. Others, such as *publican* and the French *artisan*, are used only as nouns. This suffix is used especially to forms adjectives and nouns denoting religious sects etc., such as *Anglican*, *Puritan*, *Mahometan*, and nations, as in *Roman*, *German*, *American*; it has a similar function in *Elizabethan*.

1736. The popular French form of this suffix was -*ain*, which is preserved in a few English words, such as *captain*, *villain*.

1737. -ane, as in *humane*, *mundane* was in Early MnE a mere orthographic variant of -*an*, *human* and *humane* being written at random without any distinction of meaning. We now pronounce -*ane* (·ein) apparently in imitation of the English pronunciation of Latin -*anus*.

1738. -ean, French -*een*, which has the same meaning as -*an(e)*, is a lengthened form of Latin -*aeus*, -*eus*, the lengthening -*aeānus* occurring in Latin itself in some words. By the influence of the English pronunciation of Latin the ending is in most words pronounced (·iən), but the older pronunciation, in which the suffix is short and weak, is still kept up in such words as *Mediterranean, cerulean, herculean.* Strong *-ean* in : *Manichean, Pythogorean* ; *Chaldean, European.*

1739. -ian = Latin *-iānus* also has the same meaning as *-an*, being especially frequent in adjectives and nouns expressing occupation, rank etc.: *historian, librarian, musician, physician, tragedian* ; *patrician, plebeian* ; *Christian, presbyterian* ; *barbarian, Arabian, Italian, Turanian.*

1740. -ine, -in from Latin *-inus, -inus* forms numerous adjectives, some of which are also used as nouns : *Alpine, crystalline, saline* ; *elephantine, vulpine* ; *divine, feminine* ; *Palatine, Philistine* ; *clandestine—Latin.* In Early MnE *-ine* was short, = (in), when weak-stressed, and this is still the pronunciation in many words, such as *feminine,* while others, such as *Alpine,* have weak (-ain) in imitation of those which throw the stress on the ending, such as *divine.* The pronunciation (·ijn) in *marine, machine* is an imitation of modern French.

1741. There are many original nouns in Latin *-in(e),* such as *libertine, medicine, discipline* ; *dolphin, resin.* There is a large number of chemical words in *-ine, -in,* such as *casein(e), fibrin(e), protein, iodine.* When such words become familiar they are generally written *-ine* and pronounced with the French (-ijn), as in *gelatine, glycerine.* So also in numerous newly formed trade-words, such as *brillantine, butterine.*

1742. -ant, -ent from the Latin pres. partic. endings *-ans* (*-antem*), *-ens* (*-entem*), form adjectives and nouns from verbs. Adjectives : *arrogant, reluctant, ignorant* ; *eminent, innocent, penitent.* Nouns : *dependant* [adjective *dependent*], *inhabitant, agent, student* ; *torrent* ; *instant, accident.* Many words in *-ant* are French formations : *brilliant,* Early MnE, Old French *brillant* ; *pleasant* ; *merchant, servant.*

1743. -lent, from Latin *-lentus* and *-lens* (*-lentem*) ; *opulent* ; *pestilent, violent, turbulent.*

From these must be distinguished adjectives formed from present participles (1741), such as *benevol-ent, insol-ent.*

-ple, see -ble.

1744. -ar from Latin *-aris*: *familiar, popular, regular, similar, singular.* The popular Old French form of this suffix was *-er*, and some of the above words were introduced in ME English with it. such as *singuler*, but the ending was Latinized in MnE.

1745. -ary from Latin *-arius* forms adjectives and personal nouns : *extraordinary, primary, necessary, temporary; dignitary, incendiary, secretary.*

1746. -ior. In Latin *-ior (-iorem)* is the comparative ending of adjectives. which are also used as nouns : *inferior, superior, junior, senior.*

-ior is the masc. and fem. ending. the corresponding neut. ending being *-ius*, which is used also adverbially. as in *excelsius* 'higher,' for which *Excelsior* is incorrectly substituted as an interjection—originally the title of a poem.

1747. -ese from Latin *-ensis, -esis* forms adjectives and nouns from names of countries : *Chinese, Japanese, Maltese, Portuguese.* It is also used familiarly in derivatives from names of authors to express their language or style. such as *Johnsonese* 'language of Dr. Johnson,' 'a pompous and long-winded style resembling his,' *Macaulayese.*

1748. -ose. *-ous from Latin *-onsus, -osus*, which was used to form adjectives from nouns : *bellicose, jocose, verbose ; fabulous. furious, glorious, luminous, monstrous.* So also in the new-formations *mischievous, murderous.*

1749. In MnE many Latin words were imported into the written language in the nom. masc. sing. inflection, because that was the one that came first in the dictionaries and grammars, *-us*—which is the most frequent form of this case in Latin—being written *-ous* on the analogy of *-ous =* Latin *-osus*; thus in MnE we have *barbarous* from Latin *barbarus* (fem. sing. nom. *barbara* etc.), the popular Old French *barbar* being also the ME form ; so also in *credulous, erroneous, obvious, spurious.* The less frequent nom. sing. masc. ending *-is* is made into *-ious*, as in *illustrious* [Latin *inlustris, illustris*]. *scurrilous.*

1750. *-esque from Italian *-esco*, Latin *-iscus*, forms adjectives and nouns: *arabesque, grotesque*, literally 'grotto-like,' 'belonging to a grotto,' *picturesque, statuesque.* The noun *burlesque* is also used as a verb.

1751. -t, -te, -ate, -ite, -ute. *-t* often represents the ending of the Latin pret. passive partic., preceded sometimes by a consonant, but generally by the vowel *a*, and occasionally by other vowels. Thus the following English adjectives come from Latin passive participles in *-t*: *ontent* [generally made into *contented*], *abrupt, extinct*; *accurate, legitimate, private, temperate*; *complete*; *definite, exquisite, infinite*; *absolute, destitute, minute.* Others come from Latin passive participles with the Latin change of *t* into *s* in certain combinations : *dense, diverse, sparse.* Some of these—such as *content*—existed as popular words in Old French, the others being afterwards —in English as well as French—formed directly from the Latin passive participles on the analogy of the popular forms. In Latin, adjective-participles in *-atus* were sometimes formed directly from nouns, as in the Latin words corresponding to *caudate* 'tailed,' *insensate* ; and in MnE—especially in scientific terminology—many more adjectives of this kind have been formed directly from Latin nouns, even where there are no such formations in Latin itself; thus we have *lunulate* 'shaped like a little moon,' 'crescent-shaped' [Latin *lunula* 'little moon'], *angustifoliate* 'with narrow leaves.' *-ate* was also substituted for the French ending of the passive partic., as in *affectionate.*

1752. Many of these adjectives naturally developed into nouns. In Latin itself we have personal (masc.) nouns such as *legatus* 'one deputed,' 'legate,' and in Late Latin *curātus*, which in Classical Latin is used only as an adjective ' careful,' has developed the meaning 'curate.'   In Latin we have also neuter nouns in *-um* formed from these participle-adjectives, such as *mandātum* 'what is commanded,' 'mandate,' *edictum* 'edict,' *tribūtum* 'tribute,' and Late Latin *manuscrīptum* 'hand-written,' 'manuscript.'   Many others have been formed in modern times, some of which are used only as nouns, some also as adjectives: *delegate, reprobate, favourite; extract, dupli-cate, precipitate.*   Some of these nouns are formed from the Latin pret. partic. of deponent verbs, which have an active meaning, such as *adept* 'one who has attained proficiency,' from the deponent verb *adipīscor* 'obtain.'

1753. The chemical noun-suffix *-ate* arose from the Latin technical terms of the older chemists, who called the result of the action of vinegar (Latin *acetum*) on lead (Latin *plumbum*) *plumbum acetātum* 'vinegared lead,' or simply *acetātum*, which was regarded as a noun, whence we now say *acetate of lead, carbonate of potash, nitrate of soda*, shortened into *nitrate*.   To express a less degree of chemical action the ending *-ite* has been arbitrarily formed from *-ate*—*nitrite, sulphite of soda.*

1754. In accordance with the general tendencies of English many of these adjectives were made into verbs ; thus, as the adjectives *dry* and *clear* (OE *drȳge*, Old French *cler*) had become indistinguishable from the verbs *to dry, to clear* (OE *ādrȳgan*, Old French *clairier*) so that the verbs seemed to be formed directly from the adjectives, so also such adjective-participles as *content, corrupt, direct, aggravate, desolate, moderate, separate* came to be used as verbs.   At first the ending *-ate* did duty for the passive partic. of these new verbs, as in *he was contract to Lady Lucy* (Shakespere), *they have degenerate*, but they soon began to take the English inflection *-ed*, so that a distinction was made be-tween *the land was desolate* (adj.) and *the land was deso-lated* (earlier *desolate*) *by war*.   By degrees some of the new participles came themselves to be used as adjectives, such as *contented, situated* = the older *content, situate*.   The ending -*ate* having now the function of a verb, it became usual to adopt Latin verbs into English in the form of their passive participles, especially when these were formed in -*atus*; hence such verbs as *asseverate, fascinate, venerate* were formed direct from the Latin verbs *asseverare* etc. without the intervention of an adjective-partic. in -*ate*, although, of course, it is not always certain in individual cases whether there was such an intervening form or not. This verb-forming -*ate* was extended to verbs imported from French, as in *isolate* [French *isoler* from Latin *insulāre*, whence the more learned form *insulate*], *felicitate*. Lastly -*ate* has been used to form verbs from Latin words where there was no corresponding Latin verb in -*are*, as in *incapacitate*, formed from Latin *capacitas, incapax, substantiate, vaccinate*. -*ate* is also used to form verbs from words of non-Latin origin, such as *assassinate*.

1755. -**ive** from Latin -*ivus* forms adjectives and nouns: *active, passive, extensive, furtive, primitive; captive, native, representative; alternative, motive, prerogative*. The popular Old French form of this suffix was -*if*, preserved in MnE *caitiff*—of which *captive* is the learned doublet—*plaintiff*. In some of these the ending was afterwards Latinized as in *plaintive* from *plaintif, restive* from older *restiff* which was originally applied to a horse which 'remained' (French *rester*) in one place.

Verb-forming.

1756. *-**fy**, French -*fier* from Latin -*ficare*, a weakening of *facere* 'do,' 'make,' forms causative verbs from nouns and adjectives (pronouns): *deify, edify, modify; fortify, purify, qualify* [*qvālis* 'such'].

1757. *-**ish**. Many French verbs in -*ir* conjugate partly with -*iss* before the inflections, which is taken from the Latin ending -*sco* (-*esco, -īsco* etc.) of inchoative verbs (**290.** 1). In Old French this *ss* = Latin *sc* had the sound (ʃ), and in ME it was extended to the infin. and all the other parts of the verbs that had it, as in *finisshen* ' finish,' *florisshen* 'flourish ' = Old French *fenir* [Modern French *finir*], *florir*, 1st pers. plur. pres. indic. *fenissons, florissons* from Latin *finīre*, **finīscere*, *florere, florescere.* So also in *abolish, cherish, nourish, perish, punish.* From such as these it was extended in ME to many French verbs which never had any iss-forms, as in *astonish* from Old French *estoner, diminish, distinguish, publish, vanquish.* It was also used in purely English verb-formations, such as *famish* from *famine.*

The original Latin inchoative *-scere* occurs only in words taken directly from Latin or which were Latinized in French : *acquiesce, effervesce, effloresce(nt).*

-ate, see under ' Adjective-forming.'

1758. †-ize, -ise, French *-iser*, Latin *-isare, -issāre* from Greek *-izein*, is used to form verbs from nouns and adjectives. It occurs in Greek formations, such as *agonize, crystallize, theorize*; forms derivatives from Latin words, such as *civilize, patronize, realize*; from French words, as in *authorize*; and is freely employed in new-formations, such as *galvanize, mesmerize, hypnotize.* The spelling *-ize* in imitation of the Greek form of the suffix has now supplanted the older *-ise.*

END OF PART I.

Clarendon Press Series.

The English Language and Literature.

HELPS TO THE STUDY OF THE LANGUAGE.

1. DICTIONARIES.

A NEW ENGLISH DICTIONARY ON HISTORICAL PRIN-CIPLES, founded mainly on the materials collected by the Philological Society Imperial 4to. Parts I-IV, price 12s. 6d. each.

Vol. I (**A** and **B**), half-morocco, 2l. 12s. 6d.

Vol. II (**C** and **D**). *In the Press.*

Part IV, Section 2, **C—CASS**, beginning Vol. II, price 5s.

Part V, **CAST—CLIVY**, price 12s. 6d.

Part VI, **CLO—CONSIGNER**, price 12s. 6d.

Edited by JAMES A. H. MURRAY, LL. D., sometime President of the Philological Society; with the assistance of many Scholars and Men of Science.

Vol. III (**E, F, G,**) Part I, **E—EVERY**, Edited by HENRY BRADLEY, M.A., price 12s. 6d.

Bosworth and **Toller.** *An Anglo-Saxon Dictionary*, based on the MS. Collections of the late JOSEPH BOSWORTH, D.D. Edited and enlarged by Prof. T. N. TOLLER, M.A. Parts I-III, A-SAR. . . . [4to, 15s. each.
Part IV, Section I, SAR—SWIÐRIAN. . . . [4to, 8s. 6d.

Mayhew and **Skeat.** *A Concise Dictionary of Middle English,* from A. D. 1150 to 1580. By A. L. MAYHEW, M.A., and W. W. SKEAT, Litt. D.
[Crown 8vo, half-roan, 7s. 6d.

Skeat. *A Concise Etymological Dictionary of the English Language.* By W. W. SKEAT, Litt. D. *Fourth Edition* . . . [Crown 8vo, 5s. 6d.

2. GRAMMARS, READING BOOKS, &c.

Earle. *The Philology of the English Tongue.* By J. EARLE, M.A., Professor of Anglo-Saxon. *Fifth Edition.* . . [Extra fcap. 8vo, 8s. 6d.

———— *A Book for the Beginner in Anglo-Saxon.* By J. EARLE, M.A., Professor of Anglo-Saxon. *Third Edition.* . . [Extra fcap. 8vo, 2s. 6d.

Mayhew. *Synopsis of Old-English Phonology.* By A. L. MAYHEW, M.A. . . . . . [Extra fcap. 8vo, bevelled boards, 8s. 6d.

Morris and **Skeat**. *Specimens of Early English.* A New and Revised Edition. With Introduction, Notes, and Glossarial Index :—

Part I. From Old English Homilies to King Horn (A.D. 1150 to A.D. 1300). By R. MORRIS, LL.D. *Second Edition.* . . [Extra fcap. 8vo, 9s.

Part II. From Robert of Gloucester to Gower (A.D. 1298 to A.D. 1393). By R. MORRIS, LL.D., and W. W. SKEAT, Litt.D. *Third Edition.* 7s. 6d.

Skeat. *Specimens of English Literature*, from the 'Ploughmans Crede' to the 'Shepheardes Calender' (A.D. 1394 to A.D. 1579). By W. W. SKEAT, Litt.D. *Fifth Edition.* . . . . [Extra fcap. 8vo, 7s. 6d.

———— *The Principles of English Etymology :*

First Series. The Native Element. . . . [Crown 8vo, 9s.

Second Series. The Foreign Element. . . . [Crown 8vo, 10s. 6d.

Sweet. *An Anglo-Saxon Primer, with Grammar, Notes, and Glossary.* By HENRY SWEET, M.A. *Third Edition.* . . [Extra fcap. 8vo, 2s. 6d.

———— *An Anglo-Saxon Reader.* In Prose and Verse. With Grammatical Introduction, Notes, and Glossary. By the same Author. *Sixth Edition, Revised and Enlarged.* . . . . [Extra fcap. 8vo, 8s. 6d.

———— *A Second Anglo-Saxon Reader.* By the same Author. [4s. 6d.

———— *Old English Reading Primers.* By the same Author :—

I. *Selected Homilies of Ælfric.* [Extra fcap. 8vo, *stiff covers*, 1s. 6d.

II. *Extracts from Alfred's Orosius.* [Extra fcap. 8vo, *stiff covers*, 1s. 6d.

———— *First Middle English Primer, with Grammar and Glossary.* By the same Author. *Second Edition.* . . . . [Extra fcap. 8vo, 2s.

———— *Second Middle English Primer.* Extracts from Chaucer, with Grammar and Glossary. By the same Author. . . [Extra fcap. 8vo, 2s.

———— *A Primer of Spoken English.* . . [Extra fcap. 8vo, 3s. 6d.

———— *A Primer of Phonetics.* . . . [Extra fcap. 8vo, 3s. 6d.

Tancock. *An Elementary English Grammar and Exercise Book.* By O. W. TANCOCK, M.A. *Second Edition.* . . [Extra fcap. 8vo, 1s. 6d.

———— *An English Grammar and Reading Book*, for Lower Forms in Classical Schools. By O. W. TANCOCK, M.A. *Fourth Edition.* 3s. 6d.

Wright. *A Primer of the Gothic Language.* With Grammar, Notes, and Glossary. By JOSEPH WRIGHT, Ph.D. . . [Extra fcap. 8vo, 4s. 6d.

A SERIES OF ENGLISH CLASSICS.

(CHRONOLOGICALLY ARRANGED.)

Chaucer. I. *The Prologue to the Canterbury Tales.* (*School Edition.*) Edited by W. W. SKEAT, Litt.D. . . [Extra fcap. 8vo, *stiff covers*, 1s.

—— II. *The Prologue ; The Knightes Tale ; The Nonne Prestes Tale.* Edited by R. MORRIS, LL.D. *A New Edition, with Collations and Additional Notes,* by W. W. SKEAT, Litt.D. . . [Extra fcap. 8vo, 2s. 6d.

—— III. *The Prioresses Tale ; Sir Thopas ; The Monkes Tale ; The Clerkes Tale ; The Squieres Tale, &c.* Edited by W. W. SKEAT, Litt.D. *Fourth Edition.* . . . . . [Extra fcap. 8vo, 4s. 6d.

—— IV. *The Tale of the Man of Lawe ; The Pardoneres Tale ; The Second Nonnes Tale ; The Chanouns Yemannes Tale.* By the same Editor. *New Edition, Revised.* . . . [Extra fcap. 8vo, 4s. 6d.

—— V. *Minor Poems.* By the same Editor. [Crown 8vo, 10s. 6d.

—— VI. *The Legend of Good Women.* By the same Editor.
[Crown 8vo, 6s.

Langland. *The Vision of William concerning Piers the Plowman,* by WILLIAM LANGLAND. Edited by W. W. SKEAT, Litt.D. *Fourth Edition.*
[Extra fcap. 8vo, 4s. 6d.

Gamelyn, The Tale of. Edited by W. W. SKEAT, Litt.D.
[Extra fcap. 8vo, *stiff covers*, 1s. 6d.

Wycliffe. *The New Testament in English,* according to the Version by JOHN WYCLIFFE, about A.D. 1380, and Revised by JOHN PURVEY, about A.D. 1388. With Introduction and Glossary by W. W. SKEAT, Litt.D.
[Extra fcap. 8vo, 6s.

—— *The Books of Job, Psalms, Proverbs, Ecclesiastes, and the Song of Solomon :* according to the Wycliffite Version made by NICHOLAS DE HEREFORD, about A.D. 1381, and Revised by JOHN PURVEY, about A.D. 1388. With Introduction and Glossary by W.W.SKEAT, Litt.D. [Extra fcap. 8vo, 3s. 6d.

Minot. *The Poems of Laurence Minot.* Edited, with Introduction and Notes, by JOSEPH HALL, M.A. . . . . [Extra fcap. 8vo, 4s. 6d.

Spenser. *The Faery Queene.* Books I and II. Edited by G. W. KITCHIN, D.D., with Glossary by A. L. MAYHEW, M.A.

    Book I. *Tenth Edition.* . . . [Extra fcap. 8vo, 2s. 6d.
    Book II. *Sixth Edition.* . . . [Extra fcap. 8vo, 2s. 6d.

Hooker. *Ecclesiastical Polity,* Book I. Edited by R. W. CHURCH, M.A., Dean of St. Paul's. *Second Edition.* . . . [Extra fcap. 8vo, 2s.

Marlowe and Greene. MARLOWE'S *Tragical History of Dr. Faustus,* and GREENE'S *Honourable History of Friar Bacon and Friar Bungay.* Edited by A. W. WARD, Litt.D. *New Edition.* . [Extra fcap. 8vo, 6s. 6d.

Marlowe. *Edward II.* Edited by O. W. TANCOCK, M.A. *Second Edition.* . . . . . [Extra fcap. 8vo. *Paper covers,* 2s. ; *cloth,* 3s.

Shakespeare. Select Plays. Edited by W. G. CLARK, M.A., and W. ALDIS WRIGHT, D.C.L. . . . . [Extra fcap. 8vo, *stiff covers.*

  The Merchant of Venice. 1s.   *Macbeth.* 1s. 6d.
  Richard the Second. 1s. 6d.   *Hamlet.* 2s.

Edited by W. ALDIS WRIGHT, D.C.L.

The Tempest. 1s. 6d.	*Coriolanus.* 2s. 6d.
As You Like It. 1s. 6d.	*Richard the Third.* 2s. 6d.
A Midsummer Night's Dream. 1s. 6d.	*Henry the Fifth.* 2s.
Twelfth Night. 1s. 6d.	*King John.* 1s. 6d.
Julius Cæsar. 2s.	*King Lear.* 1s. 6d.

Henry the Eighth. 2s.

Shakespeare as a Dramatic Artist; *a popular Illustration of the Principles of Scientific Criticism.* By R. G. MOULTON, M.A. *Second Edition, Enlarged.* . . . . [Crown 8vo, 6s.

Bacon. *Advancement of Learning.* Edited by W. ALDIS WRIGHT, D.C.L. *Third Edition.* . . . . . . [Extra fcap. 8vo, 4s. 6d.

Bacon. *The Essays.* Edited, with Introduction and Illustrative Notes, by S. H. REYNOLDS, M.A. . . . . [Demy 8vo, *half-bound,* 12s. 6d.

Milton. I. *Areopagitica.* With Introduction and Notes. By JOHN W. HALES, M.A. *Third Edition.* . . . . [Extra fcap. 8vo, 3s.

———— II. *Poems.* Edited by R. C. BROWNE, M.A. In two Volumes. *Fifth Edition.*
  [Extra fcap. 8vo, 6s. 6d. Sold separately, Vol. I. 4s., Vol. II. 3s.
In paper covers:—

  Lycidas, 3d.   *L'Allegro,* 3d.   *Il Penseroso,* 4d.   *Comus,* 6d.

———— III. *Paradise Lost.* Book I. Edited with Notes, by H. C. BEECHING, M.A. . . [Extra fcap. 8vo, 1s. 6d. *In Parchment,* 3s. 6d.

———— IV. *Samson Agonistes.* Edited, with Introduction and Notes, by JOHN CHURTON COLLINS, M.A. . . [Extra fcap. 8vo, *stiff covers,* 1s.

Bunyan. *The Pilgrim's Progress, Grace Abounding, Relation of the Imprisonment of Mr. John Bunyan.* Edited by E. VENABLES, M.A.
  [Extra fcap. 8vo, 5s. *In Parchment,* 6s.

Clarendon. I. *History of the Rebellion.* Book VI. Edited with Introduction and Notes by T. ARNOLD, M.A. . . . [Extra fcap. 8vo, 4s. 6d.

———— II. *Selections.* Edited by G. BOYLE, M.A., Dean of Salisbury.
  [Crown 8vo, 7s. 6d.

Dryden. *Select Poems.* (*Stanzas on the Death of Oliver Cromwell; Astræa Redux; Annus Mirabilis; Absalom and Achitophel; Religio Laici; The Hind and the Panther.*) Edited by W. D. CHRISTIE, M.A.
  [Extra fcap. 8vo, 3s. 6d.

———— *Essay of Dramatic Poesy.* Edited, with Notes, by T. ARNOLD, M.A. . . . . [Extra fcap. 8vo, 3s. 6d.

Locke. *Conduct of the Understanding.* Edited, with Introduction, Notes, &c., by T. FOWLER, D.D. *Third Edition.* . [Extra fcap. 8vo, 2s. 6d.

Addison. *Selections from Papers in the 'Spectator.'* By T. ARNOLD, M.A. *Sixteenth Thousand.* . [Extra fcap. 8vo, 4s. 6d. *In Parchment,* 6s.

Steele. *Selected Essays from the Tatler, Spectator, and Guardian.* By
AUSTIN DOBSON. . . . [Extra fcap. 8vo, 5s. *In Parchment, 7s. 6d.*

Pope. I. *Essay on Man.* Edited by MARK PATTISON, B.D. *Sixth
Edition*. . . . . [Extra fcap. 8vo, 1s. 6d.

———— II. *Satires and Epistles.* By the same Editor. *Second Edition.*
[Extra fcap. 8vo, 2s.

Parnell. *The Hermit.* . . . . . [*Paper covers, 2d.*

Thomson. *The Seasons, and the Castle of Indolence.* Edited by
J. LOGIE ROBERTSON, M.A [Extra fcap. 8vo, 4s. 6d.

Berkeley. *Selections.* With Introduction and Notes. By A. C. FRASER,
LL.D. *Fourth Edition.* . . . . . . [Crown 8vo, 8s. 6d.

Johnson. I. *Rasselas.* Edited, with Introduction and Notes, by
G. BIRKBECK HILL, D.C.L.
[Extra fcap. 8vo, *limp,* 2s. ; *Bevelled boards,* 3s. 6d. ; *in Parchment,* 4s. 6d.

———— II. *Rasselas ; Lives of Dryden and Pope.* Edited by
ALFRED MILNES, M.A. . . . . . . [Extra fcap. 8vo, 4s. 6d.

———— *Lives of Dryden and Pope.* By the same Editor.
[*Stiff covers,* 2s. 6d.

———— III. *Life of Milton.* Edited, with Notes, &c., by C. H.
FIRTH, M.A. . . . [Extra fcap. 8vo, *stiff covers,* 1s. 6d. ; *cloth,* 2s. 6d.

———— IV. *Vanity of Human Wishes.* With Notes, by E. J.
PAYNE, M.A. . . . . [*Paper covers,* 4d.

Gray. *Selected Poems.* Edited by EDMUND GOSSE, M.A.
[*In Parchment,* 3s.

———— *The same,* together with Supplementary Notes for Schools. By
FOSTER WATSON, M.A. . . . . [Extra fcap. 8vo, *stiff covers,* 1s. 6d.

———— *Elegy, and Ode on Eton College.* . . . [*Paper covers,* 2d.

Goldsmith. *Selected Poems.* Edited, with Introduction and Notes, by
AUSTIN DOBSON . . [Extra fcap. 8vo, 3s. 6d. *In Parchment,* 4s. 6d.

———— *The Traveller.* Edited by G. BIRKBECK HILL, D.C.L.
[Extra fcap. 8vo, *stiff covers,* 1s.

———— *The Deserted Village.* . . . . . [*Paper covers,* 2d.

Cowper. I. *The Didactic Poems of* 1782, with Selections from the
Minor Pieces, A.D. 1779–1783. Edited by H. T. GRIFFITH, B.A.
[Extra fcap. 8vo, 3s

———— II. *The Task, with Tirocinium,* and Selections from the
Minor Poems, A.D. 1784–1799. By the same Editor. *Second Edition.*
[Extra fcap. 8vo, 3s.

Burke. I. *Thoughts on the Present Discontents ; the two Speeches on
America.* Edited by E. J. PAYNE, M.A. *Second Edition.*
[Extra fcap. 8vo, 4s. 6d.

———— II. *Reflections on the French Revolution.* By the same
Editor. *Second Edition.* . . . . . . [Extra fcap. 8vo, 5s.

———— III. *Four Letters on the Proposals for Peace with the
Regicide Directory of France.* By the same Editor. *Second Edition.*
[Extra fcap. 8vo, 5s.

Burns. *Selected Poems.* Edited by J. LOGIE ROBERTSON, M.A.
[Crown 8vo, 6s.

Keats. *Hyperion*, Book I. With Notes, by W. T. ARNOLD, B.A. 4d.

Byron. *Childe Harold.* With Introduction and Notes, by H. F. TOZER, M.A. . . . . . [Extra fcap. 8vo, 3s. 6d. *In Parchment*, 5s.

Shelley. *Adonais.* With Introduction and Notes. By W. M. ROSSETTI. . . . . [Crown 8vo, 5s.

Scott. *Lady of the Lake.* Edited, with Preface and Notes, by W. MINTO, M.A. With Map. . . . . [Extra fcap. 8vo, 3s. 6d.

———— *Lay of the Last Minstrel.* Edited by W. MINTO, M.A. With Map. . . . [Extra fcap. 8vo, *stiff covers*, 2s. *In Parchment*, 3s. 6d.

———— *Lay of the Last Minstrel.* Introduction and Canto I, with Preface and Notes, by W. MINTO, M.A. . . . . [*Paper covers*, 6d.

———— *Marmion.* Edited by T. BAYNE. . [Extra fcap. 8vo, 3s. 6d.

Campbell. *Gertrude of Wyoming.* Edited, with Introduction and Notes, by H. MACAULAY FITZGIBBON, M.A. *Second Edition* . [Extra fcap. 8vo, 1s.

Wordsworth. *The White Doe of Rylstone.* Edited by WILLIAM KNIGHT, LL.D., University of St. Andrews. . . [Extra fcap. 8vo, 2s. 6d.

Typical Selections *from the best English Writers. Second Edition.* In Two Volumes. . . . . . . [Extra fcap. 8vo, 3s. 6d. each.

HISTORY AND GEOGRAPHY, &c.

Freeman. *A Short History of the Norman Conquest of England.* By E. A. FREEMAN, M.A. *Second Edition.* . . [Extra fcap. 8vo, 2s. 6d.

George. *Genealogical Tables illustrative of Modern History.* By H. B. GEORGE, M.A. *Third Edition, Revised and Enlarged.* [Small 4to, 12s.

Greswell. *History of the Dominion of Canada.* By W. PARR GRESWELL, M.A. . . . . [Crown 8vo, 7s. 6d.

———— *Geography of the Dominion of Canada and Newfoundland.* By the same Author. . . . . [Crown 8vo, 6s.

Hughes (Alfred). *Geography for Schools.* Part I, *Practical Geography.* With Diagrams. . . . . . . [Extra fcap. 8vo, 2s. 6d.

Kitchin. *A History of France.* With Numerous Maps, Plans, and Tables. By G. W. KITCHIN, D.D., Dean of Winchester. *Second Edition.* Vol. I. To 1453. Vol. II. 1453-1624. Vol. III. 1624-1793. Each 10s. 6d.

Lucas. *Introduction to a Historical Geography of the British Colonies.* By C. P. LUCAS, B.A. . . . [Crown 8vo, with 8 maps, 4s. 6d.

———— *Historical Geography of the British Colonies :—*

    I. *The Mediterranean and Eastern Colonies* (exclusive of India).
[Crown 8vo, with 11 maps, 5s.

    II. *The West Indian Dependencies.* With Twelve Maps.
[Crown 8vo, 7s. 6d.

MATHEMATICS AND PHYSICAL SCIENCE.

Aldis. *A Text Book of Algebra (with Answers to the Examples).* By W. STEADMAN ALDIS, M.A. . . . . . . [Crown 8vo, 7s. 6d.

Combination Chemical Labels. In Two Parts, gummed ready for use. Part I, Basic Radicles and Names of Elements. Part II, Acid Radicles.
[Price 3s. 6d.

Hamilton and **Ball.** *Book-keeping.* By Sir R. G. C. HAMILTON, K.C.B., and JOHN BALL (of the firm of Quilter, Ball, & Co.). *New and Enlarged Edition.* . . . . [Extra fcap. 8vo, 2s.

** *Ruled Exercise Books adapted to the above;* fcap. folio, 1s. 6d. *Ruled Book adapted to the Preliminary Course;* small 4to, 4d.

Hensley. *Figures made Easy: a first Arithmetic Book.* By LEWIS HENSLEY, M.A. . . . . [Crown 8vo, 6d.

—— *Answers to the Examples in Figures made Easy,* together with 2000 additional Examples formed from the Tables in the same, with Answers. By the same Author. . . . . . [Crown 8vo, 1s.

—— *The Scholar's Arithmetic.* By the same Author.
[Crown 8vo, 2s. 6d.

—— *Answers to the Examples in the Scholar's Arithmetic.* By the same Author. . . . . [Crown 8vo, 1s. 6d.

—— *The Scholar's Algebra.* An Introductory work on Algebra. By the same Author. . . . . . . [Crown 8vo, 2s. 6d.

Nixon. *Euclid Revised.* Containing the essentials of the Elements of Plane Geometry as given by Euclid in his First Six Books. Edited by R. C. J. NIXON, M.A. *Second Edition.* . . . . . . [Crown 8vo, 6s.
May likewise be had in parts as follows :—
Book I, 1s. Books I, II, 1s. 6d. Books I-IV, 3s. Books V, VI, 3s.

—— *Supplement to Euclid Revised.* By the same Author.
[Stiff covers, 6d.

—— *Geometry in Space.* Containing parts of Euclid's Eleventh and Twelfth Books. By the same Editor. . . . [Crown 8vo, 3s. 6d.

Fisher. *Class-Book of Chemistry.* By W. W. FISHER, M.A., F.C.S. *Second Edition* . . . . [Crown 8vo, 4s. 6d.

Harcourt and **Madan.** *Exercises in Practical Chemistry.* Vol. I. *Elementary Exercises.* By A. G. VERNON HARCOURT, M.A., and H. G. MADAN, M.A. *Fourth Edition.* Revised by H. G. MADAN, M.A.
[Crown 8vo, 10s. 6d.

Williamson. *Chemistry for Students.* By A. W. WILLIAMSON, Phil. Doc., F.R.S. . . . . . . [Extra fcap. 8vo, 8s. 6d.

Hullah. *The Cultivation of the Speaking Voice.* By JOHN HULLAH.
[Extra fcap. 8vo, 2s. 6d.

Maclaren. *A System of Physical Education : Theoretical and Practical.* With 346 Illustrations drawn by A. MACDONALD, of the Oxford School of Art. By ARCHIBALD MACLAREN, the Gymnasium, Oxford. *Second Edition.*
[Extra fcap. 8vo, 7s. 6d.

Troutbeck and **Dale.** *A Music Primer for Schools.* By J. TROUTBECK, D.D., formerly Music Master in Westminster School, and R. F. DALE, M.A., B.Mus., late Assistant Master in Westminster School. [Crown 8vo, 1s. 6d.

Tyrwhitt. *A Handbook of Pictorial Art.* By R. St. J. TYRWHITT, M.A. With coloured Illustrations, Photographs, and a chapter on Perspective, by A. MACDONALD. *Second Edition.* . . . [8vo, *half-morocco*, 18s.

Upcott. *An Introduction to Greek Sculpture.* By L. E. UPCOTT, M.A. . . . . [Crown 8vo, 4s. 6d.

Student's Handbook to the University and Colleges of Oxford. *Eleventh Edition.* . . . . [Crown 8vo, 2s. 6d.

Helps to the Study of the Bible, taken from the *Oxford Bible for Teachers,* comprising Summaries of the several Books, with copious Explanatory Notes and Tables illustrative of Scripture History and the Characteristics of Bible Lands ; with a complete Index of Subjects, a Concordance, a Dictionary of Proper Names, and a series of Maps. . . . . [Crown 8vo, 3s. 6d.

*** A READING ROOM *has been opened at the* CLARENDON PRESS WAREHOUSE, AMEN CORNER, *where visitors will find every facility for examining old and new works issued from the Press, and for consulting all official publications.*

☞ *All communications on Literary Matters and suggestions of new Books or new Editions, should be addressed to*

THE SECRETARY TO THE DELEGATES,

CLARENDON PRESS,

OXFORD.

London: HENRY FROWDE,
OXFORD UNIVERSITY PRESS WAREHOUSE, AMEN CORNER.
Edinburgh: 12 FREDERICK STREET.
Oxford: CLARENDON PRESS DEPOSITORY,
116 HIGH STREET.

PLEASE DO NOT REMOVE
SLIPS FROM THIS POCKET

UNIVERSITY OF TORONTO
LIBRARY

Printed in Great Britain
by Amazon

42438492R00297